Edward Blair Michell

A Siamese-English dictionary

Edward Blair Michell

A Siamese-English dictionary

ISBN/EAN: 9783742891396

Manufactured in Europe, USA, Canada, Australia, Japa

Cover: Foto ©Andreas Hilbeck / pixelio.de

Manufactured and distributed by brebook publishing software
(www.brebook.com)

Edward Blair Michell

A Siamese-English dictionary

สีบิ้กรมายน ภาษา ไทย

แปล เปน ภาษา อังกฤษ

มิศเตอร์ อิ. บิ. มิเซล

เนติ บัณฑิตย์ เปรียนชั้น ม. อ.

เปน ผู้ เรียบ เรียง

—•••◦◦◦◦•••—

กรุงเทพ ฯ รัตนโกสินทร ศก ๑๒๐

ด้วย

พระบาท สมเด็จ พระ ปรมินทร์ มหาจุฬาลงกรณ์

พระ จุลจอม เกล้า เจ้า อยู่ หัว

พระ.จ้า แผ่น ดิน สยาม

ผู้ ทรง พระคุณ ธรรม มหา บ่ระเสริฐ   ทรง

พระ มหา กรุณา อุปถัมภ์ บำรุง ศิลปาสาคร วิชา การ

ทั้ง อาณา บ่ระชา ราชฎร ให้ ได้ ร่ม เย็น เป็น สุข ด้วย

ทรง พระ ยฏิบัติ โดย ราชการ ธรรม นริยานุวัติ แล สังคหะวัถถุ

ได้ ทรง พระ กรุณา โปรด เกล้า ฯ พระ ราชทาน พระ บรมราชานุญาก

ได้ ลง พิมพ์ หนังสือ เล่ม นี้

ข้า พระ พุทธเจ้า

ขอ รับ พระราชทาน นฉอง ยัง ได้ ฝ่า ลออง ธุลี พระบาท

ควร มิ ควร แล้วแต่ จะ ทรง พระ กรุณา โปรก

ขอ เกชะ

บาน แพนก

ถ้อย คำ ทั้งปวง ใน หนังสือ ดิกชันเนริ เล่ม นี้ ข้าพเจ้า ได้ จัด เรียบ เรียง ตาม ตัว อักษร ใน ภาษา ไทย เรียง กัน ไป โดย ลำดับ ตัว ก ข. แต่ อักษร อ. นั้น ข้าพเจ้า เห็น ว่า ไม่ สมควร ที่ จะ ยก เข้า รวม กับ พยัญชน ชึ่ง ได้ จัด รวม เข้า ไว้ ให้ เปน ตัว ต้น ใน หมู่ สระ

ใน วิธี ที่ ฝึก สอน กัน ฝ่าย ไทย นั้น เรียก หัน อากาศ แล วิสัญชะนิ ว่า เปน วรรณยุต หรือ เครื่อง ประกอบ กับ อักษร แต่ ใน หนังสือ เล่ม นี้ ข้าพเจ้า จัด เข้า เปน สระ ทั้ง สอง อย่าง โดย เหตุ ว่า หัน อากาศ แล วิสัญชะนิ ก็ มิ สำเนียง ออก ดัง เช่น กับ สระ ตัว อื่น ไม่ ใช่ เปน เครื่อง หมาย เสียง ให้ หนัก เบา ดัง เช่น ไม้ เอก ไม้ โท ไม้ ได้ คู้

อนึ่ง ฤ ฤๅ ฦ ฦๅ นั้น ข้าพเจ้า จัด เรียบ เรียง เข้า รวม กับ พวก อักษร ริ รี ลิ ลี หา ได้ จัด เปน สระ ต่าง หาก ไม่

ประการ หนึ่ง ความ หมาย ที่ เปน ถ้อย คำ ภาษา อังกฤษ ตรง กับ คำ ไทย นั้น ถ้า แห่ง ใด มี คุณ ศัพท์ " a " ข้าง น่า คำ ขึ้น แล้ว คำ นั้น หมาย ว่า เปน สิ่ง ของ หรือ ชะนิด ที่ ทำ เภาะ เปน อย่าง นั้ ชะนิด เดียว เช่น กับ ไทย ว่า " มะฮึก " ความ หมาย อังกฤษ ข้าพเจ้า ใส่ ว่า " a tree " คือ เปน ต้น ไม้ ทำเภาะ อย่าง นั้ ชะนิด เดียว แต่ แห่ง ใด ที่ คำ ไทย ว่า ต้น จะ เปน ต้น ชะนิด หนึ่ง ชะนิด ใด ก็ ได้ เช่น นี้ ข้าพเจ้า ใส่ ความ หมาย อังกฤษ ไว้ แต่ เพียง ว่า " tree " ไม่ มี คุณ ศัพท์ ข้าง น่า เลย ทั้ง คำ ว่า ปลา แล สรรพ ผัก พืชน์ พรรณ ต่าง ๆ ข้าพเจ้า ก็ ใส่ ความ หมาย ภาษา อังกฤษ ดัง เช่น ที่ ชี้ แจง มา แล้ว นี้

ถ้า ท่าน ผู้ ซึ่ง ใช้ หนังสือ เล่ม นี้ ภบ ถ้อย คำ อังกฤษ แห่ง หนึ่ง แห่ง ใด ที่ ใช้ โดย ย่อ ข้าพเจ้า ได้ อธิบาย คำ เหล่า นี้ ไว้ ใน ยาน แผนก ที่ เปน ภาษา อังกฤษ ใน หนังสือ เล่ม นี้ โดย พิศดาร กว้าง ขวาง แล้ว ขอ เชิญ ท่าน พลิก อ่าน ดู ถ้า ท่าน ผู้ ที่ อ่าน หนังสือ เล่ม นี้ แม้น ภบ แห่ง หนึ่ง แห่ง ใด ผิด ไป ก็ ขอ ให้ อะไภย เสีย เถิด แล ขอ เชิญ ท่าน แจ้ง ความ ให้ ผู้ เรียบ เรียง ทราบ เพื่อ จะ ได้ แก้ไข ไว้ จะ ได้ ทำ เล่ม อื่น ใน ใบ น่า เทอญ

PREFACE.

In this Volume an attempt has been made, for the first time, to provide students with a cheap and handy dictionary, giving English equivalents for the Siamese words and expressions most commonly in use.

The only existing Dictionary in which such equivalents are given is the handsome work published by Bishop Pallegoix, in 1854. That book has long been out of print ; and the few copies which are to be found are picked up rather as curiosities than otherwise at what may be called the fancy price of about seven guineas.

This fact would in itself be a sufficient excuse for publishing a smaller dictionary, the size and cost of which bring it within the reach of ordinary students. Other reasons are, however, not wanting to justify the present very humble effort. In the first place, the arrangement of Siamese words in the Bishop's book is neither Siamese nor European, but has been planned upon a very elaborate system, which can only be understood after considerable study. Thus, under the letter *a* are ranged all the words which begin with the 1st, 3rd, 16th, 17th, and 18th Siamese vowels. And under the letter *s* are placed indiscriminately all words beginning with the 11th 38th 39th, and 40th of the Siamese consonants. But on the other hand, the Siamese words beginning with *ch* are ranged partly in their natural place under *ch*, and partly at the end of the alphabet, under x. Much difficulty is consequently experienced by European, and still more by Siamese readers in finding words which they seek to trace, either by their sound, when spoken, or by their spelling, when written or printed.

It should be mentioned also, without any disrespect to Monseigneur Pallegoix (whose work must always remain as a noble monument of his learning and energy), that, both in the orthography and in the rendering of many Siamese words, it leaves much to be desired. Scarcely any attempt is therein made to give the etymology, or origin, of the longer words, which are derived, in a vast number of instances, from Indian sources.

The scope and arrangement of the present work are essentially different. The order of the words follows, as a rule, that of the Siamese alphabet, without any reference to European modes of pronunciation, and thus resembles the order adopted in the Greek, Latin, and Sanscrit dictionaries which are most generally in use. The Latin and French equivalents which are given in the Bishop's book (and given with compicuous success) have not here been introduced : but on the other hand it has been thought worth while to add to words of foreign derivation a brief mention of the source from which they are derived.

It may be assumed that there are at least 14,000 words, exclusive of phrases, in the Siamese language, as now spoken. Of these the present dictionary contains about 8,000. It does not therefore pretend to be an exhaustive work. If such had been its aim or scope, its cost must have been far greater, and its size more voluminous. What the author has intended is to lay before the reader, and more especially before Siamese students, a compact volume containing the words required in ordinary conversation and for the reading of ordinary books. Many technical words, especially theological and mythological, have been designedly omitted: and others, which it would have been desirable to include, have no doubt escaped the notice of the author, in spite of all the assistance which could be obtained from Siamese scholars and teachers. The difficulties of obtaining correct information, even as to comparitively simple words, are almost incredible ; and the author is profoundly conscious how unable he has been to cope satisfactorily with such obstacles. He regrets most heartily that the work did not fall into abler hands, such, for instance, as his predecessor in office, Mr. Alabaster; and he craves a large measure of indulgence from readers on the ground, amongst many others, that while a demand for a dictionary of this kind was becoming more and more urgent every year, no other and more competent person seemed at all likely to undertake the work.

It has already been said that in the main the order is that of the Siamese alphabet: and in the case of all the true consonants, this is accurately correct. The reader is therefore requested to peruse the following list,—

ก—k	(middle)	ฐ—t	(high)	ฟ—f	(low)
ข—kh	(high)	ฑ—t	(low)	ภ—p	(low)
ฃ—kh	(high)	ฒ—t	(low)	ม—m	(low)
ค—kh	(low)	ณ—n	(low)	ย—y	(low)
ฅ—kh	(low)	ด—d	(middle)	ร—r	(low)
ฆ—kh	(low)	ต—t	(middle)	ล—l	(low)
ง—ng	(low)	ถ—t	(high)	ว—w	(low)
จ—ch	(middle)	ท—t	(low)	ศ—s	(high)
ฉ—ch	(high)	ธ—t	(low)	ษ—s	(high)
ช—ch	(low)	น—n	(low)	ส—s	(high)
ซ—s	(low)	บ—b	(middle	ห—h	(high
ฌ—ch	(low)	ป—p	(middle)	ฬ—l	(low)
ญ—y	(low)	ผ—p	high	อ—h	(middle)
ฎ—d	low	ฝ—f	(high)	ฮ—au, see vowels)
ฏ—t	(middle)	พ—p	(low)		

A more detailed account of each consonant sound is given at the head of the list of words beginning with it.

As the aspirated form of the letter *t* does not exist in English, it seemed better to render the Siamese aspirated *t* by the unaspirated English *t*, in order to avoid any risk that the reader should pronounce the *th* as a soft sound.

The letter *h*, when used in combination with another consonant, performs the part merely of an accent. It has therefore been so treated in the arrangement of words; and such sounds as *hmar* have been placed next to and immediately after such sounds as *mar*.

A somewhat troublesome question arose as to ใ๖, *rr*, which, though a double consonant in form, in pronounced as a vowel, a'. But, after full reflection, it was thought best to leave it in its natural place among the consonants, where readers would be most likely to look for it.

Words beginning with ใ๖, pronounced *s*, have of course been placed under *t*, and not under any of the letters *s*. And the beginner, who is searching for letters by the aid of their sound only, should remember that in this case, as in the case of double *r*, above mentioned, and some others, he may not find his word where he would naturally expect it.

Another warning which it will be well to give to beginners is that the common people constantly pronounce the letter *t* as a *k*, and not unfrequently pronounce the *k*, as a *t*. A sufficiently absurd example of the former practice is to be found in the case of a word which is actually used as the name of a letter. This is the word *trah*, meaning a seal, which is commonly used as the name of the 20th consonant (*tur trah*). The vulgar practice being to pronounce the word *trah* as *krah*, it thus happens that the very name of a common letter is habitually mispronounced.

Almost the whole enormous colony of Chinese living in Siam habitually pronounce the *r* as an *l:* and many persons who are of mixed descent, partly Siamese and partly Chinese, adopt from habit, or from the difficulty which they experience in pronouncing the *r*, a similar vulgarism. Others find a difficulty in pronouncing not only the *r*, but the *l*, and coolly omit the latter when a convenient opportunity occurs, talking, for example, of Bang-pa-soi, when the real word is Bang-pla-soi.

A great many Siamese letters suffer a degradation of sound when placed at the end of a word or syllable. For instance, the final *r* and *l* are both pronounced, almost universally, as *n;* and the same thing occurs with the curious letter *law bahlee*.

On the other hand several letters, when found at the end of a word or syllable, become hardened into a stronger form, losing the soft sound which originally belonged to them. These include all the letters *d*, and all the forms of *s* and *ch*, which are developed by their position into the hard letter *t* or *tt*. So strong is the inclination to harden these final letters, that in acclimatising English words, such as *office*, and *police*, the Siamese usually pronounce them *ofitt*, and *politt*. The letter *b*, occurring at the end a syllable, is, on a similar principle, hardened into *p*. The imported letter *y* (͡) corresponding to the Pali *ny*, when occurring at the end of a word or syllable, is pronounced as *n*. These changes, however, are not of sufficient importance in altering the sound to give any trouble to the reader in finding any word.

The arrangement of the vowels demands a fuller explanation. They are given as in the following list.

ะ   short *au,* short *o,* or short *a*

เอ = *au* and *aw*

อา *ah* or *ar*

อิ = short *i* or short *ee*

อี = *ee*

อึ short *eu*

อื long *eu*

อุ short *oo* or short *u*

อู *oo* or long *u*

เอ long *u*

แอ *aa* or broad *a*

ไอ long *i* or *ai*

ใอ long *i* or *ai*

โอ long *o*

เอา *ow* or *ou*

อำ short *am* or *a'm*

อะ short *a* with stopped breath

อั very short *a*

Siamese scholars will at once observe that in the case of อ, the established sequence of letters has been departed from. This difficult letter has been deposed from its place as the last but one of the consonants, and placed at the head of the list of vowels. An excuse may be found for this slight change (1) in the fact that, strictly speaking, อ has no consonant sound at all: (2) that it very frequently represents the Sanscrit short *a*, which in that very scientific language is the first of the vowels: (3) that some Siamese Grammarians, while claiming a place for ฮ as a consonant, also allow it a place amongst the vowels, thus forcing upon it an ambiguity of character, which, if admitted in a dictionary, would lead to incalculable trouble and confusion.

There seems to be little doubt (though it has not been before observed) that ฮ and ฮ once represented the Greek soft and hard breathings 'and' But, as ฮ has lost its original character and become solidified in practice into. a consonant, it seems reasonable to allow ฮ to assume the place which practically belongs to it as a true vowel.

One of the chief uses of this curious letter is to serve as a mute prop for other vowels, which in the Siamese system appear unable to stand alone. If the author's theory as to breathings should be correct, the occurrence of ฮ before each vowel which begins a word would be quite easily accounted for, as it would merely show that the initial vowel of the word has a soft breathing. Thus โฮเกล and โฮเกล would represent merely the English and French models of pronouncing " hotel."

Occasionally the mute ฮ is used before a consonant, as before *y*, which of course has a sort of semi-vowel sound. In the few cases in which it so occurs the word has, for the reader's convenience, been placed both under ฮ and ย.

The remainder of the simple vowels present little difficulty except in so far as their position is concerned. They are however, in this respect, somewhat peculiar, and in some cases partake rather of the character of accents than that of pure vowels. Thus the short and long *i* or *ee* and the short and long *eu* present the appearance of a crescent moon, with strokes or other marks attached, and are placed over the consonant which they follow in pronunciation. The short and long *u* or *oo* are placed, as in Sanskrit, under the consonant. The short and long *e* English *(ay* and *aa)* are written before the consonant, as are the two forms of *ai* or *i* (*mai menan*, and *mai malai)*, and the long *o* or *oh*. The composite letter *am* is reckoned in Siamese as a vowel sound,—a practice which will remind classical scholars of the Latin rule of prosody, whereby the *am* occurring at the end of a word, is elided, or cut off, like a vowel, before a following vowel sound. This curious letter consists of a circle or sun, placed over the consonant which preceeds it in pronunciation, and a stick resembling long *ah* placed after that consonant. Finally the vowel *ou*, or *ou*, consists of two sticks or vowels, *ay* and *ah*, placed the one before, and the other after, the consonant or consonants which they follow in speaking. This vowel, when followed at the end of a word by the vowel ๕, changes its sound entirely, and is pronounced *ou* with a catch or check of the breath.

The short *a* (ha'n arkart) has here been regarded as a true vowel, though Siamese Grammarians generally refuse it that title. This however necessitates no change in the order, as the letter (ha'n arkart) has been placed at the end of all the vowels.

The joint vowels or diphthongs have been arranged, in accordance with Siamese practice, in the following order.

เอ̂	(long *ee)* comes next after		อ̂	long *ee*
เอ̂	(long *eu)*	,,	,,	อ̂	long *eu*
เออ	*(ur)*	,,	,,	ไ	*ay*
เอ̂	*(er)*	,,	,,	เออ;	

One of the longest diphthong sounds in Siamese, which has been rendered here by *ow* and *owr*, is formed by placing the consonant *r* after the long *a*, thus bringing into combination the two vowel sounds *ah* and *oo*. It will be observed that in this case *r* plays the part of a vowel ; and it does so likewise when found at the beginning of a word before any short vowel sound, so that the combination *ram* will be pronounced *owa'm*.

As regards the accents, property so called, but very few words can here be said. They include *mai ayk* as in ไม้ *mai toh*. as in น้ำ, and three others of very minor importance.

The effect of the first three of these accents is to raise or lower the tone given to the syllables affected ; and a similar use is made of the letter *ห h*. Any attempt to explain these tones would involve a discussion of very great length, with a disquisition upon phonetic principles requiring an accurate and elaborate knowledge of musical science. Indeed the only way of explaining on paper the six or seven different tones which can be given to any given vowel or syllable would be to note them down according to a chromatic scale, like notes in a music score. Little or no attempt has therefore been made at the very hopeless task of explaining to readers the tones in any word; but occasionally where two or three words, differing only in accent, occur in juxtaposition, the English equivalent given to them has been varied as to indicate roughly what distinction is made between them by the Siamese. No one will, however, it is to be hoped, suppose for a moment that the correct pronunciation of the Siamese language, with its infinitely varied modulations, can be learned by perusal of a dictionary.

In giving equivalents in English (which will be found in brackets, close after the Siamese words) the author has neither hoped nor attempted to express accurately the sound of the Siamese letter or letters. All that could be achieved, or even attempted, in this respect with the type at his disposal, was to render in a rough and simple way an approximation to the sound of the native word. Those who require a more correct explanation of the vowel sounds, with all the necessary ornamentation of accents and marks, must consult a work far more elaborate and costly than this.

Generally speaking, the following sounds are attributed to the vowels used in the English equivalents.

a - *as in English* aorist — *French é-as in* Léon.

a' - *as in English* America.

aa - *as in English* Canaan, *or as the* a *in* sand, *much lengthened out.*

e - *as in English* end.

ee - *as in English* see.

i - *as in English* I.

ie - *as in English* lie.

i' - *as in English* in, *or French* inutile.

o - *as in English* on.

oh - *as in English* oh! — *French-o-in* oser.

u - *as in English* undone.

oo' - *as in English* foot.

oo - *as in English* fool.

eu' - *as in French* peu.

eu - *as the* œu *in French* cœur.

ah - *as in English* ah == *French-à-as in* âne.

ay - *as in English* may.

ai - *as in English* Cairo.

Whenever a letter at the end of a word is followed by *e*, the intention is that the sound of the last syllable should be lengthened. Thus *pie* is intended to have a longer sound than *pi*; and *howe* to have a longer sound than *how*. Whenever a vowel is followed by a hyphen, the sound of it is intended to be shortened as much as possible ; and whenever a final consonant is doubled, it is intended that the syllable should be strengthened and emphasised.

The articles, both definite and indefinite, have, as a rule, been suppressed. Thus " tree," means " *a* tree " and " universe," means *the* universe." When, however the indefinite article occurs, it is intended to mean " a kind of," so that " a tree " must not be understood to mean " any kind of tree " but " one particular kind of tree, " and so also with birds, fish, flowers, and other generic expressions. In Siamese the several species included under one genus often keep the name of that genus side by side with their own specific name. Thus almost all fish are described by double names, of which the first term is *plah*, " fish," and the second is the specific name of the particular species. The same is the case with birds, which are called *Nok Kra 'chok*, *Nok Chang Tong*, etc., etc., and with a great many trees, and insects. In this dictionary the generic term has in these cases mostly been omitted; as it would have been absurd to arrange some hundreds of birds and fishes under the single headings of *nok* and *plah*, and would have been needlessly tedious to state in each case of a bird or fish that the word describing the species ought to be used together with the generic term *nok* or *plah*.

The fanciful innovations which some busy-bodies are attempting to introduce into the Siamese language have here been rejected; and on the other hand most of the obsolete and archaic forms have been omitted. The common word ເປນ has, by the advice of the most reliable guides, and after due consideration, been printed without the "lekh paat" which is often added to it.

The only authority which has been quoted is the admirable work of my predecessor, Mr. HENRY ALABASTER, whose "Wheel of the Law" contains a mine of copious and accurate information respecting the meaning of Siamese words, especially bearing upon religious or philosophical learning. Frequent references to this work will be found in all parts of the Dictionary; and the reader is strongly recommended to make use of these references whenever he is in doubt as to the exact meaning of any word which, owing to want of space, could not be discussed at length in these pages.

The excellent Pâli Dictionary of Professor Childers has been freely consulted; and I am indebted to Sir M. Monier-Williams, Boden Professor of Sanskrit in the University of Oxford, for his valuable advice in ascertaining the origin of the numerous words which have been incorporated into Siamese direct from the Sanskrit, without passing through the intermediate stage of Pali. I am inclined to think that this latter class of words is much more numerous than is usually supposed; but in allotting to the two classes of words their several origins, I have given the preference to Pali in all cases where it seemed at all probable that they had come to Siam from this source.

Before concluding this Preface I must express my gratitude to those friends, Siamese and European, who have assisted me with their advice and help, and more especially to Hluang Desah, of the Survey Department, with whom the first draft of the work was made out; to Nai Piah, who, by the permission of Phra Metah, revised that first draft; and to Nai Tuan, who, cooperated in the later work. From His Excellency Phya

Bhaskarawongse, Minister of Agriculture, from Monsieur Charles Hardouin of the French Consulate, Mr. French and Mr. Beckett of the British Consulate, M. de Sa, of the Foreign Office, and Dr. Oscar Frankfurter, of the same Department. I have obtained very useful hints and valuable items of information.

As it may probably be found necessary, before very long, to publish an amended and enlarged Edition of this work, the author will be specially grateful to any reader who will have the kindness to point out to him any particulars in which the present Edition appears faulty or incomplete.

LIST OF ABREVIATIONS.

Engl. Eng. or E.	English, or of English derivation.	
Fr.	Freach	„ „
Portug.	Portuguese	„ „
Gr.	Greek	„ „
Lat.	Latin	„ „
Cambod. or Cam	Cambodian.	„ „
Malay.	Malayan	„ „
Siam.	Siamese	„ „
Laos.	Laosian	„ „
Sanck. or San.	Sanskrit	„ „
P.	Pali	„ „
Chin.	Chinese	„ „
Javan.	Javanese	„ „

phon onomatopœie, or derived from the sound of the thing described.

Alab. or Al. Alabaster's " Wheel of the Law " (Trübner & Co., 1871.)

Obsol. - obsolete, or no longer in common use·

Prosod. term used in prosody or scanning.

Gramm. grammatical term.

Arithm. arithmetical term.

Archit. architectural term.

Myth. mythological term.

Zodiac zodiacal term.

Astr. astronomical term.

Imper. Imperative.

Conj. Conjunction.

Campos. Composition.

Conf. — compare the word or passage last mentioned with that which follows.

Exclam. or excl. exclamation.

Espec. or esp. especially

Num. design. word used to indicate the number of heads, pieces, specimens etc. of a class.

Vulg. vulgarism, or according to the vulgar usage.

q. v. refer to the word or place last mentioned.

etc. : and other words or things of the same kind.

LIST OF SUBSCRIBERS.

H. R. H. Chow Fa Krom Phra Prince Bhanuphanduwongse Waradej (10 copies.)

H. R. H. Krom Hmun Prince Putharet Damrong Sakdi, (2 copies.)

H. R. H. Krom Hmun Prince Rajasakdi Somozom.

H. R H. Krom Hmun Prince Sommot Amarabandhu.

H. R. H. Prince Chandrathat Chudhadharn.

H. R. H. Prince Sonapundit. (2 copies.)

H. H. The Rajah of Kedah.

H. E. Phya Akarat.

The Austro-Hungarian Consulate, Bangkok.

Messrs. Andersen & Co. (2 copies.)

H. E. Phya Smud Buranuraks. (2.)

The British Legation, Bangkok. (2.)

The British Legation, Chiengmai.

Capt. J. Bush. (Phya Saharadit) (2./

J. S. Black Esq. H. B. M. Legation.

K. Bethge Esq., Royal Railway Department. (2 copies.)

W. G. Barnet Esq.

Louis Blech Esq.

J. W. Benson Esq., Bond Street, London.

A. Balfour Esq.

A. Berli Esq.

Phra Boribun.

Herr Otto Beidek.

Nai Boriban.

J. McDonald Cameron Esq., M. P.

Khun Chamnan Charasutr.

J. M. da Costa Esq., (Hluang Rajayasathok).

A. M. F. da Costa, Esq., Foreign Office.

Mons. le Père Colombet, Collège de l'Assomption, Bangkok.

Nai Kachon Charatwongse.

Dr. Cheek (4 copies.)

The Duchess of Sutherland. (2.)

Rev. John Carrington.

John Clunis Esq., Chief Architect to the Siamese Government.

Nai Chaduck.

Poh Chome, Telegraph Office, Chantaburi.

G. Collmann, Esq.

Signor S. Cardu.

Monsieur F. Chalant.

Nai Cham, Telegraph Master, Kanburi.

Nai Chark.

F. Cordeiro Esq.

H. E. Phya Damrong.

H. E. Phya Siharaj Decho. (2 copies.

Messrs. Dulau & Co., London, (2.)

C. Dunlop Esq.

LIST OF SUBSCRIBER

George D. Evans Esq., (2 copies.)

E. H. French Esq., H. B. M. Consul at Bangkok.

Oscar Frankfurter Esq., Ph. D.

Dr. Fritschi.

Capt. Fowler.

P. Gowan Esq., M. D.

J. Grassi Esq.

Signor G. Geiringer.

Capt. C. von Holck, Royal Siamese Marine Infantry.

Mons. C. H. Hardouin, Chancelier au Consulat de France, Bangkok.

T. H. Hays Esq., M. D.

John Hutchinson Esq., Municipal Department.

I. W. Hendricks Esq.

F. Hurst Esq., C. E.

H. Hooker Esq.

J. M. Inglis Esq.

Monsieur A. Jourdan, Telegraph Department.

J. C. James Esq., Educational Department.

Chas. C. Jones Esq. E. C.

H. H. the Rajah of Kedah.

H. H. Mom Chow Khao.

Messrs. Kiam Hoa Heng & Co.

H. E. Phya Pipat Kosa, Under-Secretary of State for Foriegn Affairs.

Nai Kling.

Nai Korn.

Monsieur E. Lorgeou. Gérant du Consulat de France à Bangkok.

L'École Spéciale des langues Orientales à Paris.

Khun Lekhanukorn.

M. C. L. Langguth Esq.

Capt. A. J. Loftus, Hydrographer to H. S. M.

H. E. Phya Montri, late Minister at the Court of St. James.

Nai Wisut Moltecan.

Rev. S. G. McFarland, D. D.

F. C. McGregor Esq.

Herr Erwin Müller (Hluang Boribat).

James Maxwell Esq.

C. W. Mathews Esq., Public Works Department.

Mrs. Maclachlan, (Ladies' Library. Bangkok.)

J. Maclachlan Esq.

R. L. Morant Esq., B.A., (3 copies.)

J. McCarthy Esq., R. Survey Department.

D. Niewenhuis Esq., Acting Consul for the Netherlands. Bangkok.

Hon. Sir Edward L. O'Malley. Chief Justice of the Supreme Court of the Straits Settlements.

V. F. Page Esq., Barrister-at-Law.

Hluang Pithi.

Chom Hmiin Sarapitt Pakdi.

Mr. M. M. Pullie.

LIST OF SUBSCRIBERS.

Nai Pharah.

Mom Chow Phya Pakdi.

H. E. the Governor of Petchaburi.

H. E. Phya Rajah.

Capt. A. du P. de Richelieu (Phya Cholayat) Commander R. S. N.. (4.)

Lieut. A du P. de Richelieu.

C. H. Ramsay Esq.. (Hluang Chemnong Nivalskitch.)

Mom Chow Rajawarindr.

H. W. Rolfe Esq.. Education Department.

Baboo Ramsami, Head Master New School, (20 copies.)

Monsieur E. Roland.

Nai Rang. Telegraph Department.

The Royal Asiatic Society.

The Supreme Court of the Straits Settlements, (for Library.)

Choem Sri Sararaks. (2 copies.)

Phra Nai Sarapett.

Hluang Sathorn.

Capt. Schau. Royal Body Guard.

Mom Rajawongse Samreang.

Hluang Prasiti Raj Sakdi.

Hluang Srai Somoat.

Hluang Prachak Subansorn.

Mr. B. M. Sheriff. Chief Inspector of Police. Bangrak.

F. H. Smiles Esq.. C.E.

P. B. P. Simoens Esq.. International Court.

The Siamese Legation. London, (3.)

Tan Keong Seng.

A. Thurnall Esq.. B.A.

S. Tisseman Esq.

Messrs. Trübner & Co.. (15 copies.).

T. M. Upton Esq.

United States Legation. Bangkok.

Ravana Vyte Padeachee. (5 copies.)

Hluang Binit Videsband. H. S. M. Customs.

Mom Anuwongse Warapan.

O. Weber Esq.. Consul for Norway and Sweden.

D. Williams Esq.. H. S. M. Customs·

Hluang Wathitt.

E. F. W. Wilkinson Esq.. C. E.. Public Works Department. (2 copies.)

M. R. Western Esq.

H. E. Phya Swasti Wamadit.

C. Xavier Esq.

Nai Tong Yu.

Palat Pichai Yayat.

ก

ก (kaw) English hard *g* or *k*·
(initial : a middle letter)

ก็ (kaw) 1) then, also, consequently—
ก็, (intensitive) assuredly, it can—ก็
either, or แล้ว · and afterwards
ก็ : :: — ก็ although, nevertheless
(2, (sign of the present tense)

ก(อ) (kok) 1) to hold in the arms (2)
a reed or rush เสื่อ — mat (3) — ๆ
(phon.) the clucking of a hen

ก็กรม (ka'krom) weaver's comb

กึก (ka'keuk) [phon.] to laugh

กง (kong) curve, curved — วง — ข้าว
wheel   พัก water-wheel, paddle-
wheel, propeller (of steamer),
weaver's instrument

กฎ (kot) Pali and กฎหมาย act, to
decree, to legislate — ไว้ to resolve
1 royal decrees

กด (kot) to push, to press, to compress
ๆ a fish กก a water-bird
 flamingo — ขี่ to oppress

กดูบกดิบ (ka'doo'p ka'dip) just able
to move

กทุ้ง (ka'too'ng) to poke, to strike with
a stick downwards — เส้า to beat
the cadence in a boat

กน (kon) (a word used in speaking
about prununciation) — แก้ continuously

กน (kon) to reap, to mow, to cut, to
weed

กน (kon) buttocks — ก้น bottom of
a pot

กบ (kop) (1) over-full (2) frog — ริาก
big frog · บัว little frog (3) place
(4) anvil   ข top of a house

กม (kom) to bend, incline

กมพัก (kompa't) rest or foundation for
a column or post

กมลาศน์ (ka'ma'laht) [Pali] Brahma

กรก (krok) mortar for pounding

กมุท (ka'moo't) [Pali] a white lotus

กร (kon) Pali arms — กอด to
embrace

กิร (kara) Sansk. act, action, to do

กรกฎ (karakot) [Sansk. Cancer
(zodiac.)

กรกฎาคม (karakɔtahkom) [Sansk.] name of the fourth month (July)

กรง (krong) cage ลูก—trellis-work

กรด (krot) water bottle with lid and spout

กรด (krot) acid, acrid น้ำ — corrosive water, metallic acid ลม — corrosive air

กรน (kron) to snore

กร.นย (kra'nai) (with นก)the blue-and-white kingfisher

กรบ (krop) harpoon

กรม (krom) [Pali] (1) troop, division, department, chief.— สมเกจ์ title of a Royal Highness of the first grade — พระ title of a Celestial Highness — หลวง title of a Royal Highness of the third grade— ขุน title of the fourth grade-- หมื่น title of the fifth grade—ม้า Department of cavalry—นา D. of agriculture — วัง D. of the Palace — การ provincial officer

กรรณ (ka'n) [Pali] ears

กรรฐ (ka'n) [Pali] neck พระ—neck of the King

กรรถัศ (ka'nta't) [Pali] a well-bred horse

กรรไพรี (see กันไพรี)

กรรม (ka'm) [Pali] action, work, sin misfortune, ตาม บุญ ตาม—be it as it may—ฐาน meditation, private devotion —บรรพ moral precept, natural law — วาง and—วาร ecclesiastical vote or proceedings (but see Alab. 185)

กรวด (kruat) (1) rocket (2) small pebble

กรวบ (kruep) brittle, to break

กรวม (kruam) noise of chewing or crunching

กรวย (kruwy) funnel

กรอ (kraw) to loiter about

กรอก (krawk) (1) dry, lean ยาง -water-bird which has a dry note ลูก—very small child born dead, still-born (2) [Cambod.] to put in ไส้—sausage

กรอง (kraung) to filter—ทอง to embroider or weave with gold thread

กร่อน (kraun) to be eaten up by degrees

กรอบ (kraup) (1) dried by fire (2) circuit, frame, side

กรอม (kraum) lightly, softly

กรอย (kroy) briny

กราก (krahk) (1) firmly, rapidly (2) a noise

กราง (krahng) to rasp, to grate

กร่าง (krahng) a big tree with red fruit

กราด (kraht) (1) to drive in (2) scattered กราว — furious anger

กราน (krahn) (1) senile, of an old man (2) to disfigure

กราบ (krahp) (1) bulwarks (2) to prostrate oneself—ลา to take leave, goodbye

กราม (krahm) the grinding teeth, grinders

กราย (krai) to swing the arms in walking

กราว (krow) with กริว [Cambod.] a tortoise, a turtle

กริ่ง (kring) sound of a small bell

กริ่ง (kring) to suspect

กฤช (kritt) a Malay dagger

กฤดาภินิหาร (kridapp'inihahn) [Sansk.] meritorious acts done in a former state of existence

กฤดี (krit) [Sansk.] with ชำระ ceremony of the bath for a new king

กริบ (krip) [phon.] to cut with scissors

กริม (krim) a small fish

กริ่ม (krim) glad, cheerful

กริว (kriu) a turtle

กริ้ว (kriu) to get angry —กราก rage, fury

กฤษ (kritt) with ประ common idiom as opposed to Sanskrit

กฤษดาน (kritsadahn) [Sansk.] to make; it is done

กฤษดี (kritsadee) with ไว loins

กรี (kree) box

กรีด (kreet) to draw a line with a knife —น้ำ to water, —กราย vain

กรีฑา (kreetah) to raise an army

เกรียก (kreeyek) extent from the thumb to the forefinger

เกรียง ไกร (kreeyang krai) superior, excelling

เกรียน (kreean) short; worn out

เกรียบ (kreeap) dry, dry-sounding ทะกั๋ว — tin

เกรียม (kreeam) over-done, scorched

เกรียว (kreeu) in crowds, tumultuous

เกรียว (kreeu) to shout out

กริง (kreung) to nail

กรุ (kru) to cover up with leaves -- โรๆ rough

กรก (kroo'k) noise of walking on boards

กรุง (kroo'ng) capital--ศรี Ayuthia-- ศรี the beautiful city—เทพ Bangkok

กรุณ (karoo'na) [Pali] merciful, pitiful

กรุณา (karoo'nah) [Pali] pity, compassion

กรุ่น (kroo'n) a little

กรุ่ม (kroo'm) often

กรุย (kruwy) to mark by planting little sticks

กรู (kroo) to run up in crowds

กรู (kroo) at early morning

เกร่ (kray) to wander

เกรง (krayng) to respect, to fear, moderation, respect

เกริ่น (kreun) to call, to warn

แกร (see พระ แกร)

แกรก (kraak) [phon,] noise of tearing cloth

แกร่ง (kraang) (of rice grain) full, entire (2) hard, firm

ไกร (krai) powerful

ไกร ลาศ (krailaht) [Pali] lower heaven เขา the hill on which this heaven is situated; artificial hill on which the top-knot-cutting of a Prince takes place

ไกร ษร (kraison) [Sansk.] lion

โกรก (kroke) (1) deep valley (2) gurgling -- กระดาน to saw a plank into laths

โกรง (krohng) inside (as of a ship)

โกรธ (krote) to get angry

โกร่น (krone) to fall off, to be stripped หัว -- bald

โกรย (krowy) a fish

เกราะ (krau') (1) cuirass (2) brittle

กราม (kra'm) to be exposed to

กร่ำ (kra'm) with เม seed of a tree

กร่ำ (kra'm) pulp

กระ (kra') tortoise shell ศก — black spots on over-ripe fruit

กระกรี กระกรม (kra'kree kra'krom) quick, hasty

กระเกณฑ์ (kra'ken) (see กะ เกณฑ์)

กระเกษ (kara'kett) (see การะเกด) a reed ศอก — yellow sweet-smelling flower of reed

กระโก่ง (kra'kohng) (see โก่ง) to keep up the price

กระโกน (kra'kone) to call from afar

กระจก (kra'chok) and — สอง looking-glass, mirror — ตา white of the eye สอง — to look in a glass

กระจน (kra'chon) small deer

กระจิว (kra'chaw) chirping

กระจอก (kra'chawk) sparrow — เทษ ostrich

กระจอม (kra'chawm) walking in water

กระจ้อย (kra'choy) small—จ้อย like a child, childish

กระจ่าง (kra'chahng) clear, limpid

กระจาด (kra'chaht) a basket for ve-

getables or other eatables

กระจาน (kra'chahn) (see จาน)

กระจาบ (kra'charp) hedge sparrow, a small field bird

กระจิด (kra'chit) กระจ้อย and กระจิ, small, minute

กระจิป (kra'chip) (phon.) a small bird whose note is like " chip, chip "

กระจิว (kra'chew) [Chin.] small

กระจุก (kra'choo'k) sundry small things

กระจุน (kra'choo'n) to touch lightly

กระจุบ (kra'choo'p) oil bottle, small lamp

กระจูด (kra'choot) a reed

กระเจิง (kra'cheung) roaming, wandering

กระแจะ (kra'chaa') perfumes

กระโจน (kra'chone) to jump

กระโจม (kra'chome) (1) to rush upon (2) a tent for vapour baths ผ้า — swaddling clothes, tent

กระเจา (kra'chow) a kind of hemp

กระเจา (kra'chaw) white spots on the eyeball

กระระ (kra'cha`) bright

กระทั่ง (kra'cha'ng) carved *or* chased leaves

กระทับ (kra'cha'p) a water plant ปาก — indented

กระทับปี (kra'cha'p pee) guitar

กระฉง (kra'chong) a worm which eats rice

กระฉอก (kra'chawk) (1) to gush out, (2) to indent, to notch (3) to move from side to side

กระฉ้อน (kra'chawn) to be blown about, to rock

กระฉูก (kra'choo'k) ball of cotton

กระฉูด (kra'choo't) to pull gently

กระฉุ่น (kra'choo'n) to push, to poke

กระฉุย กระเฉก (kra'chuy kra'chake) to squander; prodigal

กระฉูด (kra'choot) to splash, *or* be splashed, with mud

กระเฉก (kra'chake) wearied

กระเฉด (kra'chate) a water-plant eaten as salad

กระโฉกกระแฉก (kra'choke kra'chaak) lame, limping

กระโฉม (kra'chome) [*with* ผ]a plant

กระเฉาะ (kra'chaw) to keep gushing *or* jumping out

กระชอน (kra'chawn) cullender แมลง — a cricket used in fishing

กระช้อย (kra'choy) (1) handsome (of women) (2) dancing woman

กระชาก (kra'chahk) to drag off, to drag about

กระชามาศ (kra'charmart) gold produced in water

กระชาย (kra'chai) a sort of ginger

กระชิง (kra'ching) parasol made of leaves ทีน — a tree

กระชี (kra'chee) a small fish

กระเชียง (kra'cheeang) oar ห — noose for attaching oars to the post or peg serving as a rowlock

กระเชียก (kra'cheeat) an amulet

กระชูก (kra'choo'k) one sixteenth of a เกวียน or load

กระชูม (kra'choo'm) *and* กระชุ่ม solid, firm, robust

กระเชอ (kra'cherr) a measure of five tanans

กระแชง (kra'chaang) leaves sewn together for roofing

กระแฉะ (kra'chaa'') to graze, to touch lightly

กระโชก (kra'choke) to pounce upon, to pursue

กระเชา (kra'chow) basket for washing rice or collecting anything

กระฉะ (kra'cha') long basket

กระฉัง (kra'cha'ng) (1) bamboo box for keeping fish in water (2) to hang up as a scare-crow

กระฉัน (kra'ch'an) to push, to press

กระฉับ กระฉัน (kra,cha'p kra'cha'n) to walk with firm steps

กระซิบ (kra'sip) [Sansk.] to whisper, to speak low

กระซง (kra'soo'ng) liberal, prodigal

กระเซน (kra'senn) to penetrate or get in sideways

กระเซอ (kra'serr) stupid, silly

กระเซะ (kra'say'') and กระโซย (kra'soh) weak language

กระเซ็น (kra'senn) to wander aimlessly, to stray

กระแซะ (kra'saa') to push

กระฐิน (kra'tinn) [Pali] solemn procession กฐก annual procession to the temples (in autumn) with offerings to the priests

กระณะ (kra'na') Pali] gold

กระดก (kra'dok) higher on one side than the other

กระดง (kra'dong) sciatica กระดาน boards of all kinds

กระด้ง (kra'dong) hand-fan, open basket

กระดวน (kra'dooan) to drive a wedge

กระดวม (kra'dooam) crawling

กระดอ (kra'daw) pudenda viri

กระดอง (kra'dong) like the back of a tortoise — ห clitoris feminae

กระดอน (kra'dawn) to start back, rebound

กระดอม (kra'daum) a medicinal creeping plant

กระดาก (kra'dark) to go back, to give up, abandon

กระดาง ดาง (kra'dahng lahng) rough and rude, obstinate, incorrigible

กระค้าง (kra'dahng) hard

กระคาน (kra'darn) plank, board — ชะนวน black board or slate for writing on

กระดาษ (kra'dart) [Portug.] paper

กระดิก (kra'dik) to palpitate, to move

กระดิ่ง (kra'ding) [phon.] little bell

กระดี่ (kra'dee) (1) to lift with a lever (2) a fish shaped like a leaf

กระดี่ (kra'dee) to tickle

กระเดิด (kra'decat) (1) to carry on the hip or side (2) a little, rather

กระดึง (kra'deung) and กระดิ่ง a little bell hung on buffaloes' or other animals' necks

กระเดือก (kra'deuak) to put in little by little, to swallow with difficulty

กระเดื่อง (kra'deuang) beam or fulcrum of a lever ลือ — the news spreads

กระดุ่ง (kra'doo'ng) waddling

กระดุม (kra'doo'm) button รัง button hole

กระดอมปี (kra'dompee) [Pali] mean, low, common people

กระดูก (kra'dook) bone

กระเด้น (kra'den) to leap up, rebound

กระเดิด (kra'dertt) to exceed in height

กระแดโว (kra'dayo) to drive about

กระได (kra'dai) [colloq.] ladder —ลิง a creeping plant

กระโดก (kra'doke) and กระโหก to oscillate, skip ; indecent movements

กระโดง (kra'dohng) back-bone of a fish เสา — mast

กระโดน (kra'done) a tree of which the bark is used as litter for elephants

กระเดา (kra'dow) [Cambod.] hot

กระเดา (kra'dow) and กระโดก indecent movements

กระเดาะ (kra'daw) to make a noise with the mouth like the cackling of a hen

กระดั๊ก (kra'da'k) infirm, weak

กระดังงา (kra'da'ng ngah) (and other forms) a tree

กระตอก (kra'tok) กระดาก and กระโดก [phon.] cackling of the hen after laying an egg

กระเทรย (kra'troey) *with* หญ้า a burr, a prickly plant which sticks to the clothing

กระไกร (kra'trai) scissors ขา — jaws

เหยยา — sparrow-hawk

กระทัว (kra'tooa) a parrot

กระทอย ทิวัท (kra'toy teewit) a field bird

กระต่าย (kra'tai) (1) hare, rabbit — ป่า hare — บ้าน tame rabbit (2) iron scraper in the shape of a hare for rasping cocoa-nut

กระทิก (kra'tik) (1) bottle, jug, a measure of about one pint — วิก small; lit tle child (2) beating of the pulse

กระเทือง (kra'teuang) to get gradually better, convalescent

กระทุก (kra'too'k) to pull, to disturb with noises — กระทุก restless; to make known

กระทืน (kra'tee n) to touch, to stir up

กระแทงแรง (kra'tayng rayng) a gay woman who caresses children

กระเทน (kra'tenn) a kingfisher ("halcyon omnicolor")

กระแต (kra'taa) (1) a white squirrel; to run about like a squirrel (2) a small gong or cymbal

กระแทง (kra'taang) emulation, zeal

กระไต้ (kra'to) a bird — ไม้ parrot

กระตัก (kra'ta'k) goad

กระตัง (kra'ta'ng) urine

กระตัญญู (kra'ta'n yoo) [Pali] faithful, grateful

กระตด (kra'tot) to retire

กระตาง (kra'tahng) water-jar, vase, pitcher

กระตินน (kra'tinn) (*with* ต้น) a tree having a sweet scented yellow flower

กระโถน (kra'tone) spittoon

กระตก (kra'tok) to fan, to winnow, to disentangle by pulling the end of a bow or loop — วิก a plant, a shrub

กระตง (kra'tong) (1) thwarts, seats for oarsmen, (2) baskets and floats made of leaves, rafts made of the green trunks of banana trees etc., on which are floated offerings to the river-angel ลอย — the ceremony of floating or launching the illuminated rafts (in October and November, ไก่ a young cock ปลา — a fish — นา small mound of earth bounding a paddy field — ความ argument, the fact of a matter — เหา a long thin fish เย็บ — to make a basket or tray by folding leaves or paper, etc.

กระทบ (kra'top) to strike or jump against, to attack indirectly

กระทรวง (kra'sooang) laws, edicts, jurisprudence

กระทอ (kra'taw) a basket

กระทอก (kra'tawk) masturbari

กระท้อน (kra'tawn) (1) to jump, to rebound (2) a round fruit

กระท่อม (kra'tawm) cottage, hut คิ้น — a tree of which the leaves are used for eating as an opiate

ระท่อม กระแทม้ม (kra'tawm kra'taam) parsimony, economical

กระทา (kra'tah) (1) partridge (2) male

กระทาชาย (kra'tah chai) male; man

ระท้าน (kra'tahn) to tremble, to be shaken

กระทาย (kra'tai) (1) a basket (2) to clean rice, to winnow

กระที (kra'tee') cocoa-nut oil

ระทิง (kra'ting) a long slippery fish without scales วิว — wild ox คิ้น — a tree

กระเทียม (kra'teeam) garlic

กระทืบ (kra'teup) (1) to stamp with the foot (2) sensitive plant

กระทือ (kra'teu) an edible root

กระทุง (kra'too'ng) pelican — ลอยแพ pelican when floating

กระทุ้ง (kra'too'ng) to push, to poke, to strike downwards with a stick — เส้า to beat the cadence in a boat

กระทุ่ม (kra'too'm) (1) a flowering tree (2) to beat the water with the hands and feet

กระทู้ (kra'too) pillars or columns of an enclosure; principal parts เป็น — principal thing

กระเทย (kra'toy) neither male nor female, neuter

กระเทร่ (kra'tayray) to wander about

กระแทก (kra'taak) to hit against

กระแทะ (kra'taa) a small cart

กระเทาะ (kra'taw) to be opened, split, to be peeled

กระทำ (kra'tam) to do, act

กระทะ (kra'ta') frying pan

กระทั่ง (kra'ta'ng) as far as — คิด india rubber plant

กระหนก (kra'nok) (1) to tremble with fear (2) sculptures, decorations

กระหนาก (kra'nahk) a tree

กระหนาน (kra'nahn) a tree

กระหนาบ (kra'nahp) to press together

กระนี้ (kra'nee) in this way, thus ดัง — although

กระแนะ (kra'naa) importunate

กระไน (kra'nai) a bird

กระโน้น (kra'nohn) on the other side, there

กระหน่ำ (kra'na'm) repeatedly, persistently, much

กระหนัก (kra'na'k) certain, assuredly

กระนั้น (kra'na'n) in that way, so ดัง — although

กระบก (kra'bok) wild almond tree

กระบวน (kra'booan) manner, order, coquetry

กระบวย (kra'booi) cocoa-nut drinking vessel with a handle attached, ladle

กระบอก (kra'bawk) piece of bamboo used as a drinking vessel — ตา cavity of the eye - - ฉีด syringe

กระบอง (kra'bawng) long thick stick ไม้ — thick stick

กระบาก (kra'bark) a tree

กระบาย (kra'bai) open bamboo basket with four projecting corners

กระบาล (kra'bahn) [Cambod.] (1) head (2) sacrifice offered to demons โพล - - (a word of abuse) eat

กระบี่ (kra'bee') decayed vegetable matter in pools

กระบิง (kra'bing) and กระบวน (kra'booan) dissimulation

กระบิด (kra'bitt) (1) dissimulation (2) to tie with rattan, tie, fasten

กระบิล (kra'bin) [Pali] (1) monkey (2) Kabin (town)

กระบี่ (kra'bee) sword, sword-blade

กระเบียด (kra'beeat) (1) to tighten, condense, oppress (2) the fourth part of an inch

กระเบียน (kra'beean) a tree of which the seed produces madness or intoxication

กระเบือ (kra'beu) [Cambod.] buffalo

กระเบือง (kra'beuang) tile, earthenware

กระบุง (kra'boo'ng) basket, bamboo basket round at the top and square at the bottom

กระบุน (kra'boon) a forest tree bearing fruit like a pomegranate

กระบุ่ม กระบ่าม (kra'boom kra'barm) rude, rough, badly brought up

กระเบ็ง (kra'beng) to swell

กระเบน (kra'benn) tail or end of the panang ปลา — ray or skate (a sea fish) — บิน flying fish

กระเบย (kra'baa) see แบ

กระเบา (kra'baa) a tree of which the wood is used for making oars

กระเบาง (kra'baang) to tighten with a rope, t tie, to wrap together

กระเบา (kra'baa') (1) a block, a small piece (2) net of about a hundred feet long — บิง small

กระเบม (kra'beme) [Cambod.] embrace

กระบัง (kra'bang) (1) white lead, white paint (2) hurdles — บิง หม hurdles for catching fish (3) to cover: the guard of a sword

กระบัด (kra'ba't) to defraud

กระปรบ (kra'prip) fine (of rain)

กระโปรง (kra'prong) bamboo network to protect fruit on a tree

กระเปา กระปาบ (kra'paw kra'paa) bruised, half broken, weak

กระป๋อง (kra'pong) [Chin.] tin pail

กระปิ (kra'pee') essence of prawns (used in curry)

กระปิยะ and กะปิยะ (ka'piya) (see กปิยะ)

กระปุก (kra'poo'k) jug, pitcher, bottle

กระโปก (kra'poke) scrotum ฑก — testicles

กระเป๋า (kra'pow) [Chin.] small tobacco pouch, pocket pouch strung round the waist

กระเปาะ (kra'paw) point — แหวน bezil of a ring

กระผม (kra'pom) I (to a superior)

กระเผลก (kra'ploke) to limp, to go lame

กระผีก (kra'peek) the fourth part of a หมาะ

กระพก (kra'pok) to pick up

กระพง (kra'pong) a sea fish — ไข่ hen about to lay เปย — a bivalve shell

กระพรวน (kra'pruan) small bell

กระพร่าง (kra'prahng) confusedly

กระพราก (kra'praht) dirtily, carelessly, slovenly

กระพริบ ตา (kra'prip tah) to wink

กระพรุน (kra'proo'n) mollusc

กระเพรา (kra'prow) sweet basil

กระพลอง กระแพลง (kra'plong kra'plaang) to limp, hesitate ; staggering

กระพอ (kra'paw) a tree

กระพาก (kra'pahk) a fish

กระพายน้ำ (kra'parp na'm) a river
   tortoise

กระพือ (kra'peu) to shake, to flap (the
   wings)

กระเพือม (kra'peuam) splashing of
   water

กระพุ้ง (kra'poong) cavity, hollow

กระพุ่ม (kra'poo'm) (1) thicket, plantation (2) anything of a conical
   shape มือ — hands with the finger
   tips joined

กระเพื่อ กระพก (kra'perr kra'pok) delirious from fever, careless

กระเพิก (kra'perk) to destroy, root out

กระเพิด (kra'pert) to expel, eject

กระเพาะ (kra'paw) (1) stomach (2) a
   basket — เยี่ยว bladder — ใหญ่ large
   gut — น้ำ jug

กระพัง (kra'pa'ng)' projection of rock
   or earth

กระพังโหม (kra'pa'ng hohm) a tree

กระพัน (kra'pa'n) talisman to preserve
   from wounds

กระพุ่ม (kra'phoom) to watch over —
   กระหาย greedily, excessively, a-
   bundantly

กระมล (kra'mon) [Pali] heart, chest

กระหมวด (kra'mooat) to bind round

กระหม่อม (kra'mom) top, summit ทูล
   — Prince, King; to raise — ฉัน
   (to Princes)

กระมุท (kra'moo't) [Pali] lotus

กระเม็ดไว้ (kra'met wai) and กระเม็ด
   กระไหม to reserve for the future

กระแมบ (kra'maap) to press in, to
   squeeze together, to compress

กระมัง (kra'ma'ng) perchance, perhaps

กระยง (kra'yong) to stagger

กระยา (kra'yah) [Cambod.] food, rice
   — ทาน beggar — สาท cakes for the
   end of the 10th month

กระโย (kra'yoh) falling

กระโหย่ง (kra'yohng) to run quickly on
   tip-toe

กระยา (kra'ya') (1) sweepings, off-
   scourings (2) knife with crooked
   handle for cutting grass

กระหยัด (kra'ya't) to set aside; little
   by little

กระรอก (kra'rawk) squirrel

กระร่อง (kra'rong) กระแร้ง (kra'raang) and กระริ่ง (kra'ring) imperfect, insignificant

กระเรียน (kra'reean) a bird with a red neck

กระรุ่ง (kra'roo'ng) and กระรุ้ป (kra'-roo'p) to bungle

กระไร (kra'rai) what? how? — เลย (exclam. of surprise) it cannot be understood

กระระบุน (kra'ra'boon) and การบูร (see การบูร) camphor

กระระพฤกษ (kra'ra'proo'k) and การะ พฤกษ better กัลปพฤกษ Sansk.] a fabulous tree (bearing money, jewels etc. as fruit) (Alab. 216) ลูก — limes enclosing money or tickets and thrown as largesses ต้น — pole on which such limes are fixed before being thrown ภาว— the morning star, Venus

กระรัง (kra'ra'ng) a shell fish

กระรังตนู (kra'ra'ng tanoo) Tringano

กระรัต (ka'ra't) [Engl.] carat

กระลน กระลาน (kra'lon kra'lahn) in haste

กระลา (kra'lah) nut of the palm tree

กระลาการ (kra'lah kan) and กระลากรา (better ตุลาการ) [Pali] judge

กระหลาป่า (kra'lah bar) Batavia

กระลาสี (kra'lah see) sailors

กระลาโหม (kra'la'home) [Cambod.] Minister of War and of the Western provinces

กระลิกาลี (kra'li' kahlee) corrupt, dissolute

กระลิง (kra'ling) a small green parrot แขก — black Indians

กระหลิบ (kra'lip) quickly

กระลุมพก (kra'loo'mpoo'k) (better ตลุมพก) (1) mallet (2) a fish (3) a tree

กระเลววราก (kra'laywarahk) better กเฬ วระ [Pali] dead body, corpse

กระแหลน (kra'lenn) nearly, almost

กระโล่ (kra'loh) small basket varnished over and coloured black

กระโหลก (kra'loke) (1) skull (2) a cup made of cocoa-nut

กระหล่ำ (kra'la'm) cabbage

กระล่ำพร (kra'la'mpon) a river fish

กระลาพัก (kra'la'mpa'k) a scented wood (used in medicine)

กระลำภอก (kra'lampork) a conical pointed hat (for ceremonies)

กระละบั้งหา (kra'la'pa'nghar) black coral

กระละเม็ก (kra'la'mett) secret

กระละแม (kra'la'maa) a cake

กระวน กระวาย (kra'won kra'wai) anxious, uneasy, bad health, distress, recklessness

กระวอก กระแวก (kra'wauk kra'waak) distracted, inconsistent

กระวาก กระวิก and กระวูด (kra'waht kra'witt and kra'woot) hastily

กระวาน (kra'wahn) cardamum นก — a bird

กระวิชาติ (kra'wichaht) and กระวี [Pali] wise, learned, philosopher

กระเวน (kra'wayn) and ตะเวน (ta'wayn) (1) public exposure of criminals in chains (2) to explore กอง— police station

กระเวย กระวาย (kra'woey kra'wai) cries of pain

กระเว้า กระวอก (kra'wow kra'wort) untrustworthy, deceitful

กระเหว่า (kra'wow) and กุเหว่า (doowow) a black bird which whistles and talks — ลาย a bird with variegated plumage

กระหวัก (kra'wa't) to bind together, to reflect, to revolve

กระเษียร (kra'seean) and กระษีรา (kra'sirah) [Sansk.] milk

กระเษียณ (kra'seean) (1) small piece, cutting, scrap (2) limit อายุศึษ์ limit of age within which no one can be slave

กระเษตร (kra'sett) [Sansk.] agriculture — กระเษตราธิบดี Minister of Agriculture

กระเษม (kra'semm) and เกษม (ka'semm) [Sansk.] joy, pleasure, to be free from enemies พระ — chief judge

กระษัตร (kra'sa't) and กระษัตรา (kra'sa'trah) [Sansk.] King, royal

กระษัตรี (kra'sa'tree) [Sansk.] woman

กระส่ง (kra'song) a blackish fish

กระสวย (kra'sooi) weaver's shuttle

กระสอก (kra'sawt) [Maun] betel-nut

กระสอบ (kra'sawp) large flat bag made of rushes or cloth

กระสา (kra'sah) heron

กระสาปน์ (kra'sahp') [Sansk.] coin โรง — mint

กระสาย (kra'sai) anything in which medicine is taken

กระสิณ (kra'sinn) [Pali] means of mystic meditation, object of contemplation

กระสิรา *and* กระษีรา (kra'sirah) [Sansk.] milk

กระสูด (kra'seet) *and* กระสูด (kra'soot) to breathe through the nose

กระสือ (kra'seu) female magicians or demons who eat the bowels — ไฟ will o' the wisp

กระเสือก (kra'seuak) restless wandering in search of food

กระสุน (kra'soo'n) a bow for shooting balls ลูก — balls for shooting from a bow

กระเสด (kra'seyt) a fish

กระเส็น (kra'senn) kinsman, kinship

กระแส (kra'saa) (1) utterance, speech, flow, course, progress — น้ำ current (2) sweet sounding. harmonious

กระสัง (kra'sa'ng) a plant eaten as salad

กระสัน (kra'sa'n) [Sansk.] to miss, to feel pain at the absence of

กระหอง กระแหง (kra'hong kra'haang) (*see* กระหง) to conceive hatred (obs.)

กระหาปะณะ (kra'hahpana) [Pali] (*see* กระสาปน์) tael; Hindu coin or weight

กระหิด (kra'hitt) ungrateful นก — a small bird

กระหึม (kra'heumm) thundering, threatening

กระหือ (kra'heu) groaning

กระเหิม (kra'haym) swaggerer, brawler

กระหา (kra'haa) a small fish

กระแหะ (kra'haa') merry, smiling

กระโห (kra'ho) a large fish like a dolphin

กระหำ (kra'ha'm) genitalia viri ลูก — testicles

กระหัง (kra'ha'ng) male demons which eat the bowels of the sick

กระแหม (kra'haam) hoarse, dry throated

กระโหก (kra'hoke) growl of an animal about to bite

กระออก กระแอก (kra'ort kra'aat) sickly

กระอ้อง กระแอ้ง (kra'orng kra'aang) to slouch along

กระออม (kra'orm) water pot

กระอาก *and* กระอ้ก (kra'ark *and* kra'a'k) to vomit from surfeiting

กระอิด (kra'it) sobbing

กระอุบ กระอิบ (kra'oo'p kra'ip) to talk nonsense

กระอู้ *and* กระอี้ (kra'oo *and* kra'ee) complaining, murmuring

กระออม (kra'aam) (*see* กระแอม) to give a sign by coughing

กระไอ (kra'ai) to turn sour, to ferment

กระอาก (kra'a'k) to surfeit — กระไอ to stammer

กรัก (kra'k) yellow-wood; jacea — ไม้ a tree

กรัง (kra'ng) adhering firmly

กรัด (kra't) to fasten together (with a pin, etc.) ไม้ — wooden pin

กรัน (kra'n) *with* กล้วย a kind of banana หม้อ — a large pot for drinking out of

กรับ (kra'p) [phon.] bamboo sticks used for beating time at theatres — พวง fan-shaped arrangement of sticks used for beating on the hand

กรัถ (kra't) [Pali] to speak — รู้ to know, understand

กล (kon) [Pali] art, artifice — ยล automaton — หาก conversation เชิง stand for tapers, scented sticks, etc. เล่ห์ — มายา trick, magic

กลด (klot) parasol with three tiers or storeys

กลั้ว klon several, a lot of things together

กลบ klop (1) to cover with earth etc. to hide, (2) fish spear

กลบุตร kenla'boo't [Sansk.] children, the young

กลม klom round

กลวง kloo'ang pierced, hollow

กล้วย kloo'i banana

กลัว kloo'a to dread; fear

กลั้ว klooa' to mix or swallow with water

กลโหก kalahok [Pali] liar, cheat, impostor

กลอก klauk 1 to burn 2 to rinse 3 to turn, to roll — หน้า to make faces (4) lane (5) to put in

กลอง klawng drum — แขก Malay drum

กล่อง klaung a small box, a pocket with a narrow opening — ใหม่ cigar box

กล้อง klong tube — ส่อง telescope — ยาสูบ cigar holder, pipe

กลอน (klawn) 1) verses, poems 2) tongue of wood, latch, hasp, (3) rafter

กลอน (klon) (1) swelling of the testicle (2) rotten

กล่อม (klom) 1) to lull to sleep by singing (2) half a grain (3) a quarter of an att (4) to make round

กลอย (kloi) (1) wild potato (2) amiable

กล้า (klah) (1) rice for transplanting (2) bold กล้าแข็ง brave, able เหล็กกล้า – steel

กลาก with ขี้ (kee klark) ringworm

กลาง (klahng) middle คน – mediator, artitrator ถ้า amongst ใน –– among สณ – centre เก่า –ใหม่ neither old nor new

กลาย (klai) transformation ปี last year ปลา – a flat fish

กล่าว (klow) to say, relate, speak about

กลิ้ง (kling) to roll, to be rolled up ลูก roller

กลิ่ง (kling) [phon.] sound of a hand-bell

กลิ่น (klin) smell

กลิป (klip) [phon.] to clip, to snip

กลี (klee) (1) a box for betel-nut, etc. (2) racquet

กลีบ (kleep) leaf, petal –– หู the outside of the ear

เกลี้ย กล่อม (kleea' klom) to allure, persuade, seduce, entice

เกลียง (kleeang) trowel

เกลี้ยง (kleeang) level, smooth, clean

เกลียด (kleeat) to abhor, to detest น่า – detestable

เกลียว (kleeyo) string, to twist string –– ลม apoplexy

กลึง (klenng) to turn (with a lathe)

กลืน (kleun) to swallow, drink, sip

เกลือ (kleua) salt ป – purgative salts

เกลือก (kleuek) to roll ว่า perhaps, perchance

แกลือน (kleuan) to be spread ฝี to dissipate a tumour

เกลื่อน (kleuan) chloasma, white spots

กลุ่ม (kloo'm) a packet (of tobacco, betel-leaves, thread, etc.)

กลุ้ม (kloo'nm) (1) to darken (2) in crowds — อก and — คลุ้ง troubled, sad, distracted

กลุย with ชาย (chai klooi) edge of a cloth

เกล็ด (klett) (1) scales (of a fish) (2) to eat what is best, dainty

เกลอ (kler) friend, comrade

แกล (klaa) *and* พระ - Palace windows

แกล้ง (klaang) on purpose, mischievous

แกลบ (klaap) husk, skin of rice

แกลม (klaam) (1) to insert, to repair (2) food eaten with wine

แกละ (klaa') tuft of hair left on children's head

ใกล้ (klai) *and* เ ใ ั near

ไกล (klai) far

โกลน (klone) (1) stirrup (2) trunks of trees (3) to rough hew, to do unfinished (carpenter's) work

โกลน (klohn) [Chin.] (with ...) bald (head)

เกลา (klow) to smooth with a knife, to plane

เกล้า (klow') hair, twisted hair เ..ปร -- head, hair (of a royal pursonage) โปรด - pardon me - กระหม่อม I (speaking to a Prince of lower rank than Krom Phra)

เกลาะ (klau) a pierced bamboo used for making a noise by striking it

กล่ำ (kla'm) the eighth part of a fuang; one att ... a wild pea having red fruit

กล้ำ (kla'm) (1) sediment (2) fat of pork (3) to hem กล้ำ to intrude, advance ... กลืน to swallow, to put up with

กลำพัก (ka'la'mpa'k) a valuable scented medicinal wood

กลัก (kla'k) small bamboo box

กลิ้ง (kla'ng) bamboo through which a dog's leash is passed as protection against his bite

กลัด (kla't) to fasten together, to pin up เ..ม — pin, clap, brooch ไม้ pin made of wood ...ุม anxious, anxiety

กลั่น (kla'n) to distil ..า distilled water, ...อ — a pot for distilling

กลั้น (kla'n) to retain ใ.. to hold the breath

กลับ (kla'p) back, to return ...าย to be changed ใ.ย to change one's mind -- กลอก inconstant, changeable, unreliable

กวัด (koo'at) (1) to turn round forcibly, to wind up, to twist (2) to polish ขัน carefully, vigorously, clever, skilful

กวน (koo'an) to torment, to trouble, to mix up รบ -- to disturb

กวา with แตง (taang kwar) a small cucumber

กว่า (kwah) (sign of the comparative) more, more than มาก -- มาก too much --- ปี until

กวาง (kwarng) stag

กว้าง (kwahng) wide, width ขวาง spacious, large -- ยาว length and breath ใจ -- liberal

กวาด (kwaht) to brush, to sweep ปัด -- broom

กวาน (kwarn) [Maun] home

กว้าน (kwarn) capstan เที่ยว to search, to find

กวาว (kwow) a large tree rathes like a Bo-tree with small red flower used for dyeing

เกวียน (kween) (1) cheriot, car, cart (2) (a measure of eighty สัด or bushels cartload)

แกว่ง (kwang) to swing (a thing) to oscillate, to move from side to side

กวัก (kwa'k) to call by beckoning ใกว (kwai) to swing slowly (of a thing attached by two cords or handles) นก --- [phon.] water-hen

กวัด (kwa't) to waive or swing ใกว to waive about แกว่ง to brandish, to shake

กอ (kor) a tufted plant แก่ rogue, knave

ก่อ (kaw) (1) to begin (2) to build (3) to kindle

กอ (kor) vain, boastful

กอก (kawk) and มะกอก (1) a wild olive tree บาง -- village of wild olives, Bangkok (European name for the capital of Siam) (2) to blister the skin by applying heat, draw out

กอง (kawng) heap, pile, cohort, troop นาย -- แม่ -- leader of a troop, band, or gang ซุ่ม troops in ambush

ก้อง (kawng) echo, to resound แก้ง vain, boastful

ก้อน (korn) before, first ท่าน แก่
ancertors อย่า เกอ — wait a while
โกเกียว presently, after a while

ก้อน (kaun) fragment. mass

ก๊อป (kaup) (1) gifted with (2) to mix
together (3) and — โกย to draw up
with the hand

ก๊อปปี้ (kawpee) [Engl.] copy สมุด —
copy-book

กุน (kaun and ก้อน กุ๋ย dwarfish

กะละมัง (kauma'lawi) Chinese varnish

กา (kah) crow กาฝาก a parasite plant
— กะ (1) basin (2) water-crow, dun
diver กาน้ำ copper kettle — กาก
กะ siphon กะบาก (an accent
raising the sound, as ยั้งยัง วินัก
the additional letter (in Pali words)
which is not sounded

(kah) [Pali] to note, to mark in a
book, on a board, etc.

กา and กา (kar) [Laos. and Chin.]
bold, audacious, impudent

กา (kaw') (1) cawing of crows 2) [An-
nam.] a native of Hue or Saigon

กาก (kahk) lees, refuse, dregs อ้าย —
(a word of abuse) rascal — ร่าง
rough copy หน้า — mask

กากี (karkee) female crow (word of
abuse to women)

กากะทิง and กากะทึง (karka'ting and
karka'teung) wild tree with scented
flowers

กากะบาท (karka'bart) [Pali] an accent
like a crow's foot elevating the
tone of the (middle) letters over
which it is put

การุง (karug) to stretch out, to hang up
— เขน cross นก — เขน dominican
(a red bird)

ก้าง (karng) fish bone

การ (kart) wicked, ferocious, cruel

กาญจน and กาญจเรข (karncha'nah)
Pali gold

กาญบุรี (kahnboorec) [gold town] a
Town and Province

การเปรียญ (karmpoo'reean) [Sansk.]
a hall or building for preaching

กาด (kart with ผัก turnip, mustard
ผัก mustard — หัว let-
tuce กาด — — turnip

กาน (karn) to cut branches, to lop

กานพลู (karnploo) clove

ก้าน (karn) stalk, twig, middle fibre of a leaf

กานดา (karndah) sister, lady

กานน (karnon) [Pali] grove, wood

กาบ (karp) envelope, bark, sheath — หอย shell หอย — a sea-shell

กาพย์ (kahp) [Sansk.] verses

กาม (karma') [Pali] desire, concupiscence, cupidity (Alab. 235) น้ำ — semen humanum นก — กวม a small bird

ก้าม (karm) claws (of a crab, etc.)

กามคุณ (karma'koo'n) category of sensual pleasure

กามภาพ (karma'parp) [Pali] the world of pleasures

กามราค (karma'rark) [Pali] (and several similar words) sensual pleasures

กามา (karmah) [Pali] concupiscence, desire — โลก world of sensuality — เวร or — พร (angels) of the sensual heavens (Alab. 185. 239)

กาเมศ (karmett) [Sansk.] cupidity, sensuality

กามะ (karma') [Pali] cupidity, love of riches

กามะพฤกษ (see กระระพฤกษ and กัลปพฤกษ)

กาย (kai) กายา กายะ กาย์ and กาเย [Pali] body, multitude

ก่าย (kai) to put a limb or limbs upon or over, to put upon, embrace เกน — people meet one another — กอง to heap up; a great number

กาเยนทรี (kahyenn) [Pali] bodily senses

การ (kahn) [Pali] work, business ราช — Kings service, H. M. S. ได้ and เป็น — it succeeds, it is a good business คิด — to be at work ให้ — to give an account, draw up a report ต้อง — it is needed, necessary — วิวาห — กิพ etc, wedding, funeral, etc. ไม่ เข้า — absurd, nonsense

การิณี (kahra'nee) [Pali] cause, result

การนิกา (kahra'ni'kar) a flowering tree

การบูร (kahra'boon) [Jav. and Pali] camphor

การอน (kahron) a fish

การิย (kahriya') [Pali] to act, action

การเบ็น (kahreean) a large bird with a red head and a loud cry (see also โกญฑา)

การเรียง (kahreeang) better เกรียง a Shan tribe which lived in the forest, Kareans

การะเกด (kahra'ket) a reed with a strong scented flower กอก — flower thereof

การะเวก and การเวก (kahra'wake) bird of paradise, fabulous bird without legs (Alab. 309)

การันต์ (kahra'n) [Pali] (final letter not pronounced, as the ต in this word, and having the mark ทัณฑา ฆาฏ over it)

กาล (kahn) [Pali] (1) destruction, death, (2) gangrenous tumour

กาลกะตา (kahla'ka'tah) Culcutta

กาหลง (kahlong) a tree with a small scented blossom and a large fruit

กาลบาทว์ (kahla'bart) [Pali] aerolite, meteor (sign of evil omen)

กาลอน (karlorn) to lie, tell lies

กาลิง (karling) parroquet

กาลไทย (karloo'tai) [Pali] depraved nature

กาไหล่ (kahlai) to cover (with gold silver or other metal)

กาละ (kahla') and กาไล (kahlay) [Pali] time, death

กาหลัง (kahla'ng) (1) an Indian country (2) an actor who wears a crown like a King

กาว (kow) glue, gum

ก้าว (kow) to step, to walk แล้ว — to tack a boat

กายชู (kartu) [Sansk.] pile of fire-wood

กายร (karsonn) [Sansk.] buffalo

กาลหก (karla'hok) lime twigs for bird catching

กาสาวะพัต (karsarwa'pa't) [Pali] priest's yellow dress (Alab. 203)

กาหล (karhon) [Pali] noise of trumpets

กาฬ (kahla') [Pali] black, wicked

— ปักข์ [Pali] and — ปกษ์ [Sansk.] waning of the moon

กิ่ง (king) branch, twig เรือ — large gilt and carved boat

กิ้งก่า (kingkar) chamelion

กิงกือ or กิงกือ (kingkeu) a millipede

กิงกก (kingko'k) *better* กึ่งกก a toad

กิจ (kit) [Pali] work, action — กฎกา royal decrees, laws

กิน (kin) to eat, to drink — เข้า to take a meal, to dine, breakfast, sup ใจ to suspect กำไร to lend at usury — เหลือ to stuff, to gorge — กำไร to sell at a profit กิน to work for a living

กินรา (kina'ra' *and* kinnari (and other similar words) [Pali] harpies

กิม (kim [Chin.] gold

กิรินี (kirinny [Pali] elephant

กิริยา (ki'ri'yah) [Pali] (1) action, conduct, morals กาย etc. condition of death, etc. (2) [Gram.] verb วิเศษณ์ adverb

กิเลน (ki'lenn) a wood lizard

กิเลศ (ki'lett) [Pali] concupiscence, impurity (Alab. 212)

กิว (kiu) (1) a saddle (2) narrower at the middle than at the ends; (in surveying) a depression between two hills

กิว (kioo) (a term of raillery)

กี (kee) [Sansk.] how much? how many? — กี — ครั้ง how often? — โมง what o'clock? — มากน้อย how much? how many?

กี (kee) a quantity (of panungs, cloth, etc.) — กีทอผ้า part of a weaver's loom

กี *with* เมื่อ (meua kee) just now ก่อน a little while ago

กีกระเบื้อง (kee kra'benang) [Chin.] a stool made of earthenware

กีด (keet) to prevent, hinder

กีบ (keep) horny part of the hoof

เกยิกกาย (keeyek kai) to grope about

เกียจ (keeyet) *and* ขี้ — idle

เกียง (keeyeng) to disagree, quarrel

เกียด (keeyet) flail เสา — upright post used in treading out rice — กัน to keep back the best

เกียน (keean) *and* เกวียน (1) chariot, cart (2) cart-load (a measure of eighty ถัง .. er bushels)

เกี๊ยบ (keeap) [phon.] chirping of young chickens กิ — [Chin.] chopsticks

เกียรติ (keeat) [Sansk.] honour, dignity

เกยา (keeyo) to hook up, hang up, connect — กอง associate, relation -- ธุระ (1) to have business (2) to reap

เกยา (keeyo) (1) gold ornament for children's topknot (2) to entice, allure, seduce — พาง unlawful amour ผ้า — flowered cloth

กึก (keuk) a light noise — ก้อ grand, splendid

กึกะ (keuka') stupid

กึ่ง (keung) the middle, the half — กึ่ง a noise

เกื้อ (keua') to help, assist, succour — กูล assistance

เกือก (keuak) shoes -- ส้น boot

เกือบ (keuap) near the end, soon

กุก (koo'k) noise (especially of certain animals)

กุกู (koo'koo') [Pali] royal insignia and emblems

กุกุละ (koo'koo'la') [Pali] one of the Buddhist hells

กุงกุง (koo'ngkoo'm) [the circular mark, as over ฤๅ]

กุ้ง (koo'ng) crawfish, large prawn

กุ้ยไช (koo'chai) [Chin.] leek

กุน (koo'n) pig ปี — 12th year of the Siamese cycle

กุญแจ (koo'nchaa) [Chin.] lock and key ลูก — key แม่ — lock

กุญชร (koo'nchon) [Pali] well-bred elephant

กุฏฐัง (koo't tang) [Pali] a leprosy

กุฏิ (koo'dee) [Pali] priest's house, cell, hermitage

กุฎาคาร (koo'tahkarn) [Pali] a building with a peaked or pinnacled top

กุณฑ์ (koo'n) [Pali] fire ; to burn

กุณฑล (koo'ntonn) [Pali] earrings, head ornaments, part of a crown

กุณฑี and กุณโฑ (koo'ntee and koo'n-toh) water-pot, jug

กุด (koo't) [Laos.] to cut off; shortened, curtailed

กุดั่น (koo'da'n) a tree ลาย — painted or sculptured flowers

กุบ (koo'p) (1 to creep, to crawl, (2) paper cap worn by gold-beaters — ทอง book with gold leaves หรือ — a game with five balls

กุป (koo'p) [Pali] to get worse

กุม (koo'm) to hold with the hand

กุ่ม (koo'm) a tree with edible leaves

กุมภา (koo'mpah) [Pali] cauldron, pot, pitcher

กุมภา (koo'mpah) *and* กุมภีระ [Pali] crocodile, alligator

กุมภาพันธ์ (koo'mpahpa'n) name of the eleventh month (= February)

กุมภัณฑ์ (koo'mpa'n) [Pali] (and other forms) giants, angels (Alab.178)

กุ้ย (kooi') [Chin.] a term of raillery

กุเรา (koo'row) a large edible sea fish

กุลา (koo'lah) *and* กุละ [Laos.] (1) infidels or foreigners (2) family, race (3) shore ชาติ — people of Malabar

กุหลาบ (koo'larp) rose

กุลาหล (koo'lah-hon) *and* กุลี tumult, disturbance

กุลี (koo'lee) (1) packet of (about twenty two) panungs (2) [Chin.] coolie

กุลียุค (koo'lee-yoo'k) [Pali] tumult, sedition

กุแหละ (koo'laa') broad (boat)

กุศล (koo'son) [Sansk.] merit, virtue, health

กุสุม *and* กุสุมา (koo'soo'mah) [Pali] flowers

กู (koo) I (to inferiors, or in disdain, or to equals in joking) มึง I *or* me, thou *or* thee: to speak to in the singular number in familiarity, disdain, or anger

กู *and* กู๋ (koo) [phon.] cooing of the turtle-dove; to call from afar — ทะโกน to call from afar and tell

กู้ (koo) (1) to lend at usury — ยืม to contract debts (2) to take up, raise up — เมือง to save a country

กู๋ (koo) [Chin.] aunt

กูด (koot) (1) a bird (2) a plant

กูนขลา (koonklah) [Cambod.] young tiger

กูบ (koop) howdah, seat on an elephant หลัง — vaulted

เก (kay) too short, distorted มือ — ตีน — one-handed, lame โก — impudently — เร — เส valueless, worthless

เก้กัง (kay ka'ng) staggering

เกก (kake) against the rules, abnormal
-- เกะ เกก vain, proud

เกง (keng) robber, burglar, rogue
-- การ ferocious

เกง with อี (ee keng) a small deer

เกง (keng) [Chin.] summer-house of
Chinese shape; roof of a boat or
carriage รถ -- covered carriage

เกณฑ์ (kayn) and กะ -- [Pali] to en-
rol, levy, engage workmen without
pay

เกด (kayt) a fruit tree

เกศ (kayt) [Pali] standard -- เกศา
woman's back hair

เกญเกญ (keyn keyn) to make a loud
noise

เกน (ken) distant, far, deep

เกบ (kep) (1) to smooth, to adze, to
plane (2) to collect, to pick up,
-- ไว้ to keep

เกย (koy) (1) to be put high and dry
(2) ladder for mounting an elephant
-- ไชย portico, verandah

เกยูร (kayoo'ra') bracelet, armlet,
necklace

เกเร (kay ray) (1) useless, worthless,
good for nothing (2) [Portug.] to
be willing, desirous, desire

เกศ (kate) เกษา and เกษ [Sansk.]
hair, head (Alab. 207) -- โกนจุก ceremony of cutting the top-knot

เกษรา (kaysa'rah) and เกษรก [Pali]
pollen of flowers, scurf of the head

เกอ (kerr) disappointed, deceived

แก (kaa) (1) you (2) to sculpture

แก (kaa) (1) ripe, old -- กล้า robust,
vigorous (2) (sign of Dative) to

แก (kaa) to untie, undo, solve, correct, answer -- ตัว to excuse oneself, to make a pretext บาป to
confess, do penance -- เข็ด แค้น
and -- เผ็ด to retaliate, revenge

แก (kaa) against -- อีก for want of
anything else

แกง (kaang) condiment, curry

แกง (kang) waterfall, cascade, rapids
-- เบ้ง to disagree, not to consent
-- ไก [Cambod.] mark used for a
signature

แกง (kaang) (1) to wipe with a small
stick (2) [Laos.] carelessly, inpro-
perly

แกน (kaan) hard tasteless part of fruits
— ริก axle of a wheel

แก่น (kaan) heart of a tree

แกม (kaam) to mix

แก้ม (kaam) cheek

แกลา (kaalaa) *with* คืน yellow wood for dyeing things ย้อม — to dye with this wood

แก้ว (kaao) beautiful, amiable, valuable

แก้ว (kaao) glass, crystal หก — parrot คืน — a hard box-tree — ตา pupil of the eye — ห inside of the ear — หิน rock crystal — แหวน precious stones, personal ornaments

แกะ (kaa') (1) sheep (2) to carve รูป — statue (3) to pick out, take out

แกะ แกะ (kaa' koa') (noise of tapping or rapping)

ไก (kai) spring (of watch, etc.) ปืน trigger

ไก่ (kai) fowl, cock, hen — ต่อ decoy cock — ฟ้า pheasant — ปา *and* — เถื่อน wild fowl — วิลาศ guinea fowl — ขัน crowing of cocks

โกกเกก (koke kake) thief, rogue

โกกิลา (kohki'lah) [Pali] a small talking bird of a brown colour

โกง (kohng) bent, curved, deceitful คิด — to plan fraud

โก่ง (kohng) to bend, tighten, to raise the price of — ข้อ finger-joints

โก้ง (kohng) too tall นก — a large fishing bird, a crane

โกญจนาท (kohncha'nart) [Pali] the noise made by a wild elephant

โกญจา (kohnchar) [Pali] (1) the cry of the bird called กระเรียน (2) the bird itself

โกฏ (kote) [Pali] costly, meritorious; ten millions

โกฐ (kote) medicine ทั้งห้า เจ็ด เก้า etc. the five seven or nine kinds of wood used for medicine, etc.

โกณ (kone) [Pali] corner, angle ตรี — etc. triangle etc.

โกน (kone) to shave — ผม to shave the top-knot จุก — the 7th 14th 22nd and 29th days of the moon, when priests shave their heads

โกย (kope) to draw up or lift with both hands

โกมุท (kohmoo't) โกเมก โกมล *and* กระมล [Pali] white lotus

โกเมน (kohmenn) blood-red garnet

โกย (koee') to gather up, draw up, lift

โกลา (kohlah) tumult — หล great tumult

โกศล (kohsonn) [Pali] skilful, versed in, proficiency หัตถ์ — artist, artisan, skilled workman

โกษ (kote) [Pali] funeral urn

โกษา (kohsah) [Pali] treasure, money; (at the end of a name) a title of honour

โกษิน (kohsin) [Pali] angel; Indra

โกสุม (kosoo'm) [Sansk.] *and* โกสุม [Pali] a yellow flower

โกไสยพัตร (kohsaiya'pa't) silk cloth

โกหก (ko:hok) to lie, to tell lies

เกา (kow) to scratch

เก่า (kow) old, ancient ก่ง — as before

เก้า (kow) [Chin.] nine — สิบ ninety — อี้ chair — — เอน chair with a slanting back — — นวม stuffed chair

เกาทัณฑ์ (kowta'n) [Pali] war bow ลูก — arrows

เกาลัด (kowla't) [Chin.] chestnut

เกาะ (kaw) (1) island — หมาก (betelnut island) Penang (2) to seize, to catch hold of, to arrest — แกะ a bushy place

กำ (ka'm) to hold in the hand — กำ a game with shells — เกวน spoke of a wheel

กำ (ka'm) blood colour

กำเกิง (ka'mkeung) nearly equidistant

กำเกริน (ka'mkern) not equiditant; beyond; to intrude, to molest

กำกับ (ka'mka'p) to assist, to moderate, to take care of

กำจร (ka'mchonn) to be spread in the air, to be rumoured about

กำจัด (ka'mcha't) to disperse, drive away หนาม — a thorny creeping plant

กำชับ (ka'mcha'p) to direct, appoint, settle, order, arrange

กำดอน (ka'mdon) nape of the neck

กำเดา (ka'mdow) (1) cold in the head, disease of the nose, nasal abcess (2) warmth

กำดัด (ka'mda't) flourishing, vigorous, vigour

กำตาก (ka'mtark) *with* วัน the first day for ploughing

กำหนด (ka'mnot) to decree, decrees, laws, rules, to appoint (a time, a sum, etc.)

กำนน (ka'mnon) fee to musicians

กำเหนิด (ka'mnert) to be born; birth, origin, character

กำหนัด (ka'mna't) joy, love

กำนัน (ka'mna'n) (1) mayor of a village (2) to offer

กำนล *with* นาง (narng ka'mnonn) ladies of the Palace

กำบัง (ka'mba'ng) to veil, to cover

กำเบาะ (ka'mpaw) bezil of a ring

กำปั่น (ka'mpa'n) ship —ไฟ steamer — เหล็ก (1) iron boat (2) safe (for keeping valuables)

กำปั้น (ka'mpa'n) to close the hand

กำพล (ka'mponn) *see* กัมพล a precious sort of cloth

กำพร้า (ka'mprah) orphan, abandoned, helpless

กำพวด (ka'mpooat) a sea fish

กำแพง (ka'mpeng) wall — เพชร์ (wall of diamonds) Kampeng-Phet (a city)

กำภุฉัตร (ka'mpoocha't) [Sansk.] *see* กัมพุฉัตร Royal parasol with seven tiers and fringe

กำภุช (ka'mpoot) *see* กำพุช Cambodian

กำมพฤกษ (ka'mma'prook) (see *also* กระระพฤกษ *and* กลปพฤกษ) a tree bearing gold and silver flowers etc.

กำมา (ka'mmah) (a measure) from the elbow to the end of the closed fist

กำมะถัน (ka'mma'ta'n) sulphur

กำมะนาท (ka'mma'nart) *see* กัมปนาท [Pali] to tremble, to be excited

กำมะหยี่ (ka'mma'yee) velvet ดอก — amaranth

กำมะสิทธิ์ (ka'mma'sitt) *better* กรรมสิทธิ์ [Pali] jurisdiction, subject to

กำหมัด (ka'mma't) to strike with the closed hand

กำยาน (ka'myarn) gum-benjamin, incense — เหนื่อ benzine — ผี incense for funerals

กำยำ (ka'mya'm) tall and formidable

กำราญ (ka'mrarn) [Cambod.] mat, rug

กำราน (ka'mrarn) [Cambod.] to prostrate one self with the elbows apart

กำหราย (ka'mrarp) to repress, threaten, blame

กำเริบ (ka'mreup) to get worse

กำไร (ka'mrai) gain, profit — เท่าตัว a hundred per cent profit

กำไล (ka'mlai) bracelets

กำลัง (ka'mla'ng) force, capacity, vigour

กำสรด (ka'msot) mourning, to weep, to sob

กำสรวญ (ka'msooan) to laugh, to rejoice

กำสาบ (ka'msarp) to set, place, *or* fix, firmly

กะ (ka') to plan, estimate — เกณฑ์ to press for the King; service, to levy troops, to impress

กะ (ka') [Pali] water

กะถา (ka'tah) [Pali] text

กะบ่อ กะแบ่ (ka'paw ka'paa) bruised, half-broken, weak

กะปิ๋ยะ *better* กัปปิ๋ย [Pali] (1) science (2) priest's steward

กะปุก (ka'poo'k) jug, pitcher — หมึก inkstand

กะโผลก (ka'plake) to limp, to go lame

กะพด (ka'p'ot) *and* กะพด a pole to beat buffaloes and oxen

กะพราด (ka'praht) dirtily, slovenly, carelessly

กะพรุน (ka'proo'n) mollusc

กะ — (kah) (for all other words spelt with these initial letters see under กระ —)

กัก (ka'k) (1) to detain, to shut up, to enclose (2) noise of tapping

กั๊ก (ka'k) cross line (drawn on a surface for dice playing, etc.) square in a street สี่ — four cross roads, four lines drawn from the same point เสื้อ — a shirt without sleeves

กัง *with* อุท (oo'ta'ko'ng) [Pali] water — กัง loud noise — เกง trousers, drawers — ขา to doubt

กัง (ka'ng) monkey

กังขา (ka'ngkah) [Pali] to doubt, to suspect

กังวล (ka'ngwon) business, affair of importance

กังวาฬ (ka'ngwahn) musical, melodious

กังสดาล (ka'ngsa'darn) [Pali] concert, symphony, ; musical instruments

กังหัน (ka'ngha'n) (1) weathercock, wind mill, twirligig (2) the eighteenth vowel, q. v.

กัจฉะ (ka'cha') *with* พระ armpits (of the King)

กัญจุก (ka'nchuka') [Pali] jacket, she h, skin of a snake, etc.

กัญญา (ka'nyah) [Pali] unmarried lady, fine woman

กัญราษี (ka'nrahsee) [Pali] Virgo (Zodiac.)

กัณฐา (ka'ntah) [Pali] neck ; name of the letter ค

กัณฑ์ (ka'n) [Pali] numerical designation of sermons

กัณห์ (ka'n) [Pali] black

กัด (ka't) to bite — ฟัน to grind the teeth ปลา — fighting fish

กัน (ka'n) to hinder, protect, defend

กัน (ka'n) together, mutually ต่อ — from one to another, successively ด้วย — together — แก่ — mutually, reciprocally

กัน (ka'n) haft of knife *or* instrument (round which the handle is fitted)

กั้น (ka'n) to separate, interpose — ม่าน to hang a curtain

กันเหยก (ka'ncheeak) false ears (of actors)

กันชา (ka'nchah) a tree of which the blossom is smoked as an opiate

กันดาร (ka'ndarn) [Pali] in want of, needy, wretched

กันนิกา (ka'nni'kah) a flowering tree

กันไพร (ka'npairee) [Siam. and Pali] to repel, defend

กันยา (ka'nyah) *with* เรือ long barge for princes and nobles

กันยายน (ka'nyahyonn) [Sansk.] name of the sixth month (September)

กันหยั่น (ka'nya'n) a two-edged sword

กับ (ka'p) (1) with, together, to, for —กัน all together — เข้า condiment, dish (2) mouse trap

กัปปิยะ (ka'ppi'ya') [Pali] (1) clever, learned, able, well-behaved ; science (2) priest's steward

กัมปนาท (ka'mpa'nart) [Pali] to tremble, fear

กัมพล (ka'mpon) [Pali] a woollen cloth

กัมพฉัตร (ka'mpeccha't) [Sans.] royal parasol with seven tiers and fringes

กัมพุช and กัมโพช (ka'mphoot) Cambodian

กัลปพฤกษ์ (ka'lpa'proo'k) [Sansk.] *see* กระวะพฤกษ์ a fabulous tree

กัลยา (ka'lyah) [Pali] gracious, beautiful ; health

ข

ข (kaw khong: hard k or kh Guttural: a high letter) — ขอ name of this letter

ขง (kongchoo) [Chin.] Confucius

ขจร (ka'chon) to be dispersed, spread

ขจี (ka'chee) Cambod. soft, tender, light green

ขณะ (ka'na') [Pali] (1) time (2) soon

ขด (khot) to be rolled in spiral form, in coils, bent

ขน (khon) (1) to transport, remove, move (2) hair, quill, feather — ขา eye-lash   คิ้ว - eye-brow — แกะ wool, fleece   ลุก the hair stands on end ป่าก ก้า   ห่าน quill pen

ขน (khonn) thick (of liquids), compact

ขนก (kha'nok) ornament of painting or sculpture

ขนง (kha'nong) eye-brows

ขนด (kha'not) spiral tail

ขนบ (ka'nop) (1) manner, custom, practice (2) a hundred bales of cloth

ขนม (ka'nom) cake — ปัง [Fr.] bread , —ขั้น a common broth

ขนาม (kha'nam) market ภา, Custom-house ฝา [Cambod.] King's cushion

ขนาง (ka'narng) to doubt, to hesitate, to be ashamed, shy

ขนาด (ka'naht) mode, model, form, size โอ excessive

ขนาน (ka'nahn) (1) parallel, nearly parallel, one just in front of the other (2) mixture of remedies

ขนาบ (ka'nahp) to fasten up on both sides to attack

ขนาย (kha'nai) teeth of the female elephant

ขนิษฐ (kha'ni'tta') and ขนิษฐา [Pali] younger brother and sister

ขนุน (kha'noon) jack-fruit

เขนง (kha'neng) (1 box of gunpowder (2 party of musicians

เขนด (kha'net) weary

เขนย (kha'noy) [Cambod.] pillow

แขนง (kha'naang) shoots of trees

แขนะ (kha'neh) (1 to open or show the way (2 to ask for gifts, to keep on begging for things

ขนัด (kha'na't a plot of garden ground

ขบ (khop) to devour — พัน to grind the teeth — เขี้ยว (of the teeth), obstructed, stuffed up

ขบถ (kha'bott) rebel, rebellion, mutiny โทษ high treason

เขบ็ด ขบวน kha'bett kha'booan) cunning

ขม (khom) bitter

ขมำ (khomm) to press down, to oppress

ขมวด (kha'mooat) to tie up in a small knot

ขมวน (kha'mooan) and ตัว— an insect that eats dry fish

ขมัว kha'mooa') dark, dirty, indistinct

ขมอม and ขม่อม (kha'maung and kha'mam) top of the head

ขมิ้น kha'mi'n) turmeric; a yellow root used as powder

เขมป kha'mi'p) flatum ventris paullatim emittere

ขมี ขมัน kha'mee kha'ma'n) active, nimble, adroit

ขมุบ (kha'moo'p) soft, flexible, yielding

เขมง (kha'meng) to stretch, to tighten; tight

เขม็ด kha'mett) to collect, savings

เขม็น (kha'men) to keep on quivering, as in winking the eyes

เขม้น kha'menn) to gaze at

เขมร kha'men) Cambodian

แขมบ kha'maap) swelling and subsiding of the belly

แขม่ว (kha'mayo) [ท้อง] to puff out the belly

โขมง (kha'mohng) smoke

โขมด (kha'moht) will o' the wisp, ghost, phantom

เขม่า (kha'mow) [Cambod.] lamp black —ไฟ soot

ขมำ (kha'ma'm) to seize greedily, to eat in a vulgar way

ขมัง (kha'mang') with นาย and — ขมั a forest sportsman, a clever archer, a good shot

ขมับ (kha'ma'p) temples, side of the forehead

ขยด (kha'yot) to leave one's seat, to shift one's place

ขยน (kha'yonn) to retire, abandon, leave off

ขยอก (kha'yauk) (1) to wash a vessel by shaking (2) to swallow without chewing

ขย้อน (kha'yawn) (1) nausea, to feel sick (2) movement of trees shaken by the wind

ขยาก (kha'yart) to be horrified, to fear, to abhor

ขยาบ (kha'yahp) moveable roof of a boat

ขยาย (kha'yai) to separate, to put apart

ขยิบ (kha'yip) to nod, to wink, to make signs -- ตา to wink

ขยี (kha'yee) to rub hard with the hand or hands

ขยวน (kha'yeuan) to move or push about a little

ขยุก (kha'yook) to move by fits and starts

ขยุบ (kha'yoop) to press down, hold down

ขยุม (kha'yoom) quickly, at once

ขยุ้ม (kha'yoom) (1) handful, to pick up in the hand, to grasp (2) a spider

เขย่ง (kha'yeng) and เขย่ง to stand or walk on tip-toe

ขะยาง (kha'yaang) (1) small fish with two spikes (2) to be disgusted, to loathe

โขยก (kha'yoke) to limp, lame

โขยง (kha'yohng) consanguinity, relationship

เขย่า (kha'yow) to keep on shaking

ขย้ำ (kha'ya'm) to pound, to feel, to shampoo

ขยะ (kha'ya') sweepings, to sweep

ขยัก (kha'ya'k) to shut up what remains, to reserve

ขยัด (kha'ya't) to put by, to keep

ขยัน (kha'ya'n) skilled, clever, capable, diligent

ขยับ (kha'ya'p) to retire, to give place

ขร (kha'ra' or khon) [Pali] 1) buffalo (2) hard คิรี - mountains

เขน (kha'n) [Sansk.] sword พระ King's sword

ขรัว (khrua) abbot, chief priest - ยาย King's mother-in-law

ขลาด (khlaht) [Cambod.] timid, bashful, shy

ขลิบ (khlip) to clip, to bind; border, lace

ขลุก (khluck) [phon.] a noise (of bottles, utensils, etc.)

ขลุ่ย (khloo'i) flute

ขลู่ (khloo) a tree

เขลิง (khlayng) a hard wood

โขลก (khlohk) to pound in a mortar
— เขลก blackguard

โขลง (khlohng) (1) crowd, troop, mob of
men, elephants, etc. (2) great stench

ขโลหุ (khlohu) ladies of the Palace

เขลา (khlow) stupid, imbecile

ขลัง (khla'ng) 'Cambod.] it has happened as I wished, I have done the
(difficult) thing which I attempted

ขลับ (khla'p) shining black, dark and
lustrous

ขวด (khooat) bottle   — แก้ว glass jar
with large stopper

ขวน (khooan) to scratch

ขวบ (khooap) revolution of a period,
year

ขวย (khoo'i) bashfulness

ขวา (khah) right (hand) ซ้ายขวา   right
and left

ขวาก (khwahk) spikes to protect a
camp or garden, road, or other place

ขวาง (khwahng) cross-wise; to obstruct, opposition

ขว้าง (khwahng) to throw violently, to
hurl

ขวาน (khwahn) axe, hatchet ——
wood-pecker

ขวาบ (khwahp) noise of whipping

ขวิด (khwit) (1) to attack with the
horns (2) a fruit tree with round
fruit

แขวก (khwaak) [phon.] a bluish
river-bird

แขวง (khwaang) a district

แขวน (khwaan) to suspend, to hang

แขวะ (khwaa') to hollow out

ไขว่ and ไขว้ (khwai) to cross, to com-
plicate, to be confused

ขัว (khooa') [Laos.] bridge

ขั้ว (khooa') (1) stalk (2) to cook (meat)
brown

ขวัญ (khwa'n) (1) top of the head (2)
angel living in the head   ขวัญ to
be frightened (3) reparation, satisfaction ทำ to indemnify เสียขวัญ
to slander ก่าวขวัญ to slander

ขวั้น (khwa'n) to cut to pieces

ขอ *and* ขอ (khaw) (1) to ask — การ to beg — รับ Sir; Yes sir (phrase of assent used to a superior) สู่ — to ask a person's daughter in marriage (2) sickle, bill-hook, hook — ง้าว war-scythe — สับ hooked instrument used to goad elephants เหลือ — untameable, incorrigible

ข้อ (khor) article, articulation, joint, point, knot, question, section, circumstance — มือ wrist — ตีน ankle — ลับ mystery, secret — ความ counts, articles, charges

ของ (khaung) (1) (sign of the genitive) of (2) thing, things, goods เข้า — possessions, rickes เจ้า — owner, proprietor — กำนัน gift — กลาง disputed property deposited in court to await the decesion of the dispute

ข้อง (khong) large bulging basket for carrying fish — ระ กัน to be mixed up with, to be in bad company

ขอด (khawt) (1) to scrape round with a knife, to pare (2) to tie น้ำ — left dry by the water — หม้อ to take all the contents out of a pot

ขอน (khawn) log

ข้อน (khorn) three quarters

ขอบ (khawp) margin, edge, lace, frame — ฟ้า horizon — ตา white of the eye — ใจ — ิตวร *and* — คุณ to thank; thanks

ขอม (khaum) Cambodian

ข่อย (khoi) a tree whose bark is used for making paper

ขอรับ (khaura'p) (*see* ขอ) Yes, sir

ขา (khah) (1) voice of one answering เจ้า — Yes, Sir (in answers by a woman to a superior) (2) thigh, haunch, leg of a pair of compasses, of a tripod, etc. —หย่าง apparatus raised on legs — กะไกร jaw, handles of scissors, etc.

ข่า (khar) a root (used in making curry)

ข้า (khah) I, me, (to an inferior) — เฝ้า grandees — หลวง King's officers, Royal Commissioners — เจ้า *and* — พเจ้า I, me (speaking to an equal or superior) — แก่ (an invocation addressed to God or the King) — พระ พุทเจ้า I, me (speaking to the King or Queen or to a King's son or daughter)

ขาก (khark) to spit out

ข้าง (khaing) top, spinning top

ข้าง (khahng) part, side — ขึ้น waxing moon — แรม waning moon — คืน from the beginning — ใน the King's room — ดึก — third of the vowels, long *a* — ๆ beside, alongside

ขาด (khart) (1) entirely, altogether เป็น อัน — (2) to be broken, torn, separated — ไป to die — ทุน to suffer loss — ตัว fixed price, unalterable

ขาน (kharn) to answer — ยาม to call the hours *or* watches of the night

ขาล (khahn) *and* ขาว [Cambod.] tiger ปี — year of the Tiger (third of the cycle)

ขาบ (kharp) *with* กา (1) a millipede (2) bracelet เข้ม — gold embroidered coat worn by magnates

ขาม (khahm) to fear

ข้าม (kharm) to cross, to pass over

ขาย *or* ข่าย (khai) to sell — ปลีก to sell by retail — หน้า to put to

shame ขี้ย — commerce ค้า — to trade ผู้ — vendor

ข่าย *or* ข้าย (khaie) stake-nets ตา — meshes of a net — กรอง network of flowers

ขาล (khahn) [Cambod.] tiger

ขาว (khow) white ตา – timid, surprised

ข่าว (khowe) news, report — สถาน, legation, embassy

ขิก (khik) laughter

ขิง (khing ginger

ขิณาสพ (khinahsop) [Pali] a saint

ขิปสัจ โท (khippa'sa'toh [Pali] to sneeze

ขี่ (khee) to mount, to ride

ขี้ (khee) (1) dirt, dregs, sweeping, faeces — มูก mucus of the nose — กบ shavings of wood — ครั่ง a kind of resin — เรื้อน leprous — ผึ้ง carwax – ริ้ แตก scurf — สนิม rust — กะกรัน slack (of metals), dregs — กะติ้ว oxide of lead or tin — แมลง วัน freckles — ปลา วาฬ amber

ขุ (kheE!) unequal โด่ก คู่ — to play at odd and even (2) addicted to vice — กนิ avaricious — รว ragged, worthless

ขีด (kheet) to draw, to mark with lines ไม้ — ไฟ match (for lighting)

เขย่า (kheeya') to scatter, to throw about

เขยง (kheeang) chopping-block พัง — and ละไบ — a mode of wearing the scarf, as women do

เขียด (kheeat) a green frog

เขียน (kheean) to write, to paint

เขียร (kheean) see เขียน

เขียว (kheeyo) green, blue ตา — eyes inflamed with anger — ครัม indigo, dark blue พัร — a large cucumber

เขี่ยว (kheeo) (1) turning stream (2) to boil down (3) to torment, ill-treat (4) eye tooth

ขีระ (kheera') [Pali] milk

ขึง (kheung) to stretch — ขัง (1) proud (2) business-like — อก to stretch the top strings of a kite หลัง — อก to sleep with the body stretched out and covered up

ขึ้น (kheu'n) (1) up, going up, rising, to get up น้ำ — flood tide (2) to depend upon, to be in the power of

ขือ (kheu) (1) fetters (2) beam of a house

ขืน (kheune) to compel, to restrain — เรือ to trim a boat — คำ on compulsion — ใจ to force oneself

ขืน (kheun) rather bitter

เขือ (kheua') a river fish มะ — mad apple

เขือง (kheua'ng) rather big

เขือน (kheua'n) quay, causeway — ปากลัด Paklat (Province)

ขอก (khoo'k) noise of coughing

ขอด (khoo't) to dig, to hollow out

ขุน (kloo'n) (1) to feed (2) grandees ตก — Royal Judges — หลวง Kings — นาง chief of an order inferior to a Phra' — รม Siamese talking blackbird กรม title of a Royal Prince of the 4th class (3) (in chess) the Queen

ขุ่น (khoo'n) (1) distressed, sad, irritated, vexed (2) not clear, not pure (especially of liquids)

ขุม (khoo'm) ditch, abyss — ทอง gold mine — นรก Hell ลึ — deep; stimulating

ขอย (kho'oi') a skin disease ตก — edible bamboo seeds

ขู่ (khoo) to frighten with threats, to intimidate

ขูด (khoot) to scrape, rake

เขก (khake) to strike with the upper knuckles, having the big knuckles turned down, to rap

เข่ง (kheng) open-worked cylindrical bamboo basket

เขจร (khaychon) [Pali] to go, to walk

เข็ญใจ (khenn chai) poor, unfortunate

เขด (khett) (1) bale or packet of cotton, silk, etc. (2) to be corrected, amended; I will not do it again — ฟัน teeth set on edge — ขาม to submit through fear แก้ — to take vengeance

เขตร (khet) see เขตร

เขน (khen) (1) shield or buckler of hide (2) a dancer นก กาง — a small singing bird

เขนน (khenn) (1) to draw (a boat) ashore (2) to oppress

เข็น (khen) to forge a second time — มีด to sharpen a knife — เขี้ยว to grind the teeth

เข็ม (khem) needle — ขัด clasp — แม่ เหล็ก magnetic needle ปลา — the smaller fighting fish

เข้ม (khem) vehement, strong, much, very

เขย (khoey) son-in-law หลาน — son of the brother-in-law พี่ — elder brother-in-law น้อง — younger brother-in-law

เขฬ and เขฬะ (khaylah) [Pali] saliva

เขิน (khern) (1) a slope (2) unbecoming, extravagant

แข (khaa) [Cambod.] moon

แขก (khaak) (1) Asiatic stranger, not being Chinese or Japanese (Alab. 30) — มลายู Malay — เต้า parrot — เทศ people of India who are not black (2) visitors

แข็ง (khaang) hard, solid น้ำ — ice — มือ to devote oneself to work — แรง strong

แข่ง (khang) to contend, dispute, race

แข้ง (khaang) *with* น้ำ shin bone

แขน (khaan) arm, arm's length (measure) — ด้วน — กุด one-armed — คอก stiffness of the arm

แข้น (khaan) (1) to urge, press, solicit (2) thick (of liquids), nearly solid — ทำ to do unwillingly

แขม (khaam) a reed

ไข (khai?) (1) to unlock, to open (2) *and* — เเข็ง fat, tallow

ไข่ (khai) egg, to lay eggs — ขาว white of egg — แดง yolk — วง eggs laid by flies in meat — มุก pearl — กัน front of the hip bone

ไข้ (khaie) fever, illness — จับ intermittent fever — ป่า jungle fever — สะท้าน fever with ague — หวัด cold in the head

ไขย (khi) [Pali] beyond อายุกัม — *and* อายุ — very old age อสง — countless

โขก (khoke) to strike a hard blow with the upper knuckles, having the lower knuckles turned upwards

โขง (khong) *with* กะ a crocodile with horns แม่น้ำ — a river in Siam

โข่ง (khohng) *with* หอย snail

โข่ง (khohng) high, tall

โขด (khote) shoal, shallow water

โขน (khone) comedy, masked play หัว — mask

โขมพัตร (khohma'pa't) [Pali] fine linen

เขา (khow?) (1) horns (2) *and* ภู — mountain — ไฟ volcano นก — turtle dove — — ไฟ dove with brown spots on the neck and breast

เขา (khow?) (3) he, they, him, them the others — ว่า it is said ชั่ง — do not take any notice of him (or them)

เข่า (khow!) knee

เข้า (khow) rice — กล้อง rice half-cleaned — ต้ม rice soup, congy บิณฑ์ rice offered to priests at the New Year — ตอก rice which has burst — เปลือก rice with the husk, paddy — เหนียว glutinous rice — หลง rice sweetened with sugar and dried — สาร cleaned rice — หมาก fermented rice - สะคู cooked and dried rice — หลาม rice cooked in a bamboo stick with cocoa-nut — โพศ Indian corn - สาลี wheat — สะมาน darnel — พ้าง a rice which grows like wheat — เม่า new rice — ของ riches, effects, chattels, personal property — เช้า breakfast กิน — to dine, dinner, meal

เข้า (khow) in, to enter, to adhere to — เฝ้า to go to the King or the Princes — ไม้ to repair a boat — ออก to visit frequently

เข้า แฟ (khowfaa) [Fr.] coffee

ขำ (kha'm) (1) pretty (2) secret

ขะจัก (kha'cha't) (1) to disperse (2) to dispute

ขะนาน (kha'nahn) see ทะนาน

ขะเน็ด (kha'nett) bands of straw for tying up rice

ขะนัก (kha'na't) see ขนัก

ขะบถ (kha'bot) see ขบถ

ขะเม่น (kha'menn) see เขม่น

ขะโมย (kha'moi) thief, robber

ขะยาก (kha'yaht) see ขยาก

ขะยิก (kha'yik) quickly, nimbly, actively

ขะเย่อ (kha'yerr) to abduct, to take by force

ขะเยะ (kha'yaa') to bruise, to elbow

ขัง (kha'ng) (1) to put in prison, to shut up, to confine (2) (in compos.) full of

ขัด (kha't) and — ขวาง and — ข้อง to resist, to obstruct, obstructed, prevented, hindered — ใจ to bear or take (a thing) ill; angry, annoyed — เบา obstruction in the bladder or entrails — สน in want, poor — สมาธิ to sit cross-legged — — เพ็ก to sit cross-legged with the heels up

ขัติยะ and ขัตติยะ (kha'tiya') [Pali] royal; warrior; a Hindoo caste (Alab. 188)

ขัน (kha'n) (1) copper or brass basin — ล้าง หน้า washing basin — สากร a big basin (2) to twist, to turn (3) crowing of cocks (4) funnily, in a droll way

ขันติ (kha'ntee) [Pali] patience under opposition, moderation (Alab. 184

ขันธ์ ขันธะ *and* ขันธา (kha'ntah) [Pa-
li] the bodily senses (Alab. 237)

ขับ (kha'p) (1) to reject, drive out, drive
on (2) to sing; song

• • •

ฃ

ฃ (*kaw khet*; hard *k* or *kh* Guttural;
a high letter) — เฃฅร name of this
letter

เฃฅร (khayt) *and* -- แฃฅ bounds,
confines, limits

— · · · • • · — —

ค

ค (*kaw khit* = English *kh*. Soft Guttural: a low letter) — คฅ name
of this letter

คก (khok) *with* คัง a frog

คช (khot) คะชา *and* คะเชนทร [Pali]
elephant

คชบาล (khocha'barn) [Pali] elephant-
keepers

คชสาร (khocha'sarn) well-bred elephant

คง (khong) firm, solid, permanent

คงคา (khongkhah) [Pali] Ganges

คณิกา (kha'nikah) courtesan, bad woman

คณิตศาสตร (kha'nitsahsa'tra) [Pali]
mathematics

คด (khot) to bend, winding, crooked
— เข้า to take boiling rice out of
the pot

คดี (kha'ti') [Pali] hesitating, slow to
begin

คน (khon) man, person (of both sexes);
(numerical designation of human
beings, as) คุลาการ สอง — two
judges สาง — some persons - ทรง
inspired person พาง prisoner
with iron collar and chains, (a
term of contempt) worthless fellow
- ใช้ domestic servants

คนละแถบ (kho la'taap) each on his
own side

คน (khonn) to look after, examine,
search — คิ้ย to spin - ฝก to
make cloth

คนธรรพ (khonta'p)   Pali] inferior
angels

คณนา (kha'na'nah) [Pali] to reckon,
compute, count, to spread out

คณะ (kha'na') [Pali] multitude, crowd, assembly, association (of priests)

คบ (khop) (1) torch, lantern (2) to associate with, to confederate with

คม (khom) sharp-edged, sharp

ครก (khrok) mortar (used with a pestle)

ครบ (khrop) entire, complete

ครรภ (kha'n) ครรภา and ครรภ์ [Pali] womb, pregnancy

ครวญ (khruen) to think of with affection — ถึ to remember with love, to sigh for

ครอม (khruem) to be put upon or over

ครัว (khroca) (1) kitchen, hearth, home เฆ — to migrate (2) band (of captives, slaves, etc.) กวาด — to carry off captives

ครหา (kha'ra'har) [Pali] to calumniate slander

ครอก (khrok) (1) [phon.] noise of snoring (2) brood, litter ลูก — ๚ — son of a slave กับ ๚ — a plant with burs (3) — ไฟ to burn, burnt to death

ครอง (khraung) to rule, govern, regulate

ครอบ (khraup) cover, lid, to cover — ครัว family คัพ — medicinal mallow

ครอม (khraum) superimposed — กัน one over the other ไก่ — yoke

ครั้ (khrah) time, times

ครา (khrar) to carry off by force

คราก (khark) to be broken off, to come apart

คราง (khrahng) to groan

คราง (khrarng) thin

คราญ with นง (nong khrarn) lady, woman

คราด (khrart) rake, harrow ผัก — a vegetable

คราส (khrart) [Sansk.] part ครี — eclipse in which more than half the disk is coverd อัคฆ — eclipse in which half is covered สุริย — total eclipse

คร้าน (khrarn) lazy, cowardly

คราบ (khrarp) cast skin or shell (of snake, crab, etc.)

คราม (khrahm) (1) indigo สี — เขียว — dark blue (2) ถึง — to make war (3) — ครัน abundantly

คร้าม (khrahm) to keep back through fear, to be rather afraid of

ครรวาศ (kha'ra'waht) see ฆราวาศ

คริบ (khreep) fin

คราหวาศ (kharahwaht) see ฆรา

คฤหา (kha'reuhar) [Sansk.] house, abode

คฤหวาศ (kha'reuha'waht) [Pali] staying at home

คฤหัษฐ (kha'reuha't) [Pali] layman

ครึ่ง (and คึ่ง) (khreung) middle, half

ครึ้ม (khreum) shady, thick

ครือ (khreu) well-fitting, just fitting, just big enough

คริน (khreun) (1) bird snare (2) overhanging, threatening to fall

เครา (khreva') creeping plants, bunch, heap เสียง — rough voice ตก — to expand (of fruit)

เครื่อง (khreuang) utensils, implements — อาวุธ arms — มือ tools — ใน tripe ทรง — (of the King) to dress เสวย royal food

ครุ (kha'roo') [Pali] heavy; (in prosody) long syllables

ครุ (khroo') bamboo basket smeared with varnish or grease and used for carrying water

ครุฑ (khreo't) and ครุฑา [Pali] fabulous snake-eating eagle, Garuda

ครุย (khroo'i) fringe เสื้อ — overcoat worn by nobles on certain state occasions

ครู (khroo) teacher, tutor พระ — judicial councillor

ครู่ (khroo!) moment, instant

ครูด (khroot) to scratch, to scrape

เครง (khreng) distended, tight, severe, austere, reticent

แคร่ (khraa) bed, litter, palanquin

แครง (khraang) water-pot with long handle

แคระ (khraa') dwarfish, stunted

ใคร (khrai) who? — ๆ whoever

ใคร่ (khrie) to wish, to like

ไคร (khrai) moss, mould (on a wall, etc.) dirt on the body

ไคร้น้ำ (khrie na'm) willow

โคร่ (khroke) and ครอก snoring

โกรง (khrong) model, pattern ซี่ — rib

โกร่ง (khrohng) large, tall เสือ — tiger of the largest kind

โกรม (khrome) sound of falling down

เครา (khrow) whiskers

เคร่า (khrow) beam or bar nailed or fixed horizontally

เคราห์ (khrow) *and* เคราะห์ (khraw) [Sansk.] omen, luck (good or bad), mischance, calamity, misfortune เสีย — to avert a bad omen

ครำ (khra'm) continual, perpetual น้ำ — foul water

คร่ำ (khra'mm) (1) to inlay steel with gold (2) blackened, to blacken

กระไล (khra'lai) to retire, go away

ครั่ง (khra'ng) nest of a certain red insect used for producing gamlac from which lake is made; the colour of lake, sticklac, sealing wax

ครั้ง (khrang') times, occasions กี่ — how many times? — นั้น then

ครัด (khra't) *and* เครง distended, full, fat; severe, austere

ครัน (khra'n) sufficient

ครั่น (khra'nn) to be rather afraid of, to be feverish

ครั้น (khran') when, since, if

คลาว (khlaw) (1) to flow, run down; (2) to accompany; several together

คลุก (khlauk) to burn

คลอง (khlaung) (1) sawn plank (2) canal, creek, water course

คล่อง (khlong) nimbly, easily

คล้อง (khlaung') (1) to catch in a snare (2) rhyming

คลอด (khlaut) to give birth to

คลอน (khlaun) to be shaken, to be loose *or* loosened (of a tooth etc.), to stagger

คล้อย (khloy) hanging behind, left behind, to give way, to go down, lower, to give place

คลา *and* ไคล — (khlai khlah) to go away

คล้า (khlar) a tree

คลาง (khlarng) to be in doubt

คลาด (khlart) to be separated, disjoined

คลาน (khlarn) to creep, to bow, to prostrate oneself

คลาย (khlai) to untwist, to unroll by degrees ใจ to take new courage, to be relieved

คล้าย (khlai) like, nearly resembling

คลิ้งโคลง (khling khlong) [phon.] a black and white bird

คลี (khlee) bowl, ball เกาะ — to play at bowls or band balls or polo ฝุ่น — fine dust

คลี่ (khlee) to unroll, unfold, open

เคลีย (khleeya) to approach, to be near

คลื่น (khleun) (1) sickness, nausea (2) wave

เคลือบ (khleuap) to varnish

คลุก (khloo'k) to mix, to knead

คลุ้ง (khloo'ng) musty

คลุม (khloo'm) to cover

คลุม (khloo'mm) contracted, narrow

คลุ้ม (khloo'm!) dark, cloudy, gloomy

เคล็ด (khlett) (1) tricks (2) a sprain

เคล้น (khlenn) to caress

เคล้น (khlen) to squeeze

เคลิ้ม (khleum) aberration of mind; to make a mistake

แคลง (khlaang) (1) to doubt, suspect (2) to turn (the foot etc.) sideways, to wobble (of a boat, etc.)

แคลน (khlaan) (1) to be in need of; needy (2) flexible, moveable กู — to contemn, despise

แคล่ว (khlaao) easily

โคลง (khlohng) (1) verses (2) unsteady, wobbling — เคลง to overbalance

โคล่ง (khlong) open, extensive

โคลน (khlohn) mud

เคล้า (khlow) (1) to mix, to couple, to be together (2) to flatter

คลำ (khla'm) to touch, to feel

คล่ำ (khla'm) abundantly

คล้ำ (khlam!) rather dark สี — dull colour เขียว — dull green คลุ้ม — delirious, half-mad — เคลิ้ม to hem

คละ (khla') to mix

คลัก (khla'k) [phon.] (1) noise of walking in mud (2) abundantly, tight, close together

คลัก (khla'k) [Cambod.] to fall

คลัง (khla'ng) treasure, property stored up or stowed away

คลั่ง (khla'ng) delirious

คลับ (khla'p) to see through a fog: indistinctly

คออง (khoo'a'ng) (1) shade of a true (2) screw — ขวด corkscrew (3) to brandish, to twist a stick, etc. (4) a bracket joining two lines of writing

คออบ (khoo'a'p) (1) to spur on, to gallop — ม้า to ride fast — คุม to superintend (2) to plait, to twist, to twine

คอย (khoo'i') genitalia viri

คอน (khoo'a'n) suitable, fit, proper ค่ำ worthy, deserving: sufficiently

ควา (khwah) to reach for with the arm or hand

ควาก (khwark) too loose, too large

คว้าง (khwarng) to turn, to wheel round

ควาญ (khwarn) elephant leader

ควาน (khwarn) to extract a kernal, to scoop out thoroughly

ความ (khwarm) law-suit, affair, reason, thing (word of materiality which being prefixed to an abjective turns it into a substantive, as) — จริง truth ชำระ — to decide or settle a suit or dispute ฝัก — parties to a law-suit หมอ — Doctor of Laws, lawyer ได้ — to come to the knowledge of, succeed เบา — hasty, rash

ควาย (khwai) buffalo

ควาว (khwow) a tree

คว (khwee) a tree

แคว (khwaa) direction, diverging line, path, road, etc

แคว้ง คว้าง (khwaang khwarng) to whirl round

แคว้น (khwaan) district, division, section of country

แคว (khwaa') (1) bellowing of buffaloes (2) to scoop out a little

ใคว (khwai) implicated, entangled, mixed up

คว่ำ (khwa'm) on one's face, upside down

ควัก (khwa'k) to pick out with the hand, to tear out, extract, pick (ears, etc.) — คัว to fan, to ventilate

ควัน (khwa'n) smoke

ควั่น (khwa'nn) to twist together

คห: (kha'ha') [Pali] great

คหะบดิ (kha'ha'bodi) *better* คหบดิ [Pali] minister of high rank, householder (Alab. 188)

คหัฐ [Pali] *and* คฤหัฐ [Sansk.] (kha'ha't *and* kha'ruha't) layman

คอก (khauk) (1) enclosure, palisade, fence (2) to bend out of the straight line, bent back

คอง (khaung) (1) affair (2) trap (for birds, fish, etc.)

คอด (khaut) short, worn down, narrower, thinner

คอน (khaun) (1) to carry by means of a stick resting on the shoulder (2) to row or paddle one's own boat

คอน (khorn) (1) one of two sides — ขอก to revile (2) three-fourths

คอน (khorn?) (1) to look cross-wise, to squint (2) hammer, lever ไม้ — mallet

ค่อม (khawm) dwarf

ค้อม (khorm) bent, curved, arched

คอย (khoie) to wait, wait for

ค่อย (khoi) by degrees, gradually, without haste

คา (khah) (1) to stick, to adhere, to be stuck into (2) cangue — กรด hermit's dress หลัง — roof หญ้า tall grass used for roofing

ค่า (khar) price — ตัว ransom, debt — ไถ ransom — จ้าง wages — เช่า rent — ธรรมเนียม tax, fee, impost — คุ้ง fork of a tree — คืบ span, distance of twelve niew ข้า — slave

ค้า (kha') to trade — ขาย trade, commerce พ่อ — merchant แม่ — shopkeeper สิน — merchandize

คาง (khahng) chin คืน — a tree ปลา แข้ an edible river fish — คก toad

คาง (kharg) a black ape (eaten as a delicacy)

ค้าง (khaingh) (1) prop for plants (2) to remain, to be interrupted (3) to keep from falling, prop up ไม้ —

debt not paid — คราว the favourable moment is past — คาว bat
น้ำ — dew

คาก (khart) (1) to gird, envelope, cover
(2) to conjecture, to estimate by
guess work (3) to determine — เวร
to determine upon revenge

คาถา (khahtah) [Pali] sacred forms

คาน (khahn) stick for carrying, prop,
beam, shaft of a carriage

ค้าน (kharn) (1) parellel supports (such
as sleepers, etc.) (2) to refuse, to
reject

คาบ (kharp) (1) to hold in the mouth
or beak (2) time, times — หนึ่ง
สอง — one, twice, etc.

คาพยุก and คาพยุติ (khahpa'yoo't and
kha'pa'yoo'ti) [Sansk.] two thousand wah or fathoms; about one
league

คาม (kharm) village, town

คาย (khai) (1) rough, irritating (2) to
put out of the mouth

คาย (khai) camp, intrenchment, stock-
ade

คารม (khahrom) chicanery, specious
language

คาราว (khahrah) unfinished, imperfect

คารีคารม (khahree khahrom) judicious
speaker, eloquent, specious, plausible

คาระวะ khahra'wa') [Pali] to respect,
honour, obey, fear, to salute with
honour

คาว (khowe) smell of raw fish

คาว (khahwee) [Pali] cow คาโว ox,
bull

คาสึก (khahseuk) enemies

คิคะ khi'ka') better อิคะ [Sansk.] conduct, practice, observance (Alab-
199, 205)

คิต khitt) to think, imagine, contem-
plate ถึง to think of an absent
person — เป็น to charge (a price)
— ว่า to think ให้ to give advice
คิก — Chinese arithmetic tables

คินา (khinah) [Chin.] wide-mouthed
basket with handle, used for provisions

คินี (khinnee) [Pali] fire

คิมหันต์ (khimha'nn) [Pali] heat, hot season

คิรินทร (khirrinn) [Pali] mountains

คีต, (kheet) [Pali] (1) to play on a musical instrument (2) to sing

คีบ and คีม (kheep, kheem) pincers, forceps, tongs

คีรี (kheeree) [Pali] mountains

เคียง (kheeang) near, in front of, close to

เคียด (kheeat) to get angry

เคียน (kheean) with คะ a tree of which barges are made — คาด to tie round, tie up — ...าย [Laos.] to clothe oneself

เคียม คำ (kheeam kha'n) to prostrate oneself in adoration

เคียม (kheeam) (1) a tree (2) to postpone a debt

เคียว (kheeyo) scythe, sickle

เคี้ยว (kheeo) to chew

คึก (kheuk) with impetuosity — คึก noise

คึง (kheung) to get angry

คืน (kheun) night

คืน (kheun) to give back, restore, return, retract

คืบ (kheup) (1) a measure (the extent from the end of the thumb to the end of the middle finger; about 12 niews, or 10 inches, or half of a cubit) (2) to crawl like a leach

คือ (kheu) that is, such, such as

เคือง (kheuang) to offend, be offended, interfered with

คุก (khoo'k) to bend — คุก to threaten

คุก (khoo'k) prison for persons accused or convicted of heinous crimes

คุกคะ (khoo'kha') twisted, rude, rough

คึน — a tree

คุง (khoo'ng) [Laos.] to run ashore

คุณ and คุณา (khoo'nah) [Pali] gratitude, benefit, advantage, virtue (in addressing a person) Sir เจ้า — (in addressing a พระยา) Sir, Your Excellency พระ favour from God or the King พ่อ — benefactor

คุณสัปท์ (khoo'na'sa'p) [Pali] adjective

คุด (khoo't) (1) to bend down, turn down, double up (2) to go to sleep in a doubled up position

คักกะราก (khoo'tta'raht) a disease acusing blotches on the skin

คืน (khoo'n) witchcraft, enchantment

คุ่น (khoo'n) troubled, disturbed, muddy — แคุ่น annoyed

คุ้น (khoo'n) accustomed, familiar, intimate

คืบคับ (khoo'p kha'p) a sound (as of a horse trotting)

คุม (khoo'm) to go with, to keep close to a person — ไว้ to take care of คอม — to be in charge of คุ — gaoler

คุ่ม (khoo'mm) round (shoulders) นก — a bird

คุ้ม (khoom') (1) to be equivalent to, to fulfil (2) to protect — เข้า until

คุย (khoo'i) (1) a creeping plant (2) garrulous

คุ่ย (khoo'i) silly

คุ้ย (khoo'i) to scatter, to dig

คุรุ (khoo'roo) [Sansk.] (1) tutor (2) planet Jupiter — วาร วะ Thursday

คุลีการ (khoo'leekarn) [Pali] to mix together

คู (khoo) (1) ditch (2) to call from afar — คู้ [phon.] cooing of doves

คู่ (khoo) couple, pair — คี่ (1) odd and even (2) equal — หนึ่ง one yoke (of oxen)

คู้ (khoo?) to bend, curve, contract ไก้ — the accent ่

คูณ (khoon) [Pali] to multiply

คูถ and คูท (khoot) [Pali] ordure

คูน (khoon) and คูณ — an edible garden plant

คูหา (khoohah) [Pali] cavern, grotto, cave, den, archway

เคน (khen) [Pali] with เข้า to make offerings to priests

เค็ม (khem) salted, salt

เคย (khoy) shrimps, small prawns เข้า — pickled prawns (2) in the habit of, accustomed to คิด to get bolder

เคหะ (khayhah) [Pali] house, home

เคอะ (khu') clumsy, awkward

แค (khaa) white acacia with edible leaves and blossoms

แค่ (khan) as far as, as long as, so long, of such a size

แคน (khaan) a (Laosian) wind instrument made of long reeds

แค้น (khaan) to be sick at heart, indignation

แคบ (khaap) crowded, narrow, tight

แคม (khaam) edge, margin

'แคะ (khaa') to untie, to extract -- คน to take out and eat the inside of a fruit, etc.

ไค (khai) dirt (on the skin, on plate, etc.)

ไค (khai) to pull out

โค (khoh) [Pali] cow, ox

โคก (khoke) small hill, knoll, mound ปลา— a scaly fish

โคง (khohng) to bend a bow; arched -- ไค้ without order

โคจร (khohchon) [Pali] passage of the sun, to walk steadily

โคดม (khohdom) [Pali] Gautama Buddha (Alab. 2. 176)

โคตร (khoht) [Sansk.] (1) race, family, kindred (2) (word of abuse) to abuse a family

โคตะมะ (khohta'ma') Gautama Buddha

โคน (khone) (1) beginning (of a tree, etc.) (2) (in chess) the Bishop

โคน (khohn) to cut, cut up

โคบาล (khohbahn) [Pali] keeper of oxen, cowherd

โคม (khome) lantern, lamp ลอย fire balloon -- หวก glass lamps hanging in a temple

โครค (khohroke) [Pali] ox-gall

โคราช (khohrat) Korat (Town and Province)

โครา (khohra'm) goat

เค้า (khow) order, series, cause, beginning, principle, appearance ปลา— a big river fish without scales -- แมว a bird -- แมว owl ? -- villainous

เคารพ (khowrop) [Sansk.] to salute, to pay respect

เคาะ (khaw') to strike, knock, tap

คำ Hen) word, speech, doctrine, eloquence -- นำ notice, preface -- นม salutation -- เปรียบ parable, allegory -- สอน doctrine, teaching

คำ๋ย — advice ป่ร๕ — rosary คฏก --
a flower used for dyeing yellow
- ๋าม๋ threatening noise (2) ท๋อ๋ —
[Laos.] gold

คา (kha'm) mouthful, piece (of betel-
nut, etc.)

คำ (kha'm) night, by night (word of
computation of time in the old
Siamese Calendar, as) ๋ ๒ fifth day
of the waxing moon in the sixth
month, etc., etc. ยั๋ง -- until night

คำ (kham!) to prop up, support -- ๋
to protect

คำนุ๋ง (kha'mncung) to remember

คำนุ๋บ (kha'mna'p) salutation ค่า — สาด
law-costs

คำภี๋ร๋ (kha'mpee) [Pali] profound,
deep: sacred books, formulas —
พยากรณ๋ fortune-telling books

คำรน (kha'mron) to make a noise

คำรพ๋ (kha'mropp) [Pali] to respect,
fear, honour

คำราม (kha'mrarn) threatening sounds;
to use threats

คะ (kha') yes   พ๋อ -- (to a superior) yes
เจ๋า -- (by women to an equal or
superior) yes

คะ (kha') [Chin.] basket

คะ *with* เคอะ (khcu' kha') inexperience,
unskilfulness

คะนอ๋ง (kha'naung) to become wild or
savage

คะนึ๋ง (kha'neung) to remember

คะเนย (kha'nay) to conjecture, guess,
calculate

คะแนน (kha'naan) (1) small (2) to
mark, to make up an account

คะยี (kha'yee) to rub

คะเยอ (kha'yer) itch

คะเย่อ (kha'yerr) to take by force, to
abduct

คะแยะ (kha'yaa') to pound in a mortar

คะโย (kha'yo) *see* คโย

คะรูบ คะริบ (kha'roo'p kha'rip) nimble,
active, hurried, busy

คะหะบดี (kha'ha'bodee) [Pali] *better*
คหบดี minister of high rank, father
of a family (Alab. 188)

คคณานุก (kha'ka'narn) [Pali] celestial

คังคก (kha'ng khok) a toad

คัง (kha'ng) obstructing — แค้น angry

คัชฌะ (kha'cha') [Pali] (1) to go away
(2) a shrub with several shoots

คัด (kha't) (1) to copy (2) to raise with
a lever, to force open   ฉัตก to
hold the rudder straight — ง้าง to
steer a boat back into its course, to
make a man alter his proceedings
— เค้า a shrub — หม่อน a medicinal shrub

คัด ค้าน (kha't kharn) to contradict

คัน (kha'n) (1) to itch, itching (2)
wand, small stick, rod, handle
— นา small mounds round a field
— ซี violin-bow, fiddle-stick

คัน (kha'nn) to separate, division — บัน
ได steps or rounds of a ladder

คัน (khan!) to squeeze out

คันชั่ง (kha'nchang) balance for weigh-
ing, scales

คันทรง (kha'nsong) a tree

คันทา (kha'ntaˈ) and สัก — (better
อัณฑา) [Pali] testicles

คันธ (kha'nta') [Pali] sweet smell, perfume   - กำใร perfumery

คันธมาลา (kha'ntaˈmahlah) [Pali]
scented flower

คันโพง (kha'npohng) lever for drawing
water

คันไล (kha'nlai) [Pali] to go, to walk

คับ (kha'p) to crowd, closely fitting,
tight   - ใจ distressed

คัพโภตกร (kha'ppotonn) [Pali] state of
pregnancy

---- • ◆ • • ----

ค

ค (kaw kaˈutah   English *k*, soft
Guttural : a low letter)   - กราฐ or
— กันจ์า name of this letter

คอ (khaw) neck   ค้น — nape of the
neck   งา   throat, bosom — พอก
goitre   - หอย กลวง glutton, gourmand ง — ลอ snake with a red
neck

ฃ

ฃ (kaw rakhang = English kh or gh. Low-sounded soft Guttural: a low letter) — ระฃัง name of this letter

ฃาว (khrah) [Pali] house, domicile

ฃ้อง (khawng) gong — ฃง musical instrument composed of cymbals arranged in a circle or part of a circle ฅ้า to beat cymbals at night for mounting guard

ฃ่า (khah) to kill

ฃาต (khaht) [Pali] to kill ปิตุ - parricide มาตุ -- matricide การันต์ — the mark ์ which signifies that a consonant at the end of a word is not to be pronounced เพชฌ - executioner

เฆฅ่น (khecan) to whip, flog, scourge,

โฆษณา (khoksa'nah) [Pali] sound, resounding, loudly

- - -   •••·····   -

ง

ง (ngaw [the "bent" letter, see ฃะ] = English ng. Guttural: a low letter)

งก (ngok) to be nervous, to be agitated

งง (ngong) to be astounded, stupefied, to forget

งด (ngot) to delay, interrupt — งาม pretty, beautiful

งบ (ngop) (1) round tablet น้ำตาล - round cakes of sugar (2) cooked prawns or fish

งม (ngom) (1) besotted (2) to grope in the dark (as under water) — งาย dim eyes

งวง (ngooang) trunk (of elephants, etc.) ไก่ — turkey — กา curved handle for hanging or lifting a pot

ง่วง (ngooang) to be benumbed, stupefied, sleepy

งวด (ngooat) to be diminished, to evaporate

งวน (ngooan) to cover, to hide

ง่วน (ngooan) diligent, active, untiring, clever

ง่อย (ngoo'i) to forget, to be stupefied

งัว (ngooa) ox, bullock ปลา — a fish

งอ (ngaw) curved, hooked bent, to bend — แง incapable, clumsy

ง้อ (ngaw) to humble oneself before a person, to try to conciliate

เงาก (ngauk) to sprout out, to bud forth, to grow

เงวก (ngawk) white, white hair

เงาง (ngaung) slowly, late

เงตงาต (ngaut ngaat) angry

เงาน (ngaun) crooked, cunning

เงอน (ngonn) uncertain, infirm, overhanging, threatening to fall

เงวน (ngawn) crest, plume, crested

เงาป (ngaup) a hat made of palm leaves

เงาม (ngaum) *and* เงอม (ngomm) very ripe, very old

เงอม (ngorm) hump-back

เงอย (ngoie) bent, motionless, paralytic

เงอย (ngoi?) benumbed, negligent

เงอย (ngoi) slowly, late

งา (ngah) (1) ivory (2) sesame (tree and oil) (3) point of a fish-trap

งาร (ngar) to raise

งาง (ngarng) to pull back, to pull away, to pull open งาง — to contradict งาง — to lift with a lever

งาง (ngarng) tinkling of a bell

งาน (ngarn) (1) business (especially of preparing or elaborating a wedding or fête) works, function, duty เงา — เจา — manager of works, steward (2) (square measure) the fourth part of a ไร่

งาม (ngahm) (1) very angry (2) much addicted to

งาบ (ngarp) separated by an interval or space, to open partially, to yawn

งาม (ngarm) pretty, beautiful

งาม (ngahm) fork สอง — forked, ambiguous

เงย (ngai) [Laos.] late in the morning

งาย (ngai) easy, easily เงก — heedless, careless, reckless, inconsiderate

เงาย (ngai) leaning back, on one's back, upside down เงย moonlight

เงา (ngow) [phon.] (1) noise of cats, caterwauling (2) a kite

เงา (gow) spear with a curved head งา — the smooth silk cotton tree

งก (ngik) having the tips or edges bent back

งิด (ngit) sad งิด sulky

หงิม (ngim) mild, soft, silent, unobtrusive

งิ้ว (ngew) [Chin.] Chinese comedy งิ้ว the thorny silk cotton tree

งีบ (ngeep) to sleep for a little while, to take a nap

หงี (ngeea) to lower; to consent; to fall asleep — หู to lend an ear

เงี่ยง (ngeeang) barb, crook, hook, hooked thorn, prickles (of fishes)

เงี้ยน (ngeean) torpor caused by abstaining from opium; sensual pleasure

เงียบ (ngeeap) silence. oblivion

งึม (ngeum) [phon.] to murmur inwardly

เหงื่อ (ngeua) sweat, perspiration

เงื้อ (ngeua) to raise for striking

เงือก (ngeuak) fabulous creature, mermaid with fish's tail — มเงือก mermaid with snake's tail

เหงือก (ngeuak) gums — ปลา gills of fishes

เงื่อง (ngeuang) gaping, yawning, loitering, slow

เหงือด (ngeuat) (1) to stop, to delay (2) to raise for striking

เงื่อน (ngeuan) knot — หงวน loop

เงื้อม (ngeuam) high. elevated — เงื้อ and — มือ in the grasp of, in the power of

งุ่น (ngoo'n) to be angry

งุบ and หงุบ (ngoo'p) to nod, sleepy, dozing — หงุบ nodding; to fall asleep — งุบ to whisper

งุมงำ (ngoo'm nga'm) to mumble, to speak indistinctly

งุ้ม (ngoo'm) slightly bent

งุ่ย (ngoo'i) giddy, foolish

งู (ngoo) snake — เหลือม boa constrictor, python — งูเห่า adder — เห่า a black venomous snake

งก (ngook) to totter, to stagger

งกงัก (ngoot ngart) angry, furious

งูงี้ (ngoo ngee) buzzing of flies, low sound of talking, etc.

เง (ngay) bent

เหงก (ngayk) to strike with the knuckles

เหง่ง (ngeng) tinkling of a bell

เงย (ngoy) to look up, to admire ; surprised

เงอะ เงอะ (nger nga') silly, imbecile

เงิน (ngern) silver, money ___ — to borrow ___ เก๊ false coin, counterfeit coin ___ — capital ___ ตรา coined or stamped money, coin of the realm ___ เจ้า creditor ___ ___ ingot of silver [Chinese measure]

เงา (ngaa) angle, corner ___ ___ ___ deceitfully, crookedly, craftily ___ ___ arrogant, affected ___ — at the corner

แงง (ngaang) (1) small branch root, small pimple (2) to threaten (of a dog, etc.)

เงิน and เงิน (ngaan) to ask humbly

แงน (ngaan) to totter, vacillating

แงน (ngaan?) to raise the head or face

แงม (ngaam) (1) recess, inside angle, corner (2) half-shut (of a door, etc.)

แงว เงียว (ngao ngow) [phon.] mewing of a cat

เงาะ (ngoh) bent down, sloping

เงาะ (ngoh) stupid (as a person half awake), ignorant

โงก (ngoke) [phon.] sound of a blow

โง่ง (ngohng) beyond measure, too much

โง่ง (ngohng) curved, arched, arching, branching out

โง่ง (ngohng?) sound of a bell or cymbal

โง่น (ngohn) tottering, near ruin

เงา (ngow) lustre, gleam, reflection, shadow, shade

เงา (ngow) (1) stupid (2) root of a tree ___ — grandsons, descendants

เงา (ngow) angry

เหงา (ngow?) sad, stupefied

เงาะ (ngau) (1) curly, crisped, frizzy (2) rambootan, a tree with fruits having a hairy skin and inside like a hard egg

เหงาะ (ngaw) sound of a blow

งำ (nga'm) to gather, closed up, tight

งำ (nga'mm) hastily, without stopping; sound of lapping up water

งำ (nga'm?) jutting out, bent forwards

งง (nga'ng) (1) sound of a big bell (2) benumbed, torpid งง — a talisman protecting from blows, etc. by making the assailant powerless to strike

งั่ง (nga'ng) a metal figure used by alchemists งั่ง a short-tailed monkey

งัด (nga't) to open up from underneath, to force up, to rai e with a lever

งัน (nga'n) silent, unable to speak งัน to shake, to oscillate, to be agitate 1, nervous

งับ (nga'p) [phon.] to seize with the teeth — ปิดงับ to shut a door งับ — secretly

งาบ (nga'p) quickly, hastily

• • •

จ

จ (chow chareun = English ch. Palatal: a middle letter) เจ้าจู้ name of this letter

จก (chok) [Laos.] to pick up quickly, to snatch up

จง (chong) (aux. verb of the Imperative) may it be, let it be — จงทำ do

จด (chot) (1) to mark, to note (2) to reach, to touch — จดไว้ to record — จดชื่อ to sign — หมาย note; to note down

จน (chon) (1) poor (2) embarrassed, distressed (3) till, until — จนสิ้น until the last, entirely (4) obstacle barring the way, block, barricade

จบ (chop) to finish, end

จม (chomm) to dip, to be immersed, to sink

จมื่น (cha'meun) a superior class of King's pages having the same rank as a Phra

จมูก (cha'mook) nose จมูก - - nostril

จร (chora') and จ [Pali] to walk, go

จรเข้ (chora'kay) crocodile, alligator หาง — aloes ธง: a flag like a c.

จรจรัล (cha'ra'cha'ra'n) [Pali] to take a walk, to go

จรด พระนังคัล (cha'rot pra'na'ngka'n) [Pali] ceremony of the first ploughing of the year

จริง (ching) true

ชริก (cha'ritt) coquetry

ชริย and ชริยา (cha'riyah) [Sansk.] conduct, practice

ชรุง (cha'roo'ng) glad, joyful

เชริญ (cha'reun) [Cambod.] prosperous

ชระยง (cha'ra'yong) to do, to act

ชรัณ (cha'ra'n) [Pali] to go, road

ชวง (chooang) scent of sandal wood

ชวง (chooang) to draw water

ชวด (chooat) an edible sea fish

ชวน (chooan) (1) Governor's house and grounds (2) very near

ชวบ (chooap) to meet

ชวา (choo'a') triangle of the roof, gable-end

ชวา (choo'a') [Chin.] to turn up a card in playing

ชอ (chaw) [Cambod.] (1) dog (zodiac) (2) [Siam.] curtain for magic lantern (3) clamour, uproar

ชอ (chaw) to touch, to join, to apply (one thing to another)

ชอ (chaw') (1) an aquatic plant (2) to babble

ชอ (chaw?) monkey

ชอ (chaw?) [Chin.] to sit

ชอก (chauk) cup — บัว water-lily

ชอง (chaung) [Cambod.] (1) proud, vain (2) to mark out boundaries (3) to agree (4) to tie, fasten (5) to bear a grudge (6) to put in chains — หอง haughty, conceited — เชวียง [Pali] ceremony of putting lights on the walls to keep off demons (7) [Maun] to burn, to disturb

ชอง (chaung) (1) complaisant, yielding (2) [Laos.] umbrella

ชอง (chaung) to walk, to be ready for a thing, to aim at (with a gun, etc.)

ชอด (chort) to go to shore, to land, to moor ช: — port, harbour, landing

ชอนหู (chaun hoo) earring

ชอน (chaun) slender, small

ชอบ (chaup) a pick-axe, a hoe

ชอม (chaum) (1) the top (2) title of the King's concubines

ชอม (chomm) (1) a fish (2) to commence, to begin

ชอม (chaum?) noise of walking in water

ชอย (choie) dull, sad

ชอย (choi) (1) small, tiny, little (2) talkative

ฉอย (choi?) sad, gloomy

ฉา *with* พูด (poot chah) to talk, converse

ฉา (char) (1) shepherd, leader (2) (a dignity) chief of the King's pages (3) a spoon made of cocoa-nut for taking boiled rice out of the pot

ฉ่ำ (charr) strong, vehement, much

ฉ่ะ (chah?) Yes; Yes, Sir

ฉาก (chark) (1) from (2) a plant of which the leaves are used for roofs, attap

ฉาง (charng) insipid, not clear — วาง substitute, deputy, representative

ฉ้าง (chahng) to hire ค่า — สิน — wages ลูก — mercenary, hireling, workman, day labourer เรือ — hired boat, ferry-boat

ฉาด (chart) impudent, shameless

ฉาน (charn) (1) saucer, dish — รอง saucer — เชิง earthenware eating-vessel having a raised stand (2) to write with a stylus or iron pencil

ฉ้าน (chahn) to shine

ฉาป (charp) proud, arrogant

ฉาบัลย (charba'n) [Pali] trembling

ฉาม (charm) to sneeze

ฉามรี (charma'choo'ree) [Pali] antelope ก — crest or tuft of white antelope's hair used for ornamenting barges

ฉามร (charmonn) [Pali] a royal fan

ฉามะ (charma') [Pali] (and several derivative words) the skin or hair of animals

ฉามะร (charma'ra') *and* ฉามะรี bunches or tufts of hair, a fan of animal's hair

ฉาย (chaie) to distribute วัน — the day before a fête

ฉารี (chahree) [Pali] to go, to do, to act

ฉาริก (chahreet) [Pali] ceremonies, usages

ฉารึก (chahreuk) to engrave

ฉาเรศ (chahrett) [Pali] one of the four royal pages of highest rank

ฉาละเม็ก (charla'mett) a flat sea fish เต่า — turtle

ฉาว (chow) pulp (of cocoa-nut, etc.)

ฉิก (chik) (1) to peck ฉก — cares and troubles (2) to tear off small pieces (3) a tree

ฉิง (ching) *with* ไม้ all woods except bamboo

จิ้ง (ching) (not used alone) — จก small lizard (on walls) — จิ้งจอก fox — เหี้ย large lizard (on the ground) — โจ้ kangaroo

จิ้งเหลน (ching len) see จิ้ง

จิตตัง (chitta'ng) [Pali] (1) spirit, soul, thought (2) silently meditating

จิตตรา (chitta'ra') [Sansk.] spirit, life, soul, intelligence, idea (Alab. 223) — มาส (in dates) the 5th month

จินดา (chindah) [Pali] diamond

จินดามณี (chindahma'nee) [Pali] (1) Siamese grammar (2) a precious stone, wishing-stone

จินตา (chintah) จินตะ and จินตะนา [Pali] thought, to think

จินตะกระวี (chinta'kra'wee) [Pali] poet

จินตะรา (chinta'rah) [Pali] clever, wise, prudent

จินตะหรา (chinta'rah) [Javan.] young lady

จิบ (chip) to sip

จิม (chim) (1) touching the top of the water (2) at the moment of, near

จิ้ม (chim) to insert, to dip ไม้ — พัน toothpick

จิริก (chirit) small, puny, little

จิ๋ว (chiew) [Chin.] a Chinese intoxicating drink made with rice

จิ๋ว (chiew) [Chin.] small, puny

จิ๋ว (chiu') [Chin.] fan

จี (chee) [Chin.] pudenda feminæ

จี่ (chee) to roast, to burn ลิ้น — (lin chee) (1) a round spotted fruit (2) a red colour (3) [Annam.] elder sister

จี้ (chee!) (1) to tickle (2) ornament

จี๋ (chee?) very quick

จีก (cheet) a small fish

จี๊ด (cheet) very small, minute

จีบ (cheep) to fold up, roll up (betel leaves, etc.)

จีม (cheem) to stop up holes

จีระ (cheera') [Pali] a long time

เจียก (cheeak) (1) to divide (2) a reed with sweet flowers

เจียด (cheeat) (1) ornaments of rank (2) to buy by retail

เจียน (cheean) (1) soon (2) to cut off pieces (3) to surround, encircle

เชม (cheeam) (1) carpet (2) to be moderate, temperate

เชียว (cheeyu) (1) to fry (2) to put with oil or grease (3) (a particle intensifying the word before it)

เชียว (cheeyu) [Chin.] genitalia viri

เชียว (cheeyu) [Chin.] a Chinese pot

ชีวร (cheewonn) [Pali] the three robes of a priest (panung vest and scarf)

จึ่ง (cheung) then

จืด (cheut) fresh (of water), insipid, tasteless

เจือ (cheua) to mix, compound, dilute

เฉยเ (cheua) easily

ชุ (choo') to stuff or cram (one thing into another) full

ชุก (choo'k) (1) colic (2) to stop up (3) top-knot

ชุ่ง (choo'ng) — ชุ่ง

ชุณ (choo'n) [Pali] to pound into dust; dust, powder

ชุติ (choo'ti') [Pali] birth, migration from one state to another (M.189)

ชุน (choo'n) (1) to penetrate, to go in (2) to prop up

ชุน (choo'n) (1) monkey (2) projecting navel

ชุน (choo'n!) to push

ชุป (choo'p) to suck gently

ชุป (ch oo'p) steam pipe — แชง (1) a sea shell (2) to kiss gently

ชุม and ชุม (choo'm) to dip, to immerse, to steep

ชุย (chooi') prodigal, mischievous

ชุล จักรพรรดิ (choo'lla' cha'kra'pa't) the King

ชุล ศักราช (choo'lla' sa'ka'raht) [Pali] the old Siamese civil era

ชุลาชล (choo'lahchonn) disorder, confusion, defeat

ชุลย (choo'lla') [Pali] small

ชุฬา (choo'lah) [Pali] pin for the top-knot

ชู (choo) a small woolly dog

ชู (choo) to rush suddenly

ชู (choo) a trap (for eels)

ชูง (choong) to lead by the hand

ชูป (choop) to kiss, sound of kissing

เชก (chek) [Chin.] Chinaman

เจ็ด (chet) [Chin.] seven — สิบ seventy

เจดีย์ (cheddee) [Pali] pointed pyramid, pagoda

เจตร (chettra') *and* เจตะ [Pali] mind, thonght, spirit, life, idea (Alab. 236) เจตรมาศ the fifth month

เจตสิก (chettra'sik) [Pali] mental, mental category, mode of expression (Alab. 237)

เจน (chayn) accustomed to, able to, expert, proficient

เจ็บ (chepp) sick, ill, hurt

เจรจา (chaynchar) [Pali] to talk, converse

เจียรดา (chaytsa'dah) [Sansk.] gold ornament for the neck

เจอ *and* เจอะ (churr) to meet, to come together

เจ่อ (chur) projecting lip

เจือ (chur) confusedly

เจือเจอะ (chur cher) to come without being asked

เจิม (chern) beyond, besides; to add

เจิม (chern) to anoint, to touch with oil or unguents

แจ (chaa) to follow closely

แจ้ (chaa) light red, very red

แจ้ (chaa) to open out, expand (of flowers, etc.) ไก่ — a bird with a crest and a large tail

แจก (chaak) to distribute

แจง (chaang) to distribute, to arrange in order, to classify

แจ้ง (chaang) manifest, clear, open — ความ to inform — แจ้ง a formula used in the address on envelopes

แจ่ม (chaam) cheerful, bright

แจว (chaao) long oar (Siamese style) ห — the loop used for holding it in place

แจ้ว (chaao) warbling, chattering, noise of talking

แจะ (chaa) (1) touching, close together (2) a Laosian tribe

ใจ (chai) (1) heart, mind, character, nature, disposition — ดี benevolent ดี — glad ขัด — angry ชอบ pleased เต็ม — content, willing เอา — will น้อย — displeased คิด —

aghast, startled, frightened เสีย — despair, desperate, to disappoint, to dishearten ใจ — doubt: สิ้น — to die หาย— to breathe เอา — ใส่ to attend, take care เวียน ขน — to learn by heart — กว้าง ขวาง liberal, charitable — เป็น presence of mind — เกื้อ กัน congenial, sympathetic เข้า — to understand (2) the middle, the central part of anything as — มือ the middle of the palm of the hand, 200 grains of rice, the 64th part of a tanan — ตีน hollow of the foot, middle of the sole

โรง กระเบน (chohng kra'benn) to form the tail of the panung

โหง ฉะ (chohng cha') performance on a drum with the fingers and flat of the hand

โชค (chote) to go from one employment to another

โจทย์ or โจทนา (chote, chohta'nah) [Pali] to accuse, to rebuke, to dispute: — กัน to report, to discuss ผู้ — Plaintiff - ว่า problem

โจน (chone) to jump or leap upon, a or towards

โจร (chone) and โจระ (chohra') [Pali] thief, robber, burglar

โฆษณา (chohtcha'n) (1) to communicate (2) to make a noise

เชา (chow) a plant like hemp

เฝ้า (chow) to sit silent and still, to sit on the watch นก — a bird ปลา - a fish

เจ้า (chow!) a lord, a master: You (spoken to an inferior) — เมือง Governor of a Province — ของ proprietor — บ่าว bridegroom — สาว bride — ขา Yes, Sir (by women) — เล่ห์ cunning perfidious, unscrupulous — นี้ creditor — ที่ landlord จันทร์ — moon

เจ่า (chow?) sad and silent, melancholy

เจาะ (chaw) (1) to bore, to perforate (2) to make a noise with the tongue or mouth

เจาะ เลาะ (chaw law) handsome, agreeable

ชำ (cha'm) (1) to identify (2) to imprison (3) to remember — เป็น necessary — ขัง to imprison — น้ำ to pawn, pledge, mortgage — สอง duplicate, to copy — ไว้ to remember

ช่ำ (cha'm) (1) quickly, with quick, strokes (2) fat (3) a babbler

ชำ กัก (cha'm ka't) just enough, having none to spare

ชำนง (cha'mnong) and ชำนิอง according to one's wish

ชำนน (cha'mnon) beaten in a fight, vanquished

ชำนรรชา (cha'mna'nchah) to converse

ชำนวน (cha'mnooan) quantity, account นาย — secretary

ชำหน่าย (cha'mnai) and ชำแหนก to distribute

ชำเนียร (cha'mneean) [Sansk.] a long time past, long ago

ชำน้ำ (cha'mna'm) pawn, pledge, security, mortgage

ชำนัน (cha'mna'n) to converse, talk

ชำปะ (cha'mpah) (1) a tree with sweet-smelling yellow flowers (2) spring of a lock

ชำปากะ (cha'mparda') a delicate kind of jack-fruit

ชำปี (cha'mpee) a tree with white flowers

ชำพวก (cha'mpooak) congregation, band, assemblage

ชำปู (cha'mpoo) a tree

ชำภาะ (cha'mpaw) only, barely, just enough

ชำเริญ (cha'mreun) [Cambod.] (1) to persevere (2) to cut, dock, curtail (3) to thrive, prosper, increase, advance; good morning น้ำ favourable — สบาย good health; good morning

ชำระ (cha'mra') a part, a side

ชำลอง (cha'mlaung) to transcribe, to renew, to reprint

ชำเลย (cha'mloey) culprit, defendant, litigant

ชำศีล (cha'mseen) [Siam. and Sansk.] to fast, to observe the strict rules of conduct

ชะ (cha') (1) (aux. verb of the Future) will, shall (2) (aux. verb of the Infinitive) to

ฉเข (cha'kay) musical instrument, made like a crocodile, with strings

ฉแจ้ง (cha'chaang) clear, manifest, corrected

ฉบัง (cha'ping) leaf of gold or other metal used to hide the nakedness of female children, lappet or plate placed over a lock, etc.

ฉละ (cha'la') [Pali] to shake about a little. trembling, vibrating

ฉละเม็ด (cha'la'mett) a flat sea fish ไข่ — turtle egg

ฉละหวั่น (cha'la'wa'n) tumultuously, confusedly

ฉัก (cha'k) to cleave, to split รู้ — to know

ฉักร (cha'k) [Sansk.] (1) wheel (2) King. royal authority (so in compos.) — วาฬ and — พาฬ ends or boundaries of the world — พรรดิ very mighty King

ฉักรี (cha'kkree) [Pali] name of a throne in the Palace

ฉัง (cha'ng) with ตรง straight, true — ฉอน the eighth part of a tanan

ฉังกา (cha'ngkah) to take aim

ฉังกูด (cha'ngkoot) stern; after part of a boat

ฉังงัง (cha'ng nga'ng) stupefied, incapable

ฉังทาง (cha'ngtarn) low fellow, rascal

ฉังหรีด (cha'ngreet) a cricket

ฉังไร (cha'ngrai) unlucky, accursed, abominable

ฉังโลง (cha'nglohng) long handled instrument with bamboo plaited bowl for baling big boats

ฉังวะ (cha'ngwa') boundaries, intervals, bars, end of a rhyme, rhythm, cadence

ฉังวัด (cha'ngwa't) parish, sub-district

ฉังหัน (cha'ngha'n) food of a priest แพว — whirlegig, scarecrow

ฉันทาน (cha'ntahn) [Pali] very bad, lewd, wicked

ฉัด (cha't) (1) vehement, strong (2) to speak much (3) to prepare, adjust, arrange — แจง to get ready, fit up, regulate — ไว้ to provide — ใหม่ to revise — หา to search — ให้ to supply — การ to manage a business ผู้ — — manager

ฉัททา (cha'ta'wah) [Sansk.] four
(the fourth accent, as over เจ้า)

ฉัฏ and ฉัฏฐะ [Pali] better จัตุ four

ฉัน (cha'n) (1) a yellow shell (2) blossom of cocoa or betel-nut (3) snare,
trap เสา ฉัน mechanical crane

ฉันตาการ (cha'nta'karn) and ประ —
[Pali] inhabitants of the country
near the frontier

ฉันท (cha'n) [Pali] sandal wood ลูก
นุตเมก

ฉันทบุรี Chantaboon or Chantaboore
(Town and Province)

ฉันทร (cha'n) ฉันทรา and ฉันทร [San.]
moon (Alab. 217) วัน — Monday
กะ full moon — ดิถีดารา and
สุริยคราธ eclipse of the moon

ฉันทาน (cha'nta'n) rafter

ฉันโลง (cha'nlohng) to sustain

ฉันนับ (cha'na'p) [Chin.] dried cakes

ฉับ (cha'p) to catch, overtake ฉับ
to seize, to grip — กะ to begin
เฉา to fish — จับ to occupy ไข้
intermittent fever ฉับ guitar

ฉับเฉียว (cha'p cheeyo) [Chin.] small
earthenware kettle

ฉับปิง and ฉะปิง (cha'p-ping) leaf of
gold or silver for children, lappet
for covering a key-hole, etc., a
board forming part of the aft portion of a boat

••••••

ช

ช (chaw chan = English ch. Palatal;
a high letter) — ชอ name of this
letter

ชก (chok) (1) to steal (2) (of snakes)
to bite

ชการ (cha'ka'n) (1) adult [20 to 30
years old] (2) fierce, savage, cruel

ชงน (cha'ngon) doubtful, irresolution
ใจ mistake

ชงาย (cha'ngai) (1) to be surprised,
astonished (2) distant, far off, far

ชงวน (cha'ngoan) (1) a road reserved
for the King and the Princesses (2)
a tall tree with leaves used for
medicine

ชนาก (cha'nark) saw-fish

ไฉน (cha'nai) how? what?

โฉนก (cha'note) title deed of a garden

พ้อง — charge of forgery

ฉบับ (cha'ba'p) copy, pattern, model (numerical designation of papers)

ฉมวก (cha'mooak) harpoon with three prongs, trident

ฉมัน (cha'ma'n) stag

ฉระอ้ำ (cha'ra a'm) shaded, cloudy

ฉลวย (cha'looi) bent at both ends, arched, curved

ฉลัว (cha'looa) dull (of colours)

ฉลอ เฉลา (cha'law cha'low) elegant

ฉลอง (cha'laung) (1) to celebrate, to dedicate (2) (a royal word prefixed to the name of several articles in common use) วัน — holiday, ceremony, solemnity

ฉลอม (cha'laum) a small sea vessel

ฉลาก (cha'lark) [Pali] a lottery ticket

ลก — lime enclosing such a ticket

ฉลาง (cha'larng) Junk Ceylon [an island in Western Siam]

ฉลาด (cha'lart) cunning, prudent, subtle, discreet

ฉลาม (cha'larm) a shark

ฉลีก (cha'leek) notched, indented

เฉลียง (cha'leeang) a covered gallery, verandah

เฉลียว ฉลาด (cha'leeo cha'lart) very prudent, very cunning, clever

ฉลู (cha'loo) ox ปี — second year of the Siamese cycle

เฉลย (cha'loy) and — ไข to answer

เฉลว (cha'lao) (1) rod or stick in the river to show where the channel is deep (2) sign or mark of sale (3) ticket used by doctors for their medicine jars

เฉลิม (cha'leum) to anoint, to celebrate, to make an illumination or other fête

เฉลาป (cha'laap) obliquely, slanting-wise, zigzag

เฉลิม (cha'laam) admirable

โฉลก (cha'loke) method, model; at a good time

ฉวย (chooey) to seize, to catch

ฉวาง (cha'warng) arithmetic

ฉวี (cha'wee) [Pali] skin [of animate and inanimate things]

เฉวียง (cha'weeang) [Cambod.] to twist or turn to the left

ฉศก (chawsok) [Pali] 6th year of the Siamese cycle

ฉ๋ (chaw) to steal, fraudulent — ฉ๋น swindle

ฉอ๋อน (cha'onn) mild, affabic

ฉอุ๋ม (cha'oomm) green and shady

ฉาก (chark) with ไม้ a square rule, a screen for dividing rooms รูป — unframed picture คัก — to steer a boat

ฉาง (charng) granaries, barns (a measure of 200 เกวียน or loads)

ฉ่าง (chahng) [Chin.] sound of Chinese cymbals

ฉาน with น่า (nah charn) before the King

ฉาย (charp) (1) to seize, to pounce upon (2) to fly (3) sweetened and fried (4) cymbal - เฉียว suddenly, rapidly

ฉาย (chai) [Pali] reflection, shadow, shade พระ — (1) looking glass (for royal persons) (2) photograph of a royal person

ฉายา (charyar) [Pali] = ฉาย

ฉาว (chowe) to be spread about, to be rumoured, to babble, to gossip

ชิ (chi) and ฉี (chee) (exclam. of surprise, aversion, or anger)

ฉิ่ง (ching) cymbals

ฉิ่ง (ching) maimed, lame

ฉิน with ติ (ti' chin) slander

ฉิบ (chip) escaped

ฉิบหาย (chip hai) to perish; ruinous; destruction

ฉิม (chim) small child

ฉิว (chiew) (of wind) gentle, steady

ฉี่ (chee) noise of frying

ฉีก (cheek) to tear, rip up, lacerate

ฉีด (cheet) to inject

เฉียง (cheeang) oblique, diagonal, slanting

เฉียด (cheeat) nearly touching แล่น - to tack

เฉียบ (cheeap) sharpened, pointed

เฉียว (cheeu') quickly, rapaciously, to seize rapidly

เฉื่อย (chooey) very steadily, very slowly

ฉุ (choo') (1) damaged, spoilt (2) a swelling, bloated

ฉุก (choo'k) to be sick; anguish

ฉุง ฉิง (choo'ng ching) peevish, fretful, tiresome: noise of chains, clashing, jingling

ฉุด (choo't) to pull, to drag — ก๋ว่า to drag away, carry off

ฉุน (choo'n) sharp, keen, strong, pungent, angry

ฉุน (choo'n) กระชุ่น to give a push, to shove

ฉุย (chooi') (1) easily, neatly, quickly (2) quick easy movement of a saw through wood (3) emanation (of smells) - - ฉวย (1) foppish, idle (2) a dance

ฉูด (choot) to spout out: clyster

ฉะ (chay) oblique, leaning over

เฉโก (chaykoh) [Pali] skilful, expert, cunning, knavish, cheating

เฉะ (chate) (a word used to drive away dogs) กระ - a vegetable

เฉย (choey) phlegmatic, indifferent, aimless, besotted

เฉิด ฉาย (chert chai) เฉิด ฉิง and เฉิด ฉัง neat, cleanly

ฉ่า ๆ (chaa chaa) noise of falling rain

ฉาก (chaak) indented, serrated

แฉ่ง (chaang) healthy

แฉะ (chaa') wet, muddy ตา — bleareyed ปาก - garrulous

โฉงเฉง (chong chayng) deceiver, liar

โฉด (chote) stupid, silly

โฉบ (chepe) to seize (of falcons, etc.)

โฉม (chome) handsome, pretty

เฉา (chow) (1) stupid, silly (2) (of trees) withering, drooping

เฉาะ (chaw') to cut off

ฉ่ำ แฉะ (cha'm chaa') (1) muddy (2) negligent

ฉ่ำ (cha'm) pleasant, agreeable ฉ่ำวาน of an agreeable sweetness

ฉะ (cha') (1) (Interjection, contradicting or joking) ฉิ — (Interjection of blame) - - ฉ่า chorus in a burlesque or comic play (2) to chip, to notch (3) [Pali] six

ฉะโงก (cha'ngoke) leaning the head over, looking over the edge

ฉะเชิงเฉา (cha'serng sow) Petriew (town and province)

ฉะนี (cha'nee) in this way, thus

ฉะนั้น (cha'na'n) in that way, so เพรา -- on that account

ฉะ หวั่ง (cha'ba'ng) a rhythm of verses

ฉะ หมวย (cha'moy) to turn the eyes a little to one side, to look askance

ฉะ เลา (cha'law) (1) to cherish, foster, bring up (2) to move or transport a house bodily by digging the ground and dragging at the walls

ฉะ ลาน (cha'lan) to mow, to clear a ground, to level

ฉะเลาะ (cha'law) to disagree, embroil; broil

ฉัฐมะ (cha'ta'ma') [Sansk.] sixth

ฉัตร (cha't) [Sansk.] parasol with tiers เศวตร — white parasol over King's throne

ฉัน (cha'n) (1) I, me (2) (of priests) to eat ฉัน — I, me (by women) หม่อม (to a Prince) I, me

ฉันใด (cha'ndai) how? what?

ฉันท์ (cha'n) [Pali] a metre of verses เดียร — to be of the same mind

ฉันทา (cha'n.tah) [Pali] desire

— — — • • • — — —

ช

ช (chaw chen or small ch. = English

---

ch. Sansk. and Pali j. Palatal: a low letter) ชี name of this letter

ชก (chok) to fight with the fists

ชง (chong) [Chin.] to make tea

ชง โลง (chong lohng) a scoop for shovelling out water

ชงฆ์ (chong) [Pali] (of the King) shin, lower part of the leg (from the knee to the ankle)

ชฎิล (cha'dinn) [Sansk.] hermit, ascetic with long hair

ชน (chon) (1) fighting of animals — ไก่ cock-fighting (2) [Pali] man, people

ชนก (cha'nok) [Pali] father

ชนนี (cha'na'nee) [Pali] mother

ชนบท (chona'bot) [Pali] inhabitant, countryman

ชนม์ (chonm) age, life

ชนา (cha'nah) [Pali] men

ชโน (cha'noh) [Pali] man

ชนาธิเบศร์ (cha'narti'bett) [Pali] King

ชนิด (cha'nitt) kind, species

ชม (chom) to praise, admire, enjoy

ชมด (cha'mott) civet cat — เช็ด musk rat

ชมพู (chompoo) [Pali] a large tree having a small fruit in clusters [eugenia jambu]

ชมพู (chompoo) [Pali] continent, country — ทวีป continent inhabited by men (Alab. 13, 187)

ชมพูนท and ชมพูนท (chompoonot) [Pali] pure gold

ชมพู (chompoo) small tree having a fruit like a pear

ชรา (cha'rah) [Pali] decrepit, old

ชล (chon) and ชลา (cha'lah) [Pali] (and several similar words) water — ธิ — ธาร and ธารา river — เนตร and —ไนย tears

ชลอม (cha'laum) bamboo basket with the top end open which can be tied at the neck for keeping fruit, etc.

ชลาน (chalarn) to level

เชลย (cha'loy) booty, spoil, captives คน captive

ช่วง (chuang) shining, bright

ชวด (chooat) (1) rat 1st year of the cycle (2) finding nothing, finding all gone, having nothing left to do, stopped short

ชวน (chooan) to take with one, to persuade to a thing, to lead away ประ — sick (of a King or Prince)

ชวน (cha'wa'na') [Pali] quick, rapid, versatile, vivacity

ช่วย (chooey) to come to the aid of, to help, to succour, defend, assist, take part with — ไถ่เอา ransom — .ให้ ให้ rescue

ชวาลา (cha'wa'lah) [Sansk.] lamp

ชวลิต (cha'wa'litt) [Pali] shining, splendid

ชวา (cha'wah) better ชะวา Java

ชวาลา (cha'warlah) lamp with three branches or jets

ชู (chooa) [Hindoo] rat, mouse

ชั่ว (chooa) (1) bad, perverse, wicked (2) all (3) a generation, period, revolution น้า the future ใน — in the course of หนึ่ง — คน — prostitute

ชู (chooa) [Chin.] a Chinese box

ช่อ (chor) bunch, cluster (of flowers) (2) to cheat

ช่อง (chong) orifice, hole, aperture, gap, opportunity ได้ — at a fit opportunity   กุญ hole in a door where the bolt can be got at

ช่อง (chawng) to fasten up (hair) loosely ; wig

ช่อน (chorn) to drill กระ — a cocoanut milk receiver, a kind insect which live in paddy shell

ช่อน (chorn) a common fresh water fish

ช้อน (chaun) spoon, spoon-shaped net, to catch fish   กบ a fish-eating bird, a spoon made of shell

ชอบ (chaup) suitable, proper, right, to like   ใจ pleasing, to be agreeable — กล it seems right, it should be so

ชา (chah) [Chin.] tea ใบ — tea leaf น้ำ tea infusion

ชา (chah) torpor, numbness in the limbs, lethargy ปรี่ — canning, wise

ช้า (char) (1) a long while, to delay, too late — ๆ slow, tardy (2) rude, rough, indecent

ช่าง (chahng) workman, artificer ; employment, trade, vocation แกะ sculptor (and so of other trader and callings) - พูด orator, babbler — ประดิษฐ inventor, impostor — สลัก engraver

ช้าง (charng!) elephant . พลาย male elephant — พัง female elephant โขลง herd of elephants

ชาญ (charn) [Pali] and เชียว — vigorous, strong

ชาดก (chardok) [Pali] history (esp. of Buddha)

ชาด (chaht) vermilion

ชาตรี (chartree) [Sansk.] (1) invulnerable (2) Ligor theatre

ชาติ (chaht'i') [Pali] race, origin, existence, to be born, native (Alab. 239)

ชาน (charn) refuse of sugar cane, betelnut, etc. นอก — porch, platform attached to a house โรง gaoler

ชาม (charm) dish — ข้าง wide open dish — มี dish with a lid to it

ชาย (chaie) (1) edge, border, shore, lace (2) male, masculine ชู้ — and —ชู้ adulterous

ชายา (chahyah) [Pali] wife, fine woman

ชาร (charn) [Pali] adulterer, paramour

ชาล (chahn) and ชาลา (chahlah) [Pali] flame

ชิ! (ching) to take suddenly, to snatch away

ชิง ช้า (ching chah) swing

ชิงไชย (ching chai) to fight

ชิงชัง (ching cha'ng) hatred, to detest

ชิด (chit) connected, fitting closely, well-fitting

ชิต (chitt) [Pali] victorious, victory

ชิน (chin) (1) to be familiar, to be accustomed to (2) tin

ชิน (chin) [Pali] victor, to vanquish — สี a blue chemical substance like alum

ชิ้น (chin) piece, bit

ชิม (chim) to taste, to try

ชิวงกต (chi'wongkot) [Pali] to die (of the last King)

ชิวหา (chiewhah) [Pali] tongue

ชี (chee) nun ผัก — parsley ผัก — ล้อม chevril, an aromatic plant ยาย — old woman

ชี (chee) exudation from burning wood

ชี (chee) to show, to point out · แผ! to explain

ชีพ (cheep) [Pali] life — กิ้กไยย [San.] to die (of the King's grandsons, chiefs of vassal states, etc.)

ชีวา (cheewah) ชีวี ชีวัน and ชีวี [Pali] life

ชีวิต (cheewitt) [Sansk.] life, alive, living เจ้า — King

เชียง (cheeang) (1) veil (2) [Laos.] chief town — ใหม่ Chiengmai (capital of Laos) กวี ฝน

เชียว (cheeyo) rapid (of water, etc.)

ชื่น (cheun) joyful

ชื้น (cheune) moist, wet

ชื่อ (cheu) name — ตี้ title — เสีย fame, renown ยก — to nominate เสีย — to lose one's reputation ปลาย end of the name ผู้ กี้ the undersigned

เชื่อ (chewa) to rely, believe, credit; on credit - - ใจ to trust, reliable -- ฟัง to obey — กัน to believe

เชื้อ (chewa) (1) to ferment (2) race, family สาย posterity - เชิญ to invite

เชือก (chewak) line, rope เส้น..เชือก cable - - ป่าน cord, twine ฟั่น to twist a rope — น้ำมัน tarred rope

เชื่อง (chewang) docile, gentle, tame

เชือด (chewat) to cut, cut up

เชือน (chewan) to go in a crooked direction, to turn aside

เชือน (chewam) (1) to put into sugar, to preserve (fruits, etc.) (2) languid, ill, torpid, careless, heedless, lazy (3) to go very slow

ชุษณปักษ์ (choo'nha'pa'k) Sansk. time of the waxing moon

ชุด (choo't) (1) tinder, rope torch (2) mouse-trap, fish-trap (3) numerical designation of tea-sets, etc.

ชุน (choo'n) (1) to darn, to mend, to embroider (2) an instrument for net-making, netting needle

ชุน (choo'n) to goad, to push on

ชุบ (choo'p) (1) to steep, to dip (2) to write, to gild

ชุม (choo'm) plentiful, to abound, abundant

ชุ่ม (choo'nam) (1) to dip, to temper (steel) (2) happy, joyful

ชุมนุม (choo'nuncoom) party, meeting, to assemble, congregate - - กัน assembly เชร - - mob

ชุลี (choo'lee) [Pali] to salute with raised and closed hands

ชู (choo) to raise, to prop up ชั่ง to weigh

ชู้ (choo) adultery, adulterous ดอก ชู้ lily

เชษฐา (cheytah) [Pali] eldest brother

เช็ด (chett) to wipe

เชน (chenn) mode, species, manner

เชิง (cherng) [Cambod.] (1) foot, basis, stand เทียน candle-stick กำ behind battlements - - กราน earthenware portable stove (1) artifice, trick, deceitful

เชิญ (chern) to invite, to bid

เชิก (chert) the display of masks and figures in funeral plays, magic lantern

แช (chaa) negligent, to delay

แช่ (chaa') to saturate, soak - ชื่ม preserve (of fruit, etc.)

แช่ง (chaang) oath, imprecation: to swear, to curse

แฉล้ม (cham) open forehead วิไย pretty, amiable

เชีย (chie) it is so ใช่ — or ชิ -- not so ชิ- ชิ not only

ใช้ (chie) to use, to treat, to pay; service - ใช้ to send ข้า slaves, servants

ไช (chai) to pierce, to bore

ไชย (chaiya') ไชยา and ชไย [Pali] victory

ไชยะ (chaiya') [Pali] to vanquish, victor, victory

โชก (choke) (1) wet (2) good fortune, fortunate

โชฎึก (chohdenk) [Pali] prosperity

โชติ (chohti') [Pali] shining, glowing

เชา (chowe) citizens, people, inhabitants of - เรา all of us here บ้าน laymen; neighbours - ชั่ง ชไล peasants, rustics - นา agriculturist, farmer

เช่า (chow) to lease, to hire ให้ - to let ค่า - rent

เช้า (chow') morning — มืด before dawn รุ่ง - early morning

เชาวน์ (chow) [Pali] intelligent, quick-witted

ชำ (cha'm) a cutting from a tree, a slip; to plant

ชำใจ (cha'm chai) refreshed, satisfied

ชำ and ชำรุฎก (cha'm chank) bruised, contusion

ชำฉา (cha'mchah) fir tree, white wood, deal

ชำนาญ (cha'mnarn) and ชาน [Pali] skilful, expert, able, experienced

ชำร่วย (cha'mrooi) to thank, to recompense, to give a present in return

ชำรุด (cha'mroo't) to go to ruin; spoilt, damaged, a blot, a defect

ชำแรก (cha'mraak) to penetrate into the earth

ฉำเรา (cha'mrow) (high word) to cohabit, to copulate

ฉำระ (cha'mra') to clear, to wash, to
scour, to examine a person) or affair

ฉำลา (cha'mlah) a fish used for salting

ฉำเลียง (cha'mlenang) to look askance,
awry

ฉะ (cha') to smear over with, to sprinkle
or foment with water

ฉะงอก and ฉะงอ (cha'ngauk cha'-
ngoke) lofty, overhanging, threatening to fall

ฉะงำ (cha'nga'm) too high

ฉะฎา (cha'dah) [Pali] a crown worn
by actors

ฉะโด (cha'doh) a common river fish

ฉะตา (cha'tah) star under which a
person is born, destiny, luck ก๎ว—
astrologer's circle

ฉะนาง (cha'narng) a fish-snare made of
bamboos

ฉะนิต and ฉะนิต (cha'nitt) kind, species

ฉะนะ (cha'na') [Pali] to gain, to win,
to surmount, to excel — แว้ to
vanquish, prevail; victory ๅ๎
to outrun

ประนัก (cha'na'k) harpoon for crocodiles

ประบา (cha'bah) a flowering shrub, a
medicinal plant

ประพลู (cha'ploo) wild betel

ประมด (cha'mot) musk rat

ประรอย (cha'roi) perhaps, by chance

ประลอม (cha'laum) a bamboo basket or
case which is tied round at the top

ประลำ with ฝน (phon cha'larm) mango
showers, rains of the 3rd and 4th
months [about February]

ประลูด (cha'loot) (1) a medicinal scented
shrub 2) higher, taller, tall

ประแลง (cha'laang) iron spade or shovel,
iron lever, crow-bar

ประโลง (cha'lohng) equally balanced,
equipoise, even

ประโลม (cha'lohm) to anoint, to drench,
to pour water over

ประวา (cha'wah) [Javan.] Java

ประเอ (cha'eu) shady, cloudy

ประเอม (cha'aym) a tree of which the
branches are pounded and used as
medicine

ประโอน (cha'ohn) a fish เหรา — a tree
rather like betel

ชัก (cha'k) to pull, to draw, convulsions — ชวน to drag along, to draw on, influence สูบ to blow the bellows — หน้า to show a sad or angry face — ลาก to pull, to draw, to retard, to pull back, make slow

ชัง (cha'ng) to hate, detest, abhor, abominate

ชั่ง (cha'ng) (1) balance, to weigh (2) (weight) a catty (80 ticals) (3) let (me), allow (us, etc.) (4) to care little, not to care

ชัชวาลย (cha'tcha'wahn) [Pali] shining, brilliant

ชันสูตร (cha'nna'soot) [Pali] proof, to prove, to test, to examine to test

ชัด (cha't) visible, legible, undefaced, unobliterated — เจน distinctly

ชัน (cha'n) (1) a tree (2) resin (3) steep, upright, sticking up ผม — (hair) standing on end อัญ a flower

ชั้น (cha'n) grade, degree, storey, tier, shelf, apparatus for holding dishes

one above the other ผ้า — ใน, lining of cloth — เปรียญ a degree (of academic distinction, as M. A., etc.) — หลัง successor

ชันษา (cha'na'sah) and ชนมพรรษา [Pali] age

• • •

ซ

ซ (saw == English s. Lingual: a low letter)

ซด (sot) to swallow

ซบ (sep) to hang the head

ซม (som) dim, decrepit — ซืม to go blindly forward

ซ้ม (somm) orange ใ shaddock, pomelo

ซวดเซ (sooat say) to totter, to stagger, staggering, the staggers

ซวดทรง (sooat sohng) form, shape

ซวด (sooat) and ซวน (sooan) staggering, vacillating

ซวย (sooi) [Chin.] bad, unlucky

ซอ (saw) (1) violin, fiddle สี — to play the violin (2) stump, pollard

ซอ (saw) warbling, chattering, babbling (2) [Chin.] elder sister

ซอก (sauk) cave, corner, recess, cul-de-sac, blind alley — ซอน to start, to depart, to go

ซอง (saung) envelope, case, receptacle — มือ concavity of the palm of the hand

ซ่อง (saung) a recess — แซ่ง stagger-ing, wobbling

ซ้อง (saung!) noise, tumult

ซ่อน (saun) to put out of sight, to hide

ซ้อน (saunn!) (1) to put one upon ano-ther, to pile up — กอ to have two wives or husbands (2) a pile or set (of cups, plates, etc.)

ซ่อม (saum) (1) fork, forked (2) and — แซ่ม to mend, repair, adorn

ซ้อม (saum!) (1) to husk rice by pound-ing (2) to exercise, to train, bring out (soldiers, witnesses, etc.) — ซัก to examine evidence

ซอย (soi) to chop up, to cut in pieces, to strike or cut with quick strokes, to do quickly

ซา (sah) to swell out (as after drink-ing hot or effervescing drinks) พุ — jujube

ซา (sah) [Maun] (1) gently, quietly, (2) to be appeased, to be diminished

ซ่า (sar) (1) noise of dropping rain or water, (of fish) starting off, dash-ing away ซ่ม — an orange

ซาก (sark) (1) dead body (2) a tree used for making charcoal

ซาง (sarng) a long jointed bamboo (2) worms (a disease in children) ไม้ — a long bamboo blow-pipe for shoot-ing darts

ซาน (sahn) astray, wandering, vagrant ซม — straying blindly

ซ่าน (sarn) to be spread, to be scatter-ed about — เซ่น (1) to spatter (2) to be routed

ซาบ (sarp) to infiltrate into, to wet throughly, wet through

ซาย (saie) sand

ซ้าย (sai) left (hand)

ซาว (sowe) to wash (rice)

ซิ (si') (expletive used with the impera-tive, as) ไป — go on! get on! เอา -- begin! proceed!

ซิก ๆ (sik sik) [phon.] sound of laugh-ing, chuckling

ซิบ (sip) slight sound — ๆ trickling, rippling (of a stream, etc.) กระ — whisper

เซียว (siew) a small edible dry fish

ซี่ (see) (1) rib, lath, piece (numerical term for teeth, lathes, etc.) — โครง flank, side, ribs (2) [Laos.] to cohabit, copulate

ซี (see!) to jest, to joke : a crowd

ซี (see!) [Chin.] to die

ซีก (seek) section (numerical designation of bones, ribs, etc.) ไม้ — lath of bamboo

ซีโครง (see-krong) (see ซี) ribs

ซีด (seet) pale — เซียว pale and wrinkled

เซียะ (seeya) [Chin.] very small, puny

เซียน (seean) [Chin.] angel

เซียน or เสียน (seean) splinter — หนาม (1) thorn (2) enemy

เซียบ (seeyep) feeling of cold, cool

เซียว (seeyo) looking unwell, sickly, pale-faced

เซียว (seeyo) [Chin.] mad

ซึ่ง (seung) which, who — ว่า that is, being so

ซึ่ง (seung!) (of a hole or cave) deep, distant ลึก — profound, secret, mysterious

ซึม (seum) (1) half-asleep, drowsy, still, lethargic (2) oozing out — ซาบ to ooze or drip through หม้อ — a pot used for electricity

ซื่อ (seu) straight, direct, upright — สัตย์ true, faithful, honest ใจ — trustworthy, straightforward, honest — ตรง upright, reliable

ซื้อ (seu!) to buy รับ — to buy on commission ผู้ — purchaser แม่ — female guardian spirit of children

เซื่อง (seua'ng) slow, slowly clumsy

ซุก (soo'k) to hide (in grass, bag, etc.) — ซน restless, recklessly, childishly, naughty — ซิก zigzag, winding, in different directions

ซุง (soo'ng) (1) trunk ไม้ — log สาย — upper strings of a kite nearest to the kite (2) prodigal

ซุด (sco't) to subside, sinking, falling down — โซม to destroy

ซุบ (soo'p) [phon.] noise of the lips, whispering — ซิบ to whisper, to speak privately — ลง to push down, to bow down

ซุ่ม (soo'm) to put out of sight, to place in ambush — ซ่อน to hide, to set snares

ซุ้ม (soo'm) carved front, façade, arch; shade made by a heap of grass, etc.

ซุย (sooi) crumbling มีด — [Laos.] clasp-knife เลาะ — a yellow flower

ซูบ (soop) rather thin, lean -- ผอมลง to pine away

ซุ่มซ่าม (soo'm sahm) rude, ill-bred, rough

เซ (say) to stagger, to totter, to waver)

เซ่ง (seng) tasteless, vapid — แซ่ tumultuous, noisy

เซ็น (senn) (1) to sign ลาย — signature (2) cross pieces of wood used in building, having leaves or lathes between เข้า — Malay custom of dancing and mutilation

เซอ (surr) to wander about, vagrant, vagabond, purposeless

เซอ and เซอะ (surr) awkward, erratic, stupid

เซอะ (seu') absent-minded, making mistakes, awkward — ซะ stolid, stupid

เซิง (serng) bushy, thicket

เซิต (sert) to carry on the head

แซก (saak) to penetrate, to insinuate, to interfere, to mix ซอก — angular, blind alley

แซง (saang) joined; a pair มก — แซว a black bird with two very long tail feathers

แซบ (saap) [Laos.] savoury, well-flavoured, well tasting

แซม (saam) (1) to mend, to patch, to patch up (2) to add one thing to a lot of others, to insert one thing in others

แซว (saao) with มก แซง see แซว

แซ่ว (saao) unmoved, immoveable

แซะ (saa') (1) to cut off turf (2) to hoe (3) to separate, to open out เซาะ — (of water) to make its way, to break through

ไซ (sie) trap made of bamboo, having three flat sides and a hole at the top กิน — a large spreading tree with big roots

ไช้ (sie) (1) [particle of the apodosis, coming after ถ้า] then, assuredly; (disjunctive particle) certainly; yes; now (2) a duck

โซ (soh) beggarly, vagrant

โซ่ (soe) chain : ข้อ — link : ก้อ — chained — ตรวน fetters

เซา (sow) torpid, half asleep แซว — (1) a snake (2) a mango

เซ้า (sow!) troublesome, peevish, grumbling, vexatious

เซาะ (saw!) to scrape off, to eat away

ซ้ำ (sa'm) a second time, again; repetition

ซัก (sa'k) (1) to wash (2) to question

ซัง (sa'ng) (1) wandering, vagabond, to loiter (2) after-taste of the durien

ซัด (sa't) (1) to throw (2) driven by the wind (3) to denounce (as an accomplice) to implicate (in a charge)

— ◦◆◦ —

ฌ

ฌ (chaw chahn = English ch. a low letter) — ฌาน name of this letter

ฌาณ (chahn) [Pali] contemplation, elevation of the mind, meditative absorption, trance (Alab. 183. 192).

ฌาณาภิรติ (chahnarpi'ra'ti') [Pali] joy resulting from contemplation

เฌอ (cherr) [Cambod.] tree

— ◦◆◦◦ —

ญ

ญ (yaw yaht or big y. = English y. Guttural: a low letter) — ญาด name of this letter

หญ้า (yah) grass สนาม — lawn, grass-plot เถา — นาง a creeping plant — ยอง ไฟ (1) soot (2) a plant

ญาณ (yahn) ญาณะ and ญาณัง [Pali] supernatural power, miraculous knowledge, transcendent faculty (Alab. 182) อภิญญา — supernatural powers

ญาติ (yart) [Pali] relationship — กา and — วงษ์ relation

หญิง (ying) woman, female ผู้ — women

ใหญ่ (yai) large, big, great, important ผู้ — magnates, grandees

ฏ

ฏ (daw cha'dah or big d. English d. Dental: a low letter) — ฏะฏา name of this letter

ฏีกา (deekah) [Pali] petition, decree, law ใบ — invitation, advertisement, notice ถวาย — to present a Petition to the King

---

ฐ

ฏ (law rokcha't or big t. = English t. Dental: a middle letter) — รกชัฏ name of this letter

---

ฐ

ฐ (law sa'ntahn = aspirated English t. Dental: a high letter) — สัณฐาน name of this letter

ฐาะ ฐานา and ฐานะ (tahna') [Pali.] place, state, condition, cause, origin, event, subject

ฐานันดร (tahna'ndon) [Pali] particular post, special office, appointment

ท

ท (law prai toon = English t. French th. a low letter) — ไพร ทาย name of this letter

---

ธ

ธ (law cha'reun = English t. French th. a low letter) — เจริญ name of this letter (เจริญ [Siam.] being equivalent to Pali วัฑฒา)

เฒ่า (tow) old (person) แก่ -- (1) marriage-broker, match-maker, procuress (2) [Chin.] master

---

ณ

ณ (naw koon and naw yai = English n. Guttural: a low letter) — คณ name of this letter

ณรงค์ (na'rong) [Pali] war

เณร (nen) [Pali] disciple of the priests, neophyte

ณะ (na') conf. ใน in, at ณวัน, etc. on the ——— day, etc.

ก

ก (daw det or small d. = English d. Dental: a middle letter) — เกอ name of this letter

กก (dok) productive (of trees), abundant (of fruits, children, etc.)

ก; (dong) (1) thick deep forests with tall trees (2) to take off from the top and put at the side

กฯ with กระ (kra'dong) a flat basket for winnowing rice

กก (dot) motion from side to side, vibration

กน (don) (1) to move, to inspire (2) moment, in a moment (3) till, until

กน (don) (1) to baste (a term in needle-work) (2) to walk out of the path, to ramble ลัก — to make short cuts through roadless places

กนตรี (dontree) [Pali] concert, music of stringed instruments

กม (dom) to smell, to inhale

กฤดี (da'roo'tee) [Sansk.] and กดิ [Pali] lunar day

กรุณ (da'roo'n) [Pali] young

ก.ล (don) (1) [Pali] earth (2) [Cambod.] to reach, to arrive at

กวง (dooa'ng) (1) globe, sphere, disc, circular, spherical — ใจ heart — ชะตา astrologer's circle (2) spots of dirt, blotchy, soiled

กวง (dooa'ng) (1) a large worm which eats buds — ขหน dung beetle ขหน — a comestible like macaroni (2) mouse-trap, trap

กวด (dooa't) a game with cowries วิ — to run without looking behind; a game

กวน (dooa'n) and อุกวะ — to stop up the holes in a beam, to plug

กวน (dooa'n) hasty, hurried, pressing

กวน (dooa'n) amputated, cut off, cut short, curtailed

กวย (dooey) (1) with, at the same time, by — กน together, altogether — วา on account of — อันใก why? how? เข้า — to agree with (2) that (conj. introducing a sentence)

กอ (daw) pudenda viri หฯ — a thorny tree ส — [of elephants] fierce, savage ช้าง ส — male elephant without tusks

กอก (dauk) certainly, assuredly — กระ

ได้ perhaps, not certain

กอก (dauk) flower, produce, blossom

— ไม้ flower — ไม้ ไฟ fireworks —

เบี้ย interest, usury ผูก — to bor-

row at unlawful interest — กอง

courtesan — เล็บ white spots on the

nails — บัว lotus flower — ไม้เงิน

กอง tribute of vassal princes ลูก —

bolt of cross bow

กอง (daung) to preserve, to pickle ยา

— medicine soaked in liquid เกี่ยว

— relation, kindred ปรึง — to

consult together, to take counsel,

to agree together

กอง (daung) to go slowly

กอง (daung) *and* อ้าย — a fish found in

ponds, which, being eaten, causes

intoxication — แกว่ง oscillating

กอด (daut) to look stealthily, pry, peep

กอน (daun) high, lofty, rising far from

a river ลุ่ม — undulating

กอม (domm) to explore, spy, lie in wait

กอย (doie) [Laos.] hill, knoll

กอย (doi) stooping, bent down, sloping

forwards

กา (dah) all in line, going forward to-

gether แมลง — an edible insect

แมลง — นา a field insect แมลง —

น้ำ an edible fish with round body

and pointed tail like a cuttle fish

ก่า (darr) to curse, to revile

กาก (dark) (1) anus (2) piston in a cylin-

der, pestle in a mortar

ก่าง (darng) (1) potash (2) spotted with

white — พร้อย not clean

กาด (dart) (1) to spread (2) rather flat

ตี (1) gaoler (2) secretary — กิน

plentiful (3) full — จะ กา full —

ฟา deck of a boat ฝี — small-pox

กาดกาษ (dardaht) [Pali] abundant, full-

blown

กาน (dahn) lower earth เปน — (*see*

กาล) tumour

ก่าน (darn) custom house นาย — su-

perintendent of customs

ก้าน (dahnn) (1) stubborn, hard, cal-

lous, impudent, obstinate (2) side

สี — หา — etc. square, pentagonal,

etc. นา — separate portion of task

or work, separate place or post
หน้า — shameless

กาบ (dahp) sword ปลา — sword-fish

กาบด (dahbot) [Pali] hermit, wearing
tiger's skin and living on fruit

กาม (dahm) to mend or strengthen by
splicing, to splice

กาย (daic) (1) alone, lonely, abandoned (2) to mow, to hoe, to pick with
a pick-axe เสีย — alas! what a
pity! to regret

ก้าย (dai) cotton thread — ไหม silk
thread

การา (dahrah) การก and การากร [Pa-
li] star, constellation

การาหวัน (dahrahwa'n) [Javan.] brilliancy of the stars

กาล (darn) bolt of a door ลูก — handle
or hasp of a bolt เป็น — hard tumour in the stomach

กาล (darn) [Pali] to see ทีกร doubting, hesitating

กาว (dowe) star — ประจำเมือง evening
star — เดือน ๚ shooting stars, me-
teors — หาง comet — นักษัตรฤกษ์
[Pali] astrological stars — ไถ [as-
tron.] the sword of Orion

กาว เรือง (dowe reua'ng) with กอก Indian pink

กาวแดน (dowe daan) kingdom

กาวดึงส์ (darvadoong) [Pali] second of
the six sensual heavens (Alab. 201.
308)

ดิก (dik) to palpitate, throb

ดิง (ding) [phon.] sound of a bell

ดิง (ding) and ลิก — sounding line,
plummet — ไป to plane or straight-
en wood

ดิฐ (ditt) [Pali] permanent

ดิถี (ditt) [Pali] landing place, bathing
place

ดิน (din) earth — ภูเขา lower earth —
กล and — ก้อน upper earth, high
land ก้อน — lump of earth — เผา
earth on which plants have been
burnt as manure — ปืน gunpowder — ๚ priming — เหนียว clay
— ประสิว powder — ประสิวขาว
nitre — ดำ gunpowder — สอ pencil — สอ ของ chalk, white powder
for the face — กินา miraculous gold-
en earth — กาล hard clay at the
bottom of a river

ดิ้น (dinn) to pulpitate, toss, roll, throb, move about

ดิบ (dip) raw, unripe, half-cooked - well arranged, in good order, suitably ผ — dead bodies which are not burnt but buried

ดิเรก (di'rek) and ดิเรกเทอ [Engl.] to direct, Director

ดิลก (dee'lok) [Pali] (1) rising above others, head, top, consecrated King (2) mole, freckle, or spot on the skin (3) powder or paint for the face

ดิสเทร (dissa'tenn) [Pali] a priest who has been ordained ten years or more

ดิษ ย (ditt) [Sansk.] — ดิษ permanent

ดี (dee) gall — เกลือ purgative salts

ดี (dee) good, well — กัน mutual friends เข้า — กัน to be reconciled ผู้ — well-bred people, gentlefolk — อยู่ it is well — ร้าย by chance รอ — รอ ร้าย very nearly; perhaps คุ้ม — คุ้ม ร้าย intermittent madness

ดี with กระ (kra'dee) a fish shaped like a leaf

ดี (dee) and — เกลีย to tickle

ดีฉัน (deecha'n) I (used by women to a superior)

ดิก (deet) (1) to strike orimpel by drawing or holding back, and letting go — ฝ้าย to disentangle cotton (2) to play on a musical instrument — สี to play the violin — ดีกเปา music, a band (3) to turn away from (4) to flip (5) to lift with a lever (6) to kick like a horse — ดิก coquetry of women

ดีบุก (deel.co'k) [Pali] tin, lead

ดีปลี (deeplee) a plant used in medicine (1) long pepper (2) a bird

ดีหลี (deelee) [Laos.] love, in love

เดียง (deea'ng) to add, to join เชิญ to invite

เดียงสา (deea'ngsah) [Cambod.] not yet knowing the (Camb.) language

เดียม (deea'm) to tickle

เดียม (deea'm) to walk on tiptoe

เดียร (deea'ra') [Sansk.] on that side — ดิรัฉ [Pali] animals in general

เดียรดาษ (deea'ra'dart) [Sans.] spreading about

เดียรต (deea't) [Sansk.] landing

เดียว (deeo) alone, single, one — กัน the same — หลง so, likewise

เกียว (deeo?) moment — น now, at once

 บัวะ — directly, in a moment ปัก — presently, after a while ปัวะ — ก้อน after a while, wait a little

กิก (deu'k) late at night — ๆ very late

ดึง (deung) (1) obstinate, stubborn (2) to stretch out (3) to pull the hair

ดึง (deung) to go to the bottom

ดืน (deun) abundantly, plenty, many

ดืม (deum) to swallow, imbibe; drink

ดือ (deu) blunt, blunted, stubborn

เดือ (deua') a wild olive

เดีอก (denak) better นัวะ — (1) to swallow with difficulty (2) undulation of the waves ลูก กัวะ — apple of the throat

เดือก (deua't) boiling; to be irritated

เดือน (deua'n) worm ไส้ — a long earthworm

เดือน (deua'n) moon, month — ขึ้น (1) rising moon (2) waxing moon — แรม (1) setting moon (2) waning moon — เพ็ญ and — เต็ม full moon (15th of the waxing) — หงาย moonshine, time when the moon shines — ดับ day between two moons

เดีย (deuey) wedge, mortise, piece of wood joined to another — ไก่ spurs of a cock — ปัวะ ก staple of a door ว — mortise กัว — a plant ลูก edible fruit of it

ดุ (doo') irritable, angry, fierce — วัน disobedient

ดุก (doo'k) a fresh water fish of dirty hue with moustaches — อุย a dark fish with yellow flesh — กัน do. with white flesh — ดิก to palpitate

ดุ้ง (doo'ng) raised in the middle, crumpled up, wavy, inclined upwards, to lean on one side, to incline — เกิน down on the sides and up in the middle — ออก to mend a battered vase — กุ boasting, affected ตัว — กุ a water-worm

ดุ้ง (doo't) [Pali] and — หมัน such, like, as, the same

ดุก (doo't) to grub up, poke up — กิน to dig up with the snout like pigs

ดุน (doo'n) (1) to indent by striking, to beat into shape (2) to push

ดุ้น (doo'nn) log — ไฟ fire brand

กุย (doo'p) (1) to crawl (of insects)
(2) to palpitate, throb

กุม (doo'm) coat button, axle-tree of a
wheel รัง — button-hole — เกาะปุ๋น
axle-tree of a wheel (of cart or car)

กุ่ม doo'mm) to walk slowly with the
eyes turned down

กุล (doo'n) [Pali] a weight (of about
20 catties)

กุลารา (doo'nrahsee) [Sansk.] balance,
Libra [zodiac.]

กุยตุ๊ (doo'tsa'nee) and กุยต [Sansk.]
to be satisfied, content, quiet, silent,
salutation, happiness

กุสิต (doo'sitt) and กุสิตา [Pali] (1)
fourth of the sensual heavens (Alab.
177, 308) (2) joy, joyful, glad

กู (doo) to see หมอ — soothsayer —
แก to look at or after ลอง — to
test, to taste, to try คิด — to reflect, examine น่า — worth looking
at — หมิ่น and — ถูก to despise,
to insult

กู (doo) with ประ tree with hard wood

กู (doo?) (exclam. of indignation)

กก (dook) (1) stiff, unyielding (2) inside buttress or prop for a wall —
แก่น the inside hard part of a tree

กุกรา (dooka'ra') and กรา (sign of the
vocative) Hi! Ho!

กูต (doot) to suck

กุริยางค์ (doori'yarng) [Pali] concert,
symphony

กุริย (doori'ya') [Pali] musical instruments, concert

เก (day) vertical, upright, turned up

เด็ก (deck) child, boy

เดช (dett) เดชา and เดโช [Pali] (1)
might, power, majesty, mighty (2)
by the merit of, by means of
ขอ เดชา (a formula in Petitions
to the King) by the merit of Your
Majesty เดชาบุญ by my merits,
by good fortune, would that!

เด้ง (deng) bent upwards in the middle, arched

เด็ด (dett) to pinch off with the nails,
to pick

เดน (dayn) remnants (of dishes, of
cloth, etc.)

เดน (den) to appear clearly, exposed
to view

เดิน *better* กระ เดิน (kra'den) (1) thrown down and bounding off, ricochet (2) the biggest of the lot

เทรถ (deyra'tee) [Sansk.] impious, lawless, barbarous

เดิน (dern) to walk, travel — บก to travel by land — ความ to bribe a judge   โระ to transact another man's business ไป — to go on foot

เดิม (derm) beginning, at first, before, formerly แต่ — from the first

แด (daa) (1) motionless (2) heart

แด *and* แด่ (daa) (sign of the Dative) to (a King or great personage)

แดก (daak) (1) to push back, repulse, repel — กัน to push or, speak insolently — ออก to break out ปลา — a salt fish (2) colic — ข้น pain in the stomach (3) ironical

แดง (deng) red - ๆ bright red คั่ว — rust, rust colour — คา brown, dark red - จัด *and* กา very red ไม้ — sapan wood, a red wood used for dyeing and joinery เงิน — spurious coin ตัว — a red water worm

แดด (daat) sun

แดน (daan) limits, bounds, frontiers

แดน (dan) having a white spot on the forehead

แด้ว (dao) struggling of the body

แดะ ๆ (daa'daa') to run about causelessly, idly

ใด (dai) who? what? whoever, some one — ๆ whoever, whatever ตั — some one, any one, who? สิ่ง — something, anything อัน — *and* ประการ — (1) something (2) how?

ใด *with* แกง (kang die) [Cambod.] mark used for a signature (by illiterate person)

ได้ (dai) (1) to be able, to obtain, to get — กัน to be suited, well matched, to agree — การ it goes on well, it is a good business ตาม according to one's powers, as one may (2) (sign of the Potential) can, may, it is possible ไป you can go ไม่ — cannot, it is impossible, will not ก็ — it can, assuredly (3) (sign of past tense) as อัน ... เห็น I saw

โด (doe) post, pillar

โด (doke) to vacillate, to sway about

โดง (dohng) high, lofty

โดด (dote) to jump, to dance ลูก —
bullet

โดน (dohn) (1) to hit against, to knock,
collide, to touch (2) (of verses)
rhyming

โดย (doey) by, near, along, beside (with
subst. or adj. makes an adverb, as)
— ด่วน hastily — ดี in a friendly
way — สาร to take a passage in
another man's boat or carriage

เดา (dow) to conjecture, imagine, suppose

เดาะ (dowe) to walk with long steps

เดาะ (dor') to bend slightly, to toss
— ลูก คลี to play at ball สาวกำดัด
— grown-up girl ขันที impotent
เดาะ ตื่น — a Buddhist ceremony at
the visiting of the Temples

ดำ (da'm) to plunge in the water — นา
to transplant rice — แหม to dive
after a net

ดำ (da'm) black, bad, ungrateful ใจ —

hard-hearted แดง brown, blackish, dark — เรศ [Cambod.] delicious,
voluptuous — โหง [Cambod.] tall,
high

ดำ (da'mm) low down, deep

ด้าม (da'm) handle

ดำหนิ (da'mnee') defect

ดำเนียน (da'mneea'n) to slander

ดำเนิน (da'mnern) to go, to march, to
walk (of the King)

ดำรง (da'mrong) [Sansk.] to make
straight, direct, stand

ดำริ (da'mree') [Pali] to think, consider, resolve ห์ริะ — thought (of
a royal person)

ดำรัส (da'mra't) to command, to order
(high word)

ดะ (da') to mow

ดัก (da'k) to catch in a net, to set
snares, to watch for

ดักดาน (da'kdarn) to be condemned to
hard work, to come to misfortune

ดัง (da'ng) (1) to make a noise, to resound, to be rumoured (2) just as
— นี in this way — นั้น in that way
— เก่า as before — เช่น as much as,
such as

ดั่ง (da'ng) shield — เกิม as formerly

ดัชนี (da'cha'nee) [Pali] fore-finger

ดัด (da't) flattened out, smooth, level, straight — ผกดั [Cambod.] to get out of bed, get up

ดัน (da'r) to push, push on, break through ไข่ — the groin, kidneys

ดั้น (da'n) to go without knowing the way, to make one's way by hazard

ดับ (da'p) [phon.] to extinguish — ไฟ (and other words) to die — ความ to hush up a quarrel เดือน — when the moon is invisible ลำ — order, row, series เป็น ลำ — orderly, in order ลำ — ไว้ to put in order, arrange, arrangement

ดับ with ระ (ra'da'p) spirit-level

ดัษกร (da'tsa'kon) [Sansk.] enemy

ต

ต (taw trah vulg. krah = English t. Dental: a middle letter) — ตรา name of this letter

---

ตล (ta'la') [Pali] ground, plain, base

ตก (tok) to fall, to drop — ลูก to miscarry — เบ็ด to fish with a hook and line — กล้า to transplant paddy — แต่ง to establish — ลง กัน to come to an agreement — เงิน to advance money on goods — ใจ startled, stupefied

ตง (tong) with ไม้ cross-beams ไม้ ไผ่ — a large bamboo

ตงุด ตงิด (ta'ngoo't ta'ngitt) weak-minded, narrow-minded

โตงก (ta'ngoke) cangue, wooden frame

ตด (tot) pedere, crepitus ventris

ตติย (ta'tee'ya') [Pali] third

ตน (ton) oneself, of or to oneself, body, person

ตน (ton) trunk, tree, lower part of anything (the generic term of trees, prefixed usually to the word signifying the species) — สัก teak tree — ไม้ trees in general

ตน (ton) first, front, principally, in front — หน ship mate — คอ nape of the neck — เงิน principal เป็น — ไป and เป็น — ว่า that is to say

ศนู (ta'noo') [Pali] body, a sea turtle

โตนก (ta'note) sugar palm

ตบ (top) to give a slap *or* blow — แต่ง to dispose, to dress, to arrange ผัก — an edible plant — ไก่ indecent songs

ตม (tom) mud

ต้ม (tomm) to boil, to cook

ตร *note.* words beginning thus are vulgarly pronounced as if beginning with ตะร

ตรง (trong *cf.* ค้าวรง) straight ใจ — faithful, upright, reliable

ตรม (trom) *and* ตระม (traum) to be in pain, to languish

ตรวจ (trooa't) to verify, test, examine

ตรวน (trooa'n) (1) chain for the legs, irons (2) a ring-leader

ตรอก (trauk) narrow street, alley, crossway ตม — meretrix

ตรา (trah *culy.* krah) seal — ชู balance, scales — ชั่ง steelyard ค่อก — *and* ดี — to set one's seal ตราวา — to test เงิน — sterling coin, coin of the realm หลวง — stamped with government seal

ตราก (trark) to put a cangue on a criminal's neck, to afflict

ตรากตรำ (trark tra'm) work, compulsory work, penal servitude

ตราง (trahng *culy.* krahng) to file, to grate

ตราง (ta'rahng) prison attached to a private house, dungeon

ตรี (tree' *cf.* ค้าวรี) to examine, consider, reflect

ตฤณ (tinn) [Sansk.] grass, weed

ตริบ (trip) (1) to cut the edge of a cloth, or paper, etc., to clip, to browse, to graze

ตรี (tree) [Sansk] (1) three (2) tri lent, dagger with three blades — ศก third year of the decennial cycle — ยัมพวาย swinging festival ไม้ — an accent like the figure ๏, raising the sound ไม้ — friendship

ตรีณี (treenee') third

ตรีทูต (treetoot) [Pali] to be at the last gasp

เตรียม (treeyem) to prepare, to dispose

ตรึก (treuk) to think, to reflect

ตรึง (treung) *and* — ตรากก to tie tightly, to torment, to vex

ตรุณ (ta'roo'n) [Pali] young person
(between 13 and 19 years old)

ตรุด (troo't *vulg.* kroo't) new year (end
of the 4th month) — สังกรานต์
the second feast of the new year

ตรู (troo) (1) much, many (2) to rush
at (3) pretty, beautiful

ตรู่ (troo) *with* รุ่ง *or* เช้า at daybreak

เตร่ (tray) to wander

เตร่ะ เตร่ (tiet tray) to wander, to stroll

แตร (tiaa *vulg.* kraa) trumpet, horn —
สังข์ bugle blown to announce the
approach of the King

ไตร *and* ไตรย (trai) [Sansk.] three ผ้า
— priest's dress หอ — Library of
the Sacred Books — ปิฎก Buddha,
the law of Buddha, and the priests

ไตรยางษ์ (traiyahng) [Sansk.] three-
fold division of consonants into
high, middle and low letters

เตรา (trow) a tree

ตรำ (tra'm) to bear, to suffer

ตระกอง (tra'korng) to embrace

ตระการ (tra'kahn) beauty

ตระกูล (tra'koon) [Pali] tribe, race,
family of high descent

ตระเตรียม (tra'treeam) to prepare,
preparation

ตระหนี่ (tra'nee) miser, miserly, a-
varicious

ตระหนัก (tra'na'k) clearly, plainly

ตระโบม (tra'bome) [Cambod.] to embrace, to caress, to speak lovingly

ตระบะ (tra'ba') [Pali] (1) power, force,
austerity (2) pot

ตระบัด (tra'ba't) moment

ตระพัด (tra'pa't) to run at full speed

ตระหลบ (tra'hlop) *better* ตลบ (1) to
be dispersed, spread about in the air
— ไล่ to pursue, follow after (2) to
turn over (leaves, etc.) (3) to come
back (4) to catch birds in a net

ตระลาการ (tra'lahkahn *see* ตลาการ)
judge

ตระเวน (tra'wayn; *and* ตะเวน (ta'-
wayn) to lie in wait for, to spy, to
watch — คนโทษ to conduct criminals กอง — detachment of police

ตรัส (tra't *conj.* ตารัส) to command,
order, to speak (of royal persons)

ตลก (ta'lok) buffoonery, buffoon

ศลก ฐาคร (ta'lok bart) [Pali] silk or
other covering *or* case for priest's
alms-bowl

ศลบ (ta'lop) (1) to be spread about in
the air (2) to turn over (leaves, etc.)
to come back — คะ แล่ง deceiver,
story-teller — นก to catch birds in
a net

คลอด (ta'lawt) through — วา to the
end, throughout, for the whole length

คล้อม (ta'lawm) cylindrical bamboo
basket without lid or bottom

คลาด (ta'lart) market เปิด — to open
the market เจ้า — collector of market tax

คลิง (ta'ling) border, bank, shore

คลิงปริง (ta'ling pring) a tree with
edible fruit

คลุง (ta'loo'ng) *with* เสา stakes for tying up elephants

คลุดคูด (ta'loo't too't) curtailed, dock-
ed, mutilated

คลุ่น (ta'loo'n) lukewarm, tepid

คลุ่ม (ta'loo'm) bamboo basket shaped
like a large chalice and used by
priests — มุข do. of wood inlaid
with mother-of-pearl (not special to
priests)

คลุมพก (ta'loo'mpoo'k) (1) mallet (2)
a fish (3) a tree

เคลง (ta'layng) Peguan

คลับ (ta'la'p) a little low box

ควง (tooa'ng) to measure (by measure
of capacity or liquid measure)

ควง (tooa'ng) *with* ชก to reach out
for

ควน (tooa'n) glazed, a shiny cloth

ควาก (ta'waht) to scold loudly, to
threaten

ตัว (tooa') body, entire, himself, oneself
— ผู้ (of animals) male — เมย female ออก — to declare oneself สิ้น
— poverty-stricken เสีย — to be
spoiled, to prostitute เลี้ย! — to
make one's livelihood: (numerical
designation of animals, *as* ม้า สอง
— two horses)

ตัว (tooa) [Chin.] writ of exemption,
receipt note

ตวัก (ta'wa'k) (1) ladle made of cocoa-
nut (2) a contemptuous expression

ตวัน (ta'wa'n) sun — ออก sunrise,
Orient, East — ตก sunset, Occident,
West — สาย before noon — บ่าย
afternoon — เทียง midday, noon

กอ (taw) stump, stake — แย to torment, irritate

กอ (tor) (1) to add (2) towards, against, before : *with* กัก — to join หก — decoy — ไป henceforth, afterwards, more — สู้ to withstand — ต้าน to resist — ว่า to murmur — หน้า in the presence of — แก้ม (1) dominoes (2) to make worse, exaggerate — ตั้ง to join together

กอ (tor) (1) to build on at the side (2) to haggle (3) a wasp

กอ (torr) speck in the eye, disease of the eyes

กอก (tawk) (1) to hammer, to drive in (a nail, etc.,) to force in, insert (2) thin strip of bamboo etc. used as a string

กอง (taung) banana leaf หน — kitchen fire-wood ๕ — light green

กอง (taung) (1) sign of the passive (2) and — การ *also* — ให้ *and* — ประ สงค์ it is necessary, must, one must (3) to touch, exactly, properly — กอง spell-bound, charmed, fascinated — เก quoit

กอก (tort) to bite

กอ แก้ม (taw taam) dominoes

กอน (torn) (1) part — ที่ etc. (parts of a ship, fish, etc.) bow, front, etc. (2) to castrate, to cut (slips from a tree, etc.)

กอน (tawn) to take, to seize, to go in chace of — รับ to welcome, to receive favourably

กอบ (taup) to answer, reply — กอบ to repay one favour by another — สาร to answer by letter

กอม (torm) to suck up like an insect, an insect, fly, midge

กอม (taum) fleshy excrescence — เกย dwarf, dwarfish

กอย (toi) [Maun] done, finished

กอย (toi) (1) to strike, to attack with the fists (2) stinging insect

กอย (toy) (1) small, low — กิ่ง a medicinal plant (2) a small fowl, bantam

กา (tah) eye น้ำ — tear หาง — corner of the eye — บอด blind — เหล่ squinting ยี — short-sightedness — ปลา corns — ไม้ knot in a tree or timber — กุ้ง (1) ankle bones (2)

a tree — น้ำ hole out of which water comes — มือ whitlow

กา (tah) maternal grand-father, old gentleman — ชวด maternal great-grand-father พ่อ — father-in-law

กาก (tahk) to expose (to sun or air)

ก้าง (tahng) different, in the place of — ๆ various, diverse, of all sorts, all — ท้อง half-brothers by different mothers — ๆ — กา a representative — หน้า strange น้ำ — window — ประเทศ foreign

ก้าง (tahng) pack-saddle

กาก (tart) cloth woven with gold or silver thread

กากู่น (tartoo'n) (1) a tree (2) ankle bones

กาน (tarn) malady of children

กาน (tahn) to resist, fight

กานี (tarnee) Patani

กาบ (tarp) a jewelled gold ball

กาประขาว (tarpa'kow) (1) guardian of a pagoda (2) man in a white dress supposed to be an angel disguised

กาฬุ่น (tarpoo'n) and — ม้า a priest condemned to cut grass for the King's elephants or horses

กาม (tahm) to follow, following, according to — ใจ to yield to the wish of another, as you please — ใด as you may, as it may be — มี according to the means available, as much as there is — ๆ as he wishes ; be it so

กาย (taie) to die แทบ — on the point of dying เป็น — alive or dead ซี — faded น้ำ — low water งู กัด — snake whose bite is fatal

กาล (tahn) [Pali] fan-palm, sugar-palm น้ำ — sugar น้ำ — กรวด sugar-candy น้ำ — ทราย powdered sugar

กาหล่า (tahlah) (1) clever at kite-flying (2) Mahommedan priest

กาลีปัตร (tahleepa't) [Pali] priest's fan [oval-shaped and made of leaves]

ติ (ti') and — เตียน to blame, reprimand, reproach

กิ่ง (ting) [Cambod.] silent

กิ่ง (ting) abnormal excrescence from the flesh, as a double thumb, a fifth finger, etc.

ติก (tit) to stick, to be joined to, immersed in, impeded by — เอา to join
— ไฟ to light a fire — ใจ to apply
oneself to; to suspect — พัน attached to, fond of — การ — ธุระ
overwhelmed with business or work
เงิน — นี้ and — สิน involved in
debt - - ตาม to follow

ติณ (tin) [P. li) grass, weed

ติว (tiew) [Chin.] small sticks for counting or for fortune-telling

ตี (tee) to st.. , to beat ตีก — to
strike with the fist — พิมพ์ to
print, to strike off (from the press)
- - แฝะ to make a wall of split
bamboo

ตี and ตี (tee) quickly

ตีน (teen) foot — พา horizon ฝ่า —
sole of the foot ปลา — a fish with
two feet — เป็ด web-footed ตน —
เป็ด a medicinal plant — เทียน candle-stick — ท่า landing on the bank
of a river or canal — อุ (the letter
short u or oo') - - อู (long u or oo)

ติบ (teep) joined side by side

เตีย (teeya') [Chin.] father

เตีย (teea') dwarf

เตียง (teea'ng) bed-stead - - ที่ drawer,
side-board

เตียน (teea'n) empty and clear

เตียบ (teea'p) circular stand with rim
round it for holding edibles

เตียว (teeyo) band, bandage for closing
a crack, broad girdle of cloth for
the loins

ตึก (teuk) (1) a stone or brick building (2) — ตัก to palpitate

ตึง (teung) (1) stretched, swelled out,
tight (2) noise of a gun

ตุบตับ (teup teup) noise of moving
about

ตื (teue) stupid ตือ — a fire-work

ตื (teue') quickly

ตืน (teun) (1) to be awake (2) to stupe-
fy แตก — commotion, general a-
larm, panic

ตืน (teun) shallow, superficial, common

เตือน (teua'n) to remind, to call the attention to

ก ก กก (too'k ta'k) palpitation

กิ แก (too'k-kaa) large lizard with a loud voice, tokay

ก กะกา (too'kka'tah) and ก กก:กิย doll

กง (too'ng) clothes out of shape

ก งกา (too'ngkah) inhaler (for hemp smoke)

กน (too'n) (1) stupid (2) mole

กม (too'm) (1) swelling (2) jar กา — ankle; a tree

กม (กง) (too'm too'ng) weight, knob, or bead (attached to the string of a purse) — ห earrings ฉก — weights (of a clock or of scales)

กม (too'm?) [phon.] noise of falling into water

กมกา (too'm kah) a tall tree having medicinal leaves and fruit

กมปี (too'mpee) mitre-shaped (hat)

กย (tooi') swollen (cheeks) กย — a kite

กยกย (tooi' tooi') greedily

กลาการ กลยาการ and other forms (rdg. tra'larkarn) [Pali] judge

กลาคม (too'lahkom) [Pali] (name of the seventh month = October)

ก (too) I, me, myself, self เขา pounded rice, rice meal [= Pali sattu]

ก (too) to take fraudulently

ก (too) drawer, cupboard — หนังสือ book-case

กม (toom) (1) bud of flower (2) [phon.] booming of cannon, sound of gun

เกง (teng) small scales to weigh silver, gold, or small articles กา — a lottery-figure ไม้ — a hard wood

เกง (teng) a swelling — เกา breasts

เกง (teng?) [phon.] sound of guitar, to to steal, to rob

เกโช (taychoh) [Pali] fire, flame, heat, light, lightness, glory, power

เกน (ten) to palpitate, jump, dance

เกม (tem) full, very — ใจ willingly, with consent — ที strongly, very much, excessively (an expletive used with adjectives) — ที awful, terrible, disastrous, anoying ไกม — to the full, fully

เกย (toey) a big thorny reed having a fine and sweet flower

เกป (terp) rather large

เติม (tterm) to add

เกะ (ay') to kick, to attack by kicking

แต (taa) (sign of abl.) from, since, only, but ถูก — and แล้ว — it depends upon — ไหน whence? — ว่า but — ถ้า ว่า supposing that, if — ก่อน before เว้น — except, unless

แต่ (taa) (running) quickly

แต่ (taa?) [Chin.] tea

แตก (taak) to break, break open, to be ตื่น — noise, confused crowd ใจ — disgusted with one business and seeking another — ร้าว to be split, difference, disagreement — แหลก to be broken in pieces — ระแหง to yawn (of the earth), to open

แตง (taang) gourd — โม melon — กวา cucumber — ไทย sweet melon, musk melon

แต่ง (taang) to dispose, compose, arrange, complete — ตัว to dress

แตงไม (taangmay) a cake made of sugar

แตน (taan) wasp

แต้ม (taam) to mark, to note, to put on

— สี to paint — แผล to plaster a wound ถอ — dominoes

แตะ (taa') (1) split bamboos ฝา — house of s. b. ตี — to make a wall of s. b, เตาะ — toddling (of a child) (2) to take up by touching with the tip of the finger

ใต (tie) (tie) under, below, South ทิศ — South — ถุน lower part of a house เรือ ปาก — boats coming from the S.

ไต (tai) entrails

ไต (taie) to creep, to crawl — ถาม to question — ลวด to dance on a rope — เท้า (poetical) to go on a journey

ไต (tai) torch

ไตกู (taikoo) with ใน (short accent, as over เหลือ)

โต (toh) large, vast โตโต very large

โต ตอบ (toh taup) to contradict โต ลม to tack, to sail with difficulty against the wind

โตก (tohk) small round metal tables or stands

โตง (tohng) end

โตง (tohng) large, tall

โถง เถง (tohng tayng)　hanging　and
swinging

โถมร (tohmonn) [Pali] or โทมร short
spear, spike, javelin

โต๊ะ (toh') (1) table (2) reverend, pious
— แขก Mahommedan priest

เตา (tow) and — ไฟ hearth, fireplace,
stove

เต่า (tow) turtle

เต้า (tow) cross piece of wood on a
pest น้ำ — intoxicating juice

เต๋า (tow?) dice

เต้าหู้ (tow-hoo) [Chin.] starch made
of peas

ตำ (ta'm) to pound, to crush ; to prick

ต่ำ (ta'm) low, depressed, less ไม่ —
กว่า unless, than

ตำนาญ (ta'manahn) series, story, history

ตำหนิ (ta'mnee') fault, vice, defect

ตำเนิน (ta'mnern) to go, to walk — พล
to lead an army

ตำแหน่ง (ta'mhnaang) place

ตำหนัก (ta'mhna'k) (high word) habitation, abode [of a prince] พระ —
King's abode, royal palace

ตำบล (ta'mbonn) place, district

ตำแบ (ta'mbaa) with ปลา split and
dried fish

ตำแย (ta'myaa) nettle หมอ — ac-
coucheur, midwife

ตำรง (ta'mrong) [Sansk.] to direct,
straighten, stand, govern

ตำรวจ (ta'mrooat) King's satellites,
lictors

ตำรา (ta'mrah) code of formulas, book
of arts

ตำริ (ta'mree') to think

ตำรัส (ta'mra't) to order, to make an
edict

ตำลึง (ta'mleung) (1) a creeping plant
with red fruit　(2) the sum of four
ticals

กะ (ta') to inlay or incrust with gold

กะกรม (ta'krom) (see กะกรม)

กะกร้อ (ta'kraw) (1) light ball of cane
or leather used for playing a common Siamese game with the feet (2)
a basket used for holding fruit

กะกร้า (ta'krah) an open-work basket
made of bamboo

กะกรูด (ta'kroo't) amulet, talisman —
เบ็ด to put a hook on the line

กะกรม (ta'kroo'm) a bird like a pelican, but larger

กะแกรง (ta'kraang) rice-sieve, flat round kasket

กะไกร (ta'krai) scissors จะ - - jaws เหยี่ยว — sparrowhawk

กะกรับ (ta'kra'p) a fish

กะกลาม (ta'klahm) greedy

กะกลี (ta'klee) and กะกลาม (ta'klahm) greedy, covetous, hasty, impetuous

กะกวด (ta'kooat) a small alligator

กะกั่ว (ta'kooa) pewter, type metal — หม lead — เกรียบ tin foil ขี — oxyde of lead

กะกรอ (ta'kraw) and รุ่น — (see สะ กรอ) in the flower of youth, adult

กะกอน (ta'kawn) sediment, deposit

กะกาย (ta'kai) to seize, grasp, catch with the hands, to climb with the hands or paws

กะกี้ (ta'kee) and เมื่อ — just now

กะเกียง (ta'keeang) lamp ไส้ — wick

กะเกียบ (ta'keeap) [Chin.] chopsticks

กะกุก กะกัก (ta'koo'k-ta'ka'k) tottering walk (as of a turtle)

กะกุ่ม กะกาม (ta'koo'm-ta'kahm) rude, ill-bred man

กะกุย (ta'kooi) and — กะกาย to scratch or scrape up with the nails or claws

กะกู (ta'koo) a tall tree with blossoms but without fruit

กะกูด (ta'koot) rudder, helm

กะเกะ กะกะ (ta'kay' ta'ka') confusion

กะโก (ta'ko) a tree with yellow fruit

กะโก้ (ta'koh) (1) cake (2) a wind from the oblique corners of the compass. N.W., S.W., etc.

กะโกก (ta'koke) an edible river fish

กะโกน (ta'kone) to call or beckon from afar

กะเกาะ (ta'kaw') careless

กะขบ (ta'khop) a tree with edible brown fruit

กะขาบ (ta'kharp) (1) millipede, centipede หก — a bird ธง — lace worked standard (2) loud clapper made of bamboo

กะไข้ (ta'khay) (1) (see จระเข้) crocodile (2) (see กะไข)

กะเขบ (ta'khepp) double-sewing กุ้ง — a small prawn

ตะโขง (ta'khong) large horned crocodile

ตะคริว (ta'kriew) convulsion, cramps

ตะครุบ (ta'kroo'p) to catch by springing upon, to porence upon

ตะไคร่ (ta'khrai) froth — น้ำ mould (on a wall, rock, etc.)

ตะไคร้ (ta'khrai) aromatic herb used in cooking — น้ำ willow

ตะคอ (ta'khaw) a tree with hard wood

ตะคอก (ta'khawk) to threaten loudly, to chide

ตะคาก (ta'khark) *and* ที่ — haunch

ตะค้าน (ta'kharn) a medicinal plant

ตะเคียน (ta'kheea'n) a tall tree used for making royal barges, and having a female angel on every leaf

ตะคุก (ta'khoo'k) to bend the knee

ตะคุ่ม (ta'khoo'm) indistinctly

ตะกุย (ta'kooi) to scratch up, to scrape together with the nails or claws

ตะแคง (ta'khaang) to be bent down, inclined, to lean on one side

ตะคัน (ta'kha'n) still for making perfumes

ตะขาน (ta'kharn) (*see* ตะค้าน)

ตะเข่ (ta'khay) two-wheeled vehicle (for plants trees and heavy things)

ตะงก (ta'ngok *vulg. for* ผงก) to raise

ตะงุด (ta'ngoo't) *see* ง่ด

ตะแง้ (ta'ngaa *vulg. for* ระแง้) bunch, cluster, *or* bundle (of cocoa-nuts, etc.)

ตะจะ (ta'cha') [Pali] bark (of a tree skin, hide

ตะถาคต (ta'tahkot) [Pali] a name of Buddha (Alab. 205)

ตะนอย (ta'noi) a big red ant

ตะนาวศรี (ta'nowsee) (1) Tenasserim (2) a village near Bangkok

ตะหนี่ (ta'hnee) miserly

ตะหนุ (ta'noo') *with* เต่า big river turtle

ตะบอง (ta'bong) *see* กระบอง stick

ตะบอย (ta'boi) to stay behind, to lag; to do slowly

ตะเบียน (ta'beea'n) a tree

ตะบึง (ta'beu'ng) always, incessantly, continuously

ตะบูน (ta'boon) tree with a hard wood

ตะเบ็ง (ta'beng) to go quickly, to hasten; to puff out — มาลย์ to fasten a cloth across the breast and over the shoulders

กะแบก (ta'baak) a forest tree with hard wood

กะไบ (ta'bai) file, to file — ลม to keep on blowing into any thing

กะบะ (ta'ba') (1) wooden platter, tray (2) power

กะบน (ta'ba'n) (1) to poke, to bore, to keep on pushing (2) quickly, continually (3) tube for pounding betel nut; to pound

กะบน กะบก and กะบก (ta'ba'n ta'-loon ta'bok) a tree

กะบิง (ta'ping) gold or silver leaf attached to the belt of female children in front, placket, lappet

กะปู (ta'poo) nail — ควง screw

กะปด (ta'pot) a pole to beat buffaloes and oxen

กะปก (ta'pork) wine-party, carouse

กะปง (ta'pong) (1) axle tree (of wheel) (2) bones (of the head)

กะปาก (ta'pahk) a small fish

กะปาน (ta'pahn) bridge

กะปาย (ta'pai) (1) rope for a buffalo's nose (2) slung across the shoulder — เฉวี over the shoulder — ปาป to transfer the blame to another

กะเพียน (ta'peean) a flat fish — เงิน silver fish — ทอง gold fish

กะหน (ruly. for กะเพน) mollusc

กะปน (ta'poo'n) see ควพน

กะเพก (ta'pert) to shout at, to pat to fright, drive away

กะโพก (ta'poke) buttocks, hips

กะโพน (ta'pone) a hand-drum

กะพง (ta'pa'ng) excavation (in a rock), (spring) gushing out

กะพด (ta'pa't) continuous, persistent

กะภาย นำ (ta'parp na'm) long-necked river turtle (highly valued for food)

กะเภา (ta'pow) junk ลม — South wind

กะมยทย (ta'mooi tooi) fat (face)

กะมะรอย หลอย (ta'ma'rooi hlooi) smartly, promptly

กะยน (ta'yoo'n) flabby

กะราง (ta'rahng) grating, trellis-work, cross railings, gridiron, prison

กะรอน กะรอน etc. (see กรอน) young

กะรังกานู (ta'ra'ngkarnoo) Tringano

กะลอด (ta'laut) through

กะลุ (ta'loo') pierced, bored

กะลิง ปริง (ta'ling pring) a tree with sour fruit นก กะลิง green parrot

กะลิบ (ta'lipp) *and* กะลิ (ta'lee) quickly — กะลิบีย to work hurriedly, to
finish quickly

กะลิง (ta'leung) to look elsewhere,
star-gazing, absent-minded

กะลุง (ta'loo'ng) (*see* กลุ้ง)

กะลุ่ม (ta'loo'm) a basket *or* receptacle
for provisions — ฝุง พาก the same
with the cover on ; sound of a drum
— กะลิ่ม to heap up earth round a
tree

กะแลงแกง (ta'laang kaang) place of
execution for criminals

กะลำพอก กะลุมภก *etc.* (*see* —)

กะละ (ta'la) quite, as, like, as if — กัน
only one, the whole of it — กัน
one man like another

กะเวท (ta'wett) [Maun] image offered
to the genii

กะวะ (ta'waya) (*see* กวะ) วก —
ก a small bird

กะเวว่า (ta'wow) *and* กเวว่า (*see* กวะ
แวว่า) a talking bird

กะวัก (ta'wa'k) *and* กวัก (*see* กวัก)

กะเอ กะแอ (ta'aw ta'aa) to stammer

กะอู้ กะอี้ (ta'oo ta'ee) to speak through
the nose

กัก (ta'k) (1) to draw up (water, etc.)
— บาก to give alms to the priest
— ก to incite, urge on, give advice (2) lap, knees, on the knees

กักกะแตน (ta'kka'taan) locust, grass-
hopper

กักไสย (ta'ksai) [sansk.] to die

กัง (ta'g) bird lime

กัง (ta'ng) arm chair, long seat, bed-
stead

กัง (ta'ng) to set, place, establish —
แก่ to raise to a dignity, to appoint — แ to substitute — ท้อง
to become pregnant — ใจ to attend
to — แต่ from, since — แต่นี้, เอา
from this moment, henceforth แต่
นั้น มา from that time

กัง (ta'ng) case (of tobacco, etc.)

กังกี (ta'ngkia) [Chin.] Tonquinese

กังฮอ (ta'nghaw) Chinese purslain

กัณหา (ta'nhah) [Pali] concupiscence,
covetousness

กัด (ta't) to eat   ฟัง to slander,

affront. to mock   ตืน to give
sentence: verdict, order of court ——
ใกล to cut down to the ground ...
ขั   ขาด etc. (1) to cut in half
(2) to break off a friendship ค.ๆ —
a game with cowries —— คอ to cut
the string of a bundle

ตัน (ta'n) not pierced ฐ —— hole filled or
stopped up - เปญญา at a loss, not
knowing how to act

ตันตา (ta'nta') using an instrument

ตับ (ta'p) (1) (numerical designation of
lands of leaves used for roofing) (2)
split bamboo stick to hold fish for
boiling (3) liver — ใก entrails (4)
detachment, company [of soldiers,
police, etc.]

•••

ถ

ถ (law la'winn   English aspirated t.
Dental: a high letter) — ถือ
name of this letter

ถ (tot) to approach crawling   ถอย
to withdraw crawling

ถน (ta'non) road — หลวง public road

ตนุม (ta'naum) to cherish, take care
of, entertain

ตนัด (ta'na't) clearly, distinctly; clever
—ใจ to be persuaded

ตนัม (ta'na'm) with ดิน medicinal
earth of a yellow colour

ตบ (top) great, good ตับ - - a sorcerer

ตม (tom) (1) to fill a ditch (2) enamell-
ed (3) abundant — ถัน plentiful

ตมอ (ta'maw) [Cambod.] rock, stone

ตลม (ta'lom) to slip or slide down —
ฅลา slip of the tongue

ตลอก (ta'lauk) excoriation

ตลา (ta'lah) and ใตล (ta'lai) to stumble

ตลากใตล (ta'larhk ta'lai) to be idle
at work

ตลาย (ta'lai) with ปูน slip of the
tongue, mistake in writing

ตลึง (ta'leung) to look hard and angrily
at

ตลึง (ta'leung) to rise up, to raise oneself out, to go in front

ตลอง (ta'loo'ng) to smelt, to melt

ตลอน (ta'loo'n) to twist (a rope)   ตลู
to enter unexpectedly, to run into

แถลง (ta'laang) *and* — ไข to declare, to tell

ถลำ (ta'la'm) to slip — ถลา๋ to stumble, to make a mistake

ถลัน (ta'la'n) beyond, too far, to go beyond, to exceed

ถ่วง (too'ang) (1) hanging weight (2) to make slower (3) to sink

ถ้วน (tooa'n) right, correct, as it should be, as agreed

ถ้วย (tooi') cup — ชาม pottery — แก้ว glass

ถวาย (ta'wai) [priest's word] to offer — พระพร yes (of a priest speaking to a Royal personage)

ถวิล (ta'winn) to think lovingly of

ถั่ว (tooa') beans — เขียว grey pease — ฟ beans — ยี สง earth-nuts แทง — a game with cowries

ถวัลยราช (ta'wa'nya'raht) [Pali] to reign, kingdom, royalty

ถ่อ (taw) punt-pole

ถอก (tank) (1) projecting from the middle (2) membrum virile

ถอง (taung) to push *or* strike with the elbow

ถอง (tawng) to deliberate, to judge, decide

ถอด (taut) to take off, take away, dismiss — รูป to take a portrait

ถอน (taun) to pull up, pull out, take out

ถ่อม (tawm) lowly, humble, submissive

ถอย (toi) to go back, retire

ถ่อย (toye) (1) perverse, wicked (2) a small gnat

ถ้อย (toi) *and* — คำ words — ที one another, mutually, friendly conversation

ถา (tah) to rub with a whetstone, to sharpen ป่น — to swoop แถา — to make a swoop in a zigzag direction

ถ้า (tah) if — ว่า supposing that

ถาก (tark) to chip, to level — หญ้า to weed — ถาง ironical

ถาง (tahng) to clear the ground   ●

ถ่าง (tarng) to part, to separate, to hold apart

ถาด (taht) metal dish, small tray

ถาน (tahn) (1) basis, base, lower part (2) priest's water-closet

ถ่าน (tarn) charcoal — สีถา *and* — หิน coal

ถานานุกรม (tarnarnukrom) [Pali] from one place to another, in order

ถาปน (tahpa'nah) [Pali] to establish, re-establish

ถาม (tahm) to ask, to interrogate, to question มัก -- inquisitive

ถ่าย (taye) (1) to pour out, to decant, to purge (2) to redeem by paying duty, etc.

ถาวร (tahwon) [Pali] stationary, stable permanent, enduring, strong

ถิ่นฐาน (tintahn) [Siam. and Pali] native country

ถี่ (tee) (1) dense, close, near, close-fisted (2) in quick succession, quickly repeated

ถีบ (teep) to push with the sole of the foot — ระหัด to work a waterwheel

เถียง (teea'ng) dispute, quarrel

ถึก (teuk) wild (beasts)

ถึง (teung) until, towards, as far as; to reach — กระนั้น although — ก็น contiguous; arriving from abroad

ถึงแก่กรรม (teungkaaka'm) [Siam. and Pali] to die (of well-to-do persons)

ถือ (teu) (?) to bear, carry (2) to respect,

to observe — สัง fidelity — ท้าย to take the helm — น้ำ to drink the water of allegiance

ถือ (teu) blunt, dull, stupid

เถือ (teu-a) to cut through, to cut

เถื่อน (teuan) woods, sylvan

ถุง (too'ng) bag, wallet, purse — มือ glove — ตีน socks, stockings — ตีน ยาว stockings

ถุน (too'n) to satisfy the craving after opium-eating ใต้ — ground floor

ถุย and ถุย (too'wy) to spit upon

ถู (too) to rub, to clean

ถูก (took) (1) cheap (2) to touch, to knock (3) precisely, correctly — ต้อง properly, suitably

ถูป (toop) [Pali] pagoda, prachedee, shrine

เถน (ten) [Pali] thief, rascal

เถร (ten) [Pali] old priest, venerable man

เถิด (tert) enough, sufficient

แถก (taak) (1) to cut away (2) zigzag, crooked, to tack

แถบ (taap) quarter, part, party — นน

somewhere there ก็ะ each on his own side (2) [Laos.] rupee

แถม (taam) into the bargain, to add to

แถว (toa'o) order, series

ไถ (tai) plough, to plough

ไถ่ (tai) to redeem

ไถ้ (tai) a very long thin bag (for coins or rice)

ไถ (toh) covered dish, or vase with lid

ไถก (tohka') [Pali] small, slight

ไถง (tohng) pretty, beautiful, lofty, eminent ไถ่ — pompous

เถา (tow) (1) creeping plant (2) a lot, an assortment ก็ใ — largest of the lot ปลาย — small of the lot

เถาะ (t'aw') hare ปี — fourth yeaa of the Siamese cycle

ถ้ำ (ta'm) (1) cave, cavern (2) box — กลาง in the middle

ถัง (ta'ng) pail, bucket, a measure of twenty ka'nahns

ถัญญุะ (ta'nya') [Sansk.] milk

ถัด (ta't) since, after, next

ถัน (ta'na') [Sansk.] breast

ท

ท (taw tahn = English t. or French th. Sansk. d. Dental: a low letter) — ทาน name of this letter

ทด (tot) to dam up — สอบ to test, to try — แทน reward, recompense

ทน (ton) to support, to bear, to last out, patient, long suffering

ทนต์ (tonn) [Pali] tooth

ทนาน (ta'nahn) the contents of a cocoa-nut shell, 1800 grains of rice, one twenty-fifth of a bushal

ทนาย (ta'nai) servant of a grandee, satellite

ทนุ (ta'noo') to take care of, to support

ทบ (top) to fold สบ — to meet, come together, reinforce ขา — back of the knee; to raise the foot and so bend the knee

ทมิฬ (ta'min) [Pali] (1) bad, wicked (2) black man (3) Ceylonese

ทมุน ทนาย (ta'moo'n ta'nai) servant of a grandee

ทยาน (ta'yarn) (1) difficult to attain to (2) to go up

ทร (ton) [Sansk.] trouble, pain, suffering [as suffix] bearer of

ทรง (song) to have, to be, endowed with ; [of the King's actions] to do — ไว้วะกรุณา to pity รูป — outward appearance — ครรภ [of royal persons] pregnant

ทรชน (tora'chonn) [Pali] perverse man, wicked

ทรพล (tara'ponn) [Pali] weak, poor

ทรพิษ (ta'ra'pitt) [Pali] poison, venom, virus, small-pox, venomous creature

ทรยศ (ta'ra'yot) [Pali] wicked

ทรมาน (ta'ra'mahn) [Pali] bad, troubled, vexed, grieved

ทรวง (sooang) breast

ทราบ (sarp) (1) to know (2) damp, wet

ทราม (sarm) (1) middling, not very good (2) rude, stupid, ill-bred (3) .to flow abundantly

ทราย (sai) (1) sand (2) deer น้ำตาล — white powdered sugar

ไทร (sai) (1) a fish trap (2) fig tree เมือง — Quedah, Kedah นก — wren

ทระพี (ta'ra'pee) (1) a large spoon for taking up rice (2) a large horned animal, bison

ทวับ (sa'p) to touch with a piece of lint rag, etc.

ทวับหัว (sa'p hooa') (1) under-garment of a priest (2) water on a piece of lint, rag, etc.

ทรัพย์ (sa'p) [Sansk.] treasure, riches

ทลวง (ta'looang) (1) to pursue a flying enemy (2) to bore, to pierce

ทลิทก and ทลิทก (ta'li'tok) [Pali] poor, needy

ทลุ (ta'loo') through, pierced

ทวง (tooang) to ask back, to exact

ทัวง (too'ang) to advise ทัก — to warn

ทวด (too'at) great grandfather, great grandmother ตา — maternal great grandfather ปู่ — paternal do. ย่า — paternal great grandmother ยาย — maternal do.

ทวดึงษ์ (ta'wa'deung) and ทวดึงษ์ (ta'wa'ting) [Pali] thirty-two — าการ the 32 parts of the human body

ทวน (tooan) (1) lance (2) to beat (3) to go against wind, stream, etc.

ทวม (tooam) to over flow, to surpass

ทูยหาญ (tooi harn) brave man

ทวาทศมาศ (twarta'sa'mart) [Pali] the twelve months

ทวิ ทๅ and ทวย (tooi' tooec and tooi) [Pali] (1) two (2) to increase ; arithmetical or geometical progression

ทวีป (ta'weep) [Sansk.] island ชมพู — the continent inhabited by man (Alab. 13. 187)

ทเวศ (ta'wett) grief, sorrow

ทั่ว (tooa') the whole, all over — ไป generally

ทศ (ta'sa') [Pali.] ten — มาศ ten months

ทสางค์ (ta'sahng) [Pali] ten parts of a thing, tens

ทหาร (ta'harn) [Pali] soldier

ทอ (taw) to weave

ทอ (taw) outlet for water, aqueduct, water-course

ทอ (tor) to dread, to hesitate — ไท to draw back through fear

ทอง (tawng) gold — เหลือง brass — แดง copper — อังกฤษ tinsel — เปียก gold and quicksilver ทอก — (1) blossom of a particular tree (2) curcisan พ๊ — a red or yellow pumpkin ขุน — a black talking bird

ท้อง (taung) (1) to wade, to walk through water (2) to learn by rote, to learn by repeating over and over again — แถว order, rows, lines, columns

ท้อง (torng) belly มๅ — pregnant คๅ — to become pregnant — ฟ้า vault of the sky — แผ่น้ำ bed of a river — มๅน dropsy เสีย — diarrhœa

ทอด (tawt) (1) to throw (2) bridge, to bridge

ทอน (tawn) to cut in pieces

ท่อน (taun) a piece, a bit

ทอย (toy) (1) to pitch, to throw out (2) pegs driven into a tree to serve as ladders

ทา (tah) (1) to anoint, smear, paint — สี to colour, to paint เครื่อง — perfumes, unguents ยๅ — liniment

ท่า (tah) (1) bank, landing place, approach to a river (2) to wait for (3) gesture, condition, posture, habit, attitude ทๅ — to put oneself into an attitude — ทาง opportunity

ท้า (tar) to provoke, to excite — ทๅย a word of provocation

ทาก (talik) a blood-sucking caterpillar

ทาง (tahng) way, road, course, occasion — ๎ลง high road ง — ผะพร้าว a snake

ทาน (tahn) (1) to stop (2) to revise, to correct (3) [Pali] alms (Alab. 184) — ทวัน sun flower พระ — I pray you รับพระ — to eat (polite word), to take — บัน written promise ไว้ — place where the King's alms are distributed ไว — innocence

ท่าน (tahn) King, master; neighbour; you (to equals), he, him (speaking of magnates) — ท้าว dignity, an honourable man

ทานพ (tahnop) [Pali] a fabulous eagle, Asura angel

ทาบ (tahp) to measure, to lay (one thing) upon (another)

ทาย (tai) to solve a mystery, to guess at, to conjecture ไหร — astrologer หมอ — sorcerer, conjuror, magician

ท้าย (tai) stern, helm, steerage of a vessel สุด — last, extreme, the end

ทายก (tahyok) [Pali] donor, giver

ทายาท (tahyart) [Pali] right heir

ทารก (tahrok) [Pali] child (under thirteen)

ทารณ (tahra'na') to distribute

ทารุณ (tahroo'n) [Pali] rude, rough, wicked, dreadful

ทารมา (tahra'mah) [Pali] to afflict, to repress

ท้าว (tow) (1) to lean upon, to bear heavily upon (2) (royal title) King; (title of the old) Your Reverence — ไทย King, Emperor ผี — sorcerer, witch

ทาษ (tarse) and ทาษา (tahsab) [Pali] slave, servant

ทาษี (tahsee) [Pali] female slave

ทิ้ง (ting) to throw away — ร้าง (1) deserted, abandoned (2) divorce

ทิชา (ti'chah) [Pali] birds — กร flock of birds

ทิฏฐิ (titti') [Pali] to see, understand; doctrine

ทินกร (ti'na'kon) [Pali] sun

ทีป (ti'pay) [Pali] island

ทิพย (ti'pya') [Sansk.] and ทิพ (tip) [Pali] celestial

ทิพากร (ti'pahkon) [Pali] sun

ติม (tim) prison, lock-up house — กาบ council-chamber, armoury

ติม (tim) to poke, to prick, to push at

ติว (tiu) order, series

ติวงกต (ti'wongkot) (see ฏิวงกต) to die

ทิวา (ti'wah) [Pali] day, day time

ทิศ (titt) and ทิศา (ti'sah) [Pali] the eight points of the horizon (each having its special name, as) — บูรพ ทา — ภาคีสาน East — เหนือ North — ใต้ South, etc.

ทิศาปาโมกข (ti'sahpahmohk) [Pali] (1) philosopher, professor (2) eminent, famous

ที (tee) time, occasion, opportunity — หนึ่ง — สอง etc. once, twice, etc. ได้ — having found an opportunity ลาง — some time เกิน — too much, intolerable, distressing, annoying ทาม — (1) as it may happen (2) to neglect ท่วง — fully ก — how often ? ไม่เข้า — absurd, ridiculous, unsuitable, preposterous

ที่ (tee) (1) who, which, that — หนึ่ง — สอง etc. first, second, etc. (2) place,

— นี่ here — ไหน where ? — บน above — อยู่ dwelling-house นอน — abnormal — แอน bed — นั่ง seat เต็ม — fully, complete, very much

เทียง (teea'ng) perpendicular, true, correct; midday — คืน midnight

เทียน (teea'n) (1) candle, wax taper (2) cummin (3) a shrub

เทียม (teea'm) to compare, to equal, to place side by side, to yoke (oxen, etc.) เท็จ — false, counterfeit เงิน — counterfeit coin

เทียว (teeyo) (1) flag (2) to go over and over again, to keep on going

เทียว (teeyo) to walk about, promanade ไป — เล่น to walk about for pleasure

ตึก ตึก (teuk teuk) to palpitate, throb

ตึง (teung) to draw or pull out, tear off

ตือ (teu) blunt

เตือก (teua'k) (1) family, race — แวง series, order, pedigree (2) mal

ทุ (too') [Pah] bad

ทุก (too'k) each บรร — to load

ทุกข and — ขัง (too'k ka'ng) [Pali] pain, grief, สง — to purge

ทุกัง (too'ka'ng) a common sea fish

ทุกติ (too'ka'ti') [Pali] walking badly — รุ ม hell

ทุกฏะ (too'ka'ta') [Pali] broken down, miserable

ทุ่ง (too'ng) (1) plain, flat (2) to be purged นาก — open fields, the country — เถียง dispute

ทุ้ง (too'ng) uneven, unequal — คุ้ง winding, bed of a river

ทุจริต (tco'cha'ritt) [Pali] badly conducted, badly behaved

ทุฐ (tco't) [Pali] bad, perverse, wicked

ทุกทุ (too't tco) [phon.] great horned owl

ทุติยา (too'ti'yah) and other similar words [Pali] sound

ทุน (too'n) capital, expence, outlay

ทุ่น (too'n) (1) float, buoy, anything floating (2) plenty, abundance, much

ทุบ (too'p) to pound, to break up

ทุพล (too'yon) and ทรพล (ta'ra'pon) [Pali] weak, feeble

ทุภาสิต (tco'pahsit) [Pali] bad language

ทุม (too'm) [Pali] tree

ทุ่ม (too'm) (1) the hours of the night, counting from 6 p.m. to 6 a.m., as สอง — eight p.m. (2) to beat (the breast) — ทิ้ง to cast down, dash down — ทอด to fall backwards — เถียง to quarrel

ทุ้ม (too'm) low [especially of sounds]

ทุรน ทุราย (too'ronn too'rai) anguish, anxiety

ทุราจาร (too'rahcharn) [Pali] immorality, profanity, sin

ทุเรียน (too'reean) durien (fruit)

ทุเร (too'ray) and ทุรัศ (too'rate) [Pali] (1) calamity (2) very far

ทุย (tooi') (1) slender (2) [of animals] barren

ทุระ (too'ra') [Pali] far

ทุเลา (too'low) relieved, convalescent ขอ — to ask for a delay or for leniency

ทุลัง (too'la'ng) (1) stubborn (2) a dish — กาสา a fruit-bearing shrub

ทุ with ปลา (plah too) the Siamese herring

ทู่ (too) blunt, dull

ทูต (toot) [Pali] envoy, Minister ราช — Ambassador, Envoy

ทูล (toon) to report to the King — ฉลอง to report, to dedicate ปลัด-ฉลอง officials who recite or report to the King ข้า — ออง in the government service หัก — ไว้ god-father : a term of respect and gratitude

เท (tay) (1) to pour out, to spill (2) twenty tanans (of arak, etc.)

เท็จ (tet) false, suppositious

เท็จบาย (taytoo'bai) [colloq.] see เท็จ บาย [Pali] craft, fraud, wile

เทพ (taypa') เทพา เทพ และ เทพะ [Pali] angel

เทพบุตร (taypa'dah) [Sansk.] angel

เทพา (taypah) an edible fish

เทพากร (taypahkon) [Pali] sun

เทพาย (taypai) better เทพาย a gem

เทโพ (taypoh) a large and very delicate river fish

เทวทูต (tayva'toot) [Pali] angel-messenger, divine messenger (Alab. 211)

เทวา (tayvah) เทวะ and several similar words [Pali] angel

เทวี (taywee) woman beautiful as a nymph

เทศ and เทศา (tayt, taysah) [Pali] to show, to do openly — นา to preach

เทศน์ (tayt) [Pali] sermon

เทศ and เทศ (tayt) foreign หวาย — rattan แขก — Mahommedan

เทอญ (tern) [Laos.] expletive used at the end of any treatise

เทอบ (terp) not straight. bending at the ends, bowed downwards or upwards

แท้ (taa) true, sure

แทก (taak) to hit, to strike, to knock against, to prod

แทง (taang) (1) to prick, to pierce — กวย a tree with medicinal leaves (2) to gamble

แทง (taang) small piece, fragment [of metal, etc.] — ทอง nugget — หมึก stick of Chinese ink เหล็ก — pig of iron

แทง (taang') to miscarry

แทตย์ (taat) [Sansk.] ghost, giant

แทน (taan) in the place of, to substitute รก — to recompense, to compensate คุณ — to thank, to recompense

แท่น (tan) raised seat built in the floor, altar, throne

แทบ (taap) (1) nearly, near, ready to, on the point of (2) distressed

แทะ (taa') to browse, to graze, to nibble

แทะโลม (taa'lome) to speak plausibly to a woman, to seduce

ไท (tai) [Pali] (1) free (2) Siamese เจ้า — King

โท (toh) [Sansk.] two, second ไม้ — second accent, as over ไม้

โทง เทง (tohng tayng) oscillating, hanging and swinging โทง ๆ to go about without clothing; indecently

โทณ (tohn) [Pali] (a measure) tanan

โทน (tohn) (1) one, single (2) a bottle-shaped drum

โทมนัศ (tohma'na't) [Pali] feeling of vexation, sadness (Alab. 238)

โทร (tohra') [Pali] far, distant

โทรเลข (tohra'lek) [Pali] telegraph คำ — telegram

โทรสัพท์ (tohra'sa'p) [Pali] telephone

โทศก (tohsok) [Pali] second year of the decennial cycle

โทษ (toht) [Pali] punishment, fault,

pardon เป็น — guilty กิน — guilty, convict ขอ — I beg pardon อะไภย — to pardon, to permit กล่าว — to stigmatise, to denounce

โทษา and โทโษ (tohsah and tohsoh) (1) pain, punishment (2) anger, rage (Alab. 213)

เทา (tow) (1) to bend, to kneel, to prostrate oneself (2) of a dull or grey colour

เท่า (tow) (1) ashes (2) quantity (3) level — กัน equally —ไร and —ใด how many? how much? — นั้น so much — หนึ่ง —ใด whether much or little — ค๊ัว cent per cent —เสมอ equally

เท้า (towe) foot ทัล — infantry — สอก to lean on the elbow ไม้ — walking stick ผ้า — sole of the foot กราบ — to do obeissance, to salute with reverence

ทำ (ta'm) to make, to do — ทาม to imitate, to obey —โทษ to punish — นา to cultivate แกล้ง to do recklessly, mischievously, in a disorderly way ค่อย — little by little

ท่านบ (ta'mnop) causeway, raised path or embankment

ท่านอง (ta'mnaung) skill, art, manner, musical science

ท่านาย (ta'mnai) to foretell, prophecy

ท่านเยบ (ta'mneeyep) (1) Provincial Governor's House (2) parable, proverb

ท่านุ (ta'mnoo') to keep, to take care of

ท่านเา (ta'mnow) to let, to permit

ท่ามะรง (ta'mma'rong) gaoler

ท่าลาย and ทะลาย (ta'mlai and ta'lai) to disperse, to destroy

ท่าเล (ta'mlay) (1) domicile (2) open,

ท่าและ (ta'mlaa') [Malay] sacrifice of animals

กะเกิง (ta'keung) clean, shining

กะนง (ta'nong) fearless, arrogant; to make too much of one's dignity

กะนน (ta'non) (1) a pot for holding water (2) cushion (3) road, path

กะนาน (ta'narn) see ทนาน (a measure of capacity) tanan

ทะโมน (ta'mohn) with ลิง large monkey

กะยง (ta'yong) to wish, desire

กะยาน (ta'yarn) to desire

ทะเยียง (ta'yaang) to adjust [archit.]

ทะระกาม (ta'ra'ka'm) [Pali.] to oppress, to afflict

กะระพิศ (ta'ra'pit) see ทรพิศ

ทะลา (ta'lah) haughtily, fearlessly

ทะลาย (ta'lai) (1) to destroy, disperse (2) a bunch [of betel-nuts, etc.]

ทะลูด ทะลาด (ta'loo't ta'laht) slippery and sloping

ทะลูย ทะลาย (ta'looi' ta'lai) to go at random amongst breakable things, to destroy, be destroyed, go to ruin

ทะเล (ta'lay) sea

ทะเลาะ (ta'law) to dispute, quarrel

ทะวาย (ta'wai) of Tavoy

ทะวา and ทะวารา (ta'wahn and ta'wah-rah) [Pali] door, entrance — เยา urinary duct — หนุก fundiment

ทะสางคลี (ta'sahngkoo'lee) [Pali] (1) to join the hands in adoration (2) a measure of ten niews

ทัก (ta'k) to address, to interrogate

ทักขิณะ (ta'kki'na') [Pali] ทักษิณ [Sansk.] and ทักขิณาวัตร [Pali] going round and round a sacred thing from left to right in token of respect (Alab. 98, 198)

ทักษิณทิศ (ta'ksina'titt) [Sansk.] South

ทะกะติน (ta'ka'tin) [Pali] unlucky day

ทั่ง (ta'ng) anvil

ทั้ง (ta'ng) — ปวง and — หลาย all —
นั้น nevertheless — ใด — ใด whatever it may be — สิ้น altogether —
สอง both กัน — together

ทันตฆาฏ (ta'nta'kart) [Pali] the dead
accent, as over ปี๋,ทว

ทัด (ta't) (1) to equal (2) to oppose (3)
to fix behind the top of the car

ทัน (ta'n) to come up with, to overtake, to accompany — ใจ soon, immediately ใส่ — to catch up ใหม่ —
รู้ตัว unawares

ทันต์ (ta'n) and ทันตะ (ta'nta') [Pali]
tooth มูลิก — upper part of the
accent, as over เอ or ที

ทับ (ta'p) (1) cottage (2) to oppress,
to compress, to superimpose

ทับทา (tha'ptbah) a rake ง — a snake

ทับทิม (ta'ptim) (1) pomegranate (2)
ruby colour หลอย — ruby

ทัพ (ta'p) army, war แม่ — general —

หลวง middle of an army

ทัมกะหรก (ta'ma'ka'rok) filter

ทัศ (ta't) [Sansk.] ten

ทัศนะ (ta'tsa'nah) and ทัศไนย (ta'tsa'-
nai) [Pali] to see, to look at

ทัส (ta'sa) [Pali] ten

              ◆◆◆◆◆

ธ

ธ (low ter   English t. or French th.
Sansk. and Pali dh. Dental : a low
letter) — เธอ name of this letter

ธง (tong) flag

ธน (ton or ta'na') [Pali] treasure, riches

ธนิต (ta'nitt) [Pali] long syllables

ธน and ทนุ (ta'noo') to take care of

ธนู (ta'noo) [Pali] bow ลูก — arrow
ราษี — Sagittarius (zodiac.)

ธร (ton) [Pali] (a final suffix, meaning)
bearer of

ธรณินทร (ta'ra'nin) [Sansk.] King

ธรณีศร (ta'ra'nison) [Pali] King

ธรณี (ta'ra'nee) [Pali] earth, globe เทพ
— angels of the earth (Alab. 225)

ธรรม (ta'm) [San.] condition, quality, function, practice, doctrine, duty, laws, teachings of Buddah (see Alab. 170) — วิไสย religious research (Alab. 196) ยุติ - (1) justice (2) the new sect of Siamese priests ลูก บุญ — adopted son จักร Wheel of the Law (Alab 169)

ธรรมดา (ta'ma'dah) [Pali] usual, common ; habit, nature

ธรรมเนียม (ta'mneea'm) [Sansk.] custom, usage

ธรรมนูญ (ta'mnoon) [Pali] written charge or summons or document, officially sealed

ธรรมากติ and ธรรมาคติ (ta'mmaht) [Pali] public

ธรรมะ and ธารไม see ธรรม.

ธรา (ta'rah) and ธระ (ta'ra') [Pali] (a final suffix, meaning) bearer of

ธราดล (tarahdon) [Sansk.] surface of the earth

ธราไลย (ta'rahlai) [Sansk.] earth, world

ธเรศ (ta'rett) [Sansk.] lord of the earth.

ธเรษธร (ta'rettree) [Pali] lord of many women

ธวัช (ta'wa't) [Sansk.] flag

ทอ (taw) to weave (cloth, etc)

ธาตรี (tahtree) [Sansk.] world, universe, earth

ธาตุ (taht) (1) matter, elements, first principles (2) relics แปร - alchemy

ธานิน and ธานี (tahnin, tahnee) province

ธาร and ธารา (tahn, tahra', tahrah' [Pali] (1) King's baton (2) watercourse, stream

ธาระณะ (tahra'na') [Pali] (1) bearing, holding (2) everywhere, ubiquitous

ธายธร (taht-tree) [Sansk.] earth, world

ธิดา (tidah) [Pali] daughter

ธิบดี (ti'bodee) [Pali] chief, headman

ธิเบศ (ti'bett) [Pali] (1) a royal title (2) Thibet

ธุช (too'cha') [Pali] gold

ธุดงค์ (too'dong) [Pali] ascetic practices

ธุม (too'm) [Pali] smoke   เขา .. luan of smoke

ธุมา and ธูโม (too'mah and too'moh) [Pali] smoke

ธุระ (too'ra') [Pali] yoke, burden, office, business, affair

ทุลิ (too'lee) [Pali] fine dust ละออง dust sticking to the feet ละออง พระบาท I (speaking to the King)

ธูป (toop) [Pali] small scented sticks for burning

เธอ (ter) he, she พระองค์ He, Him (of the King) ลูก — King's child พี่ เธอ — elder brother of a King น้อง ยา — younger brother of a K. หลาน — nephew of a reigning K. วงศ์ใย — a prince of a lower grade than น้อง ยา ประยูร — uncle or great-uncle of the K.

ธำรง (ta'mrong) [see ทรง] [Pali] to make straight

ธ (ta') (1) he (2) bearer, supporter

ธช (ta't) [Pali] flag

ธนูวาคม (ta'nwahkhom) [Sansk.] name of the ninth month, (Sagittarius) [= December]

— — — ◆◆◆ —

น

น (naw nin or small n. English n. Guttural: a low letter) — นิล name of this letter

นก (nok) bird — นก a clinging and hanging bird — สีบ woodpecker, flint lock of a gun, hammer of a gun — สอง หัว double-faced, double-dealing ดัก — to catch birds — ฝูง flock of birds [Note. almost all wild birds are in Siamese called by this generic term as well as the specific name which follows; q.v.]

นขา (na'kah) [Pali] nail of the finger or toe

นคร (na'ka'ra' and na'khon) and นคเร [Pali] town

นครบาล (na'khonbarn) [Pali] royal tribunal, capital of a country, ruler of a country

นครโสภินี (na'khonsohpinee) [Sansk.] beauty of the town, courtesan

นคเรศ (na'kha'rett) [Pali] chief town, capital

นงนุช (nong-noo't) beautiful woman

นงโพธ (nong-poht) young and beautiful woman

นที (na'tee) [Pali] river

นนท์ (non) and นนทะ [Sansk.] joy

นนทรี (nonsee) a tree

นนทะลี (nonta'lee) mother

นบ (nop) to bend the head, to bow, to salute ; (of barbets) to hammer — นบอ *and* -- นอบ to obey, to submit — ยบ to bend the head to the ground, to adore

นพ (na'pa') [Pali] nine -- ศก ninth year of the Siamese cycle

นพคุณ (noppa'koo'n) (1) gold (2) [Pali] nine attributes of Buddah

นพนิต (noppa'nitt) [Pali] milk and butter

นพบุรี (noppa'booree) [Sansk.] Lopburi (New Town)

นพดล (noppa'don) [Sansk.] the nine tiers of the Royal umbrella

นพพ with นม (maa nop-pon) element, arithmetic

นพสูญ (noppa'-soo'n) [Sansk.] obelisk

นภดล (noppa'don) [Sansk.] air, atmosphere, sky

นภากาศ (noppahkart) *and* นภาลัย (na'pahlai) [Pali] air

นม (nom) pap, breast, udder หัว — nipple น้ำ - milk เนย butter, cheese แม่ — wet nurse, nurse อย่า — to wean เสวย -- (of princes) to

suck the breast   แนว a wild shrub with strong-scented flower

นมัศการ (na'ma'tsa'karn) Pali; salute, worship

นร (na'ra') Pali man

นรสิงค (na'ra'sing) man who has committed fornication in a temple and is turned into a monster

นรสิงห (na'ra'sing) (1) representation of a swan-footed woman (2) [Pali] man-lion

นรมาต (na'ra'mart) rhinoceros horn

นรามาต (na'ra'mart) [Sansk.] superior person

นฤ (na'rea) [Sansk.] free from — บาล *and* — เบศร title of the King

นฤคหิต นิคหิต q. v.

นเรนทร์ (na'renn) *and* นรินทร์ (na'rien) [Sansk.] superior man

นลาต (na'lart) [Pali] forehead

หนวก (hnooak) deaf -- ม to deafen

หนวง (hnooang) to hold on to — เหนี่ยว not to let go -- ไป to let go a little and pull back again

นวด (nooat) to shampoo เข้า to thresh rice by treading it out

หนวด (hnooat) beard, wattles of a fish,
feelers of a craw-fish — เครา whiskers — นางกราว the plant called
Venus' hair

นวม (nooam) cloak, lined cloth นวม --
boxing gloves

นวล (nooam) soft, smooth

นวย (nooi') (1) unity, one -- ตา
orbit of the eye (between the eyelids) (2) numerical designation of
eggs and other round things

นวล (nooan) down on fruits, bloom on
the cheeks นวล — gull นก นวล --
wormwood, absinthe นวล -- a fruit
ปลา — ปน a fish

นวลละออ (noo'anla'aw) *and* นวลละออง
(noo'anla'hong) *etc.* soft and fair

นอ (naw) *and* โน (noh) swelling, tumour

หนอ (nor?) [sign of interrogation, command, or admiration] เถิด — leave
off! งาม — how beautiful !

หนอ (naw) shoot, bud, offspring - กบ
ก natural son of the King แรก
skin of the head, horn, etc. — ช้าง
elephant's forehead

นอก (nauk) out of, outside, out เมือง
abroad, foreign country บ้าน -- village, country place — ใจ unfaith-
ful, infidelity — เกิน besides, also —
ทุ่ง open field, plain — แก except
-- ว่าเกิน besides that

หนอก (nawk) hump of a bull; swelling,
tumour ผัก — a plant with edible
fruit

นอง (naung) to flow

นอง (nong) calf of the leg

นอง แนง (nong nang) joined together

น้อง (norng) younger — ชาย younger
brother -- สาว *and* — หญิง younger sister — เมีย wife's sister -- สะ
ใภ้ younger brother's wife - เจ้า
เธอ King's younger brother ที่ --
relations

หนอง (naung) (1) marsh, bog (2) ulcer, corrupted blood, pus

หนอง *with* จ้อง (chong hnong) spinet,
musical instrument made of bamboo and held in the mouth, Jew's
harp

นอน (naun) to lie down to sleep, to
sleep — คว่ำ to sleep on the face

— หงาย to sleep on the back พระ

— sleeping Buddha หาว — heavy with sleep, falling asleep

หนอน (norn) worm

นอบ (naup) *and* น้อม to bend, to salute น้อม (naum) *and* นอบ — to bend, to salute

น้อย (noi) small, little

น้อย (noi) little, a little นิด — very little — ใจ to be dejected, aggrieved, indignant ใจ — timid, faint-hearted — ตัว a few (men etc.)

นา (nah) (1) field ทำ — to cultivate ทุ่ง — open field, plain ไร่ — arable field — หว่าน f. for sowing rice — ปัก f. for transplanting rice เจ้า — peasants, husbandmen, rustics (2) a measure of dignity varying (in proportion to the acreage) according to the royal grant

น่า (nar) (1) front, in front, before ข้าง — straight on, in future — ลาด sloping forwards — ต่าง window — แข้ง shin, front of the leg — ใน (1) cross-bow (2) elements of arith-

metic — ผ้า flowered cloth ภาค — *and* เบื้อง — future หัว — chief, president, general (2) season, time — ตะเภา time when the Chinese junks come

น้า (narr) mother's younger brother or sister — ชาย mother's younger brother — สาว mother's younger sister

หนา (nar?) much, heavy, thick, close เถิด — you can, you may ; enough, neither too much nor too little เร็ว — quick !

หน่า *with* น้อย (noi bnah) custard apple

หน้า (nah) face, front, in front, before — ตา face, countenance ต่อ — in the presence of เอา — to lead on น้ำ — incompetent, incapable, in bad condition สม น้ำ — you deserved your fate เอา — *and* ได้ — to obtain a person's favour

นาก (nark) alloy of gold and copper, red gold

นาค (nark) [Pali] naked ; to strip เปลือย — to be ordained เข้า — candidate for the priesthood

นาค, นาคา, นาโค and นาคินท์ร (nark, narkhah etc.) [Pali] serpent, dragon (Mab. 218. 300)

นาคิน and นาคี (narkin, narkee) female naga

นาโค and นาเค นาค q. v.

นาง (narng) Madam, lady — ชี nun — พา female angels — ห้าม Royal concubines — ยา goddess of the Chinese junks — นวล gull กัน — นวล absinth — แย้ม a flowering plant เกา — นห a plant ขน — chief officer ย่า — a creeping plant

หนาง (nahng) to suspect, doubt

นางเรัล (narngcha'ra'n) road on the ramparts of a city

นางหน (narngnoon) eatable plant

นาฏ (nart) [Pali] and — นารี beautiful woman

หนาก (nart) a tree

นาถา and นาโถ (nartah, nartoh) [Pali] protector, saviour, charitable

นาที (nartee) part of an hour [formerly usually the tenth part, now usually the 60th part]

นาโท (nartoh) [Pali] loud voice

นาน (narn) a long time ช้า — and — แล้ว long ago — ไป long after, in future เนิน — slowly, dilatory

นน (nahn) a Laos province

นานา (narnah) different, diverse

นาบ (narp) to apply heat, to scorch

นาภี (nahpee) [Pali] navel

นาม (nahm) [Pali] (1) name ทรง พระ — (of the King) he is called (2) noun [gramm.]

หนาม (narm) thorn

นาย (nai) chief, lord, master, Sir (the ordinary title of a man) เจ้า — Princes, potentates — ร้อย etc. centurion, etc. — เรือ captain — เงิน creditor, money-master — ท้าย steersman — น้ำ fishery-farmer

นาย (nie) to melt, dissolve

หน่าย (naie) offended, disgusted — แหนง hating the sight of (a person) — เหนื่อย who won't work

นายก (nahyok) [Pali] leader of men ; highest officials in the kingdom

นารถ (naht) [Sansk.] protector, saviour นร — superior person

นารายน์ (nahrai) [Sansk.] a Hindu god with four hands ; a Hindu caste

นารี (nahree) [Pali] lady นางฏ — beautiful lady

นเรศ (nahret) [Pali] superior, excellent (a royal title)

น้าว (now) to bend (a bow, etc.)

หนาว (hnow?) cold — เย็น rather cold, cool

นาวา (nahwah) and นาวี (nahwee) [Pali] boat, vessel

นาวะ (nahwa') [Pali] nine

นาฬิกา (narli'kar) clock — แดด sundial — น้ำ water-clock, clepsydra — พก watch

นาฬิเก (nahli'kay) [Pali] cocoa-nut tree

นาสิก (nahsica') [Pali] nose

นิ (ni') [Pali] (1) [prefix meaning] outward, without, down (2) hither, here

นิกขะ (nikkha') or เนกข (naykha') [Pali] relinquishment of the world [Alab. 184]

นิกร (nikkonn) and นิกาย (nikkai) [Pali] crowd, multitude, flock

นิกูล (nikkoon) tribe, family, relations

นิคม (nikkhom) [Pali] domicile, village, town

นิโครธ (ni'khrote) [Sansk.] a tall tree with hanging roots

นิคคหิต (nikka'hit) and นฤคหิต [Pali] the circular mark, as over นำ

นิ่ง (ning) to keep silence, to be silent — เถิด hold your tongue !

นิจ (nitt) [Pali] constant, perpetual, lasting

นิจจา- นิจจัง and นิจะ (nitchah, etc.) permanent, continual, always

นิด (nit) small — เดียว very little

นิติ (nitti') [Pali] sayings of the ancients, good counsels, institutions

นิตยภัตร (nittya'pa't) [Sansk.] monthly pay of a priest

นิทรา (nitsah) [Sansk.] to sleep

นิทาน (ni'tahn) [Pali] tale, story

นิเทศ (ni'tayt) [Pali] to disclose, to explain, to point out

นินทา (nintah) [Pali] slander, defamation, blame

หนีบ (nipp) [phon.] to peck, to nip หนีบ — to push and pull out and in ; sting, prick, palpitation

หนูบ (noo'p) to walk like a crab

นิบาต (nibaht) [Pali] (1) falling, descending (2) a particle (3) tale, story

นิบุณณะ (niboo'nna') [Pali] completely, subtle, clever

นิพนธ์ (nipponn) [Pali] to bind; to compose; songs or compositions made by the King

นิพาน (nip-arn) [Pali] extinction of pain and care, Nirvana (Alab. 165)

นิพพาน and นิพานิ etc. = นิพาน

นิโภค (ni'pohk) [Pali] without fortune

นิ่ม (nim) soft, tender ตัว — an animal which rolls itself up — นิ่ม fine woman

นิมนต์ (ni'monn) [Pali] to invite priests (to anything, as) — เทศน์ to invite a priest to preach

นิมาน (ni'marn) [Pali] department of the heaven

นิมิตร (ni'mitt) [Pali] (1) to dream, dream (2) to shew ศิลา — front stone of a temple, under which a treasure is hidden — อัศจรรย์ to do a miracle, to shew wonders

นิยม (ni'yomm) [Pali] ascertaining, recognizing; restraint, voluntary penance, training

นิยาย (ni'yai) [Pali] old story, tale, fable

นิราไลย (ni'rarlai) [Pali] (1) away from, departing from, separation, departure (2) unloving, unloved

นิราศ (ni'rart) [Pali] to be separated from, far from, exiled

นิรมล (ni'roo'mon) [Pali] title of the Queen, or ladies of high position

นิรุทธ (ni'roo'tta') [Pali] destroyed, annihilated

นิโรธ (ni'roht) [Pali] to extinguish, extinction, annihilation

นิระ (ni'ra') [Pali] without, out of

นิรันดร (ni'ra'ndon) [Pali] without interstices, compact, continuous, incessant, perpetual

นิรพพุท (ni'ra'ppoo't) [Pali] ten millions, a thousand millions

นิล (nin) [Pali] dark blue, black, a precious stone of a dark blue colour, sapphire กา — and ศ — black ยา — a famous medicine

นิโล (ni'lo) [Pali] black, dark blue, dark green

นิละยา (ni'la'yah) [Pali] dwelling, habitation, abode

นิ่ว (new) retention of urine หน้า — sad-looking, sulky

นิ้ว (niew) finger, Siamese inch = about ·833 of an inch — ก้น toe — ซี้ fore-finger — กลาง middle finger — นาง ring finger — ก้อย little finger

นิวรณ์ (ni'wonn) [Pali] to hinder, prevent, hindrance, obstruction

นิวาส and นิเวศ (ni'wart, ni'wett) [Pali] dwelling, residence, resting-place

นิวัตนาการ (ni'wa'tta'narkarn) [Pali] returning, turning back

นิสัย (ni'sai) [Pali] refuge, shelter, protection, cause, event, habit บอก — to report what took place

นิสากร (ni'sarkon) [Pali] moon

นี่ (nee) this, here — ที — here มา — come here — แน่ะ look! lo! behold! to point out

นี้ (nee) debt — สิน debts เจ้า — creditor, money-master ลูก — debtor เป็น — to be in debt ท่วม — deeply in debt

นี่ (nee) this, here — นั่น this and that —ในนี้ here and there — แล้ะ so it is

หนี (nee?) to fly, to escape, to avoid — เริ่น to fly and hide - - หาย to disappear

นีติ (neeti') [Pali] old sayings, traditions, good counsels

หนีบ (hneep) [phon.] to clip, to snip

เหนียง (hneea'ng) crop (of a bird) maw (of an animal)

เหนียง (hneea'ng) with ควาย shiny black คือ — an animal

แนบ and แน่น — (naap, neea'n) well joined, well fitted, even, level

แนม (neeam) with ช้าง elephant with short teeth

เหนียม with อาย (ai hneeam?) to be much ashamed

เนียร and เนียระ (neeara') [Sansk.] without, exempt, free from — เทศ exile

เนียรภาค (neeara'park) [San.] without a share

เนียรมิตร (neeara'mitt) [Sansk.] to appear, to create, to work miracles. apparition

เหนียว (hneeyo) consistent, sticking together, sticky ดิน — potter's earth. clay คน — parsimonious ใจ — avaricious, miserly

เหนียว (hneeo) to grasp, to pull, to retain

นึก (neuk) to think

นึ่ง (neung) to cook with steam ใช่ — custard

หนึ่ง (neu'ng) one ที่ — first ประ — as, just as อัน — อันเดียว one and the same

เนื้อ (neua') (1) deer — เป็ด venison (2) flesh - - หนัง carnal, fleshly — ความ the gist of a matter -- แท้ genuine เค้า — ย่อย a delicate fish

เหนือ (neua') North, above ทิศ — North ก้าไปน — beazine — ผ้า adulterous

เนื่อง (neua'ng) continual, continuous

เหนื่อย (hneuey) tired, fatigue

นุง (noo'ng) entangled, confused, disorderly

นุ่ง (noo'ng) to put on, to clothe the lower part of the body ผ้า — the panung — ผ้า to put on the panung -- จีบ to plait

นุช (noo't) young (woman) นั้น — dear — นาฎ beautiful, graceful, well-mannered

นน นั้น (noo'n na'n) a fish

นุ่น (noo'n) [Pali too'l] down of three kinds of trees, tree cotton ต้นนุ่น — a cotton tree

หนุน (noo'n) to support, to prop up, to keep up ยก — to raise up out of misery ทัพ — reinforcement

หนุบ and — หนุบ (hnoo'phnip) [phon.] sting, sudden bite, palpitation

นุพล (noo'pon, noo'pa'la') [Pali] (1) according to one's strength (2) unity [arithm.]

นุ่ม (noo'm!) soft, flabby, yielding to the touch

หนุ่ม (noo'm) of age, neither young nor old

น้อย (nooi) small

หนู (hnoo) rat — ตุ่น guinea-pig — ผี musk-rat หาง — hair like a rat's tail, pig-tail ด้วย — and อี — (a name for little boys and girls)

เนง (neng) quiet, motionless

เหนง (nengg) (1) clear, limpid (2) and เหนง sound of striking

เหนด เหนื่อย (hnett hneuey) very tired, exhausted, worn out

เนตร (nett) [Sansk.] eyes ชล — tears

เนติบัณฑิตย์ (nayti'ba'ntitt) [Pali] lawyer, councillor

เหน็บ (hnepp) (1) to push in, to stick in — ๓ to embrace closely, to hug — กระเบน to fasten up the end of the panung — ชี to tuck up the panung มีด — dagger worn in the panung (2) numbness, contraction

เนย (neu-i') cheese, butter เป็น — curdled — แข็ง cheese — เหลว butter

เนร (nayra') see เหยร [Sansk.] without, except — หิต fierce, cruel — คุณ white ant — คุณ unthankful

เนสาท (naysart) [Pali] (1) hunter, sportsman (2) skilful

เหนียว (hner) and — เหนียะ sticky, glutinous

เนิน (nern) hillock, incline

เนิ่น (nern) to linger; slow — นาน for a long time

เนิบ (nerp) slow, sluggish — นาบ slowly, lazily

แน่ (naa) certain, certainly, surely, assuredly — นอน stedfast, con-

stant — นิ่ง motionless

แหนง and น้อย (neng noy) slender, thin, graceful

แหนง (hnaang) to suspect

แน่น (nan) solid, close, thick, compact, sticking together, sticking fast — อก heart oppressed with grief หนา — stedfast, firm

แนบ (naap) to join (oneself with), to embrace

แหนบ (hnaap) tweezers, small pincers

แนม (naam) to compress, to press, to add สืบ — to explore; spy

แนว (naao) crack, crevice, crease, line, weal เป็น — streaked; leaky ชัน — — tar for stopping cracks — แถว row, line, file

แน่ว (nao) (1) straight, direct (2) unmoved, stedfast

แนะ (naa') (1) to point out, show, direct, indicate, appoint นัด — to appoint a time (2) [Pali] here, here it is — นี่ look here!

ใน (nai) in, into, within ข้าง —, ท. — กาย — inside เครื่อง — edible entrails of an animal, tripe ตับ —, เล็ก

— kernel or stone of a fruit — ตา
pupil and iris of the eye

ใน หก (nai hook) spinning-wheel

ไหน (nai?) which? where? whither?
ก — where? อยู่ — where is (it)?
ไร — where are you going to? — ๆ
wherever it may be, whatever happens

ในย (nai) [Pali] (1) manner (2) eye —
เนตร (of the King) eyes

ใน and โหนก (no and noke) swelling,
lump, tumour

โหนง เหน่ง (nohng neng) sound of a
gong

โน่น (nohn) there, that — อะไร what is
that?

โน้น (nohn?) there, yonder, that ข้าง —
on that side, there ฟาก and ฟากข้า
— on the other side of the river

โน้น (nohn) to bend down — น้าว to
cajole, flatter

โนรี (nohree) and โนเรศ [Malay] parrot

เนา (now) [Cambed.] to remain —
เนนน to remain for a long time, to
continue ทำ — let him do what he
likes

เหนา (now?) fading, faded ถี — fabulous
story (in plays)

เหน่า (now) with หัว lower part of the
belly

เหน้า (now) (1) putrid (2) earth that
has been manured

เหนา (now) [Pali] nine

นำ (na'm) to lead, to head — ร่อง
harbour-pilot ผู้ — leader, guide,
introducer

น้ำ (na'm) water, liquid, rainy season
ท้อง — bed of a stream or water-
course, bottom ตา — holes through
which water runs ลง — to put into
the water, to launch, to enter the
water หัว — beginning of the rains
สระ — artificial pond กิน — to
drink the water of allegiance ทวน
— to go against the current หยาก
— to be thirsty, thirst สรง — (of
royal persons or priests) to bathe
— ตา tears — ฝน rain water —
มัน oil — นม milk — ตาล sugar
— ชา tea — เต้า a gourd — มูก
mucus of the nose — ไหล running

water — ลาย saliva, spittle —
เหลือง pus, corrupted blood — ปะ
สาน solder — ปะ สาน ทอง borax
— ปะ สานกันยก sal ammoniac —
พุ water-spout, spring — อ้อย molasses — อ้อย สด juice of sugar cane
— พริก seasoning of red pepper —
แข็ง ice — ขึ้น flood tide — ลง ebb
tide — เอื่อ slack water — หนัก
amount, price สี — เงิน sky-blue
— เหอ sweat — ใจ will, love — กรด
corrosive water, metallic acid

น้ำ (na'm) enough, sufficient, satiated,
content, pleasure — ใจ contented-
ness, joy

นำพา (na'mpah) officious, busybody,
volunteering, restless, active

นะ (na') [word of command, sign of
vocative] ยัง — until, as far as
นะ with เหนอะ (nerr na') sticky, glutinous

นะปุงสะกะ (na'poo'ngsa'ka') [Pali] of
neither sex — ลิงค hermaphrodite

นะพะ (na'pa') [Sansk.] (1) nine (2) new

นะโม (na'moh) [Pali] to salute, to re-
vere, honour (to Buddha)

นะรก (na'rok) [Pali] hell

นะรา and นะระ (na'ra') [Pali] man

นัก (na'k) [Cambod.] (1) man (2)
prince, ruler (3) filled with, endowed with — โทษ guilty, convict —
เทศน์ preacher — บุญ meritorious,
saint — เรียน student, pupil, scholar — พรต hermit — เลง gambler,
rogue — สนม royal concubines —
สวด musicians at a funeral

นัก and — หนา (na'k nah) many, much,
too much

หนัก (na'k) heavy — ไป to grow worse
— หน่วง to retain, not to let go —
แน่น firm, constant เบา — weight

นักข (na'k) and นรขา [Pali] better
แขา nail (of the finger or toe)

นักข (na'k) [Pali] star

นักขัตฤกษ (na'kka'ta'roo'k) [Pali] 5th
day of the 6th month, when the
augurs are consulted

นั่ง (na'ng) to sit พระที่ — throne, seat
for the King or Queen

หนัง (na'ng?) (1) a magic lantern used at funerals (2) skin, leather — ตา eyelids เนื้อ — body, flesh, corporeal

นังกุฏ (na'ngkoo't) [Pali] tail (of animals)

นังคัล (na'ngka'n) [Pali] plough

หนังสือ (hna'ngseu) letter, writing, document — สัญญา written agreement — ข้าง ที่ books placed by the King's bed, King's favourite books

นัด and นัดถุ์ (na't) [Pali] (1) to inhale through the nostrils ยา — powder for inhaling, snuff (2) a charge of powder (3) to fix, to appoint ผัด — to put off, to delay

นัดดา (na'dah) [Pali] grandchild

นัที (na'tee) see แม่น้ำ river

นั้น (na'n) that, there อะไร — what is that ? นี่ — here and there — และ that is, what it is

นั่น (na'n!) he, she, it ที่ — there แล้ว — then เท่า — only — และ look there !

นันท์ and นันทา (na'n, na'nta') [Pali] joy, joyful, to rejoice

นับ (na'p) to count — ถือ to respect, fear คำ — salutation

- - - • • •

บ

บ (baw   English b. Pali and Sansk. p. Labial : a middle letter. Note : at the end of a word this letter is pronounced rather as p.)

บ่ (baw) [Laos.] not — มิ ได้ not at all

บก (bok) earth, land ขึ้น — to disembark

บง (bong) [Laos.] to look, to see

บ่ง (bong) to pick out, to open — หนาม to extract a thorn — ผี to open an abscess

บงกช (bongkot) [Pali] lotus

บด (bot) (1) to crush, to grind to powder (2) to iron (3) cloudy

บดินทร์ (bodinn) [Sansk.] great (royal title)

บดี (bodee) [Pali] magnates, grandees

บถ (bot) [Pali] path, road, course

บท (bot) lesson, poem, chapter, article — กลอน verse, song — เพลง hymn ช่าง แต่ง — poet

บท: (ba'ta') [Pali] feet, footsteps

บน (bon) (1) above, on, up (2) bribe
สิน — bribe

บ่น (bonn) to murmur, grumble — หา
and — ถึง to complain of a person's
absence, to desire lovingly ; keep-
sake

บพิธ (bopitt) [Pali] to make, found,
construct วัด — name of a temple

บ่ม (bom) to ripen fruit indoors

บร (bon) [Pali] another ซ่าย — ambush
artifice of an enemy ผ่าย — enemy

บรเพ็ธ (bora'pett) a medicinal plant

บรม and บรม: (bo'ro'ma') [Pali] great,
excellent, royal (used as title of
Kings, etc.)

บรมถ and บรมรรถ (ba'ra'ma't) superior truths, perfection of truth,
metaphysics [Alab. 167]

บรรจง (ba'nchong) to do carefully

บรรจถรณ์ (ba'ncha'tonn) [Pali] bed-
stead

บรรจบ (ba'nchop) to complete (a circle, etc.)

บรรจางค (ba'ncharng) [Pali] five qualities, to place five parts of the body

on the ground in saluting

บรรจร (ba'ntonn) [P.] bed, carpet, mat

บรรณ (ba'n) [Sansk.] tree-leaves —
ศาลา rest-house roofed with t.

บรรณา (ba'nnah) [Pali] to offer worship, to go — การ royal gift, state
present

บรรท (ba't) [Pali] (obsol.) (1) yellow,
gold-coloured, throne (2) a leaf, a
sheet [of paper, etc.] สุวรรณ —
yellow, gold-coloured

บรรดาณึก (ba'ntahneuk) [Pali] very
large collection of persons on foot

บรรทึก (ba'nteuk) [Pali] to take a note
of, to write down, to jot down

บรรพชา (ba'ppa'chah) and บรรพชิต
[Sansk.] to be ordained, to become
a priest or monk

บรรพต (ba'npot) and บรรพตา [Sansk.]
mountain

บรรยาย (ba'nra'yai) [Sansk.] to relate,
to teach, exposition

บรรหา (ba'nhah) [Sansk.] to question,
interrogate

บรรหาร (ba'nharn) [Pali] (1) answer,
order, rescript, edict (2) to take care
of, to guard

บรา (ba'rah) [Pali] (obsol.) behind, after, in future

บริ (ba'ri') [Pali] around, round about, perfectly

บริกำม์ (bori'ka'm) [Pali] to pray, to make one's devotions

บริขาร (bori'kahn) [Pali] outfit of a priest (Alab. 202) — โรพ์ scarf or kerchief of a priest

บริจาร (borri'chah) [Pali] servant, concubine, wife

บริจาค (borri'chark) [Pali] to give, to make liberal gifts

บริจาริกา (borri'chahri'kah) [Pali] maid servant, wife

บริเฉท (borri'chett) and บริเฉท [Pali] to determine, to regulate

บรินายก (borri'nahyok) [Pali] leader of a crowd, supreme power, chief

บรินิพพาน (borri'ni'pahn) [Pali] spiritual heaven, total extinction

บริบาล (borri'barn) [Pali] to watch over, to take care of

บริบูณ (borri'boon) [Pali] abundant, full, entire, perfect

บริภาษ (borri'part) [Sansk.] to speak ironically, to mock

บริโภก (borripoke) [Pali] to eat, possessions, food and clothing

บริมณฑาณ (borri'monton) บริมณฑาส [Pali] circle, circumference

บริรักษ (borri'ra'k) [Sansk.] to maintain, bring up, educate

บริวาร (borri'wahn) [Pali] retainers, retinue

บริเวณ (borri'wayn) [Pali] surrounding. entourage, vicinity

บริษการ (borri'sa'karn) [Sansk.] apparatus, outfit of a priest

บริสุทธิ (borri'soo't) [Pali] clean, pure, white, neat, clear

บริมาณ (borri'marn) [Pali] measure. rate, size

บริมาน (borri'mahn) paste

บรั่น (ba'ra'n) and บาหรั่น brandy

บวก (booa'k) addition

บวง สรวง (booa'ng sooa'ng) offering of food, wine, etc. to angels or goblins

บ่วง (booa'ng) loop, snare — แร้ว snare, trap นกหาง — a black bird with long forked tail

บวช (booa't) [Pali] to be ordained เวลา — time of ordination

บวก (booa't) to be cheated แกง — Siamese syrop

บ้วน (booa'n) to spit

บวบ (booa'p) pumpkin สูก — lathes in a roof etc., sections of a raft

บวม (booa'm) to swell; bleated; swelling, tumour

บัว (booa') (1) top of a pillar, capital (2) border, rim (3) water lily — แดน small red w. สาย — stalk of w. นก กอก — flamingo

บ่หอน (bawhaun) [Laos.] never, not

บ่อ (bau) pit, well

บอก (bauk) to tell, inform, announce คำ — advice, advertisement — ให้ รู้ to notify

บอด (baut) and ตา — blind

บอน (bawn) a water plant with broad leaves ปาก — busybody, scandalmonger มือ — mischievous, destructive

บ่อน (baun) [Laos.] gambling-house

บอบ (baup) broken down, worn out with ill-usage

บ่อย (boi) often — ๆ very often

ปอย (boi?) [Engl.] cabin boy, male domestic servant, waiter, flunkey

บ่อหอน (bauhaun) [Laos.] never, not

บ่อหง (bauheung) [Laos.] soon

บ่า (bah) (1) shoulder (2) over-full, overflow

บ้า (bar) idiotic, mad, mad after — ยอ eager for flattery — หมู epileptic — เลือด puerperal fever — ใจ (1) dare-devil, reckless (2) a cake

บาก (bark) (1) to cut, to carve (2) to turn, to avert

บาง (bahng) (1) thin, slender ผ้า — gauze — ๆ more seldom than before — คราย sometimes

บาง (bahng) (1) village — กอก European name for the Capital of Siam (2) land surrounded on several sides by water — ปลาสร้อย a town

บ้าง (barng) some, partly

บางสุ (bahngsoo') [Pali] dust, dirt, soil

บาญชี (barnchee) schedule, account, catalogue, list, index สมุห — secretary

บาด (bart) (1) a cut, mark, scar — แผล wound (2) the tenth part of an hour (3) throwing dice for a lottery or a prize — หมาง difference, dissention

บากทะยัก (bahtta'ya'k) gangrenous wound

บากหมาย (bartmai?) written summons, Court notice

บาดาล (bardarn) [San.] under-ground, regions of the Nagas, infernal regions

บาตร (bart) [Sansk.] priest's bowl for collecting food [Alab. 232] ตัก — to give alms to a priest

บาท (baht) tical: a coin three-fifths of a Mexican dollar — หลวง European priest

บาท (baht) บาทา and บาทะ [Pali] feet, footsteps พระ — the foot-print of Buddha; the King's foot รอง — shoe, slipper, boot (of royal person)

บาทบริจา (bahtbori'char) [Pali] maid-servant, concubine, wife

บาทยุคล (bahtyoo'kon) [Pali] feet of the King

บาน (bahn) [to open, to bloom, full-blown [Fr. épanouir] ใจ — gay, merry ดอก — เย็น a plant which

blooms at night — พับ hinge — ประตู leaf of a door, blind, window, etc. — แพนก or — พะแนก preface

บ้าน (bahn) home, house, village

บานทะโรค (bahnta'rohk) piles

บาป (bahp) and บาปะ [Pali] sin, sinful

บาย (baie) [Cambod.] cooked rice — ศรี ornaments made of the central fibre of banana leaves — สุหรี่ [Malay.] marsh, bog

บ่าย (bai) (1) to turn บาก — to turn aside (2) afternoon

บ้าย (baie) to rub on, to smear

บารมี (bahra'mee) [Pali] perfection, complete, merit, virtue, authority [Alab. 184]

บาล (bahn) [Pali] to keep, guardian, ruler นคร — municipal department ก — King, ruler

บาหลี (bahlee) [Chin.] small seat in the prow of Chinese junks

บ่าว (bowe) slave, servant, attendant — ไพร่ slaves (2) see เบ้า young man

บาศ (baht) [Sansk.] cord, string, rope บ่วง — loop

บาพี่(bahlee) [Pali] (1) order, series, line, row (2) Pali [the sacred Buddhist language]

บิ (bi') to break off a small piece, to chip, to pick off a fragment

บิณฑ์ (binn) [Pali] with เข้า rice offered to Buddha, to priests, or to spirits — บาทร to go after alms

บิด (bit) (1) to twist, to distort — หล่า gimlet เป็น — dysentery (2) lazy

บิดา (bidar) บิดา and บิดๅ [Pali] father, papa

บิดหล่า (bitlah) gimlet

บิตุ (bittoo') [Pali] father — ลา father's younger brother — ลา uncle

บิน (bin) to fly

บิ่น (bin) to make or grow blunt by notching of the edge or blade

บิด (bin) with เกา to tell one's beads

บิล [Engl.] bill

บี (bee) crushed, pushed in

บี่ (bee) [Chin.] rice

บีฑา (beetah) [Pali] to molest

บีบ (beep) to squeeze — คอ คาย to strangle

เบ็ย (beca) and — หอย cowrie, a small shell used for coin in some places (as in Laos) กอก — interest เล่น — to gamble [usually with shells] บ่อน — gambling-house ผัก — pur slain — หวก annual salary

เบ็ยก (beca'k) to distribute, to take what one can get

เบ็ยง (beca'ng) distorted, crooked; to speak in an ambiguous or insincere way

เบ็ยง (beca'ng) awry, distorted, deformed

เบ็ยด (beca't) to press closely, to molest, torment — ลัก to take by stealth

เเบ็ยน (beca'n) to torment, to importune

บุก (beu'k) a river fish — บ้น idiocy, irreligion

บุง (beu'ng) large marsh or swamp, flood-land — บาง swamp; bank excavated by a river

บุง (beu'ng) (1) sulky, surly, ill-humoured (2) a large edible spider

เบ็อ (beuwa') in large quantities สาก กระ — a pestle for pounding pepper

เบ็อ (beua') (1) poison (2) tired, dis-

gusted — ใจ indisposed, unwilling
— หน่าย disgust น่า — easily disgusted, fastidious

เบอ (beua') *with* คัว wild man of the
woods, idiot, dumb person

เบือง (beua'ng) on the side of, on one
side — น่า in future

เบือน (beua'n) to turn aside

บุ (boo') to beat copper into vessels
ทอง — ductile gold, gold leaf

บุก (boo'k) to go through pathless places:
across country คัน — *and* — เบือน
aquatic plants ก — [Pali] tin

บุคล (boo'konn) whoever, any one

บุหงา (boo'ngah) [Malay] flowers

บุ้ง (boo'ng) caterpillar, large file for
wood, rasp

บุญ (boo'n) [Pali] merit, luck ใจ —
goodwill; beneficent รู้ — คุณ
grateful — ธรรม to adopt บุตร —
ธรรม adopted child ตาม — as may
be, as it happens มา — ไม่ dead

บุตร *and* บุตรา (boo'tra', boo'trah)
[Sansk.] child — ชาย son

บุตรี (boo'tree) daughter

บุถุ (boo'too') [Pali] unconverted, sin-
ner, low fellow

บุถุชน (boo'too'chon) [Pali] common
fellows

บุตคล (boo'tta'khonn) [San.] whoever

บุนนาก (boo'nnahk) [Pali] white and
yellow blossom of a large tree [Rot-
tleria tinctoria]

บุบ (boo'p) distorted, battered, out of
shape — ดสาบ to make a slip *or*
mistake

บุปผา *and* บุปผะ (boo'ppa') [Pali] flower, blossom

บุปโพ (boo'ppoh) [Pali] matter of a
tumour or sore place

บุ๋ย (booi') grimaces

บุหรง (boo'rong) [Malay.] peacock,
bird

บูรณ (boo'ra'na') [Sansk.] full

บุรพการี (boo'ra'pa'kahree) [Pali] an-
cestral teacher

บุรพนิมิตร (boo'pa'ni'mitt) [San.] omen,
presage, token

บุรพบท (boo'pa'bott) [Pali] preposition.

บุราณ (boo'rahn) [Pali] old, ancient

บุริน (boo'rinn) [Pali] large city, King of a city

บุริสา (boo'ri'sah) *and* บุริโส [Pali] male, man

บุรี (boo'ree) [Pali] town, city

บุหรี่ (boo'ree) cigar, cigarette เข้า — pillau

บุรุต (boo'roo't) [Sansk.] *and* บุรุโส [Pali] male

บุระ (boo'ra') future

บุหลัน (boo'la'n) [Malay.] moon

บุศย (boo'sya') [Sansk.] white — น้ำ ทอง *and* — ราคา topaz

เบ *and* บุบผา (boo'su'bah) [Sansk.] flowers, garlands

บู (boo) barbel

บู้ (boo) distorted, crushed, indented

บูชา (boochah) [Pali] sacrifice (Mab. 201) — บิณ burnt offering — ใทย to return evil for good

บูด (boot) [Pali] sour, rancid, putrid

บู๊ต [Engl.] boot

บูต (boot) [Pali] putrid, stinking

บูม (boom) [Engl.] boom [of a ship]

บูม (boomm?) [phon.] noise of a thing falling into water

บมบาม (boombahm) uncouth, rough, rude

บูรณ (boon) [Pali] abundant, full, complete

บูรพ (boon *and* boora'pa') [Pali] East — ทิศ East

บูรพา (boora'pah) [Sansk.] East

เบูย (boon) *with* ไพ (pai-boon) [San.] fine, large

เบ (bay) *with* ปาก wry mouth, lower lip protruding like a shelf

เบ่ง (beng) to swell, to be swollen, ready to burst

เบญจ (bencha') [Pali] five — คีม fifth year in the decennial cycle

เบญจรงศ์ (bencha'rong) *with* เครื่อง [Pali] the five elementary colours

เบญจวรรณ (bencha'wa'n) [Pali] (a bird) adorned with five colours

เบญจา (benchah) [Pali] (1) funeral pile (2) seat for hair-cutting (3) five

เบญจางค์ (benchahng) [Pali] having the five good qualities

เบ็ด (bet) fish-hook — เสร็จ all together

เบน (bayn) to turn — ยาก *and* — เบยง to turn aside, to go obliquely

เบิก (berk) (1) to open a little (2) account, bill, request for payment (3) to ask for a thing without offering to pay — บาน to rejoice, to delight

เบ่ง (beu'ng) to stare (like buffaloes)

แบ (baa) to open

แบก (baak) to carry on the back or shoulders — ไป to carry — ไว้ to support, sustain

แบ่ง (baang) to separate, to divi de

แบงก์ [Engl.] bank

แบน (baan) even, flat, level

แบบ (baap) scheme, pattern, plan, model, mould, form, shape, method, system, standard, specimen, copy — อย่าง plan, example

แบะ (baa) to split open, to sever

แบะ (baa) open at the middle, gaping open — แคะ lazy, indolent, idling about, littering about

ใบ (bai) leaf, sail, (numerical designation of leaves, fruits, plates, etc.) — ไม้ leaf — ลาน palm leaves for writing upon — สัญญา copy of an agreement of which the original is kept by an official แล้น — to set

sail, to go sailing ลด — to shorten sail ปลา — ไม้ a small flat river fish — เสร็จ receipt, discharge

ใบสัตย์ (bai sa't) judge's sentence in writing

ใบ้ (bai) dumb, mute

โบก (boke) (1) to ventilate, to air, to wave away, waft away (2) to daub, to plaster

โบกขระ (bohkka'ra') [Pali] (1) lotus (2) water

โบ๊ต (bote) [Engl.] boat

โบถ (bote)]Pali] place in a templo containing an image of Buddha and surrounded by pillars; confession-house (Alab. 190) — ฝรั่ง European church

โบย (boi) to beat unmercifully

โบราณ (bohrahn) [Pali] ancient, primi-tive, old

โบษขรณี (bohska'ra'nee) [Sansk.] lotus pond

เบา (bow) (1) to make water (2) light — ๆ soft, gently — ความ unskilful, imprudent หัว — fanciful — บาง (1) less busy (2) to be alleviated (3)

not so many as before ก — to despise

เบ่า (bow) young man, bridegroom —
— สาว bride and bridegroom งาน
— สาว wedding

เบ้า (bow) crucible, melting-pot

เบาะ (bau') cushion — ม้า saddle

บำเหน็จ (ba'mhnett) remuneration, compensation, reward, premium

บำบวง (ba'mbooa'ng) to offer sacrifices

บำไบ (ba'mbai) Bombay

บำบัด (ba'mba't) to cure

บำเพ็ญ (ba'mpen) [Pali] to keep, observe, execute religious duties

บำราบ (ba'mrahp) [Sansk.] to overcome, to clear a place of enemies, to
tranquillise a district

บำราศ (ba'mraht) [Sansk.] to reject,
to relinquish, to go away

บำรุง (ba'mroo'ng) [Sansk.] to protect,
keep, take care of, repair

บำเรอ (ba'mrerr) to feed, keep, support, maintain

บะ (ba') (exclam. of surprise)

บัก (ba'k) [Laos.] prepuce

บัง (ba'ng) to veil, to hide — คน water-
closet (of the King)

ยัง (ba'ng) (1) to notch (2) guard of a
sword (3) grater

บังเกิด (ba'ngkert) to happen, to come
into existence, to be created, birth,
born วัน — birthday

บังกะหล่า (ba'ngka'lah) Bengal

บังคม (ba'ngkhom) to salute, homage
ถวาย — to do homage, to offer
(speaking to the King) กราบ —
ทูล to speak to the King, after making obeisance

บังควร (ba'ngkooa'n) suitable, proper

บังคับ (ba'ngka'p) to rule, to regulate,
ordain; command, control ผู้ —
imperious คำ — mandate ให้ —
subject

บังใบ (ba'ngbai) overlapping boards,
plates, or strips, streaks, Venetian
blinds

บังเวียน (ba'ngweean) compasses

บังสุ (ba'ngsoo') [Pali] dust

บังสุกุล (ba'ngsoo'koo'n) [Pali] funeral recitation over a dead body

บังเหียน (ba'ngheean) bit, bridle สาย
— rein, bridle

บังเหฏ (ba'nghett) [Pali] accident, unexpected event

บังธาฯ (ba'ng-aht) to dare, daring, bold

บำใฯ (ba'tchai) [Pali] faith, religion, alms

บฏ (ba't) [Pali] cloth (used for making flags), bunting

บญฯ (ba'ncha') [Pali] five

บญฯฯ (ba'nchon) [Pali] palace windows with bars

บญฯฯ (ba'nchah) [Pali] to make a declaration, to give precepts, to make ordinances, to command

บญหาร   บญฯฯ

บฑฺารฯ (ba'nta'ra') [Pali] white

บนฑฺาฏ (ba'nnaht) and บญญาฏ (ba'nyaht) [Pali] fifty

บฺฺฺ [Pali] and บรรฌ [San.] (ba'nna') leaves, letters

บฺฺฺ (ba'nhah) [Pali] question

บฏ (ba't) a moment — ฯ now, at this moment — เดียว directly, presently — ฯฯ (1) beginning of a song (2) immediately — ฦฺ immediately

บฏใฯ (ba'tchai) (1) now, immediately (2) (speaking of a priest) money

บักพลี (ba'tplee) offerings to an idol or genius

บักส (ba'tsee) disgraceful

บักร (ba'tta'ra') [Pali] leaf สญญฺฯ — patent conferring a dignity สุพรรฌ — do. written on gold

บักร (ba'tree) to paste, to solder

บน (ba'n) with น่า gable-end of a house

บน (ba'n) to cut off

บน (ba'n) (1) piece, slice (2) a half cartload of rice — เอฺฺ the top of the hip, the waist, the loins

บนฑฺ (ba'nchong) elaborate, agreeable, comely

บนฑฺ (ba'nchop) to go to meet, to make to meet, to put together

บนฑฺ (ba'nchoo') to load, to fill

บนฑฺ (ba'ncheung) agreeable, affable, polite

บนฑฺฏ [Pali] and บนฑฺฏฺ [Sansk.] (ba'ntitt) one who has just left the priesthood, pundit, learned man

บนฑฺฯ (ba'ndah) whoever, all, the whole

บนฑาฦ (ba'ndahn) [Pali] to cause, produce, germinate

บนฑาศกฺ (ba'ndahsa'k) [Pali] officials, magnates

บันกาสัตว (ba'ndahsa't) [Siam. and Sansk.] animals of all kinds, creatures, beings

บันใก (commonly pronounced *ka'dai*) stair, ladder

เบันเภาะ (ba'ndaw') (1) Brahmin's little drum (2) unable to beget a child, impotent

บันถะ (ba'nta') [Pali] solitary path

เบันทม (ba'ntom) to sleep (of the King)

บันทึก (ba'ntcuk) [Pali] (1) to guide (2) to make a note of, to make a summary, to abbreviate

บันทุก (ba'ntcuk) to load, ballast

บันทูล (ba'ntoon) [Pali] order of the Second King

เบันเทา (ba'ntow) relief, consolation

เบันเทิง (ba'ntcung) to rejoice

บันทัด (ba'nta't) line, rule

เบันรอน (ba'nraun) (1) to cut into lengths (2) to decide a case point by point

บันฦๅ (ba'nreu) to resound, loud noise, report, fame

บันลุ (ba'nloo') to reach, to go as far as

เบันเลง (ba'nleng) to sing, to make music

บันไลย (ba'nlaie) [Sansk.] to die, to be destroyed

บันลาน (ba'nlahn) to mix [colours, etc.] to intermingle

บันลังก (ba'nla'ng) [Pali] (1) throne made of marble (2) a kind of dark marble (3) name of a hill

บันะตะ (ba'pa'ta') [Pali] *and* เบรรพต [Sansk.] mountains

—————•••—————

ป

ป (*paw* English *p*. Sansk. *p*. and *pr*. Labial : a middle letter)

ปก (pok) to veil, to hide, to cover, to put on a cover ใบ — cover of a book, binding

ปจิมะทิศ (pa'chimma'tit) [Pali] west

ปฏิทิน (pa'di'tinn) [Pali] calendar

ปฏิกูล (pa'ti'koon) [Pali] dirty, filthy

ปฏิญาณ (pa'ti'yarn) [Pali] to promise, to declare solemnly

ปฏิบัติ (pa'ti'ha't) [Pali] to serve, to do service ; conduct, practice, performance

ปฏิสนธิ (pa'ti'sonn' [Pali] new birth, renewed existence, new conception

ปฏิเกธ (pa'ti'sett) [Pali] to renounce, gainsay, deny, disavow, prohibit

ปฏิสังขรณ์ (pa'ti'sa'ngkorn) [Pali] to repair, to mend, to restore

ปก (pot) to conceal or evade the truth, to prevaricate

ปดง (pa'dong) a rash

ปแดง (pa'daang) attendants at a court or prison, bailiffs, tipstaffs

ปดัก ปเดิก (pa'da'k pa'dert) difficulty, vexation

ปถม (pa'ta'ma') [Pali] first, foremost

ปทุม and ประทุม (pa'too'm) [Pali] lotus, lily (Alab. 296)

ปน (pon) to mix

ปน (pon) pounded, made small

ปม (pom) knot, swelling

ปรกติ (proka'ti') [Sansk.] in its natural state, in a normal condition, in good order, unimpaired

ปรน (pron) to give a part of, to impart

ปรนนิบัติ (pronni'ba't) [Sansk.] to serve, to take care of, service, duty, function

ปรบ (prop) to clap the hands, to applaud

ปรมาณู (pa'ra'marnoo) [Pali] small particle (a Siamese measure of which there are 512 in one hair)

ปรอง กอง กัน (praung daung ka'n) unanimously, ally; allegiance, to be on good terms

ปรอก (praut) to squeeze out, squirt out

ปรอด (pa'raut) quicksilver นก — a small fruit-eating bird like a thrush

ปรากฏ (prahkot) [Sansk.] to be shown or known; publicly

ปราการ (prahkarn) [Sansk.] wall, rampart, fort สมุท — Paknam (town)

ปราง with พระ (pra'prarng) cheeks

ปรางศ์ (prarng) [Sansk.] obtuse-topped pyramidal column with metal branch coming out from the top; obelisk

ปราจิณ (prahchinn) [Sansk.] West

ปรานี (prahnee) pity, compassion, to favour

ปรารถนา (prahta'nah) [Sansk.] to wish, want, desire

ปราน (prahn) (1) Capital town of a Province (2) [Sansk.] the breath of the nostrils (3) to be indulgent (4) a measure of time

ปราน (prahnee) to like, to show favour to; pity, compassion

ปราบ (prarp) to equalise, to level, to tame, to subjugate

ปราม (prahm) *see* ห้าม

ปราโมช (prahmoht) [Sansk.] joy; to rejoice

ปราย (prai) to scatter ลูก — small shot

ปรารภ (prahrop) to be intent upon, to be anxious about, to desire

ปรารมย์ (prahrom) to be uneasy, anxious, anxiety

ปราลี (prahlee) ridge of a roof

ปราสาท (prahsart) [Sansk.] royal palace, royal residence, royal temple

ปราไสย (prahsai) to confer, to converse amicably

ปริ (pri) (1) to be worn at the edges, nearly worn out, nearly broken (2) oozing out

ปริ (pa'ri') [Pali] around, about

ปฤชา (pri'chah) *and* ปรีชา wise, prudent; knowledge

ปริบ (prip) dropping, dripping, trickling

ปริ่ม (prim) just full, brimming

ปริศนา, ปริศน *better* ปฤษนา q. v.

ปฤษดางศ (pritsa'darng) [Sansk.] the back

ปฤษนา (prissa'nah) [Sansk.] question,

ปรี, ปรีดา *and* ปรีดิ (preedee) [San.]

joyful, glad; pleasure

เปรียง (preeang) noisy, tumultuous

เปรียญ (pa'reean) [San.] student, learned man, having an academical degree, graduate

เปรียบ (preeap) side by side; of equal size, height, length, etc.

เปรียว (preeo) to pursue eagerly, to run after

เปรี้ยว (preeyo) sour, acid

ปรึก (preuk) siccative oil

ปรุ (proo') pierced, full of holes; thoroughly

ปรุง (proo'ng) to put together, to construct, to make up

เปรต (prett) [Sansk.] a kind of ghosts or spirits, shades of the departed

แปร *and* ปรวน (praa, prooa'n) to be changed, to transpose, to displace, to speak differently, to change one's note, to change one's cry

แปรง (praang) brush, mane (of horses, etc.)

แปร้ง (prang) harsh, shrill

แปรน (praan) *and* แปร้น confused, discordant noise

ไปรเวต (praivett) [Engl.] private

ไปรสนีย์ (praisa'nee) [Sansk.] postal letter

โปร่ง (prohng) pierced, having holes in it, hollow, capable of being seen through

โปรด (proht) to grant, remit, pardon, aid, please — ปราน to be kind

โปรย (prohwi') to scatter, to throw about

เปราะ (praw') fragile, breakable ทั้ว — a medicinal plant

ประ (pra') (1) to sprinkle (2) the two dots forming the 17th vowel

ประกวด (pra'kcoa't) to animate one another, to stimulate, to compete

ประกอย (pra'kaup) to put together, to mix ; endowed with, composed of

ประกาย (pra'kai) spark, flash

ประการ (pra'karn) [San.] sort, kind, way, manner, number ก — how many : ทุก — in every way

ประกาศ (pra'kart) [Sansk.] proclamation, public notice, notification

ประกัน (pra'ka'n) to guarantee ; surety, to bail

ประกับ (pra'ka'p) to connect

ประกอง (pra'kaung) to embrace, to take up gently with both hands

ประโคน (pra'kohn) chief column, protector, refuge

ประโคม (pra'kome) concert, serenade

ประจง (pra'chong) softly, carefully, accurately, graciously

ประจบ (pra'chop) (1) to join two ends (2) flattering ; พก — to talk foolishly, to please, to flatter

ประจาน (pra'charn) to insult, affront, abuse, expose

ประจิม (pra'chim) [Sansk.] West

ประจำ (pra'cha'm) to stick to, stay in

ประจักษ์ (pra'cha'k) [Sansk.] to show, manifest, evident

ประจัญ (pra'cha'n) to fight

ประจด (pra'chot) [Sansk.] (1) to make up a number, to add (2) ironical — ประจัน to mark

ประชา (pra'chah) [Sansk.] crowd, multitude, large number

ประชิด (pra'chitt) neighbouring, adjoining

ประชุม (pra'choo'm) to assemble, meeting, assembly

ประชัน (pra'cha'n) to compete in dancing, speaking, etc.

ประดา (pra'dah) whoever, all : — น้ำ diver

ประดิษฐ์ (pra'ditt) [Pali] ประดิษฐ์ [San.] (1) to invent, originate, discover, devise, contrive (2) to establish, imagine, feign, fancy

ประดุจ (pra'doo't) as, as if, like

ประแดง (pra'daang) secretary

ประดัก ประเดิด (pra'da'k pra'dert) great trouble

ประดับ and ประดา (pra'da'p pra'dah) to decorate, adorn, trim

ประตู (pra'too) door, gate

ประทวน (pra'tooan) a deed made in substitution of one that has been lost or destroyed

ประทาน (pra'tarn) [Sansk.] to provide, to give : ใบ — to beg; to eat, to take refreshment

ประทีป (pra'teep) [San.] lantern, lamp, light, enlightening

ประเทือง (pra'teuang) (1) lightly (2) with precaution

ประทุ (pra'too') to burst, to crack, to be broken open

ประทุม (pra'too'm) [Pali] lotus, lily สระ — pond for growing lotus

ประทุษฐ์ (pra'too't) [Sansk.] and ประทุษร้าย [Pali] to injure, to do damage, mischievous

ประเทศ (pra'tett) nation, country, district ต่าง — foreign affairs สากล — — international court

ประทะ (pra'ta') to come into collision, or conflict

ประทัง (pra'ta'ng) (1) to lean (2) relief, convalescence

ประทับ (pra'ta'p) (1) to stop, to encamp, to sit (cf a King or Prince) : (2) to press with the hand — ตรา to seal, to stamp

ประณต (pra'not) to salute, to adore

ประนม (pra'nom) to join hands in saluting

ประนอม (pra'naum) to agree, to consent ประนี — to agree

ประณาม (pra'narm) to exclude from a temple, to excommunicate

ประณี (pra'nee) pity, kindness, compassion — ประนอม indulgent; compassion

ประณีต (pra'necta') [Sansk.] perfected, accomplished, carefully done

ประบ่า (pra'bah) to spread over the shoulders

ประบัด (pra'ba't) to defraud, to entangle

ประพรม (pra'prom) to sprinkle

ประพรรณ (pra'pa'n) form, shape, kind

ประพฤติ (pra'preu't) [Sansk.] to do, act

ประพาศ (pra'paht) [Sansk.] to take a walk, to travel

ประเพณี (pra'paynee) [Sansk.] usage, habit, customary right

ประภาษ (pra'paht) [Sansk.] brightened, shining

ประเภท (pra'payt) [Sansk.] custom, habit, sort, kind

ประมวน (pra'mooan) to collect, total

ประมง (pra'mong) fishing, fisherman

ประหม่า (pra'mah) to tremble, fear, dread

ประมาณ (pra'mahn) [Sansk.] (1) almost, nearly, on the point of : (2) to conjecture, compute

ประมาท (pra'mart) [Sansk.] careless, besotted, stupid

ประมูล (pra'moon) (1) to bid a higher price (2) to collect, to gather

ประบูร (pra'yoon and pra'yoora') [San.] pertaining to the family

ประโยชน์ (pra'yote) [Pali] use, purpose, object, utility, advantage ; to conduct, to improve ผล — proceeds

ประหยัด (pra'ya't) to be cautious

ประราด (pra'raut) quicksilver นก — a common bird like a thrush

ประรามาท (pra'rahmart) to use insulting language, to insult

ประระมาศ (pra'ra'maht) [Sansk.] to stroke, to touch, to handle

ประรำ (pra'ra'm) bamboo shed with flat cloth roof or awning ; hut

ประหลาด (pra'laht) wonderful, marvellous, singular, strange, extraordinary

ประลาศ (pra'laht) [Sansk.] to take flight

ประไลย (pra'lai) [Sansk.] to be consumed, destroyed ; destruction

ประโลม (pra'lohm) to embrace, to caress, to woo

ประวิง (pra'wing) to delay

ประเวณี (pra'waynee) [Sansk.] custom, rule, conjugal laws

ประเวศ (pra'wett) [San.] to travel, to go

ประหวัด (pra'wa't) to remember affectionately

ประหวั่น (pra'wa'n) to fear

ประสก (pra'sok) layman

ประสงร์ (pra'song) to need, to want

ประสบ (pra'sop) to meet with, to find

ประสม (pra'som) to join, collect, unite

ประเสริฐ (pra'seut) [Sansk.] precious, excellent

ประสาน (pra'sahn) to join : น้ำ — solder : — — ทอง borax

ประสิทธิ (pra'sit) [Sansk.] to depend upon, dependence, to end, to give

ประสิว with ดิน (din pra'siew) nitre

ประสูท (pra'soot) [Sansk.] to bring forth, give birth to

ประหาร (pra'harn) [Sansk.] to strike, to hurt

ประหัสบดี better พฤหัส q. v., the planet Jupiter :

ปรัก (pra'k) [Cambod.] money

ปรักปร่ำ (pra'k pra'm) to do on compulsion, disagreeable work

ปรัด (pra't) to brush off with the hand

ปรับ (pra'p) to fine

ปรัศ (pra't) flank, side

ปลง (plong) to let down, deposit, take off (hair, kettle, etc.) — ญ to give ear : — ผ — สา a funeral — ผม to shave the head

ปลด (plot) to disengage, take off, unhook, let loose ; deposit

ปล้น (plon) to rob, pillage, plunder

ปลวก (plooa'k) white ants

ปลอก (plauk) circle, ring, hoop, bandage of cloth, etc., wrapper — นิ้ว thimble

ปล่อง (plaung) tube, hollow, cylinder, spout : — ควัน funnel, chimney

ปล้อง (plaung) jointed, knotted, having alternate lengths of different kinds or appearance ; a kind of reed

ปล้อน (plaun) (1) to eat quickly (2) to open and take out, to pick out, to extract

ปลอบ (plaup) to flatter, to sooth, to appease

ปลอม (plaum) spurious, counterfeit, disguised, adulterated, fraudulent

ปล่อย (ploi) to let go, deliver, relinquish : — เสีย to let off, release

ปลา (plah) fish น้ำ — pickle of fish or prawns ไก — rotten entrails of fish ผัก — dishes — ย่าง smoked fish — แห้ง dried fish [Note: this word is prefixed to the name of most fish]

ปลาบ *and* — แปลบ (plahp, plaap) sting, acute feeling (of grief, etc.)

ปลาย (plarp) a plant

ปลาย (plai) point, top, tail, end, extremity ข้าว — final — มือ end of all — น้ำ source of a river

ปลิง (pling) (1) leach — ทะเล edible sea leach (2) vice, clamp, rivet

ปลิด (plit) to break off, pluck off, gather (fruit, etc.)

ปลิ้น (plin) (1) to escape by prevaricating, to wriggle out (2) prominent, projecting; (3) to turn a thing inside out คน — rogue

ปลิโพธ (pa'li'poht) [Pali] obstacle, impediment, affair, business, important occupation

ปลิว (pliew) to float in the air, to be wafted

เปลีย (pleea) feeble; to stumble — น้ำ

just above the water

ปลี (plee) blossom of banana tree — น่อง calf of the leg

ปลีก (pleek) (1) to go aside (2) to divide into small pieces (3) by retail เงิน — small money

เปลี่ยน (pleean) to change — แทน to replace

เปลี่ยว (pleeoo') (1) abandoned, solitary, lonely (2) hump, hump-back วัว — a bull

เปลม (pleum) pleased, cheerful; to rejoice

เปลือก (pleua'k) rind, shell, husk, bark

เปลือง (pleua'ng) to be consumed, expended, squandered

เปลื้อง (pleua'ng) to strip, to take off

เปลือย (pleui') naked, unclothed, nude

เปลย (plewey) long enough, going far enough

ปลุก (pleo'k) (1) to awake (a person) (2) to make sacred นาฬิกา — alarum

ปลูก (plook) to plant, to build — ฝี to vaccinate — ฝัง to marry one's children, to bring up (a person)

เปล (pla) cradle, litter — ไทย hanging and swinging cradle made of bamboo — ยวน do. of net-work

เปล่ง (pleng) rounded, plump, chubby, well filled out; to shine

เปลว (plaoo) flame — หมู hog's lard

แปล (plaa) to interpret, translate, explain

แปล้ (plaa') curved outwards, flattish

แปลก (plaak) different, changed, strange, unrecognized, grown out of remembrance .

แปลง (plaang) (1) marsh, wallowing-place, quagmire, bog, slough (2) to change, transform, transmutation (3) brush

แปลน (plaan) [Engl.] plan made by a Surveyor

แปลบ (plaap) acute pain

เปลา (plowe) tall and fine, long and slender

เปล่า (plow) at leisure, vacant, empty, void, nothing, no (a negation) เสีย — in vain

เปล้า (plow!) (1) a tree (2) a dove

เปลาะ (plaw') to tie together, cord, tie

ปล้ำ (pla'm) to wrestle

ปล่ะ (pla') to let go, let loose, dismiss ปล่อย — to let go ไก่ — wild hen

ปลัก (pla'k) mud, mire, puddles

ปลั่ง (pla'ng) (1) plump, sleek, smooth, full, well-liking (2) bright, to shine

ปลัด (pla't) lieutenant, locum tenens, deputy หฺวง — Deputy Governor, Second Governor — กรม deputy official

ปวง (pooa'ng) and ทั้ง — all, the whole

ปวง (poowung) indigestion, cholera

ปวด (pooa't) pain, ache, to be in pain — ฟัน tooth-ache เจ็บ — to be seriously injured and offended

ปวน (poo'an) to be anxious, troubled, uneasy

ปวน (poowun) (1) unreasonably, wrong, (2) to be busied, busy

ปวย (pooi') to be ill — การ to waste time, to do in vain ค่า — การ compensation

ปวะหล่ำ (pa'wa'la'm) bracelet of beads

เปอ (paw) bark for making ropes

เปอ (paw) boastful, pretentions — แป weak — ยอ to give gifts

ปอก (pauk) to peel, pare, strip, take off

ปอง (paung) to conspire, to plot against, to make plans

ป่อง (paung) (1) proud, boastful แมงป่อง — scorpion (2) rounded, bulging out, swoln

ป้อง (paung) to shade the eyes

ปอด (paut) lungs

ป่อน (pawn) worn out, deciepit, delapidated, wretched

ป้อน (paun) to put anything into an aperture, (as food into the mouth)

ป้อม (pawm) fort, citadel — ล้อม วัง walls of the palace

ปอย (poi) a hank of thread, a wisp, a handful (of hair, etc.)

ป่า (pah) to throw

ป่า (parr) wood, forest ; (as adjective) wild — กึง wood of many trees, forest — ช้า cemetery, grave — แกง underwood, stunted wood

ป้า (par) elder sister of a father or mother

ป่าก (park) mouth — ไก้ and — กา pen — น้ำ mouth of a river - - คีบ compasses — ยัก quarrelsome, talkative — หวาน very polite, treacherous

ปาง and ป้าง (parng) [Laos.] time, when

ป้าง (pahng) liver complaint

ปาณา (parnah) [Pali] life, spirit

ปาด (part) (1) a green frog (2) to shave off the top or end, to make level, to smooth over

ปาติโมกข์ (parti'mohk) [Pali] sacred book of precepts (Alab. 190)

ปาน (pahn) (1) like, equal, to equal (2) black spot on the skin

ปาน (parn) string, packthread เชือก — twine

ป้าน (parn) (1) blunt, blunted, obtuse (2) Chinese earthen tea-pot

ป้านนี (parnnee) late, too late

ปาโมกข์ (parmohk) [Pali] in front, first, principal, excellent

ปาย (pai) to swing the foot out sideways

ป้าย (paie) (1) to smear over with dirt or colour, etc. (2) [Chin.] mark, signboard, notice

ปายาศ (pahyaht) [Pali] rice porridge made for Buddha, milk-rice

ปาริโส (pahri'soh) [Pali] comrade, attendant, aquaintance

เป่า (powe) to publish, divulge — ประกาศ to proclaim — ร้อง to promulgate, announce

ปาสัง (pahsa'ng) [Pali] to bind (a dead body) round with looped cords

ปิ้ง (ping) to roast, toast, boil, bake

ปิฎก (pi'dok) [Sansk.] basket ไตร — the three baskets or Treasuries containing the teachings of Buddha, Buddhist scriptures (Alab. 166)

ปิด (pit) to shut: — เงิน to cover with silver

ปิตุ (pittoo') [Sansk.] father

ปิตุลา (pittoo'lah) [Sansk.] uncle

ปิน (pinn) [Engl.] hair-pin

ปิ่ม (pim) like, as, as if — จะ on the point of, about to

ปิยะ ปิโย and ปิยะ (pi'yah, pi'yoh, pi'ya') [Pali] dear, well-behaved, agreeable, loving, pleasure, love

เปียว (pew') [Chin.] small, diminutive

ปิศาจ and ปิสาจ (pi'sart) [Sansk. and Pali] demon, devil, goblin, ghost

ปี (pee) year หัว — beginning of the year ลูก หัว — eldest child

ปี่ (pee) a reed instrument made of hard wood, oboe — ชวา Javanese oboe

ปี (pee) (1) pounded, broken (2) a small copper earthenware or glass coin (3) rosin seal which is attached every three years to the Chinese in Siam เสีย — to pay the triennial tribute and take the seal (4) to copulate, to tread

ปี่ (pee?) half closed (eyes)

ปี๋ (pee?) [Chin.] a game (with cards, etc.), numerical designation of Chinese games of cards

ปีก (peek) wing; — ไม้ slab, outside plank of tree

ปีติ (peeti') [Pali] joy, delight, satiety (Alab. 196)

ปีน (peen) to mount, to climb, to go up

ปีบ (peep) (1) roar of the tiger (2) a case or can for oil and other liquids

เปีย (peeya') [Chin.] Chinaman's pigtail ขนม — a cake

เปียก (peea'k) wet, moist, damp เข้า — boiled rice

เปี่ยม (peea'm) filled up, full to the top

เปียว (peeyo) a very small land-crab

ปึก (peuk) a lump, a cake of sugar, etc.

ปึง (peung) [phon.] sudden sound of a blow

ปึง (peung) proud, ostentatious

ปึง (peung) [Chin.] (1) rice (2) numerical designation of volumes

ปึง (peung?) to tear in two, sound of tearing

ปืน (peun) gun — สั้น pistol — โก revolver ลูก — cannon-ball, shot, bullet, cartridge, dumbbell, projectile

ปืน (peun) (1) blade (of saw) (2) blunt

เปื้อน (peuan) stained, dirty, confused หมอง — dirt

เปื่อย (peuey) worn out, rotten, decomposed, putrefying — เน่า rotten, putrid — น้ำเน่า boiled down, liquefied

ปุก (poo'k) noise of stamping or hammering ตีน — club foot

ปุ้งกี๋ (poo'ngkee) [Chin.] a shovel-shaped basket

ปุจฉา (poo'tchah) [Pali] question, to interrogate

ปุญญะ (poo'nya') [Pali] (1) full, complete (2) merit, virtue, goodworks, piety

ปุ (poo'p) and — ปุ [phon.] a sound, as of fish leaping

ปุย (pooi') tinder made of pith

ปุริสา (poo'ri'sah) and ปุริโส [Pali] man

ปุระ (poo'ra') [Sansk.] town

ปู (poo) (1) a crab (2) to spread, to lay out

ปู่ (poo) paternal grandfather — ทวด great-grandfather เจ้า — tutelary genius

ปูเปี้ย (poo peo) pounded, broken, damaged

ปูน (poon) (1) to add (2) lime — กัก quick lime (3) time — ก่อน [of fruit] first growth — หลัง last growth

ปูม (poom) calendar ผ้า — a silk cloth

เป and เป๋ (pay) inclined, oblique, out of the perpendicular

เป๊ก (payk) [phon.] noise of a small object striking anything

เปิง (peng) swoln, tumid, full

เปิง (peng) (1) a tree (2) [phon.] sound of striking (3) numerical designation of blows or strokes (4) [of a blow] direct

เป็ด (pett) duck — ไก่ poultry — น้ำ wild duck — เทศ muscovy duck

เปตา (paytah) [Pali] departed spirits, ghosts, sinners in a state of purgatory (Alab. 189. and see also Virg. Aen, VI. 329. 615)

เปน (pen) *sometimes less properly spelt* เปน to be, to be alive — การ it succeeds — คือ chiefly, principally — แค่ only — ได้ possible — มา to happen — ไป to become — ว่า that is to say, such as, for example ไม่ — unable, not knowing how ห้า — knowing how to do ไม่ — อะไร no matter: (sometimes used for forming an adjective or adverb, as) — ที่เปน painful: [this word means also " in a state of," as] — อยู่ — คือ to remain at peace

เปก (perk) torn at the edges, frayed, having, holes in it

เปง (perng) [Maun.] rice

เปง (perng) [of a roof] damaged วิ่ง เกลิก เปก — running off into hiding, absconding

เปง ๆ (perng perng) loud sound

เปง มาง (perng marng) a long-shaped drum

เบิก (pert) to open — ไว้ to reveal

เปป (perp) to take up with the hand to the mouth

เปป (perp) noise [of an animal roaring, etc.]

แปป (paa) joists

แปป (paa) weak

แปง (paang) (1) meal, flour (2) paint

แปด (paat) (1) to mix, to be mixed (2) [Chin.] eight — เก้า a game

แปน (paan) (1) flat-shaped, flat, platform, stage (2) instrument for wiredrawing ปลา — a small flat fish

แปป (paap) pinched, pressed together, slender, thin ถั่ว — a bean

แปว (paao) not quite round

แปะกัก (paa'ka'k) [Chin.] (1) a fruit (2) a long knife *or* chopper

ไป (pai) to go, to become, *as* สุก — to ripen บ้า — to go mad — ไหนมา where have you been to?

ไป (pai) [Laos.] no, not

โป (poh) [Chin.] (1) quadrilateral brass tube used in gambling (2) [Chin.] dice กัก — dice board (3) a projection (of bone, skin, etc.)

ไป๋ (poe) [Chin.] brass instrument for gambling

ไป๋ปก (poe pot) a liar, lying

ไป้ง (pohng) covering of cloth, etc., case, hiding-place, shelter

ไป้ง (pohng) [phon.] (1) sound of a blow (2) loud

ไป๊ะ (poh') [Chin.] fish-stakes, globe or shade [of a lamp]

เป้า (pow) hump, swelling

เป้า (pow) to blow

เป้า (pow!) target, mark, butt

เป้าะ (paw') [phon.] sound of blows — เหลาะ smaller in size

ปะ (pa') (1) to patch, to mend, to repair (2) to meet with, to find (3) [a prefix like pro or præ in Latin]

ปะฏิทิน (pa'di'tin) and ประฏิทิน [Pali] date

ประราชิก (pa'rahchik) [Pali] priest guilty of unpardonable sin, and deserving expulsion

ประริทา (pa'ri'tah) [Pali] (1) protection (2) one of the Buddhist heavens

ปะเรียญ (pa'reean) better ปเรียญ [San.] a man having an academical degree

ประร่ำ (pa'ra'm) stable for elephants

ประระมาณ (pa'ra'marnoo) [Pali] atom, particle

ประระนิมิตร (pa'ra'ni'mit) [Pali] created by others, pleasures produced by others — วัสวัทิ having at one's disposal pleasures produced by others (name of the highest Deva heaven. Alab. 213)

ประระมะ (pa'ra'ma') [Pali] perfection, excellence, merit

ปะลู (pa'loo) [Chin.] a hatchet

เปะเหลาะ (pa'law') to flatter, to cajole

ปะแล่ม (pa'laam) a little, partly, a taste

ประเวศน์ (pra'wayt) [Pali] to go, to proceed, to travel

ประวะล่ำ (pa'wa'la'm) bead

ประวะล่ำ กำไล (pa'wa'la'm ka'mlai) bracelets เสมา ประวะล่ำ locket

ปัก (pa'k) to plant, to fix, to set, to put in นา — a field of transplanted rice — ผ้า to embroider

ปักษา (pa'ksah) [Sansk.] male bird ปัก ษี female bird

ปัจจามิตร (pa'tchahmitt) and ปัจนึก [Pali] enemy, adversaries

ปังสุ (pa'ngsoo') [Pali] dust, fine earth

ปา (ฺpa'tchoo') to strip, to take off

ปาปัน (pa'tchoo'ba'n) *and* ปัตยปัน [Pali *and* Sansk.] the present โรคะ — cholera

ปาไสมย (pa'tchoo'sa'mai) [Pali] at early dawn, a little before sun-rise

ปาเอกะ (pa'tchayka') [Pali] by himself, one by one, each — โพธิ a Buddha who does no teaching [Alab. 187]

ปัญญา (pa'nyah) [Pali] reason, intelligence, genius, talent, sense, wisdom, intellect [Alab. 184]

ปัณหา *and* ปัญหา (pa'nhah) Pali question

ปัด (pa't) to sweep, brush, wipe away ปัดง — broom ลูก — grains of glass, beads

ปัถพี (pa'tta'pee) *and* ปัถวี (pa'ta'wee) [Pali] earth

ปัน (pa'n) to divide, to apportion

ปั่น (pa'n) to turn, to revolve, to be rolled round — ฝาย to spin cotton

ปั้น (pa'nn) to make out of mud or clay — ลม beam with projecting peak on the edge of a Siamese roof — จั่น crane (for lifting)

ปัศจัน (pa'ssa'ta'n) cartridge ปลอก — cartridge case

ปัศ (pa'ssa'ti') [Pali] to look at, observe, see, know, discover

ปัสสาวะ (pa'ssahwa') [Pali] urine

ปัสสาสะวาต (pa'ssahsa'waht) [Pali] breath

ปัสสัทธิ (pa'ssa'tti') [Pali] calmness, repose of the mind, confidence [Alab. 196]

◆ ◆ ◆ ◆

ผ

ผ (paw pee   English *p.* Pali *and* Sansk. *ph.* Labial : a high letter) — ผ name of this letter

ผก (pok) to jump up ผัน — *and* — ผัน dodging about, shying and rearing, fidgety

ผคุน (pa'khoo'n) [Pali] 4th month (of the old calendar)

ผง (pong) *and* — คลี powder, dust

ผงก (pa'ngok) (vulg. กระงก) to raise the head, to raise anything which is inclined sideways, to raise one side up from the level

ผงาก (pa'ngart) to jump, to rush

ผงะ (pa'nga') starting backwards, drawing back

ผจญ (pa'chon) [Sansk.] to fight, to attack, to invade

ผด (pot) prickly heat, spots, tumours

ผดุง (pa'doo'ng) to construct, build, support, sustain, nourish, take care of

ผน (pon) beyond bounds, beyond measure

ผนวก (pa'nooak) to add, addition

ผนวช (pa'nooa't) [Pali] ordination of priests who are princes

ผนิต (pa'nitt) to stop up

ผนึก (pa'neuk) to seal, to close up, to mount (a paper, etc.)

แผนก (pa'naak) class, order, category, division

ผนัก ผนวง (pa'na'k pa'nooa'ng) to stick fast, to be slow about going

ผนัง (pa'na'ng) walls ฝา — partition wall

ผม (pom) (1) I, me, [respectful term] (2) hair — ม้า mane

เผยอ (pa'yerr) (1) proud (2) to open the wings, to soar (3) to open partially, to raise a little (4) to come of one's own accord

ผรศ (pa'ra'soo') [Sansk.] small axe, hatchet

ผรูต (pa'roo't) [Pali] rude, insulting, harsh, unkind

ผล (pon) [Pali] fruit, produce (Alab. 200) เป็น — useful ผรรค — degrees of sanctity, stage or path of sanitification — ประโยชน์ utility advantage, use — ไม้ (ponla'mai) fruit

ผลอ (plaw) plausibly, with maoy deceitful words

ผลา and ผะลา (pa'lah) [Pali] fruit, produce, result

ผลาญ (plahn) to disperse, plunder, destroy

ผลิ (pli') bud, opening of a flower

ผลิ ผลาม (plee plahm) ill-mannered, ill-bred

ผลึก (pa'leuk) glass

ผลุน (ploo'n) suddenly — ผลัน with a sudden start, starting quickly

ผลุม ผลาม (ploo'm plarm) mischievous, vexatious

ผลุ (ploo) (1) suddenly (2) [Cambod.] a path, a road

เผล (play) crooked, not straight, with prevarication

เผลอ (pler) incautious, reckless, rash

แผล (plaa) sore place, wound ปาก — cut, gash, wound with a cutting instrument

แผลง (plaang) to put forth one's whole strength, to pull or shoot forcibly (2) to alter the form of, to substitute; derivation of one word from another — ศร to shoot with a bow and arrows — ฆ่าน to kill — ฤทธิ to exert one's full strength

ใหล เผลอ (plai pler) and เผลอไผล to forget

ไผล and ไผล่ (plie) out of the line, out of the regular order — ขา to cross the legs — หน and — ออก to go away to one side or round a corner หลด — (1) to fall over the edge (2) to go in different directions, separate, out of sight — ซ่อน to get out of sight, to go into hiding

ผละ (pla') separate from — ผลัก to push back

ผลัก (pla'k) to repel, to push

ผลัด (pla't) to change places, to change, alternate — กัน alternately

ผวน (pooa'n) back, turning back

ผวย (pooi') [Chin.] cloak, cape

ผวา (pa'wah) (1) starting up quickly, awaking suddenly (2) headlong, falling forward, swooping down — ถึง to take with a swoop, to pounce upon

ผัว (pooa') husband — เมีย husband and wife

ผสม (pa'som) to put together, to add; mixed, blended

เพก (pawk) priests' dinner time [about 11 a.m.]

ผ่อง (porng) clear, pure

ผ่อน (porn) to take out a part, to take a little at a time -- ปรน to take away parts and put them together

ผอม (paum) thin, lean, meagre

เผอย (poi) to drop suddenly, to drop off to sleep, drooping eyelids

ผา (pah) rocks

ผ่า (par) to slit, to cleave, to split; cleft, cut — ฝนไป to rush through, to make one's way through a crowd

ผ้า (par) cloth — เช็ดหน้า handkerchief — เช็ดมือ towel, napkin — นุ่ง panung, the lower garment worn by the Siamese — โปร่ง lace — ม่าน curtain — เหลือง the saffron coloured cloth of priests — ห่ม scarf, veil นุ่ง — to put on the panung — ลาย chintz — ขาว ผ้า scarf — ไหว้ cloth presented to parents of a bride

ผาก (pahk) dried up หน้า — front, brow, forehead

ผาง (pahng) [phon.] sound (of wave, etc)

ผาด (part) (1) passing, past (2) handsome, well-looking — แผด too hot, loud — โผ to jump, to flit — เส้ง to shout out loud

ผาน (parn) to plough, turn up, plough — ไถ ploughshare

ผ่าน (pahn) to pass in front of, to walk past — ราคา to ask more than the price ม้า — piebald horse

ผานิท see นาท

ผานิต (pahnitt) [Pali] molasses

ผาย (paie) to bend outwards on each side, to open, spread out, extended ยา — medicine for expelling wind — ลม pudere — ผืน to walk, to go

ผาสุข (pahsoo'k) [Pali] peace, happiness

ผิ (pee') and ผิว (pee'wa') if, if so ผี (pee') more

ผิง (ping) to put close to the fire or the heat, to expose oneself to the sun

ผิชะนาน (pitcha'na'n) and ผิชน if so

ผิด (pit) erroneous, mistaken, false, wrong, vicious, to fail, to err, to commit a fault — กัน to differ, unlike, opposite — ชอบ right or wrong, good or bad — ไป to mistake, to err — เพี้ยน discordant, erroneous — เมีย adultery ทำ — to fail; error, fault ผู้ — transgressor

ผิน (pinn) to turn round, to reverse

ผิว (piew) the outside, epidermis, cuticle, skin — พรรณ good outward appearance, conplexion — ป่าก to whistle

ผี (pee) dead body, spirit, ghost, demon, evil genius กัน — to protect from evil spirits — กระ สือ demon who eats the entrails of pregnant women — เข้า possessed by a demon ใช้ — to send a demon to any one เสือ —

and เส้น to sacrifice to a demon

หมอ — sorcerer — เสื้อ butterfly

— ฝัน nightmare

ผีก (peek) the fourth part of a tanan

ผึง (peung) noise of breaking

ผึง (peung) (1) hatchet, plane, adze (2) broad, spreading out, to dry in the sun or wind

ผึง (peung) bee น้ำ — honey รัง — bee-hive ขี้ — wax ขาง ขี้ — ointment made of wax

ผืน (peune) the length of a panung (numerical designation of panungs, mats, table-cloths, skins, etc.)

ผื่น (peun) spots or swellings on the skin

เผื่อ (peua') [Laos.] companion, comrade, friend

เผื่อ (peua) that which is handed over by one person to another

เผือก (peuak) (1) white (of elephant), albino, pale (2) a kind of potato

เผือก (peua't) pale, faded, subsiding, diminishing

เผื่อน *with* บัว (booa' peua'n) small water lily

ผุ (poo') to become rotten — ผุย crumbling

ผุด (poo't) (of water) to spring out, (of fish) to jump

ผุบผับ (poo'p pa'p) noise of sudden and hurried movement

ผุย (pooi') powder, to pound ผุ — crumbling

ผู้ (poo) (1) [noun of animate things] person, persons — ใด who, some one, any body — ดี gentleman — อื่น other people : [with verb, noun of the agent, as] — ว่า governor of a Province (2) [designation of the sex, as] — ชาย male (of men) ตัว — male (of animals) — หญิง female

ผูก (pook) (1) to tie, to join, to compose (poems, etc.) to attach — โซ่ to chain — กอีก เบีย to lend at interest — ม้า to saddle — รัก to put to — เวร to be revengeful, to take vengeance — อากร etc. to farm revenues, etc.

เผง *and* แผ่ง (peng) [phoa.] sound (as of a blow)

เผ็ด (pett) pungent แผ่— to retaliate, revenge

เผ่น (penn) *and* — โผน to jump, to run with jumps

เผย (poey) to open a little

เผอ เรอ (per rer) slatternly, untidy, slovenly

เผิน (pern) ill-fitting, imperfectly filled, carelessly done, infirm

แผ่ (paa) to spread, to stretch out — ยาง to make thin, beat out flat

แผก (paak) fault, mistake

แผง (paang) bamboo mat

แผด (paat) a loud cry — แผ่ a prolonged noise

แผน (paan) figure, form, representation — ที่ map

แผ่น (paan) flat, superficies, flat piece, sheet — เงิน silver in flat sheets — ดิน globe, earth — เหล็ก sheet iron

แผ่ว (pao) lightly, to touch lightly

ไผ (pai) [Laos.] person, whoever, everyone

ไผ่ (pai) bamboo

โผ (poh) to rush — เผ feeble, weak — โผน jumping

โผง (pohng) [phon.] noise (as of waves)

โผก โผน (poht pohn) to jump

เผา (pow) to set fire to

เผ่า (pow) (1) race, family, breed — พวก kinsfolk, relations (2) feeling of warmth

เผาะ (paw') [phon.] noise of breaking or bursting

ผะเดียง (pa'deea'ng) to invite priests

ผะยูง (pa'yoo'ng) to sustain a burden

ผะลา *and* ผะละ (pa'lah *and* pa'la') [Pali] fruits, crops

ผัก (pa'k) vegetable : — ชี coriander: — ชี ล้อม cucumber - - ชี ลาว parsley : — กูด fern : — กาด radish — กาด หอม lettuce — กราด vegetable of which the leaf is eaten

ผัง (pa'ng) shape or model of bamboo house — ตรา ชู scale of a balance

ผัด (pa't) (1) to fry (2) to paint (the face) (3) to irritate (an elephant) (4) to delay (5) ไม้ — 18th vowel, q. v.

ผัน (pa'n) to turn, to roll, to turn and go away ผ่อน — to pay *or* do by degrees — อักษร to intone words

ผันทนะ (pa'nta'na') [Pali] (1) covetousness (2) a tree

————•◆•————

ผ

ผ (phaw phon = English ph. or f. Labial : a high letter) ผน na me of this letter

ผน (phon) (1) rain (2) to rub on a stone — ทอง to apply to a touchstone : the strokes over the vowel หิน — ทอง touchstone –- ชะลาน January rains, mango showers

ผรั่ง (fa'ra'ng) white men, Europeans ลูก — หิน — guava

ผรั่น (fa'ra'n) saffron

ผัว (phoo'a') to fade

ผอ (phaw) attenuated, compressed, to squeeze ใจ — to be afraid

ผอย (foy) down : — ฝน drizzle, fog กุ้ง — very small prawns — ทอง (1) fritter (2) a tree

ผา (farr) (1) wall, lid of vessel, crust or cream on a liquid : — แฝก double,

twin — ผนัง partition wall — ชี tall pointed basket-work lid for covering dishes, etc. usually covered with red cloth (2) measure of 25 inches

ผ่า (far) (1) palm (of the hand), sole (of the foot) (2) to act in opposition to any one's orders

ผ้า (fah) black spot, dusky, dark, dim — กระ ใก obscurity or blot on a glass, etc. — กลอน board covering the peak of a roof — แผล skin covering a wound

ผ่าก (fark) to deposit, entrust, send หนังสือ — letter — หนังสือ to send a letter

ผาง (farng) a red wood used for dyeing ; sapan wood

ผาก (faht) bitter, sharp-tasting, acid

ผาน (fahn) to cut into thin flat pieces, to slice

ผ่าย (fai) (1) dam for stopping water (2) a company having particular objects

ผ่าย (faie) part, on the side of — ว่า concerning, regarding, as for — ฝัก to give oneself up to

ผ้าย (fai) cotton, thread

ผ๊ก (fit) *better* พ๊ก sound of sneezing

ผิน (phinn) opium

ผี (phee) (1) boil, tumour, ulcer : — กาฬ small-pox (2) something which proceeds from, *as* — มือ dexterity — ปาก language, eloquence — พาย oarsmen

ผ (phee) snoring

ผึก (pheuk) to exercise — ใ? to restrain the desires

ผึก (pheut) with difficulty

เผือ (pheua') (1) a measure of 50 wah (2) to forget

เผือก (pheua'k) (1) splinters for setting a wound (2) a hurdle of reeds for shutting in fish (3) litter for a dead body, bier

เผือน (feua'n) (1) changed for the worse: (2) bitter, sour, ill-flavoured, unpalatable

ผุ่น (phoo'n) fine dust — ขาว white lead — ฝอย sweepings

ผุ่น (phoo'n) soft, elastic, disturbed (of water)

ผูง (foong) a crowd, a flock, a squadron, acquaintances, intimates, comrades

แผก (phaak) a grass used for roofing

แผง (phaang) to hide, conceal ; ambiguous

แผด (phaat) twin, double ยา — love philtre

ใผ ผัน (phai pha'n) to be desirous about, to think about

ใผ (phai) pimple, pustule

เผา (phow) (1) to watch, observe, attend, take care of — ยาม to stand sentry — ลัย to provoke — เลียน to mimic (2) to go to see the King or a Prince ข้า — courtiers

ผัก (pha'k) case, sheath, pod

ผัง (pha'ng) to bury, inter, put in the earth

ผัง (pha'ng) sea shore, bank

ผัด (pha't) to winnow, sift

ผัน (pha'n?) to dream

ผัน เผือ (fa'n feua) (1) to visit often, to associate with (2) to forget, not to recognise

———— •••• ————

พ

พ (*paw pin* = English *p*. Sansk. *v*. and

b. Labial: a low letter) — พฺภฺ name of this letter

พก (pok) the knot *or* pocket of the panung

พง (pong) clump, cluster [of trees, rushes, etc.] — พง *and* — ไพร jungle — พงศี wooded place

พงษ (pong) [Sansk.] *and* พงษา (pong-sah) [Pali] kindred, relations, family ฑกง — of royal blood พงษาวะดาร annals of the kingdom

พจน (pot) พจนา (potcha'nah) *and* พจนากถิ (potcha'naht) [Pali] word, expression, term เอกพจน (gramm.) singular พหุพจน plural

พจมาน (potcha'marn) [Pali] soft speech, pleasant expressions

พณ หว เจ้า ท่าน (pa'na'hooa chow tahn) title of a Minister

พดด้วง (potdooa'ng) making of a round tical [by bending in the edges]

พน (pon) [Pali] forest, wood — สณฑ์ (pona'sonn) thick forest

พน (pon) to blow out a liquid from the mouth, to squirt at

พ้น (ponn) beyond, later than, past, to

pass through, to get out, to be delivered — ก (1) off, away from, away (2) supreme

พนม (pa'nom) [Cambod.] (1) to join at the tops or edges (2) shrubbery, grove (3) mountains, hills — เปญ capital of Cambodia

พนาดอน (pa'nahdaun) [Pali] wood of full-grown trees

พนาไลย (pa'nahlai) [Pali] woods, deserts, solitudes

พนาวาศี (pa'nahwaht) *and* พนาเวศ (pa'nahwett) [Pali] living in [the wood

พนาวัน (pa'nahwa'n) [Pali] forest

พนาสณฑ์ (pa'nahsonn) [Pali] dense forest, thick covert

พนาส (pa'nahsee) [Pali] woods, wooded

พนักงาน (pa'na'kngarn) official, public servant, holder of an office; employment, ministry, duty, office

พนัน (pa'na'n) to bet, wager, to offer a bet — กัน to agree to a bet, to make a match

พนัด (pa'na't) [Pali] boundaries of a forest

พบ (pop) to meet with, fall in with, find

พม่า (pa'mah) Burmese

พยนต์ (pa'yonn) small statue or doll used for superstitious purposes, scarecrow, wheel

พยากรณ์ (pa'yahkorn) [Pali] predictions of the sages, oracles

พยาธิ (pa'yaht) [Sansk.] a malady in which the flesh is without feeling

พยาน (pa'yahn) and ผู้ญาณ (pooyahn) witness สืบ — to interrogate a witness, to examine a witness

พยาบาท (pa'yahbaht) [Pali] revenge, resentment, hatred

พยาบาล (pa'yahbahn) [Sansk.] to take care of โรง — hospital

พยายาม (pa'yahyahm) [Pali] patience, long suffering, perseverence, continuous action, exertion, contention, striving

พยุง (pa'yoong) to support, sustain, bear a weight

พยุน (pa'yoo'n) soft

พยุ (pa'yoo') [Pali] tempest, storm

พยุห (pa'yoo') [Pali] host, multitude, advancing troops

พยุหรณ์ (pa'yoo'honn) [Sansk.] sum of an addition, total

พยัก (pa'ya'k) to make signs — พะยัก to keep on repeating the same thing

พยัคฆ์ or พยัฆ (pa'ya'kh) and พยัฆ [Pali] tiger

พยัคฆี (pa'ya'kkhee) tigress

พยัญชน (pa'ya'ncha'na') [Pali] consonant

พร (paun) [Pali] blessing, benediction, boon, favour อวย — compliment, good wishes

พรต (prot) ascetic, anchorite, saint

พรม (prom) (1) rugs, carpets (2) to sprinkle — พรำ to sprinkle abundantly with small drops ไม้ — frame with handles for carrying, litter (3) a tree

พรหม (prohm) [Pali] superior angels; Brahma — จารีย virtuous, chaste, virtue

พรรค (pa'k or pa'kkha') [San.] troop, company, division — พวก followers

พรรคม and พรรคม (pa'tta', pa't) [San. health, prosperity, to succeed

พรรณ or พรรณ (pa'nna', pa'n) [San.] (1) form, colour, kind, genus, quality (2) seed

พรรณราย (pa'nna'rai) [San.] radiant, splendid

พรรณรังษี (pa'nna'ra'ngsee) [Sansk.] glitter, lustre, sheen

พรรณา (pan'nah) [Sansk.] to describe

พรษ (pa'sa') and พรรษา (pa'nsah) [Sansk.] rain, year, age

พรวน (prooa'n) a row of small bells used on the necks of animals ลูก — one or more of such bells

พรอง (prong) not full, nearly empty

พรอง (praung) to make a speech, oration, harangue

พรอน (praun) worm-eaten, spoilt

พร้อม (praum) (1) together, altogether, tightly joined, tightly closed (2) finished, completed, ready — ใจ unanimous, consenting

พรอย (proye) shining specks, tinsel — พราย of many bright colours

พร่อย (proy) at random, useless speech, idle talk

พร้อย (proi) covered with spots, spotted

พร้า (prah) big-bladed knife

พราก (prahk) (1) fast-falling, abundant (espec. of tears) (2) to be far

from พริก — bereavement, to take away altogether โกร — [Sansk.] Brahminy goose

พราง (prahng) to keep quiet, dissemble, hide

พราง (prahng) indistinct

พราน (prahn) to hunt, hunter

พราม (prahm) (1) stupid (2) cords or lines attached to the same point

พราหมณ์. พราหมณ์ and พราหมณา (prahmana) [Pali] Brahmin

พราหมณี (prahmma'nee) woman of the Brahmin caste

พราย (prai) bright, sparkling ผี — teraph, an abortive child kept as a charm

พราว (prowe) (1) bright (2) (of a boat) leaky (3) morning

พริก (prik) chili — ไทย pepper — เทศ long pepper นก — a small bird

พริ้ง (pring) (1) joyous (2) pretty, beautiful, attractive

พริบ (prip) to wink, to keep opening and shutting, to twinkle

พริ้ม (prim) beautiful, agreeable

เพรียก (preea'k) crying, bewailing, loud lamentation

เพรียง (preea'ng) a water-worm — ๆ outside of the ear หนๅ — pock-marked

เพรียม (preea'm) pretty, agreeable

เพรียว (preeyu) tapering, well-shaped

พฤกษ (preuksa') and พฤกษา[Sansk.] tree ราย — a tall tree of which the bark is used for medicine

พรึง (preung) connecting planks, side planks, beams, rafters — สกก short ends of an oblong

พรึง and พรึง น (preungnee) to-morrow

พฤฒา (preuttah) [Sansk.] old man

พฤฒามาตย์ (preuttahmaht) [Sansk.] oldest magistrates or dignitaries

พรึบ (preup) a collection of sudden noises, volley

พฤศจิกายน (preusa'chikabyon) [San.] name of the eighth month [of the Scorpion = November]

พฤษภาคม (preusa'pahkom) [Sansk.] name of the second Siamese month [of the Bull = May]

พฤหัส and พฤหัสบดี (preuha't) [San.] planet Jupiter วัน Thursday

เพรีอ (preuwa') (of a bird) shaking the wings

เพรีอ (preuwa) dispersed, spread about, situate in various places, going from place to place กิน — to eat often เสียง — drawling voice พก — to talk often, to keep on talking

พรุ่ง (proo'ng) and พรุ่งนี้ (proo'ng nee) to-morrow

พรุน (proo'n) having holes in it ขาก torn into holes

พรุย (preuwy) (1) coming out easily going smoothly (2) crumbling

พรู (proo) going in flocks, in swarms, in crowds พรา — to talk repeatedly, to instruct often

เพระ (pray') [phon.] sound of falling rain

เพริก (prert) [of buffaloes, etc.] at liberty, at large

เพริด (preut) more clean, brighter, more beautiful — เพรา do.

แพร (praa) silk

แพร (praa) and — หลาย to be scattered, propagated, to spread

แพรก (praak) cross-road, cross-way

หญ้า — turf, grass

แพร่ง (praang) cross-road, cross-way — พราย to disclose, make known, rumour

แพรว (prayo) bright, shining

แพรศียา (praasa'yah) [San.] courtesan

ไพร (prai) [Cambod.] woods, forests — สาด open space, wide tract — ทูรัย a precious stone of a green hue

ไพร่ (prai) common people, slaves บ่าว — male and female slaves — พล troops, multitudes

ไพรทูรย (prai toon) [San.] a greenish gem, light green ฆา — name of a consonant, q. v.

ไพรบูลย์ (prai boon) [Sansk.] perfect, abundant, superabundant

โพรก (proke) without pulp or flesh, empty

โพรง (prohng) hollow, a cave

เพราะ (praw') (1) sweet-sounding, melodious, agreeable (2) on account of — เหต on that account — ว่า because — อะไร why?

พร่ำ (pra'm) to fall [like dew or rain

พร่ำ (pra'm) complaining, murmuring

พระ (pra') [Sansk.] great, excellent, holy, the best [Alab. 164]: (a prefix attached to all things belonging to the King) — เจ้า God, King — พุทธิเจ้า God, King ข้า — พระเจ้า I (speaking to the King, the Queen, or certain Royal Princes) — บาท foot of the King, footprint of Buddha — อรค์ title of a King's son [Many words beginning thus will be found under the second part of the word, without this prefix]

พระกร (pra'kon) [Pali] hand of the King ธือ — King's walking stick

พระแกร (pra'kraa) Palace windows ช่อง — opening in a window

พระกลด (pra'klot) King's umbrella

พระกันแสง (pra'ka'nsaang) [of royal persons] to cry

พระขนง (pra'ka'nong) [Camb.] King's eyebrow

พระคลัง (pra'kla'ng) royal office, as of the Treasury, old title for a Minister of Foreign Affairs

พระคูยหฐาน (pra'kooi'ha'tahn) membra virilia regis

พระเจ้า (pra'chow) God ; the King's head

พระชนม์ (pra'chon) [Pali] age [of a royal person]

พระหนุ (pra'ha'noo') [Pali] King's chin

พระเดช พระคุณ (pra'dett pra'koo'n) [Sansk.] (to Princes or nobles) Your Royal Highness, Your Excellency

พระดัชนี (pra'da'cha'nee) [Pali] King's fore-finger

พระเต้า (pra'tow) (1) earthenware water-jug for the King (2) breast

พระที่ (pra'tee) the King's bed

พระที่นั่ง (pra'tee na'ng) any place or vehicle where the King sits, as เป็น — รำ —

พระนาย (pra'nai) (title of the four Phras who are highest in rank)

พระบรมราชานุญาต (pra'boroma'rah-chahnoo'yaht) [Pali] royal permission

พระบรมราชโองการ (pra'boroma'rah-cha' ongkarn) [Pali] royal mandate

พระบาง (pra'bahng) image of Buddha หลวง — Luang Prabang (a large city in Eastern Laos)

พระบัณฑูร (pra'ba'ntoon) [Pali] order of the second King

พระปราง (pra'prahng) (1) King's cheek (2) symbolical obelisk common in Siamese temples

พระพร (pra'pon) [Pali] blessing ถวาย — yes (by a priest)

พระพิเนษ (pra'pi'neck) [Pali] priest-hood

พระภมู (pra'pa'moo) [Pali] King's eye-brow

พระภูษา (pra'poosah) [Pali] King's clothes

พระยอด (pra'yaut) boil (speaking of the King)

พระยา (pra'yah, *vulg.* pa'yah) (a title of nobility, sometimes rather erroneously called " Marquis ") เจ้า — a higher title of nobility นาง — Queen, Princess สมเด็จหน้า — etc. various titles of nobility — ไก่ pheasant

พระราชทาน (pra'rahcha'tahn) [Pali] (of the King) to give

พระวงษ (pra'wong) King's relations

พระศก (pra'sok) [Cambod.] King's hair

พระสุธารศ (pra'soo'tahrot) drinking water (for the King)

พระสุพรรณราช (pra'soo'pa'nna'raht)
big spittoon (for the King)

พระสุพรรณศรี (pra'soo'pa'nna'see)
small spittoon (for the King)

พระแสง (pra'saang) King's sword or
weapon, King's sceptre

พระหฤทัย (pra'ha'ru'tai) the King's
mind

พระธนามิกา (pra'-a'nah-mi'kah) [Pali]
King's little-finger

พระอังกุฐ (pra'-a'ngkoo't) [Pali] King's
thumb or big toe

พรั่ง (pra'ng) several, more than one
— พรู crowd, multitude

พรัด (pra't) to be separated from

พรั่น (pra'n) afraid, to dread

พล (pon) [Sansk.] troop, battalion,
army — เทพ (pola'tep) troop of angels เท้า พระยา — เทพ one of the
four chief dignitaries, Minister of
Agriculture

พลบ (plop) twilight, dusk

พลวง (plooa'ng) (1) antimony (2) mi-
neral

พลั่ว (plooa') pick-axe — เหล็ก iron
spade, shovel

พลวัน (pa'la'wa'n) confusion, pell-mell

พลอ with สอ (saw plaw) to slander, to
backbite, to damn with faint praise

พลอ (plor) wooden tube for injecting
gargle into the throat

พลอง (plaung) bludgeon, stick, single-
stick

พลอด (plaut) to warble, chirp, babble

พลอม with กิน (kin plaum) large eat-
er, gourmand

พลอย (ploye) (1) precious stones (2)
to follow suit, to partake with, to
join in

พล้อย (ploi) with พก babbling, thought-
less speech

พลา (plah) a condiment made of raw
meat or fish

พลากร (plahkon) [Pali] troop, crowd,
army

พลาง (plahng) in the meantime, whilst
กิน — พก — to eat and speak at
the same time

พลาด (plaht) to stumble, fall

พลาน (plarn) (1) to boil (2) wandering
about, going aimlessly (3) many
different people

พลาม (plarm) (1) bright, shining, growing bright (2) greedily

พล่าม (plahm) talkative

พลาย (plaie) *with* ช้าง male (elephant)

พลาย (plai) to hide, hide away, hide up, keep back

พลิก (plik) to turn over — ไป — มา to turn over and over, rolling backwards and forwards, from side to side

พลี *and* พลี กำ (plee ka'm) to sacrifice to the guardian genius

เพลีย (pleeya) lame, weak

เพลี่ย (pleea) (1) a flat river fish (2) a fly which eats rice, etc. (3) jew's harp

เพลี่ยง (pleeang) to miss one's mark

พลุ (ploo') sudden movement, sudden sound กอก ไม้ — a firework

พลุก พล่าน (ploo'k plahn) a crowd

พลุก พลิก (ploo'k pla'k) [phon.] plash of oars, etc., jumping of fish

พลุ่ง (ploo'ng) to boil up, to rush up, to burst out

พลุย (ploowi') (1) crumbling, reduced to powder (2) greedily, hastily

พลุ่ย (plooi') fat, swelled out

พลู (ploo) a tree of which the leaves are used for wrapping up lime and chewing with betel-nut

เพล้ (play) crooked, not level, lopsided, on one side — ไพล้ sideways, not straight

เพลง (playng) music, sound of playing or singing

เพลิง (pleung) flame, fire ถวาย พระ — to kindle the fire for cremating a King or Prince

เพลิด (pleut) to rejoice พลาด — insecurely placed, falling off

เพลิน (pleun) to linger from pleasure เพลิก — contented

แพลง (plaang) dislocation, sprain

แพลม (plaam) projecting a little way, coming out ถัง — dark lantern, match

ไพล (plai) a bulbous plant used as embrocation for swellings

ไพล่ (plai) cross-legged, crossed

ไพล่ (plai) *and* — หนี to fly to one side, to swerve, to separate

ไพล่ (plo) a scoop for taking up and scattering water

ไพล้ เพล้ (ploh play) at evening, at dusk

ไพลก (plohk) to empty; too wide, too large

ไพลง (plohng) brightness

ไพลง (plohng) noise (of fish jumping, etc.) in the water

ไพลง (plohng) big, huge เป๋า — a shell

เพลา (plow) thighs —ใบ yards for la-teen sails สนับ — drawers

เพลาะ (plaw') sound

เพลาะ (plaw') to sew together (two pieces of cloth, etc.) ผ้า — two pieces of cloth sewn together

พล่ำ (pla'm) inconsiderately, at ran-dom ผก — jumping of fish

พลัง (pla'ng) [Pali] force, strength, forces

พลัง ๆ (pla'ng-pla'ng) [phon.] sound of a big drum

พลัง (pla'ng) impetuously

พลัง (pla'ng) to slip down, to be de-ceived, mistake, miss, forget

พลัด (pla't) to fall out, to be separated — พ่อ one whose father is absent or lost — พราก afflicted by absence

พลัน (pla'n) quickly, smartly, all at once

พลับ (pla'p) Chinese fig-tree ย้อม —

to dye in the juice of the fig-tree — พลัง a tree — พลา bamboo pavi-lion for the King

พวก (pooa'k) flock, troop, company

พวง (pooa'ng) (1) garland, nosegay, bouquet (2) strung together

พ่วง (pooa'ng) (1) swollen, getting big-ger (2) to attach one boat to ano-ther, to make fast, to tow

พวน (pooa'n) a rope made with rattan อ้อย — to press sugar-canes the second time

พวย (pooi') (1) emission; to issue forth, to radiate — พุ่ง to shoot [like a star] ลูก — ไป to get up and go away without saluting the host (2) point like a beak, spout

พวาย (pa'wai) with ก้ายย้ำ swing

พสุธร (pa'soo'nn) the earth

พสักการ (pa'sa'kkarn) [Pali] rain, rainy season, work for the rainy season

พหล (pa'honn) [Pali] army

พหู (pa'hoo) [Pali] many, plural — สูกร (1) much (2) learned (3) or-namented

พอ (paw) see เพอ enough

พ่อ (paw) father — ค้า merchant — ครัว cook — ตา father-in-law (f. of the wife) — หม้าย widower — เลี้ยง step father — ขุ,อ หัว god father (a term used by suppliants)

พ่อ (paw) a cry used by rowers

พื้อ (paw) to speak angrily, to protest

พอก (pauk) to cover คอ — swollen throat ยา — plaster

พอง (paung) to swell, tumour ขน — hair bristling with fear กิน สอ — chalk, carbonate of lime

พอง with พวก (pooa'k paung) comrades, friends, relations

พองพาน (paung parn) to be connected with, interested in

พองหมองปาก (paung maung park) difference, dissension

พอน (paun) to cover with tar

พอม (paum) large basket (like a hive with the top cut off) used for rice

พา (pah) to lead

พากหนัง (park hna'ng) speakers in a Punch-and-Judy show, or marionette exhibition

พากน่า (park nah) future state of existence

พากย์ (pahk) [Pali] language

พางเพียง (parng peeya'ng) almost, nearly, on the point of

พ่างพืน (parng peun) space [of the sky, earth, etc.]

พาชี (parchee) horse

พานรเรศ (parna'rett) [Pali] King of the monkeys

พาด (part) to apply, to put on, to rest one thing on or against another — บ่า to put on the shoulders — พิง to get close to, to lean against, to attach oneself to — พะอง to put a bamboo ladder against a tree

พาทย์ with พิณ (pin paht) [Sansk.] guitar, musical instrument

พาทา (partar) [Pali] quarrel

พาที (partee) [Pali] conversation

พาน (pahn) (1) vase of copper or metal (2) to stop with a cord, to snare แห — net — ท้าย steersman of the King's boat

พานร (parnon) [Pali] a monkey

พาย (pai) to paddle

พาย (pai) and พายุ also พระ — [Pali] angels of the wind or tempest (Alab. 90. 185)

พ่ายแพ้ (pai paa) to be defeated

พายัพ (pabya'p) [Pali] North-West

พาล (pahn) (1) young and ignorant, stupid, fool, (2) to speak evil of กรุง — grinning, giant, goblin — พาไล to accuse the wrong person, to punish an innocent person

พาลิก (pahlik) [Pali] a precious stone, sand

พาลี (pahlee) [Pali] monkey

พาลุก (pahlenk) body of men, troop, crowd

พาลุกา (pahlukah) [Pali] sand

พาโล (pahloh) to charge falsely, to calumniate

พาสนา (pahsa'nah) [Sansk. result of past actions on the mind and feelings

พาสุกรี (pahsoo'kree) [Sansk.] serpents living under ground

พาห (pah-ha') [Pali] (1) vehicle (2) upper arm

พาห (pah) seal (for sealing)

พาหา (pah-har) upper arm, arm

พาหล (pah-hon) [Pali] army

พาเหียร (pah-heea'n) [Pali] externally, outside

พาหนะ (pah-ha'na) [Pali] carrying, bearing, carrier, bearer, leader, conductor

พิกัต (pi'ka't) (1) to divide according to law (2) a term used in fixing the value of teak logs

พิคราะห (pi'kraw) [Pali] to consider, examine, determine

พฆาฏ (pi'kart) [Pali] to kill, destroy

พิง (ping) to lean on, lean against

พิจารณ (pi'charn) [Pali] to closely examine, scrutinize, investigate

พิจิก (pi'chik) [Pali] constellation of the Scorpion

พิจิตร (pi'chitt) [Pali] variegated, magnificent, splendid

พิชิต (pi'chitt) [Pali] victory

พิเชียร (pi'cheea'n) [Sansk.] precious stone, diamond, adamant

พิณ and พิน (pin) [Pali] guitar — พาทย์ musical instrument

พิโกร (pi'done) [Cambod.] fragrant, odoriferous

พิถี (pi'tee) road, street

พิทักษ (pi'ta'k) [Pali] to take care of, to keep

พิน (pin) *see* พิณ

พินฑู (pintoo') *and* พินฑุ (pin) [Pali] drop, accent — เอก the first accent (as over พ็อ) — โท the second accent (as over ผ้า)

พินาศ (pi'nart) [Sansk.] ruin, destruction, loss ; to be ruined

พินิต (pi'nitt) [Pali] to consider, examine, investigate

พินิจไฉย (pi'nitchai) [Sansk.] to decide a law suit (Pali)

พินัย (pi'nai) [Pali] (1) rule of morals [Alab. 166] (2) legal fine กรรม trial of an offending priest

พินัยกรรม (pi'naika'n) [Pali] schedule (of legacies, etc.) , will, testament

พิบูรณ (pi'boon) [Pali] full, too full

พิบูลย (pi'boon) [Pali] perfect, beautiful

พิบัติ (pi'ba't) [Pali] calamity, adversity, misfortune

พิบ่ราย (pi'prai) to declare, to explain

พิพาท (pi'part) [Pali] to dispute, quarrel, accuse

พิพิธ (pi'pitt) [Pali] various, manifold, abounding in various things

พิพังน์ (pi'pa't) [Pali] prosperous, to flourish

พิภพ (pi'pop) [Pali] universe, world

พิภากษา (pi'parksah) [Pali] to judge, determine

พิภาค (pi'part) [Pali] to travel over, to walk across

พิเภก (pi'pake) [Sansk.] a fortune-telling giant

พิเภท (pi'pett) [San.] a Palmyra tree

พิมพ (pimm) [Pali] to cast in a form, to print ก — to strike off, to print ตัว — type for printing

พิมพา (pimpah) [Pali] the wife of Buddha, Yasodharu

พิมพาภรณ (pimpahponn) [Pali] ornaments, costly clothing

พิมล (pi'monn) [Pali] spotless, pure, clear

พิมเสน (pimsenn) camphor

พิมาน (pi'mahn) [Pali] Heaven, the dwelling of angels or genii

พิมุข (pi'moo'k) [Pali] averted, turned aside, neglectful ; name of a gate in the Palace

พิโมกข (pi'moke) [Pali] release, deliverance, salvation

พิโยก (pi'yoke) [Pali] to separate, to be left alone, deprived of, separation, alienation

พิรม (pi'rom) [Pali] joy, delight, pleasure

พิรมณ์ (pi'rom) [Pali] fasting, abstinence

พิราบ (pi'rarp) (more properly พิลาบ) pigeon

พิริย (pi'ri'ya') [Pali] effort, vigour, fortitude, energy [Alab. 184]

พิรุณ (pi'roo'n) [Pali] rain พิร: — rain angel

พิรุณหก (pi'roo'nhek) (see also ?) [Pali] rain angel

พิรุธ (pi'roo't) culprit รู้ to detect

พิเรนทร์ (pi'renn) [Pali] mighty, heroic, formidable to the enemy

พิไร (pi'rai) to go on grumbling

พิโรธ (pi'rote) [Pali] hostile, adverse, angry, to be angry

พิลาป (pi'larp) [Pali] to mourn, deplore, wail นก — pigeon

พิลาย (pi'lai) beautiful

พิลาศ (pi'lart) and พิลาลาศ [Pali] pretty, beautiful

พิฤก (pi'leuk) terrible, strange, curious, monstrous

พิไลย and พิไลย (pi'laie) pretty, beautiful

พิส (pi'sa') [Pali] to see, to look at

ปัง talisman, chain   วาส to like, to be familiar with   เพ็ง to gaze at — เพ็ง to be like

พิศณุโลกย์ (Pitsa'noo'lok) [Pali] (ancient Capital of Siam)

พิศทาร (pitsa'dahn) [Pali] (1) extensive (2) a fabulous island

พิศ (pit) [Pali] poison

พิศาล (pi'sahn) [Pali] broad, wide, ample, extensive

พิศุทธิ (pi'soo'tti') pure, clean, immaculate

พิสูทร (pi'soot) [Pali] to try, to weigh, to tempt

พิเศศ (pi'sett) [Pali] precious เง — the King's kitchen นาย — purveyor for the same, chief cook

พิหาร (pi'harn) and วิหาร [Pali] temple, monastery, dwelling (of priest)

พี (pee) fat, big

พี่ (pee) elder brother or sister — ชาย

elder brother — ร้าว elder sister —
ช้าย eldest brother — เอือย eldest
sister — เขย elder sister's husband
— สะใภ้ elder brother's wife — น้อง
kinsfolk, brethren — น้อง งาย male
relations — เลี้ย nurse

เพียง (peea'ng) until, as far as — ใด
until when? how much? แพ่ งส —
middling, not too much

เพี้ยน (peea'n) (1) to be different, to
mistake, discordant (2) to put off,
defer, delay

เพียบ (peea'p) over-loaded เต็ม
quite full

เพียร (peea'n) [Sansk. patient : fortitude

พึง (peung) (1) it is necessary (sign
of the Imperative), must (2) just
now — ใจ suitable, agreeable

พึ่ง (peung) to ask the aid of, to seek
the protection of

พึบ พับ (peup pa'p) noise of starting
up

พืชน (peut) [Pali] seed, gem, species
— ภูมิ climate — พรรณ species,
family

พืด (peut) (1) blade (of saw, etc.) เหล็ก
— sheet of iron (2) long drawn out,
monotonous

พื้น (peun) surface, pavement, floor,
ground of a cloth worked with flow -
ers โรค — ulcer on the sole of
the foot

เพื่อ (peua) in order that, to produce,
to proceed from — ว่า so that

เพื่อน (peuan) companion, comrade,
friend

พุ (poo') (1) to gush out (2) ulcer —
พุ swollen, fat น้ำ — spout, spring

พุกาม (poo'karm) Burmese

พุง (poo'ng) belly, entrails กราย a
tree whose fruit splits when soaked
— ปลา fish fins from which glue is
made — กะ a thorny shrub

พุ่ง (poo'ng) to throw, throw at, break
out, get out, leap

พู่ง (poo'ng) convexity, concavity — ใน
concavity — นอก convexity

พุธ (poo't) [Pali] Mercury (planet)
วัน — Wednesday

พุ่ง กะ (poo'ng daw) a thorny shrub

พุก (poo't) a smell shrub with white scented flowers ผ้า พุกฎก — flowered cloth

พุกทาน (poo't-tahn) a tree with big blossoms

พุทฮ (pooo't) พุทฮะ (poo'tta') พุทฮิ (poo'tti) [Pali] omniscient, august, divine พุทฮ — Buddha — รำพา a tree with white yellow and red flowers — ศักราช Buddhistic era — ชาติ a tree with small white flowers

พุกโธ ๆ (poo'tto) (exclam. of pity or wonder)

พุทฮันคร (poo'tta'ndon) [Pali] intermediate age between the death of one Buddha and the birth of another

พุทรา (poo'sah) jujube tree

พุ่ม (poo'm) (1) shrub, shady place, grove (2) pointed ornament made of wax and given to priests, pointed covering for a basket

พุ่มเสน (poo'msenn) a camphor used for inhaling

พู่ (poo) tuft, crest, aigrette — หางม้า tassel

พู่กัน (pooka'n) [Chin.] small brush for painting or writing

พูด (poot) to speak, to talk อย่าง — dialect — ๆ conversation

พูน (poon) to heap up, to fill full

พู้น (poon) [La.] yon der, beyond, there

พูม (poom) well-dressed

เพ (pay) broken open, destroyed เเพ strewed about, littered about

เพกา (paykah) a tree with long-shaped bitter fruit

เพ่ง (payng) to stare, to gaze at

เพ็ญ (peng) full เดือน — the day of the full Moon (15 of the waxing)

เพชร (pett) [Sansk.] diamond กาก — d. for cutting glass — หนุ a yellowish precious stone with a flaw in it — บุรี Petchaburi, a town on the West coast of the Gulf

เพชฆาฎ (petcha'kart) [Pali] executioner

เพชหนาท (petcha'nartee) [Pali] a short measure of time, a second

เพชหึง (petcha'heung) [Pali] with ลม whirlwind, tornado

เพ็ญบูรณ (penboon) Cambod. and Pali, full

.เพณี (paynee) [Pali] custom ประ —
custom, law

เพ็กทูล (pett-toon) [Siam. and Pali] to
relate or report to the King

เพ็กไม้ (petmai) dwarf branch (of a tree)

เพดาน (paydahn) ceiling, wainscote,
palate (of the mouth)

เพท (payt) [Pali] (1) knowing, knowledge ไตรย — the three Vedas
[Alab. 175] (2) destiny, accident,
lot

เพทยาธร (paytyahton) [Sansk.] 1) one
who succeeds in doing a miracle
(2) a lower angel (3) a supposed
husband of all girls

เพทาย (paytai) a dull red gem

เพโธบาย (paytohbai) (see เทกบาย) [Pa-
li] knowledge of stratagems, craft,
cunning

เพน (payn) to wobble from side to side

เพล (penn) [Pali] hour of the priest's
dinner (11 a.m.) ฉัน — (of priests)
to dine, dinner

เพลา (paylah) [Pali] time, occasion

เพศ (payt) [Sansk.] disguise จำแลง —
metamorphosis

เพอ (perr) stop, wait, not yet

เพ้ (perr) delirious from fever, at ran-
dom

เพาเฉย (peuk choi) quiet, still, silent,
listless, negligent — หิน to exca-
vate or remove rock หิน — rock
having a hollow underneath, overhanging or arched rock

เพิง (peung) outside roof, outside gallery, verandah

เพิน (pern) better ที่ เพิน shifting, wandering about, unsettled

เพิ่ม (perm) to add

แพ (paa) raft, floating house

แพ้ (paa) to be defeated, overcome, to
yield

แพง (paang) dear, precious — ผัก
water-cress

แพง (pang) lower tribunal, insignificant
lawsuit

แพทย์ (paat) [Sansk.] physician, medical art

แพน (paan) to unfold ล่า — bamboo
mat รำ — (of peacocks) to spread
the tail

แพ้น ลง (paan lohng) to strike a blow
downwards

เเพญ (paap) a thin grass used for partitions

เเพว (pao) to sweep, to clean

เเพว (payo) anything set up on high (as a weather-cock on a bamboo rod) ปว notice flag or notice paper ฟ้า เปน whirligig, scarecrow — ฟ้า เปน weather-cock, whirligig

เเพศย (paasa'ya') [San.] trader, merchant, the Vaisya class

เเพศยา (paasa'yah) [Sansk.] courtesan

เเพะ (paa') goat — โลภ to seduce

เไพ (pai) [Chin.] playing cards

เไพทูรย (paitoon) [Pali] a light green precious stone

ไพรี (pai ree) [Sansk.] enemy, hostile, revengeful

ไพโรจ (pai-rote) [San.] shining, bright

ไพเราะ (pairau') [Sansk.] musical, melodious

ไพศาล (pai sahn) [Sansk.] extensive, wide, prosperous

ไพ (poh) a tree — เพ effeminate

โพก (poke) to wrap round the head, to cover

โพง (pohng) to bale out (water); earthen bottle, water-pot — พง a deep net for fish or prawns

โพด with เข้า (kow pote) Indian corn

โพธิ (pote or pohti) [Pali] (1) wisdom, wise, superior, excellent, august (2) sacred fig-tree [ficus religiosa] (Alab. xxxiv, 163) — สัตว superior animal, previous existences of a Buddha (Alab. 162) — ญาณ omniscience (Alab. 164)

โพน (pohn) horizontal — เพน to swing or wobble from the base, to climb, to mount, to come up

โพน (pohn) [Laos.] yonder, beyond, on the further side

โพระดก (pohra'dok) a chattering bird

โพระใน (pohra'nai) a leprosy

โพศก (pohsop) [Sansk.] rice พระ แม่ Goddess of rice

เพาะ (paw) to plant, to sow the seeds of

ฟ้า (pa'm) speech of a mad person

ฟ้า หยุด (pa'una'k) to halt, to rest ที่ — resting place

พะกา (pa'kah) [Cambod.] (1) flower, pollen (2) [Pali] a water bird

พะเชย (pa'soi) [Chin.] trickery, cheating (at cards)

พะนา (pa'nah) [Pali] winding borders of a forest — ๆๆ wandering in the forests or deserts

พะนิดา (pa'ni'dah) beloved and beautiful [used of younger sisters and young girls]

พะเนียง (pa'neea'ng) with ไฟ tube for fireworks ไฟ — water-pot, jug

พะเนียด (pa'neea't) trap

พะเนิน (pa'neun) (1) small hammer (2) large quantity, large heap

พะแนง (pa'nang) roast, roasted

พะนัก (pa'na'k) back of a bench

พะบู (pa'boo) [Chin.] acting of a fight, stage fighting

พะเผา (pa'pow) sensation of heat

พะยด (pa'yot) restive, ill-behaved

พะยอม (pa'yaum) a tree

พะยาธิ (pa'yahti') [Pali] descease, maladies — ขี้เรื้อน leper

พะเยิบ (pa'yerp) to rise or be lifted into the air ละออง pimples, small spots on the skin

พะโยม (pa'yome) air, upper air

พะรุง พะรัง (pa'roo'ng pa'rang) ill-fitting and superabundant clothing embarrassed, inconvenienced

พะลา (pa'lah) [Pali] strength, strong

พาลากร (pa'lahkon) [Pali] army, troop

พะลาน (pa'lahn) (with น้ำ) open (place)

พะลาหก (pa'lah-hok) [Pali] rain genius. cloud

พะลึก with พิลึก (palm pa'leuk) [Pali] better พิลึก horrible, terrific, spectre

พะไล (pa'lai) lower tier of a roof รอบ verandah round a house

พะไลย (pa'lai) [Sansk.] bracelet

พะลัง (pa'lang) [Pali] force, strength

พะวง (pa'wong) uneasy, doubting, to hesitate

พะวา (pa'wah) a tree — พะ วา to hesitate between two things, to do one thing and think of another

พะสุทา (pa'soo'tah) [Pali] earth, surface of the earth

พะหิ (pa'hi') [Pali] outside

พะหุ (pa'hoo') and พะหุ (pa'hoo) [Pali] plural, many, much

พะอง (pa'ong) *with* ไม้ bamboo ladder

พะอบ (pa'opp) box, casket

พะอืม *with* พะอม (pa'eut pa'omm) bilious, dyspeptic

พะอึ (pa'eu) cough, obstacle in the throat

พะเอิน (pa'ern) accident, it happened

พะโอน (pa'ohn) [Cambod.] younger sister, younger brother

พัก (pa'k) to rest, stop, sleep

พักตร์ (pa'k) and other forms [Sansk.] face

พัง (pa'ng) (1) stirrups (2) to fall in ruins, tumble down

พัง (pa'ng) *with* ช้าง female elephant

พังกาบ (pa'ng parp) with the body bent

พัง เผือก (pa'ng peut) peritoneum, inner skin

พังพอน (pa'ng paun) animal that eats snakes, mongoose

พังพาน (pa' ngpahn) snake's head shaped like a spoon

พังพาบ (*better* พังพาบ) (pa'ngpahp) bent down, head foremost

พัชนี (pa' cha'nee) [Pali] long-handled fan [Alab. 170]

พัด (pa't) to blow, to fan ; fan, punkah

— ขึ้น spoon-shaped fan or screen made of feathers (used by priest or grandee.) — จันทน์ sandal-wood fan —โยก a long-handled fan used in processions — แฉ้ว a root used in medicine ชัก — to pull the punkah

พัทราภรณ์ (pa'trahpon) [Pali] ornaments

พัทระ (pa'tra') [Pali] clothes, dress

พัน (pa'n) a thousand นาย — chief of a battalion, major

พัน (pa'n) to envelope, encircle, surround, ens nare, tie up

พันธนา (pa'nta'nah) *and* — การ [Pali] bonds, chains, chained

พันธุ์ *and* พันธุ (pa'ntoo') [Pali] relationship

พับ (pa'p) to fold, fold, crease — บาน metal hinge — เพียบ with the feet and legs bent back

พลรัน *see* ปั้นจั่น crane (machine)

พลวัน (pa'la'wa'n) in all directions, confusedly, complicated

พัศดา (pa'sa'dah) *see* ภัสดา husband

พัศดุ (pa'sa'doo') *and* พัสถาร [Pali] riches

พ

พ (*phaw phai* — English *ph.* or *f.* Labial: a high letter) — ไพ name of this letter

พก (phok) to swell, a tumour

พอ (phaw) [phon.] noise of a snake

พอ (phaw!) flourishing, healthy

พอก (phauk) to clean, to purify, to tan (leather, etc.)

พอง (phaung) (1) foam — ไข่ the mark ๏ placed at the beginning of a document (2) egg

พอง (phaung) to float

พอง (phaung) to accuse, denounce, accusation, charge, complaint — ร้อง to appeal

พอก (fort) rotten, decaying, going bad, fermenting, turning sour

พอน (faun) [Laos.] remnants from a fire etc., débris

พอน (faun) to kiss

พอน (phaun) sheaf, bundle, handful

พอน (faun) a gesture or movement in dancing : — การ (of peacocks) to spread the tail

พ้า (phah) obscured, not clear, shade [of a lamp, etc.]

พ้า (far) sky ก้น — horizon : — ผ่า and — ผ thunderbolt (an oath) — — เกิด may the thunderbolt destroy me — ลั่น — ร้อง thunder — แลบ lightning ดาก — deck of a ship

พาก (fark) (1) bamboo or wood floor (2) beyond, the shore, bank : — ข้าง โน่น and — ขะโน่น the other bank or side เหล็ก — iron girder

พาง (farng) (1) straw (2) dark, cloudy, indistinct

พ้ง with เข้า (kow farng) millet (used for cage birds)

พาด (phaht) to strike or beat [clothes on a stone, etc.]

พาน (farn) [Laos.] deer

พาย (phai) (1) to take up with the hollow of the hand (2) abundant, liberal, lavish — มือ a measure of capacity, the fourth part of a ka'm

พ้าย (phai!) cotton, thread

พิก (phitt) (1) [phon.] sound of sneezing (2) [Chin.] brush for writing

พิบ (phip) (1) depressed, crushed พิบๆ
— snub nose (2) sound of striking

พี (phee) confused muttering of a person asleep

ฟืน (pheun) firewood, fuel — ฟ้อย
small chips of wood

ฟื้น (pheune) to renew, to escape, to
rise again, to recover from — คืน
to turn up the ground ไถ — to recover

ฟืม (feum) a weaver's instrument

เฟือ (feuwa') to overflow, well-filled,
satisfied

เฟือง (feua'ng) coils of thread etc.,
round a reel, fluting (of wood, of
columns, etc.)

เฟื่อง (feua'ng) (1) to be divulged, to
be noised abroad (2) to know quite
well, able to answer off-hand (3)
festooned, hanging in loops

เฟื้อง (feua'ng) (small silver coin worth
8 atts, one-eighth of a tical) fuang

เฟือน (feua'n) to wander in mind, to
lose one's mind or one's head

เฟือย (feuey) aquatic plants on the
bank of a river

เฟื้อย (feuey) long, prolonged, extended

ฟูฟะ (foo'fa') not firm, rotten, decaying

ฟุ้ง (foo'ng) to be wafted about in the
air, to spread, to be noised abroad

ฟุด (foo't) (1) to blow, kindle by blowing (2) tinder (3) noise of sneezing

ฟุต (foo't) [Engl.] foot, feet ไม้ — carpenter's rule

ฟุบ (foo'p) to stoop, to be depressed

ฟูม (phoo'm) crying, shedding tears

ฟู (phoo) (1) to ferment (2) to be on
the road to wealth, to become rich
— ฟ้า like a monkey

ฟู่ (phoo!) hissing (of vipers or other
animals)

ฟูก (phook) mattress

ฟูง (phoong) (แห) to mend (a net)

ฟูด (phoot) a noise (as of a big fire,
of an elephant eating, of blowing
the nose, etc.) — ฟาด vulgar manner of eating

ฟูม (phoom) abundant — ฟาย greedily,
excessively, abundantly เลือก —
covered with blood

แฟ (phaa) small bead, berry or seed

แฟ (phaa) Laos. dense, crowded

แพ่ง (phaang) small pumpkin

แพ็ก (phaat) grunting of pigs

แพ็ก (phaat) [Laos.] flat, level

แพ็น (phaan) thick, solid

แพ็บ (phaap) *and* แพน (phaan) [Laos.]
(1) flat, flattened, thin, dried up
(2) a flat basket for travellers —
ะ ย ะ pack-saddle for bullocks or
elephants

ไฟ (phai) fire -- พาง straw fire, short-
lived anger - พา thunderbolt,
electric light — ธาๆ heat or fever
in the stomach, heart-burn ลูก—
spark, firebrand

พัก (pha'k) (1) large pumpkin, gourd
(and such-like vegetables) (2) to
warm, to hatch, to brood — ผ้าย
to associate with, to join *or* belong
to a party

พัง (pha'ng) to hear, listen, obey

พัด (pha't) to knock about, to shake,
shatter กลอน — กัน verses with
alternating rhymes

พัน (pha'n) tooth — กราม molar teeth,
grinders ยา — tooth powder, den-
tifrice — ผง the stroke or strokes

over two of the vowels ◌ั and ◌ั

พัน (pha'n) to cut off, to strike with
the sword

พันเผือ (pha'n fena) to visit frequently,
to associate with, to frequent, to do
often

พันเผือน (pha'n pheua'n) to wander
in mind, to forget

- ---•• - -

ภ

ภ (*paw pa'nyah* = English *p.* Sansk.
bh. Labial: a low letter) — ภิริยา
name of this letter

ภควา (pa'kha'wah) [Pali] worshipful.
venerable, admirable, blessed, holy

ภคินี (pa'ki'nee) [Pali] younger sister.
a term of address by priests

ภพ (pop) [Pali] existence, world — ช:
สาร world of dying and being born
again, state of transmigration

ภมร (pa'monn) [Pali] bee

ภมู (pa'moo) [Pali] eyebrow

ภยัน (pa'ya'n) [Pali] to fear, dread

ภรรยา (pa'nyah) *or* ภิริยา [Pali] wife

ภอ (paw) *and* พอ (1) to suffice, sufficient, enough — ใจ satisfied, content — ดี pretty middling, pretty fair — ได้ that will do, it is good enough — ว่า *and* แค่ — as soon as — แรง (1) much (2) able to be lifted or taken away — กิน satisfied; comfort — ใช้ still useful

ภอ (paw) then, when

ภาคย (pahk) [Pali] part, share, lot, destiny — หญัท [San.] to blame, reprimand

ภาคินัย (pahkhi'nee) [Pali] nephew

ภาชน (pahcha'na') [Pali] vessel, dish, bowl, receptacle

ภา (pah) [Pali] rays, brightness, splendour

ภานุ (pahnoo') [Pali] sun

ภานุมา (pahnoo'mah) [and other similar words] radiant, shining, rays

ภาดา (pahtah) [Pali] brother, male relation

ภานิช (pahnitt) [Pali] merchant

ภาพ (pahp) [Pali] to exist, person, nature, form, image ยาพ — power,

strength เขียน — to draw portrait ดากูมา — I (by a priest speaking to a magnate)

ภาย (pai) side, part — นอก outside — ใน inside — น่า future — หลั : afterwards

ภารฐีระ (pahra'too'ra') [Pali] important affair, business, serious occupation

ภารา (pahrah) [Pali] (1) heavy weight (2) four hundred catties (of gold, in weight) (3) chief city

ภาราณะสี (pahrahna'see) *better* พาราะ ณะสี [Pali] Benares

ภาระ (pahra') [Pali] bearing, supporting, carrying, load, weight

ภาวะ (pahwa') [Pali] essence, substance, being, condition, state

ภาวะนา (pahwa'nah) [Pali] meditation, (Alab. 168)

ภาษกร (pahsa'ka'ra) [Sansk.] sun

ภาษา (pahsah) [Sansk.] language, idiom, in the manner of — เด็ก like boys

ภาษิต (pahsitt) [Sansk.] to speak, utter

ภาสา (pahsah) [Pali] light, lustre

ภาษี (pahsee) gain, profit, taxes โรง — Custom House ตาม — ภาษา according to his wish, in his own way

ภิกขา (pikkhah) [Pali] and — ชร (of priests) to beg, to go round for alms

ภิกษุ and ภิกษุ (pikkhoo' and piksoo') [Sansk.] mendicant priest

ภิกษุนี (pikkhoo'nee) [Pali] nun

ภิญโย ภิยโย and ภิโย (peeyoh) [Pali] more, better, improving, best

ภินิหาร (pi'ni'hahn) [Pali] to do great acts (good or bad) to have great success, ambition

ภิมพา (pimpah) [Pali] better พิมพา cast in a mould (a name of Buddha's wife Yasodhara)

ภิริยา (pi'ri'yah) [Pali] wife

ภิเศก (pi'sayk) [Sansk.] to consecrate with holy water, to crown ราชา — to come regularly to the throne ปราบดา — to succeed by right of arms

ภุชงค์ (poo'chong) [Pali] King of serpents, King of the subterranean regions

ภุชพากย์ with กัม (ka'mpoo'cha'park) [Pali] Cambodian language

ภุชะ (poo'cha') and ภุช [Pali] trunk (of elephant, etc.), the arm bent back, arm

ภุญช (poo'n) [Pali] eat, possess; rich

ภู (poo) [Pali] plain, earth, land

ภู เขา (poo kow) mountain — ธโร mountain — ธร and — บาล King, lord, master

ภู (poo) with แมลง big beetle

ภูต and ภูตะ (poot, poota') [Pali] demons, devils, bad genii

ภูธร (pootonn) [Pali] royal title, King

ภูบดี (pooba'dee) ภูบาล ภูเบศร (and other like words) [Pali] King, ruler

ภูผา (poopah) [Pali and Siam.] cliff

ภูมินทร (poominn) [Pali] lord of the earth

ภูม (poom) [Pali] place, terrestrial พระ — guardian of a place สนาม — battle-field

ภูมี (poomee) [Pali] earth พรา — angel of the earth, King

ภูวดล (poowa'donn) [Pali] surface of the earth, King of the earth

ภูวไนย (poowa'nai) [Pali] King

ภูษา (poosah) [Sansk.] panung, clothing of the lower part of the body, apparel, garments, adornments

เภตรา (paytrah) junk, ship

เภทุบาย (paytoo'bai) [Pali] art of sowing dissension

เภรีาคาร (payrahkhahn) [Pali] tower for keeping a drum or tocsin

เภรี (payree) [Pali] drum, kettle-drum, toesin

เภสัช (paysa't) [Pali] (1) medicine (2) betel-nut ฉัน — to chew betel-nut (of a priest)

เภอ (peu) better เพอ stop, wait, not yet

ไภย (pai) [Pali] fear, fright, danger, misfortune, calamity

โภ (poh') [Pali] (in addressing equals or inferiors) my good sir, my friend, my good man

โภคา (pohkah) and โภไคย [Pali] riches, fortune

โภคินี (pohki'nee) [Pali] (1) wealthy (2) royal concubine

โภชน์ (poht) and โภชนา (pohcha'nah) [Pali] food

ภะมอน (pa'mann) Pali' lathe with two wheels

ภะสะ (pa'sa') Pali] a-hes

ภักดี (pa'kdee) [Sansk.] benevolence, charity, good works, to cherish

ภักตร์ and ภักตรา and พักตร (pa'k-trah) [Cambod.] face, countenance

ภักษ (pa'ksa') [Sansk.] food, diet

ภัณฑ์ (pa'nta') [Pali] utensil, parcel, article ค:ร — heavy article ล:ห — light article, too light วร — (wa'ra'pa'n) precious articles

ภัตร (pa't) [Sansk.] boiled rice, a meal

ภัทรบิฐ (pa'tra'bitt) [San.] the throne used when the King is crowned

ภันเต (pa'ntay) [Pali] my Lord, my excellent Sir

ภัสดา (pa'ssa'dah) [Pali] husband

ภัสมะ (pa'sa'ma') [Pali] ashes

• • •

ม

ม (maw [Sansk.] English m. Labial: a low letter)

หมก (mok) [Laos.] to cover, hide — หมก — to roast, to put to the fire — มุ roasted, enraged (2) uneasy, sad หอ — fish cooked in banana leaves หอ — หม pork do.

มกฏา (ma'ka'tah) *and* มกัฏ [Pali]
monkey

มกราคม (ma'ka'r ahkom) [Pali] month
of the Scorpion, name of the 10th
month (January)

มคธ *and* มะคะธะ (ma'ka'ta') [Pali]
the country (in India) where Pali
was spoken, Pali

มงกุฎ (mongkoo't) [Pali] crown, dia-
dem — รัด เกล้า crown for women

มงคล (mongkhonn) [Pali] auspicious,
lucky, festive, good fortune, blessing, festival — ราชสิก coronation of
a King

มงครุ่ม (mongkhroo'm) music used at
comedies

มณฑก (montok) [Pali] frog

มณฑล (monton) [Pali] disc, circle,
circuit บริ — perfectly round

มณฑารพ (montahrop) [Pali] *and* มณ
ฑา a strong-scented flower [Ery-
thrina fulgens]

มณเฑียร (monteea'n) [Sansk] King's
palace, edifice

มด (mot) ant — หมอ physician แม่ —
sorceress, witch — ลูก after-birth

— ยอบ myrrh

หมด (mott) (1) all, the whole — ไป
clean, pure, beautiful ทั้ง — all
(of things) — ไป 'more and more,
one after another — แล้ว it is
finished (2) all gone, empty, nothing — ตัว to be stripped of all

มดาย (ma'dai) [Cambod.] mother

มธุ มธุระ (ma'too', ma'too'ra') [Pali]
honey, sweet

มน (mon) (1) curved in irregular form
ใบ — leaf (2) ash colour, dirty
colour

หมน (monn) dirty-coloured, darkish,
blackish, sad, dull — หมอง sad —
ไหม้ half-burned, sad

มนตร์ (monn) มนตร (montra') *and* มน
ตรา (montrah) [Sansk.] sacred formulas — ฤทธิ์ effect of reciting a
sacred formula น้ำ — holy water
เสก — to pray

มนตรี (montree) [Sansk.] counsel-
councillor, minister

มณฑา (montah) a shrub with sweet-
scented flowers

มนุส *and* มนุษย (ma'noo't) [Pali and Sansk.] man, mankind

มรกฏ (ma'ra'kot) [Sansk.] (1) emerald (2) monkey

มรคา (mora'kah) *and* มรรค [Pali and Sansk.] road, way, path, track, course, passage

มรฎก (mora'dok) [Sansk.] inheritance ผู้ รับ — heir, executor

มรฎบ (mora'dop) [Sansk.] dome, spire (Alab. 290)

มรณา *and* มรณะ (ma'ra'na') [Pali] death, dying

มรรค (ma'k) *and* มรรคา [Pali] *conf.* มรคา road, way, path, passage

มรสุม (monsoo'm) [Engl.] monsoon, season

มฤค (ma'reuk) มฤคา *and* มฤค [San.] deer, stag, hind, doe

มฤตยู (ma'reuta'yoo) [Sansk.] death, unlucky day; Siva

มระแหม่ง (mo'ra'maang) Moulmein

มลทิน (montin) [Pali] defect, stain, blot, fault, taint มาก — free from stains or blots

มลละ (molla') [Pali] wrestling, pugilism, boxing

มลาย *with* ไม้ (mai ma'lai) the thirteenth vowel, q. v.

เมล็ด (ma'lett) grains — เข้า measure of which 19,200 go to a tanan (2, one-eighth of an att

แมลง (ma'laang *vulg.* maang) fly, insect — ทับ green beetle — ป่อง scorpion — ปู big beetle — วัน house-fly

มวก (mooa'k) a medicinal wood

หมวก (mooa'k) hat, cap

ม่วง (mooa'ng) dark purple, brown with a purple shade

หมวด (mooa't) (1) to bind up (the hair), to curl (the hair) (2) division, troop, company

มวน (mooa'n) (1) all เป็น มล เป็น — by wholesale (2) a moth which eats fish (3) covering (4) to roll up ท้อง — colic, stomach-ache

ม้วน (mooa'n) a ball *or* roll of thread *or* silk ใม้ — the twelfth vowel, q. v.

มหรรณพ (ma'ha'nopp) [Pali] ocean, great sea, large lake

มหา (ma'har) [Pali] great - ราช great King — ชาติ past lives of

Buddha — บรม superior man, grandee — หิง assa fœtida

มหากไทย (ma'hahtthai) Minister of the North ผม — a tuft worn in the old Siamese fashion

มหากเล็ก (ma'hart lek) Royal Pages

มหาวัน (ma'hah wa'n) [Pali] deep forest

มหาสาล (ma'hahsarn) [Pali] man of great wealth, magnate (Alab. 188; but see also Childers 230)

มหาหง (ma'hah hong) root of a certain plant used for medicine

มหาหิง (ma'hah hing) foul-smelling medicinal exudation from a tree

มหิ (ma'hee') [Pali] (1) earth, world, ground (2) great ปลา — a fabulous fish — มา very great

มหิงษ (ma'bing) [Sansk.] buffalo

มหิก (ma'hit) fierce, brave, cruel

มหิก (ma'hitt) sacrifice, worship, worshipped, revered

มหิทธิ มหิกรา and มหิสร etc. (ma'hitti', etc.) [Pali] powerful in the earth, excellent, great

มหินทร์ (ma'hinn) great, powerful; Indra

มหิบาล (ma'hi'barn) [Pali] King

มหึมมา (ma'heummah)[Pali] immense, vast, great

มโห (ma'hoh) = มหา

มโหรณพ (ma'hohra'nopp) great sea, ocean, large lake

มโหรศพ (ma'hohra'sopp) games and ceremonies at Royal funerals

มหัศจรรย์ (ma'ha'tsa'cha'n) [Pali] strange, curious, marvellous, extraordinary

มอ (maw) [phon.] bellowing, noise of cows สี — ash colour หน้า — ซอ dirty-looking ง — ซีอ a snake

หมอ (maw) doctor, professor — ความ (1) lawyer (2) [of a Siamese] swindler, deceiver — ช้าง elephant-driver — ก soothsayer — ยากแผน surgeon — ง snake-charmer — ผี magician — ยา medical man, physician, doctor ปลา — a common fresh-water fish

หม้อ (maw) pot — แกง earthen pot for cooking มิน — soot sticking to the pot โรง — potter's work-shop; earthenware

มอก (mauk) unevenly (of painting), in patches

หมอก (mauk) cloud ตา — seeing indistinctly

มอง (maung) to look for, search for คอ̊ม — to examine secretly

หมอง (maung?) soiled, stained, dirty เศร้า — uneasy, sad หมน̊ — sad, melancholy — หมาง covered with shame — พระ ภักตร์ having a sad countenance (of royal persons)

ฆม้อง (mong) sound of the cymbal or gong

มอญ (maun) Peguan, Maun — รำ a lascivious dance

มอด (maut) an insect that eats wood — ไป to go out (of a fire)

มอน (maun) mulberry-tree

หมอน (maun?) (1) pillow, bolster — ข้าง long pillow, "dutch lady" (2) rollers for moving beams upon

มอบ (maup) to deliver, hand over — เวน สมบัติ to give over a kingdom

หมอบ (maup) to fall down before, to kneel before — กราน to remain prostrate or kneeling

มอม (maum) dirty, hideous

ม่อม (mom) with ท้าว ยาย a shrub

หม่อม (momm) and — แม่ wives of princes and superior nobles, concubines of the King — เจ้า child of a พระ องค์ เจ้า grandson of a King

หม่อม (momm) I [speaking to a superior] — ฉัน I [speaking to a หม่อม เจ้า]

มอย with ตา (tah moi) whitlow

ม่อย (moy) to slumber; light sleep — ๆ and — หลับ dozing, half asleep

ม้อย (moi) and จะ ม้อย to look askance, sidelong glance

หมอย (moi?) hair appearing at the age of puberty

มา (mah) to come กลับ — to come back — หา to visit, to come and see อยู่ — it happened ไป — หา กัน to frequent

ม้า (mar) horse, mare ขี่ — to ride ลาย zebra — น้ำ hippopotamus — ลา mule ปลา — a river fish

ม้า (mar) and — ตั่ง bench

หมา (mah?) dog — ใน and — ป่า wolf

— จิ้ หวก fox — หมู and หมู่ —
pigs and dogs! a term of contempt
— ๆ little long-haired dog

หม่า (mah) and — ไว้ to keep by soak-
ing in water

มาก (mark) much — มาย abundant,
much, many — มี rich — น้อย
much or little? กี — น้อย how
much?

มาก (mahk) betel-nut — พลู betel-nut
and leaves ชาน — the remains of
betel-nut which are spit out เหยั
— to mix the ingredients forchew-
ing betel เข้า — sweet fermented
rice — รก chess — แกบ a Laosian
game with balls

มาง with เปิง (perng marng) a long
drum struck with both hands

มาง (mahng) to endure with shame,
to be ashamed

มารคมาศ (marka'mart) [Pali] the third
month

มายา (mahyah) Maia, the mother of
Buddha [Alab. 79]

มาศ (mart) trunk hollowed out for
making a boat ลิก — stick for
stopping up a hole in a boat

หมาก (maht?) half-dry เหล็ก — awl.
boring tool

มาดร and มาดรา (mahdonn and mah-
drah) [Pali] mother

มาตยา (martyah) [Pali] grandees, chief
magistrates

มาตรา (martrah) [Sansk.] chapter,
section, clause

มาตุ (mahtoo') [Pali] mother — ราช
King's mother

มาตุลี (mahtoo'lee) [Pali] Indra's chari-
oteer

มาตุลังค์ (mahtoo'la'ng) [Pali] uncle

มาท (maht) มาทว่า (and other similar
words) although — หมาย to decree.
determine, resolution — ไว้ to resolve, to determine upon a future
course of action, espec. upon pun-
ishing any one

มาน (mahn) dropsy ท้อง - - swelling in
the stomach

ม่าน (marn) screen, curtain กั้น — to
draw the curtain

ม้าน (marn) nearly dry

มานพ (mahnop) [Pali] young man

ม่านลาย (marnlai) a large long-necked
river turtle

มานะ and มะนะ (mahna', ma'na') [Sansk.] to determine, determination, purpose

มานัด and มานัศา (mahna't, mahna'-sah) [Sansk.] will, mind, intention

ม้าม (marm) and กับ — spleen

มะหมุ่ย (marmooi') a creeping plant the fruit of which, if touched, produces a rash

มาย (maie) and มาก — many, plenty

หมาย (mai) to make a decree, law ยาก — sealed order of the King — ว่า to intend, to think of มัน — to expect — ใจ to resolve, to intend มาก — intention

หม้าย (mai) widow, widower, widowed

มายา (mahyah) [Pali] fraud, guile, artifice, coquetry

มาร (mahra') [Pali] (1) giant, demon King of the bad angels นาง — giantess, female demon (2) death

มารดร (mahra'don) and มารดา [Pali] mother

มารยา (mahnyah) fraud, coquetry

มารา (mahrah) and มาระ [Pali] giant, demon [Alab. 213]

มาริก (mahritt) with เมือง Mergui

มารุต (mahroo't) [Pali] wind

มาระยาทร (mahra'yart) [San.] morals, manners

มาลก (marlok) [Pali] see มาพ้าก

มาลย (mahl) with เยาว young and pretty woman

มาลา (mahlah) มาลาคี and มาลาไลย [Pali] flowers, garlands พระ — a royal crown or hat สุวรรณ — gold flowers sent as a token of homage

มาลหลี (mahloo'lee) a tree with yellow blossoms

มาไลย (marlai) and มาลับ [Pali] flowers in bloom

มาศ (mart) and มาศะ [Pali] (1) gold (2) sulphur (3) month

มาศก (marsok) [Pali] as much money as one-fifth of a tical

มาพ้าก (marlok) [Pali] enclosure, yard

มาพ้ด (mahlaw) [Chin.] cymbals

มิ (mi') [shortened from of ไม] not, no — ได้ not possible, cannot — ใช่ for fear that, so as prevent — ใช่ not so, no, not at all

มิคะลุทธิ (mikkha'loo't) [Pali] hunter

มิ่ง (ming) (1) the top (2) lady (3) soft ยอก — *and* — มเหษี Queen

มิ่งขวัญ (ming khwa'n) tutelary genius of children

มิจฉา (mitchah) [Pali] false, wrong, mistake, disagreeable, grudging — ทิฐิ infidel, irreligious

มิด (mit) well-closed, well-joined

มิตร (mitt) [Sansk.] friend

มิถุนายน (mi'too'nahyon) [Pali] the third month (new style) Pisces June]

มีน (min) [Pali] fish, Pisces [zodiac.] — เหม้า soot

หมิ่น (min) (1) to despise, disdain ก — to disparage (2) near the edge

มิญชัง (mincha'ng) [Pali] marrow, brains

มินาคม (mi'nahkhom) [Pali] the 12th month [new style] = March

มินิต (mi'nitt) [Engl.] minute

หมิบ (mip) outer part of the lips

มิศ (mitt) [Engl.] Mister, "Mr."

มิฬห (minha') [Pali] excrement

มี (mee) to have, to be — อยู่ there is

มาก — rich, riches — คุณ benefactor, to do good

มี (mee!) uproar, noise — ข่าว to be published, talked about

หมี (mee?) bear

มี (mee) vermicelli soup made of rice

มีด (meet) knife — โกน razor — แกะ sculptor's chisel — คลอก knife for splitting osiers — เหน็บ dagger — ผ่า ผ surgeon's scalpel — พร้า sabre, sword, kitchen-knife — พับ clasp-knife, pocket-knife

เมีย (meea') wife — น้อย concubine ตัว — (of animals) female มัว — not get fully awake

เมียง (meea'ng) to watch, observe

เมียง (meea'ng) tea-leaves used [in Laos] for chewing like betel

เมียน *and* เหมียน (meea'n) to gather up, shut up, hide

เมียว (meeyo) [Chin.] cat

มี่ซั่ว (meesooa') [Chin.] vermicelli

หมึก (meuk) ink ปลา — cuttle fish แท่ง stick of Chinese ink

มึง (meung) thou, thee [speak'ng to

children, or in contempt] ก – to address in the second person [Fr. tutoyer]

หมึ (meun) stunned — กืน secret enemies — หงิ to sulk, to pout — หัว dazed, bewildered

มืด (meut) darkness เช้า — early morning หน้า — fainting fit, swoon

หมื่น (meun) (1) ten thousand หัว — chief of the King's secretaries (2) lowest title of nobility กรม — a little of royal Princes

มือ (meu) hand เข้า — to participate, help ลง — to begin แก้ — (1) revenge (2) to recommence, to do over again เครื่อง — instrument, tool ฝ่า — palm of the hand ผี — skill, industry ลก — artisan, workman ลาย — good hand-writing — ก้วน one-handed — ลิ่ง ribs of a boat

เมื่อ (meu) a minute ago

เมื่อ (meue) times

เมื่อ (meua') when — หน้า future — กระ นั้น then — ไร when ?

เมือก (meua'k) gluten, glutinous liquor

เมือง (meua'ng) kingdom, city, country — ขึ้น tributary kingdom — เอก — โท — ตรี town of 1st, 2nd, 3rd rank เจ้า — Governor of a Province — ใหม่ Singapore

เหมือง (mooa'ng) flooded country, low-lying land, marsh

เหมือด (mooa't) vermicelli — กิน a tree with medicinal wool

เหมือน (mooa'n) like — กัน in the same way, equally, all the same

เหมือย (mooi') out of health, unwell

เมื่อไร (mooa'rai) when ?

มุ (moo') to become angry — กระ วิ violent in speech, abusive, foul-mouthed

มุก (moo'k) [Sansk.] with หอย mother-of-pearl — ดา pearl — ดา ภาน a precious stone

มุข (moo'k) [Pali] (1) face, front, mouth, entrance, beginning, principal (2) triangular face or side of a house, etc., gable-end

มุง (moo'ng) (1) to roof the house (2) crowd or knot of spectators

มุ่ง (moo'ng) to pay attention, regard

attentively, to intend, intention

มุ้ง (moo'ng) mosquito net

มุจลินท์ (moo'cha'lin) [Pali] nymph of the cave หิน — a tree [Barringtonia acutangula]

มุด (moot) (1) to get underneath, to to hide under, to burrow into the mud (like fishes) (2) [Cambod.] to plunge into the water

หมุด (moo't) peg, plug (of lint, wood, etc.)

มุดกุด (moo't koo't) with สั้น shortened, curtailed

มุดตู and มุดตู (moo't too') flabby, weak, slow

มุกะกิก (moo'ta'kit) [of women] very ill

มุกะกาฎ มุกะะาฎ (moo'ta'kart) [of men] very ill

มุตตัชะ (moo'tta'cha') [Pali] corner of the tongue; Palatal [Gramm.]

มุทุ (moo'too') soft, tender, flabby, weak, mild, slow

มุ่นนาย (moo'n nai) master, owner, proprietor

มุ่น (moo'n) (1) to bind up the hair in a top-knot (2) to cover up, to cover over (3) agitated — ใจ and — หมก to be troubled, sad, anxious; to

take pains — มัว blinded inwardly

หมุน (moo'n) to turn, to whirl

หมุน (moo'nn) dark

มุนี (moo'nee) [Pali] hermit, ascetic teacher, saint

มุม (moo'm) angle, corner แมงมุม — spider

มุ่ม (moo'm) (1) blunt, obtuse, thick (2) to squeeze

มุย มุย (mooi' mooi') gluttonously, greedily

มุย (mooi') and อ้าย — [Chin.] an axe, a hatchet อ้าย — Amoi

มุย (mooi') a tree

มุ้ย มุ้ย (mooi' mooi') fat, corpulent

มุลิกา (moo'li'kah) see มุลิกา

มุลี (moo'lee) lattice-work, blinds

มูลัง and มูลัง (moola'ng) [Pali] foundation, base

มุสา (moo'sah) [Pali] lie, lying, falsely — วาท falsehood

มุสิกะ (moo'si'ka') [Pali] rat

หมู (moo?) pig, hog หัว — ploughshare ปลา — a river fish ปลา — ทะเล porpoise บ้า — epileptic

หมู่ (moo) herd, flock, troop, genus [of animals], race [of men]

มูก (mook) น้ำ — and ขี้ — mucus of the nose สั่ง ขี้ — to blow one's nose

มูต (moot) [Pali] urine

มูน (moon) to flavour rice with cocoa-nut milk (2) raised place, hillock, heap

มูน มาม (moom marm) dirty, slovenly, ill-behaved

มูล (moon) [Pali] (1) root [of trees, etc.] (2) excrement of animals (3) price

มูลของ (moola'khong) [Pali and Siam.] common things

มูลิกา or มูลิกา (mooli'kah) female shampooer, masseuse

มูลไวยากรณ์ [Pali] grammar

หมูสี (moosee) a dwarf cocoa-nut tree

เหมมิหมิน (may minn) to do imperfectly, improperly

เมขลา (maykha'lah) with นาง [Pali] female angel of the ocean

เมฆ (mayk) [Pali] clouds สี — ash-grey

เมงมอน (meng maun) Peguans, Mauns,

เหม็ง ๆ (meng-meng) sound of a gong

เม็ด (mett) seed, grain, stone of fruit, kernel [designation of pills, seeds, etc.] กล — wisdom, science, craft

เมตตา (mettah) [Pali] kindness, compassion, benevolence, charity [Alab. 168, 184]

เมไตรย with พระ (Phra-Mettrai) [San.] name of the next coming Buddha

เมถุน (may thoo'na') [Pali] (1) sexual intercourse, sensual love (2) Gemini [zodiac.] — คิน name of the third month

เมทินี (mayta'nee') [Pali] earth, world

เมโท (maytoh) [Pali] sweat, perspiration

เม่น (menn) porcupine

เม้น (men) to hem

เหม็น (menn?) to stink, bad-smelling, stinking — ขี้ musty smell — ... smell of a dead body — เขียว smell of boiled vegetables

เมย with เฉย (choy moy) careless, indifferent, taciturn

เมรุ (mayroo') [Pali] (1) Mount Meru [Alab. 13] (2) funeral shrine

เมไรย (mayrai) [Pali] intoxicating
liquors

เมศ or เมศราษี (maysa'rarsee) [Pali]
Aries [zodiac.]

เมควิถี (maysa'wi'tee) [Pali] passage
of the sun through Aries

เมษายน (maysahyonn) [Sansk.] name
of the 1st month [April]

เมอ (mer) [Cambod.] to turn the face
towards, to look

เมิน (mern) to turn away the head, take
no notice — บุง sulky — เฉิก not
to take care, not to look

แม (maa) mother, [a title something
like English "Mrs."] — ผัว mother-
in-law, mother of the husband —
ยาย mother-in-law, wife's mother
— เลี้ยง step-mother — นม nurse
— ซื้อ tutelary genius of children
— ครัว female cook, cook-maid —
เจ้า — คุณ [in addressing women]
my Lady, Madam — ชาว ladies
of the Palace — กอง superinten-
dant — ทัพ General-in-chief — ตีน
and หัว — ตีน big toe — มือ and หัว

— มือ thumb — บันได upright of a
ladder — ประ ตู door-posts — ฝา
posts for a wall of plank or bamboo
— มด sorceress, witch, poisoner
— หม้าย widow — แรง vice, machine
for lifting — เหล็ก magnet — แม่
สื่อ mould for type — น้ำ river —
เฮย Hi ! (to women)

แม้ (maa!) certainly, although, if —
ว่า even if

เเหม and แม่ (maa) [exclam. of surprise
disapprobation or blame]

แมง ruly. for แมลง

แมง with แอ้ง (ang mang) stuck fast,
immoveable, unable to move

แมงคุด (maangkoo't) mangosteen

แมงลัก (maang la'k) sesame

แมน (maan) [Cambod.] sky, heavens

แม่น (man) hitting the mark, correctly,
rightly, skilful

แม้น (maan) although, even if มาก
nevertheless . — ถ้า ว่า if, although ;
alike, similar

แมบ with นอน (naun maap) to lie on
the face

แหม่ม (memm) [of foreigners] Madame

แมว (maao) [phon.] cat, caterwauling the cry of cats — เฝ้า sentinel, spy (2) a mango

ใหม่ (mai) new, recent, again — ๆ not yet used ทำ — to recommence, repair

ไม่ (mai) not — ได้ it is impossible, cannot — รู้ ได้ do not know — ใช่ ไม่ก็ not so — เอา not to wish; no, thank you เท่า — by no means บุญ เท่า — if I die — ไหว too heavy — เป็น not able

ไม (maie) a roll (of silk, cloth, etc.)

ไม้ (mai) wood ต้น — tree, stick ดอก — flower, blossom ลูก — fruit ผล — [high word] fruit หน่อ — shoots of bamboo — หอม a sweet wood used for burning น้า — cross-bow ช่าง — carpenter — วา a measuring stick about 80 inches long — กวาด broom — เท้า walking stick — เรียว rod for whipping children — สอย pole, hair-pin — ตุง tree trunks — ราว

bulustrade, banister — เอก — โท — ตรี etc. [names of various letters and accents, q. v.]

ไหม (mai?) (1) silk ตัว — silkworm ก้อน — and เส้น — silk thread (2) fine สิน — ปรับ — fine, to fine

ไหม้ (maie) to be on fire ไฟ — conflagration — เกรียม half-burned

ไมตรี (maitree) [Sansk.] friendship, charity [Alab. 168] มิตร — close friendship ราช — treaty of alliance (2) name of a Buddha [Alab. 177]

โม (moh) call for a dog แตง — watermelon

โมก (moke) jasmine — มัน a tree used for carving

โมง (mohng) hour กี่ — what o'clock?

โม่ง (mohng) large ปิด — blind-man's-buff

เหม่ง (mohng) gong hanging on a three-legged stand กรับ sound of gongs and drums used at hair-cutting ceremonies

โหมด (moht) cloth embroidered with gold and silver

โมทนา (mohta'nah) [Pali] to rejoice, give thanks, congratulate

โมรา (mohrah) [Pali] (1) peacock (2) a precious stone

โมฬี (mohlee) [Pali] top-knot, crest

โมหา โมหะ โมโห and โมหันธ์ (mohah etc.) [Pali] ignorance, error, illusion of the passions, anger [Alab. 37, 218]

เมา (mow) drunk, intoxicated ๛ — drunkard ผัว — addicted to — ยา intoxicated with tobacco เบื่อ — (1) disgusted with drinking (2) a poison

เมา with เข้า (kow mow) new rice bruised in a mortar ปลา — a white river fish แมลง — poisonous gnat

เข้าใหญ่ (mow kow) too big, strange-looking

เหมา (mow?) and จ้าง — to contract for work

เมาฬี (mowlee) and โมฬี [Pali] top-knot

เมาะ (maw') mattress for children

เหมาะ (maw') properly, suitably, elegantly — เจาะ well-wrought — เหมง well-fitted

มะ (ma') [Maun] mother

มะ (ma') [a prefix] fruit, fruit-tree

มะกรูก (ma'kroot) a lime or lemon with rough skin

มะเกลือ (ma'kleua) (1) ebony (2) a tree ลูก — fruit used for dying black

มะกล่ำ (ma'kla'm) a creeping plant having a red fruit

มะกอก (ma'kauk) olive

มะกา (ma'kah) a medicinal tree

มะกูฏ (ma'koo't) [Pali] top, summit

มะโก (ma'koh) a tree

มะกัก (ma'ka'k) an olive tree

มะขบ (ma'khop) a tree with red fruit, pomegranate

มะขวาท (ma'khwart) a tree with round edible fruit

มะขวิด (ma'khwit) a fruit tree

มะขาม (ma'kharm) tamarind — เปียก a round fruit used for medicine — เทศ an edible fruit — เปียก t. jam

มะเขก (ma'khayk) to threaten to strike with the back of the knuckles

มะโขก (ma'khoke) to threaten with the front knuckles

มะเขือ (ma'kheua) and — เทศ tomato

มะคำ and มะคะ (ma'kha') a tree with black seeds used for medicine

มะคำไก่ (ma'kha'mkai) a tree with medicinal fruit

มะงั่ว (ma'ngooa') a large sour lemon

มะราหู่ (ma'chahroo) [Malay] a cloth

มะซาง (ma'sahng) a fruit tree

มะณี (ma'nee) [Pali] precious stone, jewel ทินตา — Siamese grammar and prosody

มะดูก (ma'dook) a fruit tree

มะดัน (ma'da'n) a large tree with small sour fruit

มะตาด (ma'tart) a large tree with sour fruit

มะติ (ma'ti') [Malay.] dead

มะตูม (ma'toom) a tree with large oval fruit used as a remedy for diarrhœa ลูก — bale-fruit

มะธุ (ma'too') มะธุระ etc. [Pali] honey, sweet, savoury, melodious

มะโน (ma'noh) [Pali] mind, thought, intellect — ไมย (1) right, conformable, springing from the mind (2) horse — ธรรม conscience

มะโนรถ (ma'nohrot) [P.] wish, desire

มะโนรา (ma'nohrah) nymph of the forest [theatr.]

มะนะ (ma'na') and มานะ to try, effort, to know

มะนะสิการ (ma'na'si'karn) and มะนะสิการะ [Pali] attention, to take heed, consider carefully

มะนะโส (ma'na'soh) [Pali] will, purpose, intention

มะปราง (ma'prarng) a yellow plum

มะปริง (ma'pring) a small sour plum

มะแปน (ma'paan) with ส้ม a small orange

มะฝ่อ (ma'faw) chestnut

มะพร้าว (ma'prow) cocoa-nut

มะพลับ (m a'pla'p) a fruit tree

มะเฟือง (ma'fooa'ng) a sour yellow fruit

มะไฟ (ma'fai) a fruit tree

มะภูด (ma'poot) a yellow fruit very like a large pear

มะม่วง (ma'mooa'ng) mango — พิมเสน a common mango

มะม (ma'mee) noise, shouting

มะเมีย (ma'meea) horse ปี — seventh year of the cycle

มะเหมียว (ma'meeyo) (1) a small black beetle (2) a forest animal

มะมูง (ma'moo'ng) [Ca.] cockroach

มะแม (ma'maa) goat ปี — eighth year of the cycle

มะยม (ma'yomm) a fruit tree

มะยูร (ma'yoo'ra') มะยูรา and other forms [Pali] peacock, peafowl

มะรายืน (ma'rainee) fourth day after

มะรึง (ma'reung) a tree with bitter fruit

มะรืนนื (ma'reunnee) the day after to-morrow

มะเรือง (ma'reua'ng) and — the third day after, three days hence

มะรุม (ma'roo'm) a tree with pods used for curry

มะเหรกเหก (ma'rayk kayk) senseless (talk), unprincipled (action)

มะเริง (ma'rayng) venereal ulcer

มะรอย with เฉย (choy ma'roy) idle, apathetic

มะโรง (ma'rohng) the great dragon ปี — fifth year of the cycle

มะระ (ma'ra') bitter pulse

มะลาก (ma'lark) to rejoice

มะลากอ (ma'larkaw) papaw

มะลาย (ma'lai) and มลาย with ไม้ the 13th vowel, q. v.

มะลายู (ma'layoo) Malay

มะลิ (ma'lee') a tree with white flowers — ลา do. with a single flower — ซ้อน do. with large flowers

มะไล (ma'lai) [Pali] chaplet of flowers, wreath, garland

มะแวง (ma'waang) a medicinal plant

มะสุ (ma'soo') [Pali] beard

มะเสง (ma'sayng) small snake or dragon ปี — sixth year of the cycle

มะละกอ (ma'la'kaw) papaw

มะสะหรู (ma'sa'roo) a striped silk cloth

มะหวด (ma'hooa't) a tree with small red fruit

มะหิ (ma'hee') [Pali] earth

มะหู (ma'hoo') omen, presage, fortune, fate, luck

มะเห (ma'hay) [Pali] great — Queen — ศวร a King of angels

มะไหย (ma'hai) มะหนิศ [Pali] great

มะโหรี (ma'hohree) music, concert

มะโหระทึก (ma'hohra'teuk) a metal kettle-drum beaten before the King

มะโหรศพ (ma'hohra'sop) [San.] games and amusements at Royal funerals

มะโหสถ (ma'hohsot) [Pali] a generation of Buddha

มะโหฬาร (ma'hohlạrn) [Pali] excellent, full of good things

มะอึม (ma'om) a tree

มะอึก (ma'euk) a tree with small round
fruit

มัก (ma'k) desirous of, addicted to อุ๋
— having a bad habit — ง่าย careless — ใก้ covetous — ผัว (woman)
who desires men other than her
husband — หลง constantly making
mistakes

หมัก (ma'k) fermentation, to leave a
thing to ferment, to leave dirty
clothes undried — แบ่ง to dilute
and ferment meal — หมม accumu-
lation of dirty things

หมักขัก with อ้วน (ooa'n ma'k kha'k)
big and fat man

มัค (ma'k) [Pali] road, way, path,
stage, degree [Alab. 170]

มัควาฬ (ma'kha'wahr) better มัฆ!พาน
[Sansk.] Indra

มั่ง (ma'ng) bulging out, swollen, thick
— มี wealthy, rather rich — คึ่ง
very bulky, very rich, opulent

มังกง (ma'ngkong) a small fish

มังกร (mangkonn) fabulous sea dragon

มังกู (ma'ngkoo') (1) a fabulous animal
(2) liar

มังกุณะ (ma'ngkoo'na') bug

มังคะไล (ma'ngkha'loh) [Pali] auspicious, lucky, joyous, festive

มังคุ (ma'ngkoo') with เรือ long barge
rowed by oars

มังคุก = แมงคุก mangoosteen

มังษา (ma'ngsah) มังษะ and มังษ่
[Pali] flesh

มัจฉา (ma'tchah) and มัจโฉ [Pali] fish

มัจฉริยะ (ma'tchi'ri'ya') [Pali] avarice
[Alab. 206]

มัจโฉ (ma'tchoh) a theatrical term

มัชฌิมา (ma'tchi'mah) and มัชฌิมะ
[Pali] middle, the middle country,
Central India [Alab. 187]

มันเชฏฐู่กากร (ma'nchetti'karkon) [Pa-
li] tax on sapan wood

มัด (ma't) to tie, to bind, to tie up; a
bundle [of torches, faggots, etc.]

หมัด (hma't) (1) flea (2) fist กำ —
to clench the fist

มักถลุงค์ *and* มัทถลุงค์ (ma'tta'loo'ng)
[Pali] brain, skull

มัตติกา (ma'tti'kah) [Pali] earth, soil,
mud

มัตะกะ (ma'ta'ka') [Pali] dead, stupid,
senseless

มัทธยม (ma'tta'yom) [Sansk.] middling

มัทยัต (ma'ta'ya't) [Pali] prudent,
careful, moderation

มัน (ma'n) (1) he, she, you [word of
contempt] (2) bright, shining

มัน (ma'n) Siamese potato — เทษ
potato — เสา yam

มั่น (ma'nn) firm, stedfast, constant
— คำ to keep a promise — แม่น it
is true, certainly — ถึ very fat

หมัน (ma'n?) barren ต้น — a tree with
brown leaves ปลา — a fish

! มัน (ma'n?) tow, worn-out net ยาก
— to caulk (a boat)

! มั่น (ma'nn) diligent, industrious

มัม มั้ม and หมัม (ma'm) to eat greedily, dirtily

มัศการ *see* นมัศการ

มัศยาการ (ma'sa'yahkonn) [San.] a fish

ย

ย (yaw yon   English *y*. Guttural : a
low letter) — ยอ name of this letter

ยก (yok) (1) to lift, raise, take away,
to rise (2) a measure of planks one
sok wide and sixteen wah long (3)
time, times — โทษ to pardon, forgive — ยอ (1) to praise, to commend (2) to pull up a net

หยก (yok) (1) action of people walking
or running slowly (2) a stone worn
on the wrist by Chinamen (3) shade
for a lamp

ยกกระบัตร (yokkra'ba't) *better* ยกระ
บัตร [Cambod.] third Governor of
town or province

ยง (yong) (1) fine, strong, pretty (2) to
urge on, instigate ยุ — to urge on,
to a fight — ยุทธ to fight, to make
a hard fight

หยง (yong) to raise a little, to raise
oneself on tip-toe, to comb up the
hair หยิบ — to pick up gently

หยก (yot) drop

ย่น (yon) to abridge, to contract, folded, wrinkled หน้า — angry-looking

(2) to come back, go back — ยัง to
retire, withdraw, give up

ยนตร์ (yon) [San.] instrument worked
by machinery, automaton, machine
แยน — secret mode of instruction.
ไพรฑ Palace of Indra

ยม (yom, yoma') and derivatives [Pali]
the King of the infernal regions

หยม or หย่อม (yaum) a small quantity
of anything, tuft of grass, sprig of
tree, etc.

ยมบาล (yomma'barn) and ยมพบาล
satellites of พระยายม see ยม

ยมุนา (ya'moo'nah) Jumna, one of the
five rivers of the Punjab

ยรรยง (ya'nyong) strong

ยล (yon) to see, to look

หยวก (yooa'k) soft inside of the plan-
tain tree

ยวง (yooa'ng) pulpy seed of fruits —
ใย fine

ยวด (yooa't) more, increase, to be in-
creased

ยวน (yooa'n) (1) pleasure, voluptuous-
ness (2) Annamese, Cochin-Chinese
— แกว Tonquinese

ยวบ (yooa'p) bending, flexible, yielding
หยวบ (yoca'p?) (1) all in unison, keeping time together (2) to shake about

ยวย (yooi') in a curved line. winding.
not straight

ยั่ว (yooa') to strike or touch playfully.
to tiekle, to caress

ยศ (yot) [Pali] dignity, honour, reputation, renown ยั่วใหญ่ — well at-
tended, with large retinue ยิ่งใหญ่ —
superior in rank เต็ม — in full force
แต่งเต็ม — full dress

ยอ (yaw) (1) fruit tree (2) a square net
(3) to flatter, to praise, to extol (4
[to ponies and buffaloes] stop!
ยอ a shrub of which the roots are
used for dyeing red

ย่อ (yaw) to abridge, abbreviate, curtail, bow down — เกล to make oneself lower — ยอให้ to give way —
ท้อ cowardice — แย to stagger, to
lose strength

ยอก (yauk) prick, sting, sharp pain —
ย้อน incoherent

เยอก (yawk) to caress, to play with

ยอง (yaung) (1) squatting with the knees up, sitting (2) fine, pretty

ย่อง (yong) to walk gently — แย่ง to walk throwing the feet side-ways

หยอง (yawng) to fear, to be afraid, to be frightened away, to have the hair or crest standing on end

หย่อง (yong) (1) carved work (2) socket (3) nimble, quick

ยอด (yaut) summit, top

หยอด (yawt) to soak, to ferment, to drop one thing on or into another

ยอน (yawn) to pick out of a hole, to take wax out of the ear

ย่อน (yaun) to sway, to bend (like a carrying pole)

ย้อน (yorn) to fail, to refuse, to rebound

หยอน (yawn?) to respect, fear

หย่อน (yonn) to slacken, let loose, let go ยุก — ไป fastened loosely

ยอบ (yaup) to contract, make smaller, become lower, to lower oneself, to go down (of a swelling) — แยบ nearly all gone

ยอม (yaum) to consent, to agree ใบ — written relinquishment of a charge ตัว to give up one's liberty (by marrying, becoming a slave, etc.) — ให้ to lend, to let

ย่อม (yom) (1) habitually, according to custom (2) middling, small (3) part of the price

ย้อม (yawm) to dip, to dye

หย่อม (yomm) (1) anything which tapers off towards the top (2) cluster, clump, tuft (of grass, hair, etc.)

ย่อย (yoi) to break into pieces ซื้อ — to buy by retail

ย้อย (yoie) to trickle down, to slip down, to drop, to run down ยาน — long and pendulous

หยอย (yoye) (1) [to run] eagerly (2) small lock of hair, scanty hair

หย่อย (yoi) one after another

ยอระยาตร *see* บุรยาตร

ยา (yah) medicine, medicament, drug, tobacco — ดำ black extract from aloes — เม็ด pills — ลง purgative — ทา liniment — ขี้ผึ้ง ointment — สวน clyster — พอก poultice — ถ่าย — ถุเลา — รุ various kinds of purging — แก้ ลง remedy for diarrhœa — หยอด ตา ointment for the eyes, collyrium สี ย — to smoke — น้ก snuff — เลือก medicine for women

ยา (yah) to tar (a boat)

ยา ยี (yah yee) to molest, trouble, annoy, torment

ย่า (yar) paternal grandmother ปู่ — ancestors

เหย่า *less properly* อย่า (yar?) (1) *negative Imper.* not, do not — เพ่อ not yet — เพ่อก่อน wait a bit — ว่า not only (2) to separate, repudiate, desert, go away — ร้างกัน divorce

ยาก (yahk) difficult, laborious, poor — เข็ญ ประ ศา too difficult, very poor

เหยาก *and less properly* อยาก (yark) to desire, want — เข้า hunger (2) rather thick — นัก very thick

เหยากเยื่อ (yark yeua') rubbish, refuse, litter

ยากร (yahkonn) companies, troops แสน - - 100,000 men, large army

ยาคู (yarkhoo) [Pali] soup made of young rice shoots, rice-gruel

ยาง (yarng) (1) a genus of river fishing birds — กรอก a species of this genus — เสวย (sa'woy) royal species very good for the table (2) glutinous soup เห็ด — mushroom น้ำ มัน --- thick varnish

ย่าง (yahng) (1) to smoke (meat) (2) to walk slowly

หย่าง *with* ขา (khar yarng) cross pieces used as a support

หย่าง *and* อย่าง (yarng) mode, way, manner, kind, species, custom, fashion — ไร *and* - อะไร how? — ไร ใย why? ตัว — pattern — หได — ใด in any way

อย่างกุ้ง (yarng ka'ng) *or* ย่างกุ้ง Rangoon

ยาจก (yahchok) [San.] poor, beggarly

ยาจะนา *and* ยาจะนะ (yahcha'nah) [Sansk.] (1) to wish, ask, beg (2) to go

หยาด (yart) drop

ยาด เยียง (yart yeea'ng) [Sansk. and Siam.] to walk with the body bent

ยาตร (yaht) and other forms [Pali and Sansk.] to walk, to go

ยาน (yarn) too long, hanging down

ยาน (yarn) [Pali] moveable, moving, palanquin, litter

ย่าน (yahn) extent, distance — กว้าง in width, space of

ย่านาง *and* ย้านาง (yahnahng) spirit or genius attached to ships [Virg. Æn. X. 235.]

ย่านาง (yahnarng) a tree, shrub

ยานี (yarnee) verse of five syllables

ยานุมาศ (yarnoo'mart) [Pali and Cam.] state palanquin

ยานัง (yarna'ng) [Sansk.] palanquin, beast of burden

ยาบ (yahp) beating of the air, to wave

ยยาบ (yarp) rough, rude, ill-bred

ยาม (yahm) [Pali] (1) watches of the night — หนึ่ง 9 p.m. สอง mid- night สาม — 3 a. m. (2) handle [of plough]

ย่าม (yarm) (1) wallet, bag (2) to get bolder

ยยาม (yarm') *and* — หยาบ proud, ar- rogant, insolent, rude

ยามา (yahmah) [Pali] (1) the third heaven (2) = ยาม q. v.

ยาย (yaie) maternal grandmother, a

common term for old women แม่- mother-in-law คา — ancestor — ทวด maternal great grandmother — ท่าว [honourable appellation] old lady — แก่ old woman — ชี old nun คิว — ชี a night insect

ย่าย (yai) strings, threads or rags, etc. hanging or dropping from a ceiling or wall, etc.

ย้าย (yie) [Pali] to displace, remove, go to another place

ยาเยย (yahyee') [Malay.] my dear

ยาว (yowe) long, length คำ — long syllables, long stories เพลง - amorous songs, love ballads, ditties โยน — spreading from one to ano- ther, wide-spread, garrulous

ยาสง (yahsong) *letter* อะ สง *with* ถิ่ earth-nuts

ยิก (yik) in quick repetition, with quick movements — ๆ quickly

หยิก (yik) (1) frizzy, curled (2) to pinch, to scratch หยิก — tiresome, rest- less — ๆ quickly

ยิง (ying) to propel, shoot out, shoot

— ยิง to fire a gun, to shoot with a gun — นก to shoot at a bird — ฟัน to shoot out the teeth

ยิ่ง (ying) more, the more, improved — วัน advanced hour in the day ขึ้น — better, more ๆ — better, chiefly, best ยุ่ง — entangled, complicated, confused

หยิ่ง (ying) vain, ostentatious, conceited, conceit

ยิน (yin) (1) to hear (2) liqueur made of junipers, gin

ยินดี (yindee) glad, joyful, to rejoice ความ — pleasure

ยินร้าย (yinrai) displeased, annoyed, angry

ยิบ (yip) to prick, stinging, violent ; closed, shut up

หยิบ (yip) a pinch with the fingers — ยิม to borrow trifles here and there - ฟาย to pick up and put into the palm of the hand, a handfull - มือ a measure of 50 (formerly 150) grains of rice

ยิ้ม (yim) smiling

หยิม (yim?) scanty; little หยิม — continually asking, tiresome, troublesome

ยี (yee) (1) to rub on, to anoint (2) to fondle, to excite by caressing - ยวน to cheer up

ยี่ (yee) [Chin.] two — สิบ twenty ที่ — second

ยี่โถ (yee toh) a tree flower

ยี่เข่ง (yee kheng) etc. a flower หยี with กำมะ (ka'mma' yee) velvet

ยี่ซั่ว (yee sooa) [Chin.] (1) vermicelli (2) fennel (3) pig-tail,

ยี่โถ (yee toh) flowering laurel

ยี่ปุ่น (yee poo'n) Japanese

ยี่ภู่ (yeepoo) [Cambod.] mattress (of the King)

ยี่สง with ตัว (tooa' yeesong) better ดิน ถั่ว earth-nut

ยี่สน (yeesonn) a large flower ปลา — a sea fish

ยี่สุ่น (yeesoo'n) Indian rose

ยี่หวน (yeehooa'n) (1) pleasure, delight (2) a sweet-scented flower

ยี่หุบ (yeeh oo'p) a flowering shrub with large leaves

เยีย (yeea') [Laos.] by chance, if by chance — ไก why? how? ไก่ — a cock which looks like a hen

เยียง (yeeya'ng) example, manners

เยียด (yeeya't) (1) condensed, close-fitted, compact, crowded (2) far

เหยียด (yeeya't) to stretch oneself out, at full length

เยียบ (yeeyep) coolness of a forest, chill, sheltered place ปลา ซ้าย — a flat fish

เหยียบ (yeeyep) to trample upon

เยียม (yeeya'm) (1) to come out, put out (2) and — เยียม to visit, call upon

เหยียม (yeea'm?) first

เยียรยง (yeea'ra'yong) *better* เยียยง fine, handsome, strong, vigorous

เยียวยา (yeeyo yah) an aperient medicine

เยียว (yeeyo) to make water ก้อง — bladder

เหยียว (yee'o) *and* อ — hawk, kite, generic term for birds of prey — กะไก่ sparrow-hawk หาง - joint of planks resembling a kite's tail

ยึก (yeu'tt) (1) to hammer in [a nail] (2) to take hold of and keep fast, to hold back (by a cord, etc.)

ยึง (yeung) [ยิ่ง] more

ยึด (yeut) to stretch out; long, lasting — ยาว at length — ยาก slipping down and being pulled back again [espec. of the mucus of the nose]

ยืน (yeune) to stand up, stand to - - ยืน to stand up to, to contend with, to oppose with both hands ยั่ง — to stand to one's word ให้ อายุกับ — long life to you !

ยืน (yeun) to reach out, to put forward, to push out, to offer

ยืน ๆ (yeun! yeun!) long, lasting, further on, continuing

ยืม (yeum) to borrow

ยือ (yeu) to pull away, to pull off, to distrain, to seize in satisfaction of a debt

เยือ (yeua') thin skin, pellicule, sheath, covering — อรู *and* — กระ marrow — มะพร้าว pulp of coconut — อ to break, to pull apart — ยาง stuck together

เหยอ (yeua') bait

เหยอก (yeua'k) (1) to be blown about by the wind (2) cold sensation arising from solitude or fear

เหยง (yeua'ng) to go out of the straight line, to turn aside — กัน uneven, inconsistent, incongruous — ย้าย to take away พก — ย้าย to resort to a subterfuge

เหยือน (yeuan') to go to visit

ยุ (yoo') to lead into evil, to incite to mischief

ยุกเข็ญ (yoo'kken) poor, needy, destitute

ยุกหยิก (yoo'k yik) querulous, troublesome

ยุกระบัตร (yoo'kra'ba't) [Camb.] Third Governor

ยุค (yoo'kh) [Pali] time — ยุค time of confusion

ยุคล (yoo'khonn) [Pali] a pair, two

ยุคะบัตร (yoo'ka'ba't) [Pali] the proper moment, the right time

ยุง (yoo'ng) mosquito — กวาด broom หก — peacock หัวการเหยก — a common tree with light red blossom

ยุ่ง (yoo'ng) and — ยุง intricate, confused

ยุ้ง (yoo'ng) loft, barn: a measure of twenty เกวียน

ยุต (yoo't) to retain, detain, hold, keep

หยุด (yoo't?) to stop, to stay, to cease, to leave off

ยุติ (yoo'ti') (1) to cease (2) [Pali] true, perfect, right — ธรรม justice

ยุทธ์ ยุทธะ ยุทธนา and ยุทธ์ (yoo'tt etc.) [Sansk.] to light, to wage war ยุทนาธิการ and ยุทธิการ barrack

ยุทนาธิการ (yoo'ta'nahti'karn) [San.] War Department

ยุ่น (yoo'n) soft, yielding, flabby

ยุบ (yoo'p) to go down (of a swelling), to be lowered

หยุบ (yoo'p) to keep pushing down

ยุบล (yoo'bonn) contents of a letter, story

ยุพิน (yoo'pinn) and ยุไพ line girl

ยุพา (yoo'pah) and ยุพ่ young man or woman; handsome

หยุม (yoo'm?) ill-bred — หยุม peevish, to molest, vex, tease

ยุ่ย (yooey) crumbling to pieces, reduced to dust — ย่่ยุ reduced to a paste

ยุ้ย (yooi') swelled, full, round

ยุ้ย (yooi?) working quickly, cutting quickly ยุก — disordered, disorderly

ยุรยาตร (yoo'ra'yaht) *and* ยุรยาตรา to walk like a peacock, pompous

ยู่ (yoo) blunt, obtuse, blunted, with the edge off

อยู่ (yoo) to remain, to be, to inhabit — มา it so happened — ไป for the future — ไฟ to be in childbed กิน — to spend one's life: food — กิน to cohabit ฯลฯ — หัว the King

ยุง (yoong) to give as alms

ยุงยาง (yoong yarng) a tall resinous tree

ยุ่มย่าม (yoom yahm) long and tangled (hair)

ยุพัก (yoo pa'k) to keep quiet, rest

ยูร (yoora') tribe, family, kindred

ยูง (yoon) peacock

เย (yay) crying of children

เย่ (yae) crooked, distorted, pouting, distortion of the mouth, in crying, etc.

เย้ (yey!) leaning to one side, toppling over

เหย (yey?) pouting, pale-faced, unhealthy-looking

เหยก (yayk?) cunning, meddlesome, deceitful ไหยก — deceitful, untrustworthy

เย็ด (yett) indecent movements — กับ sodomy — แม่ [word of insult or abuse]

เย็น (yen) (1) evening (2) cool, cold, cold weather — ไป to grow cold — ใจ to refresh, to be terrified ใจ estrangement อยู่ to be at peace

เย็บ (yep) to sew จ้าง — tailor — เกือก shoe-maker

เยา (yao) shouts of rowers

เยด (yayt) *with* ใจ pleasant

เยอ (yerr) to desire, itching

เย่อ (yer) to pull at, to drag, to do by force — อย่าง ostentations, pretentious — ลาก to drag away violently, to abduct

เย่อ (yerr) proud, vain, affected — อย่าง ostentations, pretentions เย่อ — pretentions

แยะ (yerr?) beyond one's strength

แยะ (yeu') (1) to be split open, to break open, (of a boil) to burst (2) many, much

เยิก (yerk) shout of encouragement when dragging trees, etc.

เยิ่ง (yerrg) ignorant, ill-mannered พระ — (of the King) tumour

เยิ่ง (yerng) with ยุ่ง intricate, confused, entangled

เยิน (yern) broken, spoilt, or damaged at the edge ยับ — spoilt, altogether damage

เยิ่น (yurn) protracted, prolonged, lengthy ยืด — flexible from its length

เยิ่ม (yerm) half-melted, to liquefy

แย (yaa) capricious, inclined to cry (of children) — แย keen, eager for ตำ — nettle

แย (yaa) (1) to stoop by bending the knees (2) exhaustion, fatigue, heavily laden เพลีย — weighed down by a heavy weight

ตัว with ตัว (tooa' yaa) (1) edible wood lizard (2) walking with the knees bent (3) prostitution

แย (yaa?) to push with a stick

แยก (yaak) to disjoin, separate

แยง (yaang) to prod, to prick, to sting — รู and ร to prod into a hole with a stick, to probe มุม to determine the angles so that a house may be built square

แยง (yaang) to take away by force

แย้ง (yaang') to contradict — กัน to dispute — แย้ง to keep on contradicting — กระแหยง elaborate, having many cross lines or marks ย่าง — to walk throwing the feet out sideways

แยงขน (yaa ng khon) hair standing on end

แยง (yaang) howdah without roof ยืน to stand on tip-toe with the knees bent

แยบ (yaap) secret art, concealed plan ยับ — nearly all gone

แย้ม (yaam) to open a little, opened, gay, cheerful

แยม (yaam?) rare, scattered, scanty เยิม — nearly bald, patchy (of turf, etc.)

แยง (yaao?) alert, nimble, springy

แยะ (yaa') (1) to push with the elbow, to elbow, to push on (2) to split open, to burst asunder, to crack (3) very many

ใย (yai) (1) well-looking, clean, fair, fine (2) down, [on fruit, etc.] — ใข่ white of egg

ใย (yai) fibre of leaf or plant, thread of spider's web, etc. — ใฟ soot — แมลงมุม spider's web เยื่อ — attachment, liaison เยิ่น — glutinous, fibrous

ใย่ (yai) movement of the lips

ใยดี (yai dee) to be eager for, to hanker after

โยยะ (yaiya') liberation, absolution, emancipation — ธรรม purification, liberation from sin

โย (yoh) fat, round, having many seeds in it [of a durien]

โย (yoh) [Pali] whoever, whatever — โส worthless, scamp, rascal

โย้ โยก and โยยก (yoke) staggering, wavering, shaken about

โยคาวจร (yohkahwa'chon) and โยค [Pali] ascetic or mendicant priest

โยง (yohng) to tow, to drag through the water with a rope เสาวะ — shrouds ตุ่ — blind man's buff

โย่งเย่ง (yohng yeng) to get up on tiptoe, to reach up

โหยง (yohng?) quick, nimble โย่ — proud, arrogant, boastful

โยชน์ (yote) [Pali] a distance of 8000 wah = about 10 miles

โยทะกา (yohta'kah) (1) anchor (2) a thorny bush with white flowers.

โยธา โยธ and โยธ (yohtah, etc.) [Pali] soldier, warrior — กณ a battalion, a division, an army

โยน (yone) (1) to throw forward with underhanded or backhanded action (2) to swing (3) a load (of earth, wood, etc.) which can be thrown

โยนี (yohnee) [Pali] pudenda feminae; source, cause

โยปน (yohpa'na') [Pali] any, every

โยม (yohm) parishioners, people attached to a temple or related to a priest — อุปถาก one who has made up his mind to be attached to a priest

โยโส (yohsoh) [Pali] he, who, whoever,

any one, man of the lowest caste, worthless, rascal

เย่า (yow) house

เย้า (yow!) to pat, stroke, caress

เยาะ (yau') softly, gently, (running) with light quick steps

เยาว์ (yowe) [Pali] young

เยาวมาล (yowwa'marn) young girl

เยาะ (yau') to desire, to jeer

ยำ (ya'm) to cut in pieces, to collect ingredients — ผัก to make a salad ระ — crushed, pounded, broken up (a curse)

ย่ำ (ya'm) (1) to trample upon, to tread down — เทือก muddy field prepared for planting any thing (2) to beat, strike — ยาม to strike the watches of the night — ค่ำ and — สนธยา six p. m.

ย้ำ (ya'm) (1) to press gently with the teeth (2) to repeat what is said by another

ยะ (ya') yes

ยะถา (ya'tah) [Pali] as, as it ought, properly [a word of blessing or thanks used by priests]

ยก (ya'k) and หยก ๆ to make a sign

(2) to change the position, to move — แยก and — ยอก to set apart, put by — ย้าย to remove, to displace — ไว้ to hide away — ป morose, crabbed — หลัง hollow between or near the shoulders

หยัก (ya'k) to indent, to cut, to notch — หย่อน carelessly

ยักษ์ (ya'kk) and other similar forms [Pali] goblins, demons, superhuman creatures [Alab. 178]

ยักโสก (ya'ksok) curled, curly (hair)

ยัง (ya'ng) yet, still, not yet, until; [in a letter] to — รุ่ง till dawn — ก่อน not yet — ชั่ว getting better — ไม่ มา not yet arrived

ยั่ง (ya'ng) enduring, permanent, lasting — ยืน to testify, to keep one's promise

ยะ (ya'ng) to stop, to keep stopping, to loiter

หยั่ง (ya'ng) to sound, examine, explore, presume

ยัญญัง (ya'nya'ng) [Pali] the glomerous fig-tree

ยัด (ya't) to push in, to fill in, to load

(a gum); vulg. to eat

หยัก (ya't) (1) fine, pretty (2) to fall by drops, to leak

ยัน (ya'n) (1) intoxication caused by betel-nut (2) palpitation, convulsion (3) to touch, push against

ย่าน (ya'n | Laos.] to fear, dread

เย้ย (ya'n) to jeer, to deride, to make fun of

ยันตร์ (ya'nn) [Pali] (1) machine (2) braiding

ยับ (ya'p) (1) sound of flapping or beating the wind, blowing about (2) crushed, broken, torn (3) to defer, put off (4) effulgent, shining

หยุย (ya'y) alacrity, joyousness, in good spirits

· • •

ร

ร (row ra'ksah — English r, and at the end of a word r. Guttural: a low letter) -- รักษา name of this letter

ร (rok) (1) confused, disarranged, disorderly (2) after-birth

รกชัฏ (rokcha't) [Pali] forest, wooded, over-grown, full of rubbish or litter

รง (rong) yellow gum, gamboge

รจนา (rocha'nah) [Pali] painting. colouring, dye, painted, paintings

รณ (ronn) and รณรงค์ [Pali] battle. fight, enemy

รด (rot) to sprinkle, to water

รถ (rot) [Pali] carriage — ไฟ locomotive steam engine -- คลุม covered carriage

รน (ron) and — รี่ to go into danger. restless รวน — troubled in mind. uneasy, disquieted ปืน -- gunmaker

รน and รั้น (ronn) to retire, to draw back

รบ (rop) to fight กวน to molest เรือ – fighting ship, man-of-war

หรบ (rop) to dance, writhe, wriggle about

ระบิล (ra'bin) and ระบอบ — (ra'baup ra'bin) law, custom

รม (rom) to smoke, to steam

ร่ม (rom) shade, umbrella, parasol

รมณี (romni) [Pali] agreeable, pleasing. charming, delightful

รเมยศรี (romyett) [Pali and Sansk. pleasant

อรร see under อ

รวก (rooa'k) (1) to scald, to cover with boiling water (2) small bamboo

รวง (rooa'ng) (1) ear of corn (2) hive (3) crumbling (4) to dig; pit

ร่วง (rooa'ng) to fall off, drop off

รวด (rooa't) quickly

รวน (rooa'n) (1) [of a crowd] to rush about, to move hither and thither (2) to bend out of the perpendicular, bent, stooping, crumpled up (3) to stir in a pot, to cook

ร่วน (rooa'n) crumbling, brittle

รวบ (rooa'p) and รวม to heap up, to add up; to take up in a bundle, to gather up รวม — to include, altogether

รวม (rooa'm) to collect, gather together

ร่วม (rooa'm) to live together, cohabit

รวย (rooey) (1) rich, lucky, well off (2) to gain — ริน gently, moderately, wafted slowly

รัว (roon) (1) to tremble, palpitate (2) to beat a small drum with quick strokes

รั่ว (rooa) leaky

รั้ว (rooa!) hedge, enclosure, fence

รศ (rot) [Sansk.] taste, flavour, relish, savour

รอ (raw) to stop, restrain, delay, floodgate, sluice, to take rain water, to wait for ปัก — to bank up with stakes, camp-shedding

รอ (rau) contiguous, adjoining หัว — to laugh

หรอ (ror?) ragged, in holes, worn-out

รอก (rauk) pulley

รอง (raung) to put in, to take rainwater — ท้า [high word] shoe

ร้อง (raung) to cry out — ไห้ to cry, to weep

รอด (raut) to rescue, to save

รอน (rawn) and ตัด — to cut into pieces, to cut off pieces

ร้อน (raun) hot การ — urgent, pressing business เจ็ด — injured, suffering from an injury — ใจ troublesome

รอบ (raup) round about — คอบ skilful in management

ร่อม (raum) (1) pointed, forming an angle (2) to collect

รอย (roye) tracing, mark, vestige, trace — แผล scar

ร่อย (roi) blunted, having lost its edge

ร้อย (roy) (1) to insert, to thread (2)

hundred (3) to arrange

รา (rah) (1) mouldy, musty ปลา — salt fish (2) to stop — พาย to ease off rowing or paddling — ระ to back water

ร่า (rah) to ramble — เริง gay, cheerful, merry

ร้า (rar) half-rotten and pickled fish

ราก (rark) (1) root, foundation (2) to vomit

รากษ (rark) bloodthirsty, savage

ราค (rahk) and ราคะ [Pali] concupiscence

ราคา (rarkhah) price, purchase money

ราคี (rarkhee) ill-humour, defect

ราง (rahng) (1) rather obscure, confusedly (2) conduit, canal, trough, spout — ปืน stock or carriage of gun or cannon

ร่าง (rarng) form, shape, sketch — แห meshes of net กัน — copy

ร้าง (rarng) to leave, to desert, to be separated from

รางวัด (rahngwa't) suburbs, fine paid by the inhabitants of a district when a crime has been committed there

รางวัน (rahngwa'n) reward, recompense

ราช ราชะ and ราชา (rart, rarcha', rarchah) [Sansk. and Pali] King, royal [a common prefix, as] — การ royal service, Government service — ปาทว confiscation of money or property — นิกุล royal family — สีห lion, fabulous Siamese animal — สัจ royal good faith — ทูก envoy, ambassador — ทัณฑ์ royal punishment — หริศง สนาน ceremony of exhibiting the royal elephants and ponies — สาร royal letter, ambassador, envoy — วน r. treasure — ปาน r. palanquin

ราชี (rahchee) [Pali] and ราคี order

ราคี (rarchee) Queen

ราโช (rahchoh) the bent part (of a ship, etc.)

ราก (rart) to spread about, to pour out

รากกก (rarta'kot) girdle of a priest

ราตรี (rartree) [Sansk.] night

ราน (rahn) to rush in, to burst in — รอน to cut (branches), to lop

ราน (rarn) (1) gnat (2) desirous, eager

ร้าน (rarn!) tavern, shop

ราบ (rarp) flat, level

ราม (rarm) [Sansk.] gay, pleasant, joy, delight

รามๅย (rarmoh) [Pali] agreeable, delightful

รามัญ (rahma'n) [Pali] Pegu, Peguan, Maun

ราย (rai) (1) numerical design. of lawsuits, letters, documents, sums of money (2) posted at intervals, having spaces between, deployed

ราย (rai) music เร — up and down, zigzag, winding, in a serpentine line — หน running away in a sideways or crooked direction

ร้าย (rai!) cruel, harsh, brutal, fierce ก — fickle, changeable, of uncertain temper

ราว (rowe) and ไม — hand-rail เรือง — event, affair, history, petition, address

ร้าว (row) to cleave, to split, cracked

— ราน to be different, to become unfriendly

ราวี (rahwee) to attack, harass

ราศี and ราศรี (varsee) [Sansk.] beauty, splendour, orderly, well-order, arranged

ราษฎร (rahsa'donn) [Sansk.] people, multitude, citizens

ราษี (rarsee) [Pali] (1) quantity, mass (2) sign of the zodiac

ราห (rah-hoo) [Pali] celestial monster which causes eclipses by eating the sun or moon [Alab. 218]

รี (ree') to consult, resolve

ริก and หริก (rick) lightly, gently, tapping gently

ริศดวง (ritseedoou'ng) obstinate malady, hæmorrhoid, piles — พลวง obstinate dysentery

ริทธิ ฤทธิ and ริทธา (ritti', rittah) [Sansk.] power, strength, authority, virtue [Alab. 195]

ริน (rin) to pour out gently

ริน (rinn) a small gnat

ริบ (rip) to carry off, to confiscate, spoil, plunder, pillage

รีบ (reep) hastily, precipitately

ริม (rim) rim, shore, bank, edge, lace, border

ริว (rew) long strips แผก — (1) a fish (2) Petriew (town)

ริศยา (rissa'yah) [San.] to envy, covet, covetousness

รี (ree) [Pali] length

รี (ree) rather quickly, moving straight to the point

รี *with* ริก (rik ree!) to fawn upon, to allure, to play the siren

หรี (ree) half shut, half extinguished — ๆ cry of the grass-hopper

รีๆ *with* ค่า (khah reechah) tax, duty, court fee

รีก (reet) (1) to lengthen by squeezing or pressing, to beat out (metals, etc.) (2) rule, custom, sect เข้า — *and* ทารีก to become a member of a different sect, to be converted, to be perverted

หรีก (reete) a cricket

รีปู (reepoo) [Pali] enemy

รีพล (reeponn) army, troop, battalion

เรีย (reea') scattered, confusedly

เรียก (reea'k) to call, to call out

เรียง (reea'ng) to arrange

เรียด (reea't) long, full length

เรียน (reea'n) (1) to learn, to study — บนไว to know a lesson (2) to inform — มา ยัง a formula used on

the envelopes of letters addressed to officials below the rank of Phraya กราบ — to inform (of an inferior)

เหรียน (reea'n?) a flat iron; the Spanish or Mexican dollar — หยก dollar

เรียบ (reea'p) level, well-arranged, in order ผู้ — เรียบ author of a publication — รียบ orderly, well arranged

เรียว (reeoo') to end in a point

เรียว แรง (reeo raang) strength

ฦ = รี

ฦก (reuk) [San.] favourable moment

รึง (reu'ng) tightly

หฦทัย (ha'reu'tai) *see under* ห

ฦๅ = รี (reu) word of interrogation สบาย — are you well ?

รี (reu) *and* รีอ to pull to pieces, destroy, upset

หรี *or* หรีอ (reu?) *or* รๅ (reu) *and* — ว่า either, or

ฦๅดี (reudee) *see* สัมปฤๅดี a joyful heart

รืน (reun) clean, well cared for, well-looking. sweet-smelling

ฦๅสาย (reusaie) cherished, darling

เรือ (reua) boat — กำปั่น ship — ไฟ better — กลไฟ steamboat, steamer — แจว boat with Siamese oars — สำปั้น small boat rowed gondolier fashion, or with paddles

เรือ (reua) fading, faint (of colours)

เรื่อ (rewa) slow, lingering (of an illness)

เรือก (reua'k) hurdles, fence, palisade

เรือง (reua'ng) shining, glittering, rather bright

เรื่อง (reua'ng) history, account, piece of writing ไม่เปน — nonsense — ความ charge, indictment, legal, document — ราว Petition, charge, report

เรือน (reua'n) (1) manner of arranging the hair (2) house, family เข้า — married — เบี้ย family reduced to slavery — แหวน setting of a ring

เรื้อน (rooa'n) leprosy

เรื่อย (reuey) delaying, slow, dilatory, lingering

ฤๅษี (reusee) [Sansk.] hermit

รู (roo') to pull out, take away, throw away — หยัง to purge

รุก (roo'k) to advance, push on, go forward หมากรุก — chess

หรูกหริก (roo'k rik) vexation, troublesome, naughty

รุกข (roo'kh) [Pali] tree

รุ่ง (roo'ng) (1) shining (2) dawn — เช้า early on the morrow

รุ้ง (roo'ng) (1) in a line forwards, stretching forwards (2) rainbow — กินน้ำ rainbow resting on the sea

รุจี (roo'chee) [Pali] agreeable

รุด (roo't) moving by little and little

รุดม see รุดม

รุน (roo'n) to push, to urge on, to purge

รุ่น (roo'n) growing up, adolescence

รุบรุบ (roo'p rip) indistinct, not fully visible, flickering, twinkling

รุม (roo'm) to flock together, to be collected เมือง -- Constantinople

รุ่ม (roo'm) warm, tepid - ร่าม badly dressed, having ill-fitting clothes

รุ่ย (ruee') ragged, having jagged edges

รู (roo) hole, orifice — จมูก nostril

รู (roo) very thin (cloth), very fine

รู้ (roo!) and -- ได้ to know

รก (root) to milk, to rub

รูป (roop) *and* รูปา [Pali] form, figure, shape, image, representation [Alab. 172] — ถ่าย photograph — ฉากก painted image — พรรณ (1) form and appearance (2) wrought gold, silver, etc.

เร (ray) common, worthless — รวน doubting, undecided

เร่ (ray') to wander about, to go in a crooked course

เร่ง (reng) to urge on, hasten

เร้น (renn) to hide

เรไร (ray rai) grass-hopper, cricket

เรว (raoo') cardamum

เร็ว (rew) quickly — ๆ very quickly

เรอ (reu'r) to belch

เรื่อ (reu'r) to wander, to stray

เริก (rerk) favourable moment

เริง (rerng) content, glad

เริด (rert) to interrupt, to stop, to leave off

เริม (rerm) pimples

เริ่ม (rerm) beginning

แร (raa) (1) to make a number of

strokes with a pen, pencil, or brush (2) to keep things in a disorderly condition, untidily

แร่ (raa) mines, metals, minerals, ore

แร่รวย สวย (raa rooi' sooi') well dressed, clean, pretty

แหร่ (raa) gait of an immodest woman

แรก (raak) beginning, to begin — นา ploughing ceremony [Alab. 208]

แรง (raang) strength, force แรน — vice, crane แข็ง — strong

แร่ง (rang) sieve

แร้ง (raang) vulture — กา birds of prey

แรม (raam) (1) long absence, remaining away (2) waning of the moon; [in dates] latter part of the month เดือน อ้าย — สอง ค่ำ second day of the waning in the first month

แรว (raao) sponge, noose for catching birds

แระ แหง Raheng (town)

ไร (rai) (1) a louse (2) marks of hair pulled out (3) who? what? someone เป็น — what is the matter?

ไร่ (rai) (1) field, plantation — นา plantations (2) a square measure including 400 square wah

ไร่ (rai) poor, needy

โร (roh) swollen, without strength

โร้ (roh) continuous, uninterrupted

โรกเหรก (rohk reyk) lean

โรค (rohk) [Pali] sickness, malady, disease

โรง (rong) shed, outhouse, depôt, court, place, room, warehouse, hall — โม่ mill ท้อง พระ — hall of the King or a Prince

โรจ (roht) and โรจนา (rohcha'na') [Pali] resplendent [Alab. 207]

โรม (rome) to rush at — วิ่น to fight

โรย (roey) (1) to fade, wither (2) to scatter, spread

โรไร (roh-ray) very lean, feeble, without strength

เรา (row) we, I (of a great personage)

เร้า (row) eagerly, repeatedly, urgent, pressing

เราะ (rau') (1) to chip, to indent, to nibble (2) a bean หัว — to laugh

รำ (ra'm) (1) to gesticulate, dance, pantomime (2) white powder

ร่ำ (ra'm) uninterruptedly, continuously — ไร (1) slowly (2) to keep on weeping or grumbling

รำคาญ (ra'mkharn) vexed, anxious, vexatious, annoying

ร่ำจวน (ra'mchoo'n) to sigh (with love), to think of

ร่ำดับ (ra'mda'p) to set in order

รำทวน (ra'mtooa'n) a show of horse exercise with lances, tournament

ร่ำเพ ร่ำพัก (ra'mpay-ra'mpa't) possessed with a devil

ร่ำพึง (ra'mpeung) to think of, to meditate, ponder

ร่ำเพย (ra'mpoey) (1) breath, breeze, to puff, to blow gently (2) a tree with long yellow blossoms

ร่ำแพน (ra'mpaan) [of peacocks] to spread the tail

ร่ำพรรณ (ra'mpa'n) [Pali] to keep on complaining

ร่ำพายุ (ra'mpai) gusts, puffs of wind

รำมะนา (ra'mma'nah) a small drum

ร่ำมะนาด (ra'mma'nart) tooth-ache

รำไย (ra'myai) better ลำไย a fruit tree

ระ (ra') one after another, to strike first on one side and then on another

ระกา (ra'kah) cock ปี — 10th year of the Siamese cycle

ระกำ (ra'ka'm) (1) to repress, to afflict, afflicted (2) a thorny bush producing fruit

ระกับ (ra'ka'p) *better* กับ to join, to fit on at the side

ระกำ (ra'ka'm) uneasy, anxious, vexed

ระฆัง (ra'kha'ng) bell ลูก — clapper หอ - - belfry, bell-tower ๆ — name of a letter

ระคน (ra'khon) to mix

ระคาง (ra'kharng) chagrin, resentment, to doubt

ระคาย (ra'khai) anger, displeasure — หมาง to pout, to sulk

ระงา (ra'ngaa) bundles (of fruit, cocoanuts, etc.)

ระงับ (ra'nga'p) to repress one's anger, to moderate, to mitigate

ระสัง (ra'sa'ng) to turn back without accomplishing one's object

ระดม (ra'dom) together, general ปล้น — concerted robbery, gang of burglars or robbers

ระดา ๆ (ra'dah) *and* ระดาย spread about

ระดู (ra'doo) (1) season, weather (2) menstruation

รถ ๆ (ra'tah) [Pali] car, carriage

ระกาณึก (ra'tahneuk) a large number of carriages together

ระทด (ra'tot) to groan, to sigh ; sorry

ระนาด (ra'nart) (1) a musical instrument with plates of wood, glass, or metal, harmonica (2) bamboo flooring of a boat

ระเนียด (ra'neea't) balustrade

ระแนง (ra'naang) (1) sieve (2) lathes supporting a tile roof

ระนะ (ra'naa') ship's bottom, keel

ระบบ (ra'bop) *and* ระบอบ custom

ระบม (ra'bom) (1) sore, inflamed (2) baked — ใจ vexed

ระบาย (ra'bai) (1) fringe, border (2) to inhale, breath (3) to purge (4) to let out wind, pedere

ระเบียง (ra'beea'ng) gallery, portico, verandah

ระเบียบ (ra'beea'p) to arrange, well arranged, well ordered, in good order, well done

ระเบียน (ra'beea'n) public registers ทำ — registry

ระเบิด (ra'bert) explosion, to break, to crack

ระเบือ (ra'beua) to be spread, divulged, rumoured

ระแบบ (ra'baap) rule, manner, form

ระบำ (ra'ba'm) to dance, to leap

ระบัก (ra'ba't) (1) short scanty hair (2) to cheat (3) to form a bud, to grow

ระพี (ra'pee') [Pali] sun

ระพะพาน (ra'pa'pahn) to strike together, to speak indirectly to, to seek a quarrel

ระมาศ (ra'mart) elk

ระมัก (ra'ma't) to take care of oneself, to be on one's guard

ระย่อ (ra'yaw) fear

ระย่อม (ra'yom) a tree whose root is used for medicine

ระย้า (ra'yah) hanging ornament with several branches or tassels โคม — chandelier

ระยำ (ra'ya'm) to spoil, damage, to curse

ระยะ (ra'ya') interval, space, distance

ระยับ (ra'ya'p) (1) to flutter, to glitter (2) changing weather — ฝน rain about to fall — แดด sun about to shine

ระราน (ra'rarn) to oppress

ระริก (ra'rick) to palpitate

ระรึง (ra'reung) (1) to tie or fasten tightly (2) oppressed, sick at heart

ระรื่น (ra'reun) full of pleasant odours, sweet-scented

ระเรื่อย (ra'rewi') gently, smoothly (especially of wind)

ระไร (ra'ray) to wander, move about

ระลอก (ra'lauk) see ละลอก, wave

ระลึก (ra'leuk) see ลำลึก to think of

ระวาง (ra'warng) hold of a vessel, fi— charterparty, receipt

ระหว่าง (ra'wahng) between, intermediate, empty, vacant

ระวิวาร (ra'wee'wahn) [Pali] Sunday

ระแวก (ra'waak) cross street, cross path, alley

ระแวง (ra'waang) to suspect, to act with caution, careful

ระไว (ra'wai) and ระวัง — to take care, to be watchful

ระหง (ra'hong) a forest of tall and straight trees

ระโหย (ra'houi') weak, broken down, languid

ระโหง ระหาง (ra'haung ra'haang) to conceive a suspicion or dislike of a person

ระหาย (ra'hai) thirst, to be thirsty

ระเหีย (ra'heea') slothful

ระเห (ra'hay) to wander about

ระเห็๓ (ra'hett) to go up, to go quickly

ระเหย (ra'hoey) to evaporate

ระแหก (ra'haak) *and* ระเหิก to break
open, break up, damage, spoil

ระแหง (ra'haang) (1) cracked, gaping
open, fissure (2) Raheng (town)

ระหั๓ (ra'ha't) water-wheel for lifting
water

ระหั๓ (ra'ha't) [Sansk.] private, secret

ระอา (ra'ah) *and* —ใจ to be disgusted,
tired

รัก (ra'k) (1) a tree whose juice is used
for gilding น้ำ — lacquer (2) to love

รักเร่ (ra'k ray) a shrub with small
flowers

รักแร้ (ra'k-raa) armpits

รักษา (ra'ksah) [Pali] to keep, to save,
to take care of, to cure

รัง (ra'ng) (1) a tall hard tree (2) nest,
hole — กระ๓ุน button-hole

รัง (ra'ng) to pull up, pull tight, pull

รัง (ra'ng) to govern ห้า — to clear a

waste field, jungle, or forest

รังเกียจ (ra'ngkeea't) (1) to transfer a
work, to get another to do (2) to
suspect, dislike, dissatisfied with

รังแก (ra'ngkaa) to vex, molest, oppress

รังษี (ra'ngsee) [Pali] ray

รังสรรค (ra'ngsa'n) shining, radiant,
sunshiny

รังสฤษดิ (ra'ngsitt) [Sansk.] (1) to
make light, light up, enlighten (2)
to build, create

รังเตึง (ra'ngteung) tin cooking utensil
in three pieces for making cakes

รัชกาล (ra'tcha'karn) [Pali] reign

รัชชะกะ (ra'tcha'ka') (1) washman (2)
dyer

รัฐ (ra't) [Pali] territory, country,
realm

รัด (ra't) to squeeze, to embrace, to
bind up, to tie — เข้า to compress
—เอา *and* —เอา เปรียบ to take the
best, grasping, covetous

รัดประคด (ra'tpra'kot) (1) girdle of a
priest (2) a breast cloth

รัตตี (ra'ttee') [Pali] night

รัตน *and* รัตนะ (ra'ta'na') [Pali] gem,

jewel, glass, crystal, precious stone

— มณี precious stone

รัตนโกสินทร์ (ra'ta'na'kohsinn) angelic
gem: new name for Bangkok —
ศก [in dates] year from the foundation of Bangkok as a capital

รัถยา (ra'tyah) [Sansk.] carriage-road,
street

รัน (ra'n) to strike, to smite

รั้น (ra'n) obstinate, headstrong

รันทด (ra'ntot) oppression, affliction

รันทวย (ra'ntooi') languishing, feeble,
likely to fall

รันแทะ (ra'ntaa') sledge

รับ (ra'p) to receive, accept, agree to
— รอง to answer for another — สั่ง
order of King or Prince — จ้าง to
take employment

ารับ (ra'p) nimble, restless, jumping
about — ๆ quickly

รัศมี (ra'ssa'mee') [San.] rays, brightness, clearness

รัษฎา (ra'ssa'dah) [Sansk.] country,
district — กรมพิพัฒน์ Treasury หอ
— Treasury

ล

ล (law wi'lart   English l, and at the
end of a word n. Guttural; a low
letter)   วิลาศ name of this letter

ลก ลาน (lok larn) to be frightened,
nervous

ลคน and ละคร (la'khon) comedy,
stage play

ลง (long) down, to come down, go
down, put down, get out (of a carriage, boat, etc.), go out (to sea) —
มือ to begin work — ผี to bewitch,
sorcery — ราก (1) to take root (2)
cholera — รัก to cover with rosin
before gilding — ชื่อ to sign — โทษ
to punish — ชาติ degenerate —
ท้อง diarrhoea ปราบ — to pacify, to
level, to smooth down

หลง (long) to miss the way, to forget,
to mistake, to be mad

ลงกรณ์ (longkon) [Pali] see จุลงกรณ์
ornament ปิ่นฟ้า — ornamented hair-
pin: name of H. M. the King

ลด (lot) to lower, to let down, to diminish — ลั่น in stages, in storeys,

storey หัก — to deduct a sum —
เลี้ยว windings, circuitous

หลก (lott) slippery, flowing, moving,
restless ปลา — small slippery fish

ลน (lon) (1) to put near the fire (2) in
a hurry, hastily, to scamp

ล้น (lonn) (1) very learned, excellent,
supreme, precious (2) to overflow
— เหลือ superabundant

หลน (lon?) to boil to a jelly

หล่น (lon) (of leaves, flowers, etc.) to
fall, to drop

ลบ (lop) to rub out, efface, deface, destroy

หลบ (lopp) to slip away, shun, avoid
— หลังคา to roof — กระเบื้อง to
roof with tiles ไข้ — internal fever

ลพ (lopp) vulg. for นพ [Pali] new —
บุรี Lopburee (Town and Province)

ลม (lom) wind, flatulence, illness เช้า
windy season หัว — beginning
of the monsoon เข้า ข้อ gout,
rheumatism — ตะกัง cramp — จับ
convulsions บ้าน — to be ill — พ

บ้า storm — ปาก language — เว่า
North wind — พัก หลวง North-
West wind — หวน whirlwind กิน
— (of sails) to catch the wind, to
be filled — เข้า ออก respiration

ล่ม (lom) to capsize

ล้ม (lomm) to fall to the ground ไม้ —
to fell a tree

หล่ม (lom?) mud บ่า — depression in
the shoulder (a deformity)

ลมุด (la'moo't) a fruit tree

ละมาะ เกาะ แกะ (la'mau' kau' kaa')
small islets round an island or promontory

ลมัก ละเมียก ไว้ (la'ma't la'meea't wai)
to reserve for the future

ลล่ำ ลลัก (la'la'm la'la'k) fatness, stammering, (walking or talking) with
difficulty or confusedly

ลวก น้ำ ร้อน (looa'k na'm raun) to boil
slightly, to put in hot water

ลวง (looa'ng) to deceive, impose upon

ล่วง (loo'wa'ng) to go on, to go too far,
to slip away; that which is past
— เกิน to go beyond, trespass
ประเวณี adultery

ลั้วง (loo'ang) to put in and take out, to grope for — มือ to put in the hand — ควัก to put in the hand and take a thing out

หลวง (looa'ng?) (1) largest, superior, royal, belonging to the State นาย — and ใน — the King ของ — Government property กรม —title of a Prince of the third rank (2) title of an inferior dignitary

ลวด (looa't, wire ได้ — to dance on a wire — หนัง small strips of hide — ลาย carving, sculptured ornament

ล้วน (looa'n) to exceed, excessive

ล้วน (looa'n) simple, simply, only, entirely

ลวม (looa'm) casket, pouch, bag, receptacle

หลวม (looa'm) (1) too large, too loose, too big for what is inserted in it (2) going without obstacle, freely, too freely

หลัว (looa') dull, dusky

ลหาร (la'harn) [Cambod.] marsh, bog

ลหุ (la'hoo) [Pali] light, small, short, quick

ลอ with ไก่ พระ ยา (kai phra'yah lau') pheasant

ลอ (law) (1) to allure, to attract (2) to come in sight ลับ — to appear and disappear

ลอ (lor) to banter, provoke, chaff

ลอ (lor) to roll, wheel

หลอ (lor?) to eat away by degrees, to pare down, to clip, to cut (a pencil)

หลอ (lu') to melt metals, to fuse

ลอก (lauk) to take off (skin, bark, etc.) — กราย (of snakes, etc.) to shed (the skin) — หนัง สือ to copy a book

หลอก (lauk) to startle, to frighten suddenly, to terrify in jest ผก — to deceive

ลอง (laung) to test, to try ว่า to exercise, to practise

ลอง (long) (1) hole pierced downwards, aperture (2) to follow a river downwards เบิก — passport — แพ — ซุง to float down a raft นก — ตัว a bird

ลอด (laut) to pass through a hole, under an arch, etc. — ลัว to go by a straighter road, short cut

หลอก (lawt) small channel, tube, pipe ไม้ — weaver's bobbin, reel — ก้าย thread rolled on a bobbin หอย — tube-shaped shell กลอง — name of a small canal in Bangkok

ลอน (laun) part of the body, part

ลอน (lon) stripped bare, denuded — กง empty purse พก — to speak deceitfully

หลอน (hlon) (a term of endearment

ลอบ (laup) (1) secretly, stealthily (2) basket-work fish trap with narrow neck and long body

ล้อม (laum) to surround with a fence, etc. — รั้ว to fence in

หลอม (laum) to melt metals, to fuse

ลอย (loy) to float (in air or water) คน — exempt from service — ชาย to walk with the panung hanging down — กระ ทง a festival

ลออ (la'-aw) [Cambod.] handsome, pretty, beautiful

ลออง (la'-aung) dust, powder — ธุลี พระบาท dust of the King feet, [a form of address meaning Your Majesty

ลา (lah) (1) ass, donkey (2) to smear, to cover over (3) and อำ — to bid farewell — ไป ก่อน good bye (4) permission, leave กราบ — (to a grandee) to ask leave to retire ราคา — to beat down the price — หนี instalment, part of a number

ล่า (lah) (1) to withdraw, retreat (2) to delay, to retard, to be left behind (3) to be tired

ล้า (lar) (1) to delay, loiter, hang behind (2) benumbed, straightened out เหนื่อย — benumbed with fatigue

หลา (lah) a yard (measure) แบ — to lie on the back with the limbs stretched out

หล่า with บิด (bit lar) [Chin.] gimlet

หล้า (lah) sky, air, firmament, world, earth ใต้ — under heaven แผ่นดิน — terrestrial plain

ลาก (lark) (1) to pull with the hands (2) a lakh of rupees (= about £8000) (3) — ข้าง name of the third vowel

หลาก (lahk) to be astonished; unexpected event, wonder, surprise

ลากข้าง (lark-kharng) third of the vowels, q. v.

ลาง (lahng) (1) destined event, calamity, misfortune (2) kind, sort — กิน certain persons (3) a tree having medicinal sap

ล่าง (lahng) below, beneath

ล้าง (larng) (1) to wash (2) to put to death by order of the King, to execute, destroy, upset

หลาง with ทอง (taung larng) a thorny tree

ลาญ (larn) to die, death แยหลา — to die เลว — rough, rude, common

ลาด (lart) (1) flat, level (2) inclined, sloping (3) to spread out

ลาน (lahn) (1) a tree with fan leaves ใบ — palm leaves for writing (2) open place, threshing-floor ฝนชะ — shower of rain which levels the threshing-floor, mango showers (3) hasty, inconsiderate — ใจ ignorant, unintelligent — ตา unable to distinguish ลน — hasty, hastening ง เห่า ลา - a viper (4) spring (of a watch, etc.)

ล้าน (larn) and หัว — bald

ล้าน (larn) a million

หลาน (lahn?) grandson, nephew — สาว grand-daughter, niece ลูก — posterity

หลาบ (lahp) to correct oneself, to be amended — ทำ corrected, effectually reprimanded, reproved เข็ด taught by experience

ลาภ (lahp) [Pali] property, possessions, profits, good fortune

ลาม (larn) (1) to advance, extend, encroach, spread (2) daring, impudent กิน — ปาม to eat dirtily

ล่าม (lahm) to know a foreign language, linguist (2) to tie up, chain up together

หลาม (larm?) (1) in crowds ๆ — a snake เข้า -- glutinous rice cooked with cocoa-nut milk (2) indigestion

ลามก (larmok) [Pali] low, ill-behaved, dirty

ลาย (lai) confusion of the eyesight, variegated ผ้า — chintz ริม — border, line of ornament ลาย confusion of colours — มือ handwriting — ระบาย ornamental border --

สิ a green and black snake หลัง — marks of the rattan on the back น้ำ — spittle, saliva

ล่าย (laie) to examine, examination

หลาย (lai?) several, many (sign of the plural)

ลาย แทง ผุด (lai taang poo't) indication of hidden treasure or of anything unknown

ลาลด (larlot) sad, grieved, sorry

ลา ลี (larlee) to go, to walk

ลาว (lah-o) Laos, Laosian

เลา (lah-o?) (1) to plane, to smooth with a knife (2) pointed wood

หลาวชะโอน (lah-o cha'-ohn) a tree

ลิ (lee') to have a piece broken off ลิก poetry

ลิง (ling) monkey ฝีปี — ribs of a boat — โลก joy, gladness

ลิขิต (li'khit) [Pali] to write, writing

ลิก (lit) to cut off the rough part with a knife, to prune

ลิน (lin) small lizard which bites

ลิ้น (linn) tongue — ไก่ uvula — หมา tongue-shaped fish — กะเล slough

of the cuttle-fish — ชัก — ลิ้น etc. drawers of a box, cupboard, etc. — เลื leaves used for polishing boats

หลิน (lin?) and แพร — [Chin.] a Chinese silk

ลินจง (linchong) lotus, water-lily

ลินี (linchee) a fruit tree

ลินลา (linlah) and ลินลาศ [Pali] to walk, to go

ลิบ (lip) a long way off, out of sight, to go right on

ลิ่ม (lim) wedge, lump

ลิ้ม (lim) to taste

หลิม (lim?) tapering, thin

ลิลา (li'lah) to walk, to go

ลิลิต (li'litt) verses, poetry

ลิว (liew) (1) to see from afar (2) to drift rapidly down [lai. ruo]

หลิว (lew?) small, minute

หลิว (lewe) and ตา — looking with one eye

ลิสิต (li'sitt) [Engl.] receipt

ลี with จร (chorra'lee) [Pali] and — ลา to walk, to go — ลาศ to go hastily

ลี (lee) bent มด — an ant

ลี (lee) to run away secretly, slip away

ลี (lee) [Chin.] (a measure of 2000 lengths of the foot)

หลี (lee?) [Chin.] the fiftieth part of a fuang ; 16 cowries

หลีก (leek) to get out of the way, to avoid, to escape sideways, to keep out of the way

ลีบ (leep) dry, pinched, stunted, thin

เลีย (leea') to lick ได้ — almost like

เลีย with ได้ (lai leea') almost alike, nearly equal

เลียง (leea'ng) to question แกง — vegetable curry

เลียง (leea'ng) to keep out of the way, avoid, shun, escape, run away

เลี้ยง (leea'ng) to nourish, bring up, keep, entertain พ — nurse of an infant prince ลูก — stepson — แขก to entertain one's friends งาว — feast, dinner-party นก — bird which is fed ไม้ — a small bamboo

เลียงผา (leea'ngpah) and เยียงผา wild goat

เลียน (leea'n) to mock, to chaff

เลียน ('eea'n) flat, polished

เหลียน (leea'n?) a long sharp knife, a scythe

เหลียน (leea'n?) and เรียน with เงิน dollar

เลียบ (leea'p) to follow the shore — ชาย to go round about, round the edge, circuitous, indirectly ต้น — a large tree พุด — เลียบ to speak indirectly, to talk with periphrasis

เลียม (leea'm) to hem, to trim, to edge (with metals, etc.)

เหลียม (leea'm) angle, corner, side เป็น — angular ย่อ — to round off บวบ — a pointed gourd with flat sides สาม — etc. triangle, etc.

เลียว (leeo) turn, circuitous, winding

เหลียว (leo?) to look round, look behind

ลี ลา (leelah) to go, to walk

ลึก (leuk) deep, profound — ซัง (1) deep and widening or branching out at the bottom (2) profound, secret — ล้ำ (1) deeper (2) secret and sacred

ลึงค์ (leung) [Pali] sex, gender, genital parts กะ - eunuch

ลือ (leu) [Cambod.] it is rumoured —

ว่า to be divulged, published เลอง — notorious

ลน (leun) slippery

ลน (leun) freed from trouble or anxiety, clear

ลม (leum) to forget — ตัว to go astray, absence of mind — ตา to open the eyes

เหลอ (leuwa') to remain, to stay, residue, remainder — ไป (1) too much (2) incapable of being taught, intractable ตก — [tree] loaded with fruits or flowers ล! — more, superior

เลอก (leua'k) (1) to choose, select (2) some, some one, (3) gum, glue

เหลอก (leua'k) open and turned up (eyes)

เลอง (leua'ng) notorious

เหลอง (leua'ng?) yellow

เลอต (leua't) (1) blood ตก — flux ยา — medicine for this malady (2) bug

เลอน (leua'n) to efface, blot out, forget

เลอน (leua'n) (1) drag or sledge for carrying rice (2) to move — ที to take another employment or title — ขน to rise to higher rank ก้าว —

shooting star

เหลอบ (leua'p) (1) to look towards (2) gadfly

เลอม (leua'm) clean, bright, shining — ใส pure, devout

เหลอม (leua'm?) python, boa-constrictor

เหลอม (leua'm) (1) unequally, uneven (2) to get down, to lower oneself, to withdraw

เลอย (leui') saw, to saw — วิลันกา hand-saw

เลอย (leui') to creep, to crawl

ลุ (loo') to reach, to attain, to obtain

ลุก (look) (1) to rise, to stand up — ลม to get up and fall down again — ลน hastily, hurriedly (2) to be lit, lighted เปา — to fan the flame, to blow up the fire

หลุกหลิก (loo'k lik) in a hurry, hastily

ลุกะโทษ (loo'ka'tote) pardon, to ask or obtain pardon

ลุง (loo'ng) elder brother of the father

ลุ้ง (loo'ng) large receptacle (usually of brass and in several pieces) for provisions

หลุด (loo't) to be untied, loosened ร่าน่า — time of forfeit for pawned things

หลิว (loo'n?) swift

หลบ (loo'p) to press down, to bend down the edges ผม — hair hanging down over the forehead — หลบ hastily, hurriedly

ม(loo'm) lower — เน่า becoming putrid — หลง to be deceived, blinded by passion

หลุม (loo'm?) ditch, well, pit, hole

ลุย (looi') (1) to destroy, to be destroyed (2) to walk across, walk through

ลุ่ย (looi') to slip down (of a panung) to come undone, become unfastened

ลู่ (loo) (1) not stiff, soft, flexible, pliant (2) to rush at

หลู่ (loo) to despise, scorn, unappreciative, ungrateful

ลูก (look) child, offspring, issue — หลาน descendant, issue, posterity — อ่อน infant, young child — จ้าง workman, employé, servant — เมอ several workmen having one master — เรือ sailors — เต้า children — แฝด and — ฝาแฝก twins — ปี๋ย illegitimate child — ศิษย์ disciple

ลูบ (loop) to touch, stroke, caress —

ใล้ to anoint with perfumes, to stroke

เล่ (lay) as, like, as if, just as

เล่ (lay) slowly, tardy, late ใล้ — dilatory, procrastinating, behind hand

เหล่ (lay) awry, athwart. to squint

เล็ก (lek) little, small — น้อย a little

เหล็ก (lek) iron แม่ — magnet — ไหล miraculous iron — จาน iron stylus for writing — วิลาศ tin — ชาว tinned sheets of iron — กล้า steel — ไข awl — สีกัด shears or knife for cutting iron — หมาด a square boring instrument — ไฟ steel for striking fire

เลข (layk) [Pali] (1) number, arithmetic, superstitious number inscribed วิชา คิด — arithmetic ผูก — and เสาว — good hand-writing (2) clients marked with a stamp ทาษ clients who have sold themselves to a master — อาษา clients appointed for certain purposes สัก — to tattoo a client

เลขา (laykah) [Pali] line, mark, drawing, writing

เลง (layng) [Cambod.] (1) gambling, play ไม้ — gambler, rogue (2) to strike on the head

เล็ง (leng) to look into, examine, refer

เล็ด ลอด (lett laut) to slip away, escape

เลน (layn) mud, mire

เล่น (len) to play, to jest — ตัว to become dissipated ไพ่ — gambler

เล็น (lenn) a louse เหา — vermin

เหลน (dayn) great-grand-child จิ้ง — a lizard

เล็บ (lep) nail (of finger or toe) — มือ a plant

เลเพ (lay pay) disarranged, out of line, out of order, scattered, confused

เล็ม (lemm) (1) to hem (2) to nibble, to forage about, to get what one can

เล่ม (lem) (numerical designation of knives, scissors, volumes, oars, etc.)

เลย (loy) beyond, more เกิน — (1) too far, too much, to exceed (2) to insult ละ — to lay aside, to desert

เลลัง (layla'ng) to hesitate

เลหลัง (layla'ng) auction

เลว and เล้ว (laoo) inferior, poor, low, ignorant, untruthful

เล่ว see เร่ว cardamum

เหลว (laoo) liquid แหลก — splintered, broken (up, crushed into small pieces or into a liquid state

เลศ (layt) [Pali] to accuse falsely, to calumniate

เลห เล่ห and เล่ห์ (lay) [Pali] fraud, artifice, cunning — กล do.

เลอ (lur) most, the most — สวาดิ to love excessively, very lovely

เลอ (lurr) negligence, careless เลิน rashly, carelessly

เหลอ (lurr) stupid, taken aback, abashed, shame-faced

เลอะ (lur) blotched, blotted, disorderly filthily

เละ (la') muddy

เลิก (leuk) (1) to raise, lift up, pull up, (2) to interrupt, to stop — ท้อง ร่อง to clean a ditch

เลิง (lerng) deceived, stupefied, mad เลิง with อี (eelerng) fat, a fat pitcher

เหลิง (lerng) to go up น้ำ — full tide

เลิน, เล่อ (lern lerr) careless, negligent, imprudent, rash

เลิศ (lert) better, superior, excellent ยิ่ง — very excellent, best

แล (laa`) (1) to look (2) and, also ไป — certainly. amen. that is all. it is finished

แล (laa) loaded according to one's strength, bearing a heavy burden

เหล (laa?) *with* กับ liar, calumniator of a woman

แลก (laak) to exchange — เข้า to give goods in exchange for rice — แหวน betrothal

แหลก (laak) crushed, reduced to dust

แลง (laang) (1) maggot that eats fruit, worm that gnaws the gums (2) (rock) with holes in it

แลง (lang) to split, to cleave, to cut up -- เข้า a small measure made of a cocoa-nut ลง — slave who carries his master's baggage

แลง (laang) dry, drought

แหลง (laang) dwelling-house, domicile, place หลัก — post, support, fixed abode, residence — หน้า terrestrial plain

แลน *with* ด้วง (dooa'ng laan) a worm

แลน (lan) (1) to run, to sail quickly (2) goldsmith's blow-pipe เป่า — to blow through a g. b.

แหลน (laan?) sharp point, pointed iron

แหลน (lan) *with* กะ all but, almost nearly, not quite

แลบ (laap) to open a little -- ลิ้น to put out the tongue ฟ้า — lightning

แลม (lam) to taste, to eat a little

แหลม (laam?) sharp, pointed โฉ promontory หลัก — ingenious, dexterous

แล้ว (lao`) already, at an end, it is done (sign of the past participle) มา — he is come — ก็ไป made of -- ใน that case, then -- กัน there is an end of that — แก to depend on -- ใย it is enough, in that case you can go - นั้น and then

และ (laa`) (1) to take off the bark, to take off *or* away (2) rest *or* foundation for a post

ไหล *with* หลง (long? lai`) infatuated, engrossed with useless things

ไล่ (laie) to put to flight, to pursue ไป — *and* ไย — (expletive used in speaking of bamboos) — เลียง to ply with questions — เลย almost alike — ๆ to discuss, compute, deliberate, count

.ไล (lie) to anoint, to smear, to rub on

ไหล (lie?) to flow — เพรื่อ to flow in several directions — ขึ้น flood tide ปลา — eel หาง — a creeping plant

ไหล่ (lai) back of the shoulders

ไล่ (loe) small round shield or buckler

ไล่ (loh) to swing, oscillate, wobble — เรือ to row a boat with one oar — ไล deceiver, cheat, liar, idler

.โหล (loh?) (1) having a gap or hole in it, hollowed, excavated ขวด — wide-mouthed bottle (2) a dozen — เหล weak, indisposed (3) stopped short, unable to go on

โลกย์ โลกา and โลกัย์ (lohk) [Pali] world, universe ความ — concupiscence, worldliness, carnal pleasure ไตร — (1) the three worlds (2) a sacred book of the Siamese — วัน destruction of the world (worst day of the week)

โลกันต์ (lohka'n) [Pali] hell of corrosive water

ไล่ ชิงช้า with พิธี (pi'tee loh-chingchah) swinging festival

โลง (lohng) bier, coffin without a lid

โล่ง (lohng) open, unoccupied, clear โกง empty, bare

โลน (lohn) (1) scamp, rogue, babbler, shameless (2) louse

โล้น (lohn) bald, nearly bald

เหลน (lohn?) great-grand-child

โลด (lote) (1) to jump, dance (2) a tree with medicinal bark

โลภ (lohp) (and other similar words) [Pali] anger, passion, greed, lust (Alab. 213)

โลม (lohm) to flatter, caress

โลมา (lohmah) [Pali] hair ปลา porpoise

โลหิต (loh-hitt) and โลหัง [Pali] blood

โลหะ (loh-ha') [Pali] iron, brass, copper, metal

เลา (low) (1) white with spots, speckly white (2) a plant (3) pipe of a wind instrument with hole in it (4) short explanation, definition

เล้า (lowe) (1) arak, intoxicating drink — แกรบ arak made from beans —

อะเห้ง essence of aniseed (2) to relate, tell, recite

เล้า (low!) (1) to caress, flatter, soothe,
appease (2) enclosure for animals

เหลา (low?) to sharpen with a knife,
to point

เหลา (low?) [Chin.] (1) old, aged (2)
relation, race, species, caste, association, society

หลา (lowe) some, several (sign of the
plural) — ทั้ all these

เหลาหลก (low? lok) a betel palm

เลาะ (lau') to unsew, unpick

เหลาะแหละ (lau' laa') (to talk) use-
lessly, vain, trifling

ลำ (la'm) (1) numerical designation of
bamboos, boats, and long-shaped
articles — คอ neck — ไม้ bamboo
(2) bed of a river or canal — รอง
deepest part of a river, ditch, or
moat — ท่อ conduit, channel, passage

ล่ำ (la'm) (1) fat, stout (2) to fasten
with ropes — ลา to bid farewell

ล้ำ (la'm) superior, excellent, precious

ลำคอง (la'mkhenang) sad

ลำเข็ญ (la'mkhayn) hard work, pover-
ty, misery

ลำเจียก (la'mcheea'k) a plant with
strong-scented flowers

ลำดวน (la'mdooa'n) a tree with small
scented blossoms

ลำดับ (la'mda'p) order, line, series, to
set out in order

ลำเนา (la'mnow) rank, place; be it as
it may — ธาร bed of a water-course

ลำบาก (la'mbark) pain, trouble, fatigue, annoyance, vexation

ลำพอง (la'mpaung) vain, haughty

ลำแพน (la'mpaan) plaited bamboo mat

ลำไพ่ (la'mpai) to make petty gains, to
appropriate, misappropriating the
master's things, embezzling

ลำพาพาน (la'mpowparn) beautiful
woman

ลำโพง (la'mpohng) plant whose fruit
causes madness

ลำพัง (la'mpa'ng) by one's own exer-
tions, by oneself

ลำพู (la'mpoo) a tree growing on river
banks having a curious-shaped fruit
not eatable

ลำเภา (la'mpow) fine woman

ลำไย (la'myai) a fruit tree

ลำเอียง (la'm-cea'ng) to prefer, to show partiality; bent, inclined, crooked

ลำลึก (la'mleuk) to think of

ลำสัน (la'msa'n) fat, very stout

ละ (la') (1) to let go, to give up, to permit, to forsake (2) etcetera — ไป not to care any more (3) every one, one by one ก — every time ก — หนึ่ง สอง etc. one, two at a time, etc.

ละคอน (la'khon) comedy, play รำ — stage dance

ละโลม (la'bome) to mitigate, appease, caress, console

ละม่อม (la'maum) well governed, good-tempered, well-mannered

ละมาด (la'maht) [Malay.] to bow in adoration

ละมาน (la'marn) darnel, tare

ละมั่ (see ฝา)

ละเมียด (la'meea't) well behaved, well mannered

ละมุดสิดา (la'moo'tsidah) a thorny fruit tree

ละมุน (la'moo'n) smooth, soft, agree-

able, affable, well behaved

ละเมง (la'mayng) comedies

ละเมอ (la'meur) and ละเมอ talking in one's sleep

ละเมิด (la'mert) not to obey orders, contumacious

ละไม (la'mai) tender, soft, sweet, pretty

ละโมบ (la'mope) greedy, gluttonous, covetous

ละมั่ง (la'ma'ng) a stag

ละลอก (la'lauk) waves — ใ big boils

ละล่าใจ (la'lah chai) to become careless and incautious

ละลาย (la'lai) to dessolve, melt, digest — คำ not to keep one's word

ละลิบ (la'lip) out of sight

ละเลง (la'leng) to knead, to spread about on a cloth, to smear

ละเลิงใจ (la'lerng chai) mad with joy

ละลัก ละลน (la'la'k la'lon) emotion, mental trouble

ละว้า (la'wah) wild tribes in the North West of Siam

ละแวก (la'waak) (1) an old town near Cambodia (2) narrow streets in a town, lanes

ละโว้ (la'woh) (1) Louvo. Lopburee (Anderson 115. n.) (2) a vegetable

ละสง (la'song) a bean with three seeds in its pod

ละหวย see ระหวย weak

ละห้อย (la'hoi) down-hearted, uneasy

ละหาน (la'harn) stream which dries up in dry weather, mountain torrent

ละเหีย (la'heea') languishing, weak

ละหุ่ง (la'hoo'ng) castor-oil plant

ละโหย (la'howi) oppressed with love, distressed, uneasy about

ละออ (la'-aw) see also ลออ [Cambod.] beautiful

ละออง (la'-ong) see also ลออง dust

ละอาย (la'aie) ashamed, shame

ละเอียก (la'eea't) fine as dust, thin, delicate, minute ใจ — attending to small details

ลัก (la'k) to steal ลัก — to snatch, to grab — ลั่น in incongruous, exceptional, different from the others beside it

หลัก (la'k) stake, root, basis, groundwork, refuge, support ปัก — to drive in a stake เป็น — the chief,

the head, the principal part แหลม skilful, expert — ใหญ่ superior in rank, very eminent — แจว peg or post for the oar

ลักขณะ (la'kkha'na') and ลักษณะ [Pali and Sansk.] bounds, limits, condition, nature, property (of anything), order, reason, sign — ทาษ code of laws (about slaves, etc.) — วุฒิ science of things นร — (nora'la'k) thin, lean, delicate, suitable, right, proper สุภ — beautiful in all respects ทร — deformed

ลักเพศ (la'kpeyt) [Pali] sham priest

ลัง (la'ng) a shallow receptable made of bamboo, basket — เล uncertain

หลัง (la'ng?) back, behind, after สัน — back (of a man, animal, knife, etc.) ก — at a later time, last, after — คา roof — เค้า bar at a river mouth — โกง hump-backed — ยาน etc. (numerical designation of houses)

หลั่ง (la'ng) pouring water into the hands

ลังกา (la'ngkah) Ceylonese

ลังสาก (la'ngsart) a fruit tree

ลัญฉกร (la'ncha'khon) [P.] royal seal

ลฎิ (la'ti') [Pali] young and soft

ลัด (la't) (1) to grow — ให้ to get fat
(2) to take the short road, a short
cut คลอง — canal cutting off a
part of a river ปาก — mouth of do.
(3) to let go a thing which has been
bent back

ทลัด (la't) quickly, soon

ลัดา (la'dah) wild jasmine

ลัทธิ (la'ttee') [Pali] religious tenets,
schism, heresy

ลัน (la'n) a bamboo eel-trap

ลัน (la'n) to explode, to make a sudden sound

หลัน (la'n) order, degree, series

ลันไท (la'ntai) and ลันเทา a bean

ลันทม (la'ntom) a flowering mountain
tree

ลับ (la'p) (1) hidden, secret ข้อ —
mystery — หลัง behind one's back
— แล to appear and disappear,
trellis-work, screen (2) to sharpen
หิน — whetstone

หลับ (la'p) to sleep, sleepy — สนิท
sound asleep

ลับ (la'p) [Sansk.] quotient

ลับแล (la'plaa) blind, screen

---- ◆ ◆ ◆ ----

ว

ว (waw = English w. Sansk. v. Guttural : a low letter)

วก (wok) to turn, turn back, return

วง (wong) circle, orb, circuit (num.
design. of circular things, as rings,
etc.) — วน to whirl, gulf, whirlpool
— เวียน (1) to draw round, encircle
(2) compasses

วกะ (wong) [Pali] crooked

วงกา (wongkah) (1) a bracket (2) the
mark showing a mistake or rejected phrase or word

วงษ์ (wong) and วงษา [Sansk.] family,
race ; [end of many proper names,
as สุริยวงษ]

วจี (wa'chi') and วจิ วาจา and วะจะ
[Pali] word, speech, discourse

วชิรญาณ (wa'chi'ra'yahn) [Pali] knowledge

วฏ (wa'ta') [Pali] transmigration

วน (won) to turn, whirl, whirling —

เวียน to transmigrate

วนา (wa'nah) and วนะ [Pali] woods, forests, deserts

วนิดา (wa'ni'dah) and วนิตา [Pali] handsome woman

วร (wa'ra) [Pali] and — วรรณ excellent, superior, precious

วรณา (wa'ra'nah) [Pali] to praise, extol

วรดิตถ์ (wa'ra'ditt) [Pali] high, precious ท่า ราช — a Palace landing

วรรค (wa'ka') [Pali] space [in writing]

วรรณิพก (wa'nni'poke) [Pali] beggar, poor, indigent

วรา — วร

วรุณ (wa'roo'na') [Pali] angel of rain

วรุตม (wa'roo'ta'ma') [Pali] first, best, superior, excellent

วระภูษณ์ (wa'ra'poo't) [Pali] ornaments

วล (wa'la') and พล [Pali] strength, force, troops, forces

วลาหก (wa'lah-hok) [Pali] clouds, cloud-angel

วว (wooa') ox, cow, cattle

วษา วัสสา วะษา and พรรษา (wa'ssah)

[Sansk. and Pali] rainy season, year; season from the 15 of the 8th month to the 15 of the 11th month [Alab. 97, 189, 229] .ข้า — to go into a monastery to stay for this season

วษ ฏก (wa'soh tok) [Pali] rain water

วสุธา (wa'soo'tah) [Pali] earth, world

วอ (waw) covered palanquin for princes

วอก (wauk) monkey ปี — 9th year of the Siameses cycle

ว่อง (waung) agile, expert — ไว active

วอด (waut) to finish, complete — วาย to die, to ruin

วอนว่า and วอน ขอ (waun wah, waun khaw) to ask often or urgently รุ ว่อน to besiege with requests

ว่อน (wonn) wander about, to roam around, to soar

วา (wah) a measure of length (= about 80 Engl. inches) ไม้ — stick or wood for measuring this length ลด — ลา ช่อก to lower the price

ว่า (war) to say ราชการ — ความ etc. to administer public business, justice, etc. — กล่าว to discourse, to speak in favour of — ทิ to hold the place of another

ว้า *and* หวา (war) [excl. of encouragement] come on! get on! ว้า เหว่ lonely, solitary, affrighted by solitude

หว้า (wah) a fruit tree

วาก แวาก (wahk waak) mental distraction, distraction, inconsistent

วาง (warng) to deposit, place — ใจ to confide — ยา to administer physic, to poison

ว่าง (warng) clear, unoccupied, open, at liberty, at leisure — เปง empty, solitary — เว้น exempt from, unoccupied

ว้าง (wahng) spacious เวิง — space arched over [by trees, etc.]

หว่าง (wahng) intermediate space, interval — เขา valley

วาจา (wahchah) วะ ๒ วาี *and* วี [Pali] words, speech, talk, discourse, advice, eloquence

วาด (waht) (1) to draw pictures (2) to back-water with a paddle

หวาด (wart) to be startled, to start back from fear

วาตะ (wahta') *and other similar forms* [Pali] wind, air

วาที (wahtee) [Pali] words, discourse

วาน (wahn) to employ the help of another person — ทำ to order (a person) to do (a thing) ผู้ — one who orders

หวาน (warn) sweet, honeyed, candied

หว่าน (wahn) to sow

หว้าน (wahn) a medicinal plant หัว — root of this plant

วานซืนนี้ (wahnseunnee) two days ago

วานนี้ (wahnnee) yesterday

วานร (wahna'ra') [Pali] monkey

วานรินท์ *and* วานเรศ (wahna'rinn, wahna'rett) [San.] King of the monkeys

วาณิช (wahnitt) [Pali] trader, dealer, merchant

วาป (wahp) to blaze forth, to burst out into light — วับ to keep blazing out

วาม (wahm) glittering, bright, palpitating, flashing out, growing bright — ๆ lightening and dying away again

วาย (wai) (1) to be deminished, de-

crease (2) to be finished, to lose --
ชนม์ to die — ปราน without breath
(3) out of stock. all sold เร่ง —
scarce

ว่าย (waie) to swim

หวาย (waie?) rattan, fasces of the lictors ย่าง — เทษ dragon's blood, a
kind of resin

วายุ (wahyoo') and วาโย [Pali] wind,
air — ภักษ a bird which lives on
wind; a seal used in the Treasury
— บุตร a monkey born of the wind

วาร (warn) and วาระ [Pali] day

วาริช (wahritt) [Pali] animals bred in
the water, fish

วาริน (wahrinn) and วารี [Pali]
water, river

วาระ (wahra') [Pali] day

วาลุกา (wahloo'kah) and พาลุกา [Pali]
sand

วาฬะ (wahla') [Sansk.] savage, wild
— มฤค beast of prey

วาวแวว (wowe wao) to sparkle, shine,
twinkle

ว่าว (wowe) kite (toy) หาง — catalogue, list of persons in the King's

service กม — North wind

วาศินา (wahsa'nah?) [Pali] mental effect of good or bad actions

วาส (wahsee) [Pali] (1) habitation,
dwelling (2) razor

วาสุกรี (wahsoo'kree) [Pali] gigantic
serpents living under the ground.
Nagas. King of these creatures

วาหะ (wah-ha') [Pali] vehicle, chariot,
carriage, to conduct, to carry วิ —
wedding

วิ (wi') [Pali] (1) (prefix meaning
separation, disjunction) (2) better

วิกล (wi'konn) and วิการ [Pali] incomplete, mutilated. spoiled, de-
fective

วิฆาฏ (wi'khaht) and วิฆาฏ [Pali] to
kill, to cause the death of

วิ่ (wing) (1) giddines (2) to keep on
asking

วิ่ง (wing) to run — หนี to escape by
running, to flee

วิงวอน (wingwaun) prayer, to entreat,
supplicate, to ask pardon

วิจารณ (witchahra'na') วิจารณ and วา
ระณะ [Pali] to examine, to consider, reflection [Alab. 195]

วิจิตร (witchitt) [Pali] ornamented, magnificent, splendid

วิชา (witchah) [Pali] art, science — ฅร one who succeeds in doing miracles, a lower angel

วิไชย (wi'chai) [Pali] victory

วิญญา (winnyah) and วิญญาณ [Pali] to know, knowledge, mind, intelligence, soul [Alab. 173]

วิด (wit) to bale out (water) drain, exhaust, evacuate

วิตก (wittock) [Pali] reflection, reasoning, consideration [Alab. 195]

วิถาร (wittahn) to explain, to discuss; at large, at length, widely, wide

วิถี (wittee) [Pali] way, road, street, course

วิธี (witti') and วิธ [Pali] art, mode, manner, method, skill

วิน (win) cloven, split, torn

วินา (wi'nah) [Pali] without, besides

วินาที (wi'nartee) [Pali] a second, an instant

วินาศ (wi'nart) [Sansk.] to be lost, destroyed, ruin

วินิจฉัย (wi'nitchai) [Pali] to investigate, scrutinize, examine with care, ascertain, decide

วิไนย (wi'naie) [Pali] avoidance, subduing, training, discipline [Alab. 166.], title of a priest, part of the Buddhist scriptures

วินะ (wi'na') [Pali] one who knows, one who commands

วิบาก (wi'bark) [Pali] good result, reward, recompense

วิบัติ (wi'ba't) [Pali] misery, misfortune, ruin

วิปริต (wi'pa'ritt) [Pali] transformed, changed, unnatural, monster

วิปลาศ (wi'pa'lart) [Sansk.] miraculous, extraordinary

วิปัสนา (wi'pa'ssa'nah) [Pali] contemplation of good and evil, thorough investigation [Alab. 226]

วิภัค (wi'pa'kh) [Pali] declensions

วิภาค (wi'pahk) [Pali] to divide, to separate into parts

วิภู (wi'poo) [Pali] (1) lord, ruler (2) manifest, evident

วิภูสิต (wi'poositt) [Pali] ornament

วิมล (wi'monn) [Pali] spotless, handsome

วิมาน (wi'marn) [Pali] heavenly abode, pagoda of seven storeys

วิมุติ (wi'moo'ti') [Pali] doubt, principles of emancipation, free thought

[Alab. 196]

วิโมกข์ (wi'mohk) [Pali] acquitted, released, escape

วิโยค (wi'yohk) [Pali] separation, deliverance, release

วิริยา (wi'ri'ya') [Pali] energy, fortitude, perseverance, patience [Alab. 184, 196]

วิรณ (wi'roo'n) [Pali] rain

วิรุฬห์ (wi'roo'n) [Pali] growth, increase, angel of growth

วิรุฬหก (wi'roo'nhok) [Pali] rain-angel [see Alab. 175]

วิโรธ (wi'roht) [Pali] anger, enmity; to become angry

วิลา วิไลย วิลาน and วิลาศ (wi'lah, etc.) [Sansk.] charming, seductive, beautiful

วิลา (wi'lah) and วิลาร [Pali] better วิฬาร cat

วิลาป (wi'larp) mourning, lamentation นก — pigeon

วิลาศ (wi'laht) [Pali] (1) an inferior heaven (2) beautiful, pretty เมือง -- London

วิลันดา (wi'la'ndah) Dutch

วิวร (wi'wonn) [Pali] to open

วิวาท (wi'wart) [Pali] quarrel, dispute, contention, litigation

วิวาห (wi'wah-ha') [Pali] marriage, wedding

วิวก (wi'wake) [Pali] solitude, seclusion, abstraction

วิศาล (wi'sarn) [Sansk.] large, huge

วิสาขะ (wi'sarkha') (1) a constellation [Alab. 101] sixth month of the old Siamese year (2) name of a female saint

วิสาสะ (wi'sarsa') [Pali] conversation, intimacy, to make acquaintance

วิสุทธิ (wi'soo'tti') [Pali] pure, holy, correct

วิสูตร (wi'soot) curtain, screen, partition

วิสิฐ or better วิเศษ (wi'sett) [Sansk. Pali] precious, excellent, magnificent โรง — the King's kitchen หลวง — a title of honour

วิไสย (wi'saio) [Pali] (1) kingdom, country, (2) character, nation, race — รูป qualities of the four senses [Alab. 237] ธรรม — legal research, jurisprudence [Alab. 196]

วิสัชนา (wi'satcha'nah) [Pali] to explain, to preach, to enlighten

วิสัญชะนี (wi'sa'ncha'nee) [Sansk.] name of the 17th vowel [see Preface]

วิสัญญี (wi'sa'nyee) [Pali] to faint, swoon

วิหก (wi'hok) [Pali] birds

วิหาร (wi'harn) [Pali] abode of a priest, monastery, temple not having the sacred leaf (ใส้มา) in it

วิฬาร (wi'larn) [Pali] cat

วี (wee) to fan

หวี (wee?) comb — กล้วย bunch of bananas

หวีด (weet) [exclam. of alarm]

เวียง (weea'ng) [Laos.] walled-in place, palace

เหวี่ยง (weea'ng) to throw with a backhanded or underhand action, to chuck

เวียน (weea'n) to whirl, to turn, to walk around — เทียน a ceremony of exchanging lights from hand to hand [Alab. 298: and see also Æsch. Ag. 299] — เทียน bilious headache

วุฒิ better วุทฒิ (woo'ttee') [Pali] (1) flourishing, permanent, increase,

prosperity (2) old man

วุก (woo't) [phon.] (1) to light by blowing (2) sound of striking the air with a whip or stick

วุตตา (woo'ttah) [Pali] to say, to speak

วุตตัญญา (woo'tta'nyah) [Pali] linguist

วุธ and วุธา (woo'ttah) [Pali] = พุธ Mercury

วุ่น (woo'n) busy

วุ้น (woo'n) jelly made of lichens

วุ่นวาย (weo'n waie) tumult, trouble, disturbance

วุป (woo'p) [phon.] (1) nodding of the head in dozing (2) [phon.] noise of an explosion

วุย and วุ้ย (wooi') [exclam. of fear] (2) excl. of calling hither

วู วู่ and หวู (woo) [phon.] buzzing, humming, noise

วูวาด (woot waht) (1) to disappear suddenly (2) [phon.] noise of the swooping of birds

เว้ (hway) Hue (capital of Annam)

เวง (wayng) with วิง soothed by a sound, abandoned, solitary, pensive

เวง (wayng) [Cambod.] Palace

เวจ (wett) water-closet

เวไชยันต์พิมาน (waychaiya'nta'pi'marn) [Pali] Palace of Indra [Alab. 171]

เวทนา (wayta'nah) [Pali] sensation, sensation of pain [Alab. 172], pity, sympathy

เวทนียา (wayta'ni'yah) [Pali] knowledge, fruition [Alab. 47]

เวน (wayn) to reject a thing which is useless, to cast off

เว้น (wayn) to except, to exempt — — ว่า exempt, free from — แต่ except, unless — ไว้ excepted — ว่าง and ว่าง — interruption, interval

เวไนไตย (wayna'taie) [Pali] fabulous eagle, Garuda, Krut [Alab. 192, 212, 300]

เวไนย (waynaie) [Pali] to lead, to teach, to convert — สัตว์ animals which can be taught

เวร (wayn) [Pali] revenge, anger, hatred, enmity, vengeance ผูก — and ร้อง — [Cambod.] vengeance, to be avenged [see also next word]

เวร เวรา and เวร (wayra', etc.) [Pali] retribution, rotation, turn, in turn, in order กัก — the turn comes round ผาย — officials who serve in rotation ผก — to pay off one bad turn by another

เวลา (waylah) [Pali] time — สาย forenoon — บ่าย afternoon — ค่ำ nighttime ใกล — the moment is near ให้ — at the proper moment

เวหน (wayhon) and เวหาศ (wayhart) [Pali] air, sky

เวหา (wayhah) [Pali] empty space, air

เวหาร (wayharn) [Pali] monastery, convent, temple, dwelling

เวฬู (wayloo') [Pali] bamboo — ปพพร spots in bamboo

แหว (hwaa) excl. of anger by children

แหวก (hwaak) to open partially, to push aside

แหวง (waang) and แหวง to turn the head round so as to bite an assailant

แหว่ง (waang) unentire, imperfect, incomplete

แวด (waat) to surround, to escort

แว่น (wen) and — ตา spectacles

แหวน (waan') ring แก้ว — precious stones หัว — bezel of a ring

แวบ (waap) (1) to fall or go with great

speed, to disappear suddenly (2) partly open

แวมๆ (waam waam) twinkling light [as of a firefly]

แวว (waao) loops, rounds — ๆ inside of the ear — หนังสือ loops of letters ใจ — intelligence เห็น — ๆ foresee

แวว (wao) indistinct — ๆ not hearing distinctly

แวะ (waa') (1) to stop in one's course (2) to turn aside and go in

ไว (wai) prompt, active, quick เห็น — ๆ to see without being sure, to have a presentiment มือ — rapacity, thieving

ไว้ (wie) to keep; [added to another verb means] continuously, permanently เก็บ — and เอา — to keep — ใจ confidence, hope

ไหว (hwai) to shake, tremble, oscillate ดิน — earthquake

ไหว้ (waie) to salute, to adore

ไวยวุฒิ (waiya'woo't) [Pali] : adolescence, youth, age of growing

โว with ปาก (park woh) boasting, vain : with ยก to boast

โว่ โหว and โหว่ (woh) hollow

โว้เว้ (woh way) bad manners, vulgarity, vagubond

โวย โว้ย and โหวย (woey) [excl. of one common fellow calling to another]

โวหาร (wo-harn) [Pali] speech, word, common use, to speak, eloquent

เว้า (wow) curved, concave, bending inwards

เว้าแหว่ง (wowe waang) mutilated, imperfect

หว่ำ (hwa'm) (1) eaten away in the middle, hollow, deep (2) [phon.] noise of falling into water

วะ (wa') [exclam. of dislike or disgust]

หวะ (wa') to be broken, to burst

วะชิราวุธ (wa'chi'rahwoo't) [Pali] adamant, a stone used to bore gems

วะชิรญาณ see วชิรญาณ

วัก (wa'k) to scoop up (water, etc.) with the hand

วัง (wa'ng) palace, royal court — หน้า (front palace) p. of the Second King — หลัง p. of the Third King — นอก p. other than the King's

วังวน (wa'ng won) gulf, whirlwind, whirlpool

วังเวง (wa'ng wayng) (1) soothed with sounds (2) oppressed with solitude

หวัง (wa'ng?) and — ว่า to expect, conjecture

วัชรินทร์ (wa'tcha'rin) [Pali] angel

วังษา   วงษา q. v.

วัฏ (wa't) and — สง สาร [Pali] to whirl, transmigration

วัฒนา (wa'tta'nah) วัฒนะ and วัฒนา การ [Pali] progress, continuation, to grow larger, increase

วัด (wa't) (1) to measure, survey (2) monastery, temple (3) to pull up (a fish out of the water, etc.)

หวัด (hwa't) (1) cold in the head (2) to write with a running hand

วัตถุ (wa'ttoo') [Pali] (1) history, plot, subject, matter [see Alab. 206] (2) fortune, money

วัตถะ (wa'tta') (1) — วัตถุ (2) [Pali] cloth garment (3) to turn, world

วัดเหวี่ยง (wa't weea'ng) to whirl, to twirl, to hurl

วัน (wa'n) day — ๆ by day — คืน (in document) date - นี้ to-day กลาง — at midday — พระ the Siamese

Sunday or holy day, at intervals of 7 or 8 days แมงลง — fly, ephemerid

หวัน (wa'n?) [Javan.] brilliancy

หนว่ (wa'nn) to shake, agitation, emotion

วันทา (wa'ntah) and วันทนา [Pali] to salute, venerate, pay homage

หวันปีหวา (wa'nyee'wah?) [Javan.] (1) life, soul (2) lady

วับแวบ (wa'p werp) to flutter (like a scarf worn on the breast) to dance (like flames), to flicker

วัยวะ (waiwa') [Pali] limb, member, body

วัลลี (wa'nlee) [Pali] creeping plant, creeper

วสวัตตี (wa'sa'wa'ttee') Pali (1) bringing into subjection (2) obtaining pleasures created by others ประวตี มิตร — highest of the Deva heavens [Alab. 113] (3) a name of King Mara

* * * * *

ศ

ศ (saw-k... ... Engl. s. Lingual: a high letter) — ศอ ศี name of this letter

ศก (sok) [added to Sansk. numerals signifies the year of the decennial cycle] เอก — โท — etc, 1st, 2nd, year of the decade, etc. รัตนโก สินทร์ — date in years from the foundation of Bangkok as a capital

ศคา (sa'kah) [Pali] crowd, assembly

ศพ (sop) [Sansk.] corpse, dead body ปลง — funeral มิไหว — or มหา — funeral fêtes, festivities, displays, ceremonies, etc.

ศาล (sarn) [Pali] hall, tribunal, court of justice — ต่าง ประเทศ International Court — เจ้า Chinese pagoda erected in honour of the guardian angel

ศรี (see) [Sansk.] handsome, beautiful, beauty, prosperity — สวัสดิ flourishing, prosperity - สรรเพชุ a name of Buddha, jewels of a bright colour — สุดา fine woman — วิลาศ fine, glorious — วิไลย civilized; beauty

ศรีสุนิสา (seesoo'ni'sah) [Pali] daughter-in-law

ศฤงคาร (singkharn) (1) love, passion (2) attendants, retinue (3) having a large retinue, wealthy

เศรีก (serk) [Sansk.] a coronet used (for women) in theatres

โศรก (soke) [Pali] sad, sorrowful

เศร้า (sow) (1) ugly (2) sad, sorrowful

ศรัทธา (sa'ttah) [Pali] faith, belief

ไศล (sa'lai) [Sansk.] rocky mountain

ศาลา (sahlah) [Pali] (1) ศาล (2) out-door shed or roofed platform for sleeping on

ศิขร (sikkhon) and เศขร (seekhon) [Pali] (1) peak, point, top, summit (2) buffalo (3) hard, rigid

ศิริ (si'ri') [Pali] = สิริ q. v. beautiful, beauty, prosperity, glory

ศิโรตม์ (si'rote) [Sansk.] to bow, to salute; pointed skull [Alab. 207]

ศิล (sin) and ศิลา (si'lah) [Pali] stone, rock

ศิลปสาคร (silpa'sart) [Sansk.] various arts, skill, mechanical knowledge [Alab. 210]

ศิษย์ (sissya') [Sansk.] and ลูก — pupil

ศีล (seen) [Pali] good conduct, moral practice, piety, religious observances — ขาด excommunicate อด fasting, Lent

ศีส: (seesa') [Pali] head, front, beginning (as of a wood, town, etc.)

เศียร (seea'n) [Pali] head

ศึก (seuk) [Sansk.] combatant, warrior ข้า — enemy ไส้ — spy, traitor — ผู้ to practise, scholar —
ษาธิการ Education Department

ศึษ see ศิศ learning, scholar, student

ศุกร (soo'k) [Sansk.] Venus (planet)
วัน — Friday

ศุกรปักษ์ and ศุกปักษ์ (soo'kkha'-
pa'k) [P.] time of the waxing moon

ศุข (soo'k) [Pali] white

ศุข (soo'k) [Pali] happy, blest, peace-
ful, easy, healthy — สบาย health
and happiness — สาน and — เษม
happiness, felicity

ศุขี (soo'khee) [Sansk.] happiness,
prosperity

ศุพลักษร (co'] a'ksonn) [Pall] King's
hand-writing

ศูล (soon) [Pali] sharp pointed instrument, spear, lance, pike, stake

ศูลี (soolee) [Pali] and ศิร — Siva:
archangeel

เศก (sake) [Pali] sprinkling, unction;
to consecrate; royal marriage

เศลา (saylah) [Pali] rock, stone

เศก = เศวีก q. v.

โศกศีลย (sokhksa'n) [Sansk.] pain of a
wound inflicted by a missile, sickness of heart, grief, pang, anguish

ศักดิ (sa'k) and ศักดิ [Sansk.] power,
authority, influence, dignity, rank
ยก — rank, reputation, glory —
สิทธิ full of strength, victorious,
saintly — ผา the measure of a
person's rank

ศักราช (sa'ka'rart) [Pali] Siamese era
พุทธ — sacred Buddist era จุล —
old civil era, beginning 638 A. D.

ศักรวา (sa'kra'wah) [Sansk.] singer,
musician (2) we, us

ศับท better ศัพท (sa'p) [Sansk.] soun l,
noise, voice, word, term กิต —
rumour โทร — telephone

ศัลละ (sa'nla') [Pali] better ศัลย (sa'n)
[Sansk.] missile, gun, point of a
weapon, lance, sharp missile, bullet

ศัลย (sa'n) sick at heart

ษ

ษ (saw baw = English s. and at end of
word t. Lingual: a high letter) ษอ
ษอ name of this letter

ษัตรี (sa'ttree) [Sansk.] woman, female

———————◆◆◆———————

ส

ส (saw law = English s. and at the
end of a word t. a high letter) สอ
สอ name of this letter

สก (sok) [Cambod.] lock of hair

สกด (sa'kot) (1) to restrain, to keep in,
to lull to sleep, to beguile หมอ —
magician สกด — consecrated beads
used as amulets — รอย to track,
to dog, to follow (2) name given to
a consonant as practically complet-
ing the end of a word

สกนธ์ (sa'konn) [Sansk.] body, troop

สกปรก (soka'prok) dirty, foul, squalid

สกรรณ์ (sa'ka'n) [Camb.] in the prime
of life, vigorous, powerful ทกขึ —
severe diarrhœa

สกล (sa'kon) [Pali] all over, in all

parts of; all the world, universe

สกุณ (sa'koo'n) flock of birds

สกุโณ (sa'koo'roh) (and other similar
forms) [Pali] male bird

สกุณี and สกุณรี female bird

สกุล (sa'koon) (1) noble, well-born,
well-bred (2) (Engl.) school

สกัด (sa'ka't) (1) the shorter sides of a
parallelogram or oblong (2) to mortise, to chisel, to chip (3) obstruct,
hinder, interrupt ไม้ — press เหล็ก
— chisel for cutting metals กัน —
to intercept, to stop by spreading
out the hands on each side

สง (song) (1) to raise or lift with the
hand, to take up (2) ripe (betel-nut)
(3) to shake the dust out of anything ถั่วยา — a bean

ส่ง (song) (1) to lead out of the house,
to see (a person) off, to escort, conduct บอก — to bring news from a
distant place เหล็ก— iron instrument for driving in nails — อากร
monopoly — เสียง to act as inter-
preter, to make a noise (2) to lift
up (3) to hand over to, to put within the reach of (4) to light (a fire)

สงกรานต์ (sorgkrarn) (1) to migrate (2) angel of the year ๗รุๅ — festival of the New Year

สงกา (songkar) to doubt, distrust, disbeleive

สงคราม (songkhrarm) war, warfare, military science

สงเคราะห์ (songkraw) [Pali] to help, to come to the rescue of

สงฆ์ (song) [Pali] (1) priest ๒ — female priest, (2) a troop (3) alike

สงบ (sa'ngop) to be tranquillised, quieted — หาย to come to an end, disappear — คน when all the people are quiet

สงวน (sa'ngooa'n) to take care of, to keep

สงสาร (songsarn) [Pali] (1) to go and come back, transmigration (2) compassion ; to pity

สงไสย (songsai) to doubt, distrust

สง่า (sa'ngar) (1) majestic, majesty, dignity, (2) dressed up

เสงี่ยม (sngee'am) moderation, modesty, humility

สงัด (sa'nga't) quiet, tranquil

สฐาน (sa'tarn) [Pali] place, site, position เคหา — site for a dwelling house — ใก where

สด (sott) fresh, vivid — ชื่ glad, merry — ใส bright, flourishing

สดมภ์ (sa'domm) (1) [Pali] sorcery, witchcraft, spell ปล้น — to rob by the help of sorcery (2) post, stake, stump (3) walk lightly, or slowly

สดวก (sa'doo'ak) quickly, easily, uninterruptedly

สดุ้ง (sa'doo'ng) to start, to be startled

สดุด (sa'doo't) to knock against with the foot, elbow, etc. — กับ to trip up, to come in contact with the feet

สดุดี (sa'doo'sa'dee) [Pali] to worship, to pay respect to, contentment, happiness, gratitude

สดูป (sa'doop) [Sansk.] and ถูป [Pali] pagoda, prachadee, shrine

เสด็จ (sa'dett) (1) (of a King or Prince) to come, to go ยัง ไม่ — he (the Prince) is not yet come (2) Prince, royal personage (3) to draw up [water]

แสดง (sa'daang) to tell, explain

สดับ (sa'da'p) to hear

สตางค์ (sa'tarng) [Sansk.] one hundredth part

สถล (sa'tonn) [Pali] by land, on land — มรรค์ conrse through the land, land-path

สถิตย์ (sa'titt) [Pali] to be domiciled, to settle — เสถียร to be permanently settled

สน (son) (1) to thread a needle, to pass a string through a buffalo's nose สัย — in crowds — ใๆ to attend busily to (2) turpentine tree ยาง — turpentine

สนทนา (sonta'nah) [Pali] to converse, to talk

สนธยา (sonta'yah) [P.] dark, evening

สนเท่ห์ (sontay) [Pali] to doubt, to be uneasy

สนธิ (sonti') [Pali] joint, combination, conception บัติ — to be born again new conception เอา — to be conceived

สนม (sa'nom) ladies of the palace

สนวน (sa'nooan) (1) a tree, (2) gateway, enclosed passage

สนอง (sa'naung) (1) to answer (2) to

do a favour — คุณ to be grateful (3) rest, socket, place for holding

สนาน (sa'narn) [Camb.] (1) to bathe, to wash (2) pleasant, to play

สนาม (sa'narm) open ground in a town, Square — มวย wrestling arena — ไก่ cockpit — เพลาะ mound in front of a soldier, breastwork

สนิท (sa'nitt) [Pali] united, associated, intimate ทา — to pretend friendship หวาน — quite sweet

สนิม (sa'nim) rust

เสนียด (sa'neea't) [Cambod.] (1) in the way, troublesome (2) a tree หวี — a comb with teeth on each side

สนุก (sa'noo'k) [P.] cheerful, cheery, agreeable, acceptable — สาน playful, amusing — สบาย well & happy

สนุ่น (sa'noo'n) (1) a tree (2) soft ground, muddy place

เสน่ห์ (sa'nay) and เสนหา [Sansk.] to love; love-potion, philtre

เสนอ (sa'neuc) (1) to run on before, outstrip (2) to take part with, intercede for, recommend

สนะ (sa'na') to bind, tie, bandage ช่าง
— tailor

สนัก (sa'na't) (1) to grasp tightly, to
hold on to (2) skilful แทก — much
broken, half-destroyed — สัก to
seize tightly, hold very tight โก
very large, huge

สนัน (sa'na'n) loud, sounding ก้อง
echo

สนับ (sa'na'p) tight-fitting — มือ sew-
ing pad — เพลา tight trowsers

สบ (sop) (1) to please (2) to find, to
meet with (3) to be acquainted with
— เสีย (1) to give presents (2) to
nourish, cherish

สบถ (sa'bot) [Pali] to swear, curse,
imprecation, oath

สบาย (sa'bai) to be in good health, to
be well ตาม — according to one's
wish — ใจ joy, to enjoy

สเบียง (sa'beea'ng) provisions

สปรศ (sa'pa'rot) pine-apple

สพรั่ง (sa'pra'ng) apparent plenty,
well to do, well off

สพาน (sa'parn) = กะ พาน bridge

สม (som) (1) to heap up, to add to, to
join (2) fit, suitable, appropriate,
worthy — อ้าง willing witness,
ready to swear to anything · ใ
and — เสพย์ to cohabit —— เข้ากัน
to have got what one deserves
ควร suitable, proper, respectable

สม (som) sour, acid ; vinegar ส้ม, —
alum

สมกบ (somkop) (1) rancid, putrid
(meat) (2) parasitical tree

สมคบ (somkhop) to associate with the
bad, to consort

สม ชร (somchon) [Pali] (1) defile, passage (2) bestiality, incest

สมณ สมณา (sa'ma'nah) and other
forms [Pali] one who does penance,
ascetic, monk, priest [Alab. 203]

สมเด็จ (somdett) excellent, superior
[title of the highest honour]

สมทบ (somtopp) to put together,
amalgamate, joint

สมนาคุณ (soma'nahkhoo'n) [Pali] to
return thanks, to remunerate

สมบูรณ (somboon) [Pali] complete,
full, superabundant, opulent

สมบัติ (somba't) [Pali] plenty, abundance of property, riches ครอง — to reign

สมประดี (sompra'dee) recovering one's senses

สมปอง (sompaung) as I wished, as I expected

สมปัก (sompa'k) embroidered cloth

สมพร (som'pon) [Pali] so be it, let it be as you wish ; to approve of

สมพาศ (sompart) [Pali] to cohabit

สมโพธิ (sompohti) [Pali] (1) enlightenment, knowledge (2) to celebrate, solemnise — ญาณ savant, learned man, History of Buddha

สมพักษร (sompa'kson) [Sansk.] year

สมภาร (somparn) [Pali] chief priest of a monastery, abbot

สมเพท (somphayt) better สมเพช [Pali] pity, pitiable, deplorable

สมมต (sommot) = สมมติ

สมมม (sommom) dirty, foul

สมมติ (sommoo'ti') (1) [Pali] consent, permission ; to respect, to esteem, to call — วงษ a respected family (2) to substitute

สมร (samn o m) (Head ใจ) - beloved

or kind lady (2) amulet สาย — string of an amulet (3) to fight, battle-field, war, battle

สมรศ (somrot) to copulate, cohabit สิน — property inherited from parents

สมรู้ (somroc) witness, accomplice, to consort

สมศักดิ์ (somsa'k) of age to be tattooed with the mark of identification

สมศักดิ์ (somsa'k) [Sansk.] of good repute, honourable

สมอ (sa'maw) gall-nut tree ลูก — gall nut

สมอ (sa'maw) anchor ถอน — to hoist the anchor — เกา anchor which does not catch hold

สมอง (sa'maung) brain

สมาคม (sa'markhom) to associate, to be familiar with

สมาต (sa'mart) [Malay.] Mahomedan priest

สมาทาน (sa'martahn) [Pali] perfect observance

สมาธิ (sa'mahtee') [Pali] cross-legged and motionless

สมาน (sa'marn) [Pali] united, to join, to patch up

สมาหาร (sa'mah-harn) [Pali] to collect victuals, to forage, to prepare food

สมิง (sa'ming) [a Peguan title] เสือ — man transformed into a tiger

สมี (sa'mee) a medicinal tree

เสมียน (sa'mee'an) clerk, copying clerk, secretary, — ตรา chief secretary

สมุก (sa'moo'k) a box, or basket with a top or lid to it

สมุด (sa'moo't) volume, book

สมุติ (soommoo't) *see* สมมติ

สมุท (Pali) *see* — ปราการ Paknam — สงคราม a Province — โคคม a name of Buddha

สมุน (sa'moo'n) (1) leaves stitched together for roofing — ละแวง a medicinal tree (2) student

สมุห (sa'moo') [Pali] battalion, regiment, body of men — นายก a dignity above all the other grades — บาญชี Chief Secretary

เสมด (samett) (1) a tree of which the leaves are used for roofing (2) a sea turtle

เสมอ (sa'men) equal, level, continuous, always — ที่ remaining in the same place — ทั่ว equal on all sides

แสม (sa'maa?) *and* — ทะเล a sea-side tree — สาร a tree with hard wood

ใสมย (sa'mai?) (1) time, occasion, season (2) religious assembly

โสมสร (sa'mohson) [Pali] to rejoice in company, to meet, assemble, unanimous

สมัค (sa'ma'kh) [Pali] agreeing, consenting, assenting, unanimous ทหาร — volunteer

สมัก (sa'ma't) to suck up หมาก — prepared betel-nut

สมัน (sa'ma'n) stag

สมันตพงษ (sa'ma'nta'pong) [Pali] of equal family, equal rank

สยบ (sa'yop) to bow the head

สยม (sa'yom) [Pali] on self — ภวิญญาณ having omniscience in on self, archangel

สยอง (sa'yaung) to be afraid of — ขน hair bristling *or* standing on end with fear

สยาม (sa'yahm) (1) brown (2) Siamese

สยุม (sa'yoo'm) to dress in fine clothes ภร nuptials, wedding, coronation of a King and Queen

สแยก (sa'yaak) tree without branches

แสยง (sa'yaang) (hair) standing on end

แสยะ (sa'yaa') half-open, a jar; to draw down the corners of the mouth

สยัมภู (sa'yampoo) [Pali] self-existent

โสรง (song) [of the king] to bathe

สรณา (sa'ra'nah) *see* สระนา

สรพู (sa'ra'poo) [Pali] lizard

สรเพชฐ (sa'ra'pett) [Sansk.] title given to one of the highest Phras

สรร (sa'n) to choose, prefer

สรร (sa'n) [Sansk.] worse than the rest, inferior

สรรพ (sa'ra'pa') [Sansk.] all, every — ใน pronoun · สัตว์ all creatures · · ยุทธ all kinds of weapons

สรรพ (sa'p) ready เครื่อง — materials ready for use

สรรพากร (sa'pahk onn) [Sansk.] collection of taxes, revenue farm

สรรเพชญ (sa'npett) [San.] omniscient, learned, Buddha

สรรลาบ (sa'nlarp) [Pali] to converse readily, to speak, jestingly

สรรเสิญ (sa'nsern) *and* สรรเสริญ [Pali] to praise, commend

สรวง (sooa'ng) to sacrifice to angels or genii

สรวม (sooa'm) to dress, clothe สรก — to put on over the head

สรวล (sooa'n) to laugh, smile

สร้อย (soi) collar — ไก่ neck feathers — ทาบ gold ball hung on the neck. sash — สัน a kind of music, a reed

สร้อย เศร้า (soi sow) sad, melancholy

สร้าง (sahng) to build, construct

สรูป (sa'roop) to add, to join, unite

เสร็จ (sett) [Pali] it is finished, ready เป็น — promiscuous, altogether, the whole lot ภาษี เป็น — general tax on property

เสริม (serm) to insert

โสรม (sohm) [Pali] orb of the moon

โสรมนัศ (sohma'na't) [Sansk.] satisfaction, enjoyment [Alab. 238]

สระ (sa') [Pali] pool, pond, lake — โบกขรณี lotus pool

สระณะ (sa'ra'nah) *and* — คมน์ [Pali] remembrance, faith, refuge, profession of faith in the Three Refuges

สระแหน่ (sa'ra'naa) mint (herb)

สลด (sa'lot) sad, melancholy

สลน (sa'lon) wriggling, going crookedly

สลบ (sa'lop) swoon, to faint

สลวน (sa'looa'n) a tree

สลวย (sa'looi') in good order, well made up, well done

สลอด (sa'laut) croton (from which croton oil is obtained)

สลอน (sa'laun) many, much

สลวย (sa'looi') waving (of tree tops)

สลากพัต (sa'larkpa't) [Pali] distribution of food to the priests by means of tickets

สลาก (sa'lart) *with* ปลา a flat fish

สลาตัน (sa'larta'n) [Malay.] North-West (wind)

สลาย (sa'laie) split, cleft, sprung

สลิด (sa'litt) (1) a common flat fish (2) a tree

เสลี่ยง (sa'leea'ng) litter of a King prince *or* grandee

สลึง (sa'leung) the fourth part of a tical (= about sixpence)

เสลด (sa'lett) phlegm

แสลง (sa'laang) noxious, unwholesome, to hurt — พระโทย (of the King) to injure

เสลา (sa'low) (1) tall and straight (2) to carve, to decorate, well-wrought (3) a fruit like an apple

สละ (sa'la') (1) to let go, to relinquish (2) a thorny fruit tree ปลา — a fish — ทิ้ง to cast off, get rid of

สลัก (sa'la'k) (1) to carve, chiselling chasing (2) bolt — สำคัญ sign, mark, evidence

สลัด (sa'la't) (1) to toss away (2) [Malay.] pirate — ใก a tree

สลับ (sa'la'p) one with another, diverse, promiscuous, manifold — สี to mix colours — ไพ่ to shuffle cards

สวด (sooa't) to recite, to read aloud, to chant [Alab. xlvii]

สวน (sooa'n, (1) to verify สอบ — to test, compare, verify (2) garden ชาว gardener — อุทยาน royal garden (3) to impale, inject ยา — clyster (4) to laugh, smile (5) to go in opposite directions

ส่วน (sooa'n) part, share มี established measure สัก — true m.

สวนา *and* สวนัง (sa'wa'nah, sa'wa'na'ng) [Pali] to hear, to listen

ส้วม (sooa'm) to evacuate [of priests]

ส้วมกอด (sooa'm kaut) to embrace

สวย (sooi') well-dressed, elegant, presentable ส่ะ — dressed up, decked out เข้า — rice boiled too dry

ส่วย (sooi') tax, duty, tythe, contribution (in money or kind) impost, monopoly ทำ — to work a m.

สวรรค์ (sa'wa'n) [Sansk.] certain of the heavens [Alab. xxxvii] — คไลย (of the last King) to die — คต (of a late King) to die

สวรรยา (sa'wa'nyah) [San.] royalty, royal property

สวา (sa'wah) monkey

สวา (sa'wah) [Sansk.] dog

สว่าง (sa'warng) light, brightness, to shine

สวาท (sa'wart) (1) love (2) a fruit tree

สว่าน (sa'wahn) a Chinese boring instrument

สวามิ and สวามี (sa'warmee) [Pali] (1) love (2) husband — ภักดี to work willingly for, good servant

สวาย (sa'waie) a well-flavoured fish

สวาศ (sa'wart) [Pali] enjoyable, loveable, pretty สุก — amiable

สวิง (sa'wing) a spoon-shaped net — สวาย mental trouble, anxiety

เสวียน (sa'weea'n) frame of rattan for holding a rice-pot

สเวตร (sa'wayt) [Sansk.] white — ฉัตร white umbrella of the King, storeyed umbrella or canopy

เสวย (sa'woy) [Cambo d.] (1) to eat, to enjoy (2) royal

แสวง (sa'wayng) to search for, to seek

ไสว (sa'wai) tall, large, abundant

สวะ (sa'wa') collection of floating weeds

สวัด with ง (ngoo sa'wa't) a snake

สวัสดิ์ (sa'wa'tt) [Sansk.] happiness, prosperity

สหัส (sa'ha't) [Pali] a thousand

สอ (sau) (1) in quick succession, one after another (2) spittle, saliva (3) chalk กิน — chalk pencil กิน — ฝรั่ง pencil

สอ (saw) to slander, to calumniate

สอก (sauk) fore-arm, cubit (a measure of about 24 niews

สอง (sorng?) [Chin.] two — น่า a long-

shaped drum — คู่ pair, couple — ไข
doubtful, doubt, undecided

ส่อง (sawng) to light up, illuminate
กล้อง — telescope — กล้อง to look
through a telescope — กระจก to
look in the looking glass

ส้อง (saung) (1) dwelling, habitation
(2) walking slowly — เสพย to cohabit — สาธุการ to thank, praise
— สุม to assemble (an army etc.)

สอก (sort) to insert, penetrate, insinuate สิน — dowry given to the
parents of a bride to keep for her
— ส่อง to inquire carefully into —
แนม to explore; shy — รู้ inquisitive

สอน (sawn) to teach, instruct เสียน —
to help one man with advice against
another

ส้อน (saun) (eyes) showing only the
white

ส้อน (sorn) to put out of sight

สอบ (saup) (1) to compare — พยาน
to confront witnesses with the accused — สวน to compare, to test
(2) a figure slightly smaller at the

top than at the bottom, truncated
cone, truncated obelisk

สอ พลอ (saw plaw) without consideration, thoughtlessly คน — intri-
guer, informer, detractor

สอย (soi') to gather with a split pole
— ผม to arrange the hair ใช้ —
to use, employ

ส้อย (soi) (1) [better สร้อย] neck feathers of a fowl ปลา ส้อย a small fish
(2) final two syllables of a verse

ส่า (sah) dregs of wine, fermentation
of spirit

ส้า (sah) noise of a crowd moving

สาก (sark) (2) pestle — กระเทือง wood-
en hammer used instead of a flail for
rice — กระเบือ pepper-mill ปลา —
a fish (2) hardened skin

สากล (sarkon) [Pali] spreading about,
comprehensive, the whole

สาเก (sarkay) with สก bread-fruit
with กัน bread-fruit tree

สาขา (sarkar) branch of a tree

สาคร (sarkhon) [Pali] ocean, sea

สาคู (sarkhoo) [Chin.] sago

สาคะเรศคร (sarka'rett) [Pali] very large
river, ocean

สาง (sahng) (1) near day break (2) to cleanse to clean (3) *and* เสือ — panther ผ — diseases ผ — demons (4) stinking เหม็น — intolerable stench (5) to comb พระ — King's comb

สาง (sarng) to get better, to improve (of a drunkard)

สาชล (sabchonn) [P.] the great rivers

สาฎก (sardok) *with* ผ้า Indian cloth

สาด (sart) (1) to sprinkle (2) mat (3) to fall sideways *or* slanting-wise

สาตร (sart) [Pali] sect — วาหะ caravan of merchants

สาตรา (sartrah) [Pali] arms, weapons

สาทาน (sartarn) poor, wretched, needy

สาธก (sartok) [Pali] (1) to accomplish, to fill, complete (2) to appeal to a higher court

สาธารณ (sartahra'na') [Pali] to be spread about, general, universal

สาธุ (sartoo') [Pali] it is well, so be it — การ *and* — ษะ to commend, praise, extol

สาเธย (sahtaye) [Sansk.] to complete, accomplish

สาน (sarn) (1) to plait (2) pleased, pleasant (3) arsenic — สัม alum

สาน (sabn) *or* สาณ *with* ผ้า [Sansk.] coarse cloth

สานุศิษย์ (sarnoo'sitt) [Sansk.] pupils, students

สาบ (sarp) inside strip of cloth at the edge of a garment with buttons on it เหม็น — stale, musty แมลง — cockroach — สูญ to vanish

สาบาล (sabbahn) [Pali] to swear, oath แช่ง — to curse

สาป (sarp) [Pali] to swear at, reprimand, abuse

สาพิภาค (sarpi'pa'k) [Pali] to volunteer, to assist

สาม (sarm?) [Chin.] three — สิบ thirty ราก — สิบ an edible root

สามเณร (sahma'nen) [Pali] pupil of a priest, neophyte

สามเณรี (sahma'nayree) young female nun, novice

สามขา (sarmkhah) tripod, three-legged stool

สามหาว (sarmhow) impudent, shameless, immodest

สามล (sarmar) [Pali] dusky, blackish brown

สามารถ (sarmart) [Pali] able, strong, bold, brave

สามานย (sarmarn) bold, impudent, insolent, harsh ร้าย — cruel

สามี (sarmee) [Pali] husband

สามัคคี (sarma'kkhee) [P.] to associate

สามัญ (sarma'n) [P.] common, general

สาย (saic) (1) late in the morning (2) (numerical designation of ropes, roads, etc.) — ยู่ iron rings for a padlock, latch — สิญจน์ a string passed round the city to keep off demons — น้ำ water course — สมร beloved lady — ฟ้า flash of lightning (3) discendant, issue

สาย (sai) (1) to move to and fro in the water, to move, to lock, to oscillate ว่าว — the kite dashes up and down or hither and thither (2) to play music with notes quickly following one another

สาย (sai) and ใส้ a bird

สายชู (saichoo) with น้ำส้ม vinegar made from arrak

สายติง (sai-ting) an aquatic plant

สายหยุด (sai-yoo't) a flower whish has a smell in the morning only

สายสิญจน์ (sai-sinn) [Pali] string hung round a house or room at a ceremony, and held at the end by a priest

สายัณห (sa'ya'nn) [Pali] evening

สาร with โดย (doey sarn) passage in another person's boat or carriage

สาร (sarn) [Pali] (1) pith, inside, hard interior, essence (2) strength, best part, superior, excellent (3) elephant — หนู arsenic เข้า — husked rice

สาร (sarn) สารา and สารน [Pali] letter — กรมธรรม์ receipt for money paid for enslaving a person, slave-paper

สารถ (sart) [Sansk.] treatise, book, art, "shastra"

สารท (sarht) [Pali] autumnal season; feast of cakes in the 10th month

สารหนู (sshra'noo) arsenic

สารบาญชี (sahra'barnchee) [Pali] general catalogue

สารวัก (sahrawa't) third master, school usher

สารศเวตร (sa hn'sawett) [Sansk.] white elephant

สารา (sah'rah) [Pali] letter

สารานิยา (sahrahniyah) [Pali] compliments, agreeable sayings

สาหร่าย (sahrai) an edible aquatic plant — ทะเล sea-lichen, bêche-de-mer

สารริกะ (sahreeri'ka') [Pali] bodily existence, corporeal

สาร (sahree) [Pali] = สาร

สารูป (sahroop) [Pali] suitable, fit, well-conducted

สาเร (sahray) vagabond, gad-about

สาแพรก (sahraak) frame of light sticks or strings for carrying a weight

สาระ (sahra') [Pali] see สาร

สาระณา (sahra'nah) see สวะณา

สาระถี (sahra'tee) and สารถี [Pali] driver, coachman

สาระทุกข์ (sahra'too'k) [Sansk.] afflictions, calamities

สาวะบาต (sahrabatt) malignant: see สันนิบาต

สาระบาล (sahra'barn) [Pali] preface

สาระประกก Javanese turtle dove

สาระพางค์ (sahra'parng) [Sansk.] the whole body

สาระพิษม์ (sahra'pitt) snake venom

สาระพี (sahra'pee) a scented flower

สาระเพชร (sahra'pett) see สรรเพช

สาระภาพ (sahra'parp) [Pali] to confess

สาระวล (sahra'won) embarrassed, harassed, busy, unsuccessful

สาระวอน (sahra'waun) to make pretences, to put on affected airs

สาล (sahn) [Pali] Royal Court of justice, tribunal, law court — ต่างประเทศ International Court

สาลิกา (sahli'kab) a talking black bird

สาลี with เข้า (kow sarlee) fabulous wheat เข้าโพด — wheat

สาลี (sarlee) (1) timber cart (2) a fruit like an apple

สาลู (sarloo) with ผ้า a Malay cloth

สาละวน (sahla'won) (1) garden (2) = สาระวล

สาว (sowe) girl, young woman พ — elder sister น้อง — younger sister หลาน — niece — ใช้ servant maid

สาวก (sahwok) [Pali] pupil, scholar, student, disciple (Alab. 187)

สาวโปฎก (sahwa'podok) [Pali] *better* สุวโปฎก a fabulous talking black bird

สาวบ้าน (sowe-parn) to pull at a rope or cord

สารศึกา (sarsa'dah) [Pali] teacher, tutor, preceptor — จริย superior teacher

สารศนา (sarsanah) [Pali] religion, religious doctrine, r. teaching

สารสน (sart) [Sansk.] letter ราช — royal letter, official despatch

สานหบ (sah-heye) to cover up

สาเหตุ (sah-hett) [Pali] cause of quarrelling, anger, provocation

สาโหต (sah-hote) harsh, cruel fierce

สาหัส (sah-ha't) [Pali] harsh, cruel

สาอากร with ส่วย (sooi-ahkorn) tax

สิกขา (sikkhah) [Pali] rules, discipline doctrine (of priests)

สิข (sikkhee) [Pali] crest, top-knot (2) flame (3) clitoris fæminœ

สิง (sing) to be in ง — a snake

สิ่ง (sing) thing, something, what? — ใก what? anything — ของ possessions, riches, property — ไร what?

สิงขร (singkhonn) [Pali] mountains

สิงคาลี (singkharlee) a jackal or wolf

สิงคาละ (singkharla') wolf or jackal

สิงโต (singtoh) [Sansk.] lion

สิงห and สิงหะ (sing, sing-ha') [Sansk.] lion จะมูก — large snub nose

สิงหนาท (singha'nart) roaring of a lion

สิงหฬ (sing-hon) [Sansk.] Ceylon

สิงหาคม (sing-hah-khom) [Sansk.] the fifth month (Leo, == August)

สิงหาสน (sing-hart) [Sansk.] seat, lair

สิญจน (sinn) [Pali] unction, holy water สาย — string passed round a city for the purpose of protecting it from evil spirits

สิทธิ (sitt) and สิทธิ [Pali] accomplishment, perfection, success. perfect, complete — ขาด altogether, it depends entirely upon — การิย complete work, treatise อาญา — absolute power ฤๅษี — hermit, saint

สิธนกร see สิธนกร

สิน (sin) (1) debts, property belonging to others กระบิด — to refuse to pay a debt — ค้า goods, merchandize — บน (1) bribery (2) riches — ไหม court fees — สมรศ inheritance, heritage — ส่วรศ property acquired after marriage — สอด money paid for a girl on her marriage

สิน (sin) to curtail, shorten ตัด — to judge, to decide a case, judgement, order of court

สิ้น (sinn) (1) end (2) all, everything — สุ๘ finite — ตัว ruined

สินเทา with เกลือ (khlooa' sintow) a cathartic resembling Epsom salts

สินธิพ (sintopp) and เสินธพ [Pali] belonging to Sindh, a Sindh horse

สินธุ (sintoo') and นธุ [Pali] (1) river, stream, sea (2) Sindh

สิ้นพระชนม์ (sin-pra'chon) [Siam. and Pali] (of a King's son) to die

สินยารคน (sinyarkonn) [Pali] tax on white sugar

สิเนรู (si'nayroo') [Pali] mount Meru (Alab. 13)

สิโนทก (si'noda'ka') [Sansk.] clear water, to pour out

สิบ (sip and sib) [Chin.] ten — เอ็ด — สอง etc. eleven, twelve, etc. ยี่ — สาม — etc. twenty, thirty, etc. นาย — sergeant

สิมพลี (simpalee) [Pali] the silk-cotton tree (Bombax heetaphyllum)

สิรา (sirah) [Pali] milk

สิรา (si'rah) salute with closed hands

สิริ (si'ri') all, the whole, together

สิปะสาการ (sinpa'sart) [Sansk.] treatises on the arts, complete science, all the arts (A'ab. 210)

สิระสา better สิรสา (sirasah) [Sansk.] to salute

สิริง (siring) [Pali] a small snake

สิโรตม (sirohtama) [Pali] of the head, perfection of shape in the head, lowing with the head

สิโรรถ (si'rohrot) [Sansk.] hair of the head, g o.y [see Alab. 207]

สิลา (si'lah) [Pali] stone

สิว (si'oo') pimples

สิว (sew) chisel

สี (see) colour — สีก bright colour — เผือก pale — ฟ้า sky-blue — เขียว green, blue — — คราม dark blue, dark green

สี (see) to grind, grindstone for rice — เข้า to husk rice — ฟักร and — ผัด circular fan โรง — mill — ลม windmill — ซอ to play the fiddle — ปาก correct language วิม — ปาก lips — พาย paddler, canoe man — เสียด a bark chewed with betel-nut

สี (see) [Chin.] four — สิบ forty

สีกา (seekah) [Laos.] (priests' word) woman

สีขร (seekhonn) *and* สิรขร [Pali] mountain

สีคาง (seekharng) flank, ribs

สีตันดอน (seeta'ndon) river with waters like air

สีพอง (seepaung) *with* กิน chalk

เสีย (seea') to be lost, spoilt, destroyed ทำ — to destroy — ชาติ degenerate — คน corrupted, demoralised — ปาก vain talk — กาย deplorable, regrettable — ทาย expenses, thefts — ที to miss the mark — ผี to sacrifice to devils ได้ — (1) profit and oss (2) they are married — วัก fanatic

เสียง (seea'ng?) (1) sound, voice, language (2) to strike — เปอง to raise or lower the voice, (gramm.) circumflex

เสียง (seea'ng) to divide into two pieces, to cast lots, to take one's chance — ทาย to consult soothsayers, oracle, omen, enigma, puzzle

เสียก (seea't) to rub, scratch, press เปียก -- to press close, rub together — เข้าไป to push one's way in

เสียน (seea'n) (1) very small thorn, small splinter — หนาม thorn, enemy, rebel (2) an edible plant

เสียบ (seea'p) (1) to impale, fix on a point, insert a point (2) pain in the stomach หอย — an edible shell fish

เสียม (seea'm) small pick-axe

เสียม สาร (seea'msahn) [Pali] to walk slowly and lightly

เสียม (seea'm) (1) to sharpen, to teach — สียม to instruct one si le how to defeat the other

เสียว (seeo?) sting of pain, qualm

เสียว (seeo') (1) thinner on one side (2) three quarters of anything

สีล (seen) [Sansk.] sacred precept, moral precept, morality (Alab. 181)

สีสง (seesong) a river fish

สีสด (seesot) light red :

สีสิท (seesit) a wood used for the roofs of house-boats

สีเสียก (seeseea't) bark of a tree ปลา a rough-skinned fish

สีสุก (seesoo'k) (1) garden bamboo (2) light

สึก (seuk) (1) blunt, worn, deteriorated (2) to leave the priesthood รู้ — to feel, to perceive, to be aware of

สืบ (seup) to inquire after, to investigate — ข่าว to inquire for the last news — พืช to use for planting or sowing again — ชาติ to propagate, to reproduce — สันดาน to reproduce, to replace, fill the place o — สวน to examine, inquire into — เสาะ to search, inquire — ราว to inquire in all directions — สาย successor — มาแต่บุราณ transmitted from antiquity

สื่อ (seu) pimp, procuress, go-between, corruptor of youth

เสือ (seua') tiger — ดาว leopard, yellow-eyed cat — ปลา tiger cat ปลา — striped spitting fish เผือก — tuber, potato — สมิง man transformed into a tiger หาง — tiller, helm ขอ — crank, axle, arm of lever คา — a large tree ต้น — a small tree with

hairy leaves

เสือ (seua') mat

เสื้อ (seua') coat, shirt — ผ้า clothing, clothes — กัก jacket ผ — butterfly

เสือก (seua'k) to push on, to shave

เสื่อม (seua'm) (1) to decrease, diminish (2) to be mollified — สูญ to disappear, vanish — คลาย to change by degrees, to recover slowly

สุ (soo') to soak in hot water, to steep

สุ (soo') [Pali] well, good

สุก (soo'k) (1) shining, bright, conspicuous — ส brightest สี — happy, prosperous, well-to-do ไผ่ สี — garden bamboo (2) ripe (3) cooked — ขึ้น ripened in a stove — กึ่ง (1) half ripe (2) the day before a ceremony กิจ — a complete game

สุกกรม (soo'kkrom) a wild tree

สุกร (soo'konn) [Pali] hog, boar, pig

สุกร with วา (wahsoo'kree) [Sansk.] King of the Nagas

สุขุม (soo'koo'm) [Pali] thin, fine, subtle ยา — an anodyne

สุคต (soo'ko't) [Pali] (1) arriving in

good time, going properly (2) holy, a name of Buddha

สคนธ (soo'khonn) (and other similar forms) [Pali] perfume, scent

สุขี (soo'khee) [Sansk.] fig

สุกะติ (soo'kha'ti') [Pali] to succeed, attain to happiness — ม heaven

สงสิง (soo'sing) vain, boastful, ostentatious

สุจริต (soo'charitt) [Sansk.] faithful, well-conducted, virtue

สุชี (soo'chee') [Sansk.] clear, pure, clean

สุชะนี (soo'cha'nee) carpet

สุชน (soo'chonn) [Sansk.] tears

สุด (soo't) last, furthest, end ที — the last เป็น ที — entirely, altogether, most (sign of the superlative) — คิด at one's wit's end — ตา and — ลับตา out of sight — ท้อง youngest child — ท้าย the end of all — มือ beyond one's strength — แล้วแต่ depending upon, in accordance with

สุดา (soo'dah) fine woman

สุทธิ (soo'tti') [Pali] pure, purification

สุทัศน (soo'ta'tt) [Pali] (1) pleasant to the eyes (2) one of the heavens (3) pleasant view

สุธา (soo'tar) [Pali] ambrosia, nectar

สุธารส (soo'tahrot) (1) scented water (2) tea for royal persons

สุนทร (soo'ntonn) and สุนทรศ [Pali] eloquent, well-spoken, good

สุนทรี (soo'nta'ree) [Pali] beautiful woman

สุนทรา (soo'nta'rar) [Pali] see พสุนธร

สุนาการ (soo'narkarn) [Pali] hearing

สุนี (soo'ni') flash of lightning

สุนิสา (soo'ni'sah) [Pali] with พระ King's daughter-in-law

สุนะกะ (soo'na'ka') [P.] (1) nail (2) dog

สุนัข (soo'na'k) and สุนขา [Pali] dog — ป่า wolf — จิ้งจอก fox

สุนัต (soo'na't) circumcision

สุบรรณ (soo'ba'n) [Pali] Garuda, fabulous eagle that preys on men and women

สุบิน (soo'binn) [Pali] dream, to dream — นิมิตร nocturnal vision

สุบรรณราช (soo'ba'na'rart) better สุบรรณราช [Pali] King of the eagles

สุพรรณ (soo'pa'n) [San.] (1) of good colour, bright, brilliant (2) [Pali] gold, golden

สุพรรณถัน (soo'pa'nta'n) [P.] sulphur

สุภะ and สุภะ (soo'pa') [Pali] (1) pretty, elegant (2) musician

สุภาพ (soo'pahp) [Pali] (1) modest, mild, affable (2) to travel

สุภาวดี (soo'pahwa'dee') good speaker, good talker, orator

สุภาสิต (soo'pahsitt) [Pali] wise sayings, instructive words

สุม (soo'm?) to burn with a slow fire — แร to expose to the fire — ไฟ to keep up a slow fire ยาสุม — (1) cooling application for the head (2) Indian smoking mixture — แกลบ to roast in the husk — หัว to plaster up the head — ทุม sacred grove

สุ่ม (soo'm) a large wicker or bamboo frame, coop — ปลา to fish with a coop — ไก่ hen-coop

สุมามาลย (soo'marmarlya') [Sansk.] beautiful as a garland of jessamine

สุมาลี (soo'marlee) [Sansk.] collection of beautiful flowers, bouquet

สุเมธา (soo'may tah) [Pali] wise, clever

สุเมรุ (soo'mayroo') [P.] Mount Meru (Alab. 13)

สุยปติ (sooi'yati') [Pali] to hear

สุรชาติ (soorachart) [Sansk.] race of divine origin, demigods

สุรา (soo'rah) [P.] intoxicating liquors

สุรามฤท (soo'rarma'ritt) [P.] miraculous water taken by angels, [nectar

สุราไลย (soo'rarlai) [Sansk.] heaven of Indra and the angels

สุริฉาย (soorichai) [Sansk.] of the sun

สุรินท (soo'rinn) [Sansk.] giants, monsters — ราห celestial monster which causes eclipses

สุริย and สุริยา (soo'riya) [Pali] sun

สุริยาตร (soo'riyart) [Sansk.] course of the sun

สุริโยภาค (soo'ri'yohpart) [Pali] morning brightness of the sun

สุริวงษ (soo'ri'wong) [Sansk.] child or descendant of the sun

สุระ (soo'ra') vulg. for สุร q. v. strong, bold — ภาพ brave and bold — สา กร rough water — ศักดิ courage and dignity

สุหรัต (soo'ra't) [Malay.] Surat ผ้า – Surat cloth

สุวกล (soo'wa'khon) a small tree with scented flowers

สุวไปฎก (soo'wa'podok) [Pali] fabulous talking bird

สุวภากย์ soo'wa'park) a tree with scented flowers

สุวรรณ (soo'wa'nn) [San.] gold, golden — บรรค gold leaf, golden sheet

สุวิมล (soo'wi'monn) [S.] spotless, pure

สู (soo) [Laos.] you

สู (soo) [Laos.] to go to — ขอ to ask a person's daughter in marriage — กัน to visit — กัน กัน (1) to go to meet, rendezvous (2) to distribute a meal

สู้ (soo) to resist, oppose, fight — ทน to endure patiently ไม่ — ดี not so good, not advisable ไม่ — เป็นไร not very important

สูง (soong) high, tall ;ครื่อง — royal ornaments คำ — pompous words, stilted language, grandiloquent — ขึ้น to rise to a higher place อายุสูม -- advanced age

สูญ (soon) [Sans.] empty, void ; to vanish — เลข zero, ought

สุก (soot) to inhale - สูก to sniff, to sniffle

สูกร (soot) [Sansk] (1) string, thread ; string of figures ; portion of scripture, text (2) web of thread, tapestry

สูน (soon) axis, centre, middle

สูบ (soob) (1) to suck, absorb (2) pump (3) bellows — ยา to smoke tobacco ยา — tobacco

สูร (soora') [Sansk.] brave, strong, bold, valiant ; giant

สูรชาติ (soora'chart) [Sansk.] race of heroes, giants

สูรย์ (soon) [Pali] sun

สูรโลกย์ (soora'lohk) [Sansk.] habitation of the giants

สูรางค์ (soorahng) culy. for สูรางค์ [S.] ladies living with the angels สูราง คนาร ladies living in the heavens สูรางคนิการ a crowd of the same สูรางคนาง verses

สูรารักษ์ (soorahra'k) [San.] courageous genii

สูรู (sooroo) to act without orders, officious, interfering

สูราะไกย (soora'kai) better สูราะไกย

see ยักษ์ [Pali] monster, ghost, apparition

เสก (sayk) recitation of religious formulas before consecrating anything — สรร (1) salvation (2) damnation

เสง (seng) a tree with red blossoms

เสรฐ (sayttee) [Pali] wealthy man

เสตุ (saytoo) [Pali] ridge, causeway, path

เสโท (saytch) [Pali] sweat, perspiration

เสน (sayn) (1) a large monkey (2) colour of red lead

เส้น (sen) (1) nerve, sinew (numerical designation of threads, cords, etc.) — ด้าย thread of cotton — สาย nerves and sinews — ชัก convulsions (2) to sacrifice to devils (3) (a measure of twenty wah) sen (4) numerical designation of ropes, etc.

เสนา *and* เสนี (saynah, saynee) [Pali] (1) army (2) grandees, high officials ธรรศมหา — chief of the officials — มาตย์ courtiers — มนตรี chief official — บดี Great Council of State

เสพย์ (sayp) [Pali] to eat, drink, partake of, use, copulate, associate

เสภา (saypah) solo singing

เสมหะ (sem-ha') phlegm

เสมา (saymah) ornament for a child's neck

เสมา (saymah) [Pali] sacred stones round a temple ราช — *and* ขันธ์ — frontiers, borders

เสย (soey) to comb up *or* push back (the hair)

เสยยา (say-yah) [Pali] to lie down

เสลา (saylah) [Pali] stone, rock

เสวกา (sayvakah) [Pali] courtiers, followers, attendants — มาตย์ [San.] council of ministers

เสศ (sayt) [Sansk.] remainder, remnant

เสิด (sert) (obsol) to run away, to go quickly

เสิม (serm) to add to, augment, enlarge, increase

แส *with* จีน (cheen saa) [Chin.] physician, master แพร — silk stuffs

แส (saa) to seek occasion, to search for an offence

แส (saa) (1) fan, small rod, switch — ม้า horsewhip — เหล็ก foil — ปืน ramrod — จามรี horse-hair tassel (2) warbling, gabbling, incoherent sounds

แสก (saak) to disjoin, divide, part (the

hair etc.) นก — a bird with a loud cry

แสง (saang) (1) arms, weapons พระ — King's sword (2) rays, radiant — ทอง rays of day-break

แสง (saang) on purpose, wilfully

แสงงอน (saa-ngorn) coquetry

แสด (saat) a tree having small yellow seeds สี — orange-red colour

แสน (saan) a hundred thousand, much, very much — ยากร officials

แสบ (saap) biting, stinging, pricking, sharp — ท้อง hungry, hunger

ใส (saie) clean, bright, pure สุก — bright ผ่อง — flourishing

ใส่ to put, to place — เสื้อ to put on a coat — ใจ to take care, to bear in mind เอาใจ — to attend to, to be careful, to take to heart — ความ to make a charge, to calumniate

ไส (sie) to push, to repulse — กบ to plane

ไส้ (sai) bowels — กรอก sausage, black pudding — ตะเกียง wick of a lamp

— ศึก secret mutineer, traitor ยก — a bird

ไส้เดือน (sai dooa'n) earth-worm

ไส้ตัน (saitan) a small fish, very good for eating, but having no entrails

ไสยา (saiyah) [Pali] to lie down, to sleep

ไสยาศน์ (saiyart) [Sansk.] bed

ไสสาตร (sai-sart) [Pali] Brahminical doctrine, magical art, black art

โสหุ้ย (sohooi) [Chin.] expenditure

โสๆ (soke) (1) dry (2) a tree of which the flower is eaten

โสกา (sohka) [Pali] sad, sorrowful tearful, to cry

โสกี (sohkee) [Pali] sadness, sorrow, mourning

โสกัน (sohka'n) [Pali] to shave the topknot (of princes)

โสโครก (sohkroke) dirty, foul, squalid

โสด (sote) bachelor, spinster, celibate, unmarried

โสดา (sohdoh) [Pali] the stream (of human passion), the first degrees of sanctity

โสตร (sote) โสต: and โสตง [Pali] ear, hearing

โสภะ (sohpa') (of the King) [Pali] to have a swelling

โสภา (sohpah) (and other similar words) [Pali] handsome, fine, well-looking

โสภิ and โสเพณี (sohpaynee) beautiful woman

เสา (sow) pillar, post — หิน boundary stone — กระโดง mast

เส้า with ไม้ กระทุ้ง (mie kra'toong sow) (1) pile-driver (2) sticks for beating time in a boat ก้อน — three leg-ged stand

เสาร์ (sow) [Pali] with พระ Saturn (planet) วัน — Saturday

เสาวคนธ์ (sowwa'khon) [Pali] per-fumes (2) flowering shrub

เสาวนี (sowwa'nee) [Pali] orders of the Queen, or the royal ladies

เสาวโปฎก (sowwa'pohdok) [Sansk] a talking bird

เสาวภาคย์ (sowwa'park) [San.] young and pretty girl

เสาวรศ (sowwa'rot) [Sansk.] a flower-ing plant

เสาะ (sau') with ท้า cowardice เด็ก — crying, peevish child

เสาะหา (sau'-har) to seek for, to search รู้ — to get information

เสาะ ค้าย (sau' daie) to pull out a thread without tangling it

สำ (sa'm) often, much, repeated

ส่ำ (sa'm) many, much

สำคัน (sa'kha'n) (1) mark, sign, evid-ence (2) principal thing, of chief importance เป็น — in witness whereof — ว่า to conjecture

สำแดง (sa'mdaang) to show, display, reveal

สำทับ (sa'mta'p) to multiply accusa-tions, to make repeated charges

สำนวน (sa'mnooa'n) evasion, artifice, prevarication, subterfuge, deceit, sophistry

สำเนียง (sa'mnooa'ng) word s, language, speech, sounds

โสม (sohm) [Pali] moon

โสม (sohm) [Chin.] a scented medicinal plant, ginseng

โสมนัศ (sohma'na't) and โสมนาการ [Pali] to rejoice, to exult

โสฬศ (sohlott) [Pali] (1) sixteen (2) a coin (= one sixteenth of a fuang, and one half of an att)

สำนึก (sa'mneuk) to reflect, to think over, conscious รู้ — to acknow-ledge a fault, to repent, — ตัว to come to ones lf, recover one's con-sciousness

สำเนา (sa'mnow) written account, report

สำนัก (sa'mnaa'k) to halt, rest-house, lodging place

สำบุกสำบัน (sa'mboo'k sa'mba'n) to do too often, to work beyond one's strength

สำปลื้ม (sa'mpleum) agreeable, exhilarating; name of a temple in Bangkok

สำเปน (sa'mpa'n) [Malay.] a small river boat

สำผัส (sa'mpa't) to touch — อ่อนนsoft, tender

สำเพง (sa'mpeng) junction of three roads, name of a street in Bangkok หนึ่ง — courtesan

สำภาระ (sa'mpahra') [Pali] materials, necessaries, furniture, ornaments

สำเภา (sa'mpow) junk

สำมโนคัว (sa'mma'nohkhrooa) census

สำมรด (sa'mma'rot) pine-apple

สำมะลอ (sa'mma'lau) a jack-fruit

สำมะเลเทเมา (sa'mma'laytaymow) to carouse in bad company, to associate with the wicked

สำมัชชา (sa'mma'char) [Pali] theatre, concert, party — กร tax on dancing places, theatres, etc.

สำรด (sa'mrot) broad belt of embroi-

dered cloth ศิริ — marriage portion

สำรวญ (sa'mrooan) to laugh, giggle

สำหรวด (sa'mrooat) to chant, intone, recite ผา — a wall made of planks and leaves

สำรวม (sa'mrooa'm) to fit together, make up, compose, regulate

สำรวย (sa'mrooi') fop, dandy, masher

สำรอก and สำราก (sa'mrank, sa'mrark) to vomit — ริ่ง to scold, chide

สำริด (sa'mri(tt) alloy of brass and dark metals

สำฤทธิ์ศก (sa'mritti'sok) [Pali] tenth year of the decennial cycle

สำหรัว (sa'mray) (1) place of execution (2) name of a canal

สำเร็จ (sa'mrett) finished, done with, completed กน — accomplished scholar, glossary, commentary

สำเริง (sa'mrerng) joy, happiness

สำโรง (sa'mrohng) a cotton tree

สำราว (sa'mrow) to abate (of fevers),

สำรับ (sa'mra'p) (1) food, meals, provisions (2) assortment, suit, set

สำหรับ (sa'mra'p) for, to, intended for, fit for กน suited for one another

— กัน for oneself

สำลี (aa'mlee) cotton

สำลัก (sa'mla'k) choking, to be half suffocated

สำสม (sa'msom) to pile up, accumulate

สำส่อน (sa'msaun) collection of various people or things, miscellany, heterogeneous, disorderly

สำหาว (sa'mhow) (high word) bold, impudent, insolent ผัก — an edible ground plant

สำออย (sa'm-oy) plausible, seductive, fawning

สำอาง (sa'marng) clean, pure, neat

สะสม (sa'-som) to heap up, collect, add

สะเกา (sa'kaw) [Cambod.] white

สะเกา (sa'kaw) [Cambod.] หนุ่ม — and วัน — in the flower of youth, adult

สะกา (sa'kar) draughts, back-gammon, dice

สะการ (sa'kar) and สะการะ [Pali] (1) to sacrifice, to offer up, to pay respect, (2) flowers

สะกิด (sa'kitt) to scratch or scrape gently so as to attract attention

สะเก็ด (sa'kett) shavings, film over a scar

สะเกย (sa'kett) to wash the hair วัด — a temple used for cremations

สะแก (sa'kaa) (1) an ash tree (2) dice

สะแก (sa'kaa) [Cambod] dog

สะคริว (sa'khrau) a tree

สะคริวง (sa'khrong) a tree with edible fruit

สะคร้าน (sa'khrarn) handsome

สะคร้าว (sa'krowc) a large tree

สะค้าน (sa'kbarn) a medicinal creeping plant

สะดายุ (sa'dahyoo') a large eagle

สะเดียง (sa'dee'ang) curtain

สะดึง (sa'deung) window-frame

สะดือ (sa'deu) navel — กะไล whirlpool in the ocean

สะเดา (sa'dow) a tree with eatable blossoms

สะเดาะ (sa'dau') to conjure, to work by magic — เคราะห์ to avert by magic, to cure by skill

สะดัม and สะดำ (sa'da'm) [Cambod.] representative of the Chief Priest

สะดำ (sa'dam') [Sansk.] pillar, post, column

สะเตา (sa'tau) a fruit tree

สะติ (sa'ti') [Pali] mind, intellect, thought, reflection, attention

สะตือ (sa'teu) (1) a large bird (2) a tall fruit tree

สะกู (sa'too') to clean, to bleach, to dry (rice etc.)

สะถา (sa'tar) [Pali] stable, enduring, permanent — ปั้น to build again, repair. set up, establish

สะถป (sa'toop) [Sansk.] pyramidal structure

สะทก สะท้าน (sa'tok sa'tarn) to tremble, to shudder, to be alarmed

สะท้อน (sa'torn) (1) to rebound (2) a fruit tree ฦๅ — it is rumoured, made known

สะท้าน (sa'tarn) to tremble, shake, quiver

สะเทือน (sa'teua'n) to shake, to make to quiver

สะเทิน (sa'tern) to be disturbed in mind, ashamed; shame

สะตำม (sa'ta'm) [Sansk.] correct law. philosophy

สะโบง (sa'bong) [Cambod] panung

สะบ้า (sa'bar) a tree with a fruit like a large bean ลูก — (1) fruit of this tree (2) knee-cap, gizzard, of birds, marble

สะบู่ (sa'boo) [Portug.] soap ต้น — soap plant ยาง — juice of this plant

สะใบย (sa'booy) content, satisfied

สะไบ (sa'bai) [Cambod.] woman's scarf — เฉียง scarf worn sideways

สะบัก (sa'ba'k) shoulder-blade — ใน hollow of the back between the shoulders — สะบ้ม knocked up, worn out

สะบัด (sa'ba't) to shake — ดิ้น to wriggle; turn-ccat, shifty — ฦๅ — นั่ง restless by getting up and again lying down, agitation — ดี — วาย mad and sane at intervals

สะบั้น (sa'ba'n) broken to pieces

สะพร้ง (sa'pra'ng) all, the whole, altogether

สะภาวะ (sa'bha'wa') and สะภาวะ [Pali] nature, essence, state of existence

สะไพ้ (sa'pai) daughter-in-law ผ — ผใ้ wife of elder and younger brother

สะผา (sa'mah) [Pali khamah] to permit, forgive; pardon, permission — โทษ pardon for a fault เครื่อง — offerings of tapers, flowers etc. made at confession

สะมาธิ (sa'marti') [Pali] steadfastness of mind, concentration of thougt tranquillity

สะมาบติ (sa'marba'ti) [Pali] attainment, result of devout meditation

สะมะณะ (sa'ma'ta') [Pali] tranquillity, quietude, cessation, self-denial, mortification of the body

สะระณา (sa'ra'nar) see สรณา

สะระณัง better สรณัง (sa'ra'na'ng refuge, asylum, protector, patron

สะระบับ (sa'ra'ba'p) cloth of gold

สะล้าง (sa'larng) [of trees etc] standing thick together, numerous

สะว่าน (sa'warn) gasping, panting, at the last gasp

สะเวตวะฉัตร (sa'waytra'chat) [Sansk.] royal white umbrella A lab. 297

สะหาย (sa'hai) [Pali] comrade, friend, associate

สะหัส (sa'hat) better สหัส a thousand

สะอม (sa'om) a tree with edible leaves

สะอาด (sa'art) clean, neat, tidy

สะอง (sa'ing) scarf or decoration worn sideways

สะอิด สะเอียน (sa'itt sa'eea'n to refuse or draw back through modesty, to have qualms, to be disgusted

สะอึก (sa'euk) hiccup

สะอึน (sa'eun) sob

สะเอว (sa'aew) loins - กาะ ว่า น้อย slender, slim

สัก (sa'k) (1) to tie the sword hilt to the wrist (2) to keep on prodding or pushing. to bore many holes (3) to tattoo — เปน ทาษ to put a mark on a slave's arm นก กา a woodcock

สัก (sak) (1) teak (2) at least — เท่าไร how much?

สักกะลาด or สักกะลาด etc. (sa'ka'lart) flannel (first known in Siam as of a scarlet colour)

สักโก (sa'kko) [Pali] a name of Indra

สักขี (sa'khee) [Pali] witness, one who knows

สัโค (sa'kkho) [Pali] heaven, the heavens, paradise

สักราช (sa'ka'rart) [Pali] era จุล — the old civil era พุทธ - the religious era คฤ ๚ — European era

สักกระวา (sa'kra'wah) a kind of poetry

สิเลาด (sa'ka'lart) [En. scarlet] flannel

สัง (sa'ng) to arrange

สั่ง (sa'ng) to order, command คำ — command, injunction, order ริบ — royal command — งาน to command positively — ไว้ to leave word — สอน to instruct — ขมูก to blow one's nose

สังกระสี (sa'ngkra'see) zinc, corrugated iron

สังกา (sangkah) [Pali] to doubt, hesitate

สังเกต (sa'ngkeyt) remembrance, to bear in mind, recognize, not to forget เคย — to know from experience กาม — in its accustomed place or state

สังกะตัง (sa'ngka'ta'ng) (1) not so well (2) confused

สังกัด (sa'ngka't) (1) to limit, boundary (2) to be in the service of

สังข (sa'ng) [Pali] sacred spiral shell, conch

สังขลิก (sa'ngka'lik) [Pali] chains

สังขา (sa'ngkhah) [Pali] to doubt, hesitate

สังขาร (sa'ngkharn) (and other similar forms) [Pali] predisposition, controlling motive power [Alab. 235] — ธรรม principle of good and evil

สังขินี (sa'ngkhi'nee) [Pali] a sacred book

สังเค็ก (sa'ngkhett) offering made to priests at a funeral

สังเขป (sa'ngkhep) [Pali] summary, compendium, to summarise, to abridge

สังกะวาก (sa'ngkha'wart) a small river fish

สัวม see สังฆะ

สังฆราช (sa'ngkha'rart) high priest

สังฆาฏิ [Pali] with ผ้า (pah sa'ngkharti') cloak of Buddhist monk

สังฆะ (sa'ngkhaa'‚ and other similar forms) [Pali] living in common, monk, priest — ราช head of all the priests — วาศ to be one of the priests — กรรม duties of a priest — ทิเลศ capital sins of a priest — การ one who looks after a number of priests [as teacher, protector, etc.]

สังโยค (sa'ngyoke) [Pali] contraction (gramm.) running together of letters

สังวร (sa'ngwon) [Pali] to keep the senses in subjection, constraint, self-restraint

สังวาลย์ (sa'ngwarn) necklace of gold or silver worn cross-wise

สังวาศ (sa'ngwart) and สมพาศ [Pali] to live together in peace, to cohabit

สังเวียน (sa'ngweea'n) enclosure of a cock-pit

สังเวท (sa'ngwayt) compassion, pity

สังวัจฉระ (sa'ngwatcha'ra') [Pali] year, revolution of the year

สังวัธยาย (sa'ngwa'ta'yai) [Sansk.] to recite, intone

สังสกฤษ [Sansk.] Sanskrit

สังสาระ (sa'ngsahra') [Pali] succession of birth, continued existence, world, universe — วัฏิร (and other forms) whirling of the world

สังหร (sa'nghon) to warn เทพ — angel warning

สังหาร (sa'ngharn) [Pali] to kill, strike, destroy

สัจ and สัจา (sa't, sa'char) true, trusty ซื่อ — faithful ใบ — judge's sentence

สัจจะ (sa'tcha'ng) [Sansk.] truth

สัญจร (sa'nchon) [Pali] to wander about, to stray, to go, to meet

สัญญุการ (sa'nya'karn) power of distinguishing, discernment [Alab 237]

สัญญา (sa'nyah) to promise, agree, agreement, หนังสือ — written contract

สัญญ (sa'nyce) [Pali] mind, senses, intellect, thought, perception

สันโกษ and กันโกก (sa'ndote) abandonment of earthly desires, contentment, happiness

สัก (sa't) (1) ta'nan, bushel (2) to copulate (of animals) (3) to drift

สัก (sa't) [Pali] seven

สัตตาห (sa'tahha') [Pali] seven days, week

สัตย and สัตยา (sa't, sa'tyah) [Sansk.] true. truth

สัตรู (sa'troo) [Sansk.] enemy, hostile

สัตว (sa't) [Sansk.] animal, creature โพธิ — chief or best of a. — หน้า ขน hairy-faced a. (expression of contempt). — เกียรฉาน irrational a.

สัตะวา (sa'ta'wab) bird — โนรี a parrot

สัตะวาร (sa'ta'warn) [San.] week

สัทธา (sa'ttah) [Pali] faith, truth (Ala. 184) trust, credit

สัน (sa'n) (1) to select the best, having a good appearance, preferable กม - intelligent (2) edge

สั่น (sa'n) to tremble, stagger, waver

สั้น (sa'n) short, brief

สันฐาน (sa'nt' hn) [Pali] shape, form

สันดอน (sa'n'laun) bar of a river, estuary

สันดาน (sa'n'larn) and สันดาโน [San.] spreading, extending, habit, usage ลม — a kind of colic

สันโดษ (sa'ndote) [Sansk.] contentment, satisfaction, happiness

สันต (sa'nta') [Pali] coarse, thick

สันตุฐิ (san'too'tti') [Pali] contentment, happiness

สันตะวา (sa'nta'wah) an edible water-plant

สันตะฆาฏ (sa'nta'khart) [San.] of the arteries ถม — corruption of the blood in the arteries ยา — physic for this disease

สันทัต (sa'nta't) (1) intermediate, middle-aged สาว — grown-up girl (2) skilful, expert

สันถาณุง (sa'ntarna'ng) [Pali] form, configuration, Conjunction [gram.]

สันนิฐาน (sa'nni'tarn) [Pali] consummation. ascertaining, intelligence, to understand

สันนิวาต (sa'nni'wart) [Pali] association, to cohabit

สันหลัง (sa'nla'ng) back-bone

สันนิบาฏ (sa'nni'bart) [Pali] assemblage, congregation; to come together

สับ (sa'p) to hack, cut up, hash — สัน coming and going, in different directions ขอ — iron goad for elephants

สับกาห (sa'pdah-ha') [San. and Hebr.] week

สับประกน (sa'ppra'don) obscene forms of speech or action

สับปลับ (sa'ppla'p) to tell lies

สับสน (sa'bsonn) coming and going, in different directions

สับคับ (sa'pa'kha'p) howdah

สับงก (sa'pa'ngauk) to go off to sleep, to nod

สับตู (sa'pa'too) [Malay.] serge

สับทน (sa'pa'tonn) coloured umbrella for grandee

สับรศ (sa'pa'rot) [Sansk.] pine apple

สับเหรอ (sa'pt'reu) appointed to conduct cremations

สับประคับ (sa'pra'kha'p) howdah made of rattan

สับประกน (sa'pra'don) one who uses obscene words or commits obscene actions

สับประยุทธ (sa'pra'yoot) to fight, weapons

สับปลับ (sa'pla'p) to tell lies

สัพพัญญู (sa'ppa'nn) versed in all sciences, omniscient

สัพยอก (sa'pa'yauk) to speak jestingly,

สัพวรศ (sa'pa'rot) (1) a tree (2) a bad omen

สันพฤดี (sa'npreu'dee) [Sansk.] enlightenment

สัมพัทธวรณน (sa'mpa'tcha'ra'chon) [P.] annual ceremony (of firing the guns, etc.)

สัมพันธะพงษ (sa'mpa'nta'pong) [San.] affinity, kindred, relations

สัมมา *(sa'mmah)* [Pali] thorough, proper, right, correct, stedfast — ส้าพหไธ having self-knowledge of all truths

สัมมัปปธาน *(sa'mma'ppa'tarn)* [Pali] right exertion, meritorious effort [Alab. 226]

ดัสดี *(sa'sa'dee)* [Sansk.] (1) sixteen (2) office of keeping the government slaves

───── ◆•◆•◆ ─────

ห

ห *(haw =* English *h.* aspirate : a high letter

หก (hok) (1) six — สิบ sixty (2) a small parrot (3) to spill, to upset, to lower on one side โก — to dissimulate, prevaricate ; liar

หงส์ (hong) [Sansk.] goose, swan

หนุ (ha'noo') [Pali] chin, jaw

หนุมาน (ha'noo'marn) a giant monkey

หด (hot) to draw back, draw in, contracted, withdrawn

หไทย (ha'taie) [Pali] heart, mind, soul [Alab. 237]

หน (hon) direction กระ — to search for, look for ล่อง — to disappear

หน (hon) time, times — หนึ่ง สอง —

etc. once, twice, etc. — แรก first time — หลัง last time

หรคุณ (horakhoo'n) line of figures, product, total

หรดี (horadee) South-west

หรรษา (ha'nsah) [Sansk.] laughter, mirth, merry. to enjoy

หริ (ha'ri') [Pali] green พระ — รักษ Vishnu

หริภุญไชย (ha'ri'poo'nchaie) Laos, Laosians

หฤทัย (ha'reutai) [Sansk.] heart

หวง (hooa'ng) to keep back, reserve — หึง jealousy

ห่วง (hooa'ng) (1) ring, hook, knot, buckle (2) obstacle, impediment

ห้วง (hooa'ng) (1) ditch, excavation, river, flood (2) stage or portion of a journey

หวด (hooa't) (1) to cut, to mow (2) whip, scourge (3) a round vessel or mould, used especially for cooking glutinous rice

หวน (hooa'n) to turn, to come back, to reverse

หวย (hooi') lottery ตัว — lottery number or figure

ห้วย (hooi') rivulet, creek, stream

หัว (hooa') (1) head — ขวาน woodpecker — เปย croupier, a tax on games — น่า president — พัน chief of the King's pages — หมืน commander of 10,000 men, General — เมือง chief town, capital — กระ เทิ.ม garlic — หอม onion แม่ ทูล — god-mother พระเจ้า อยู่ — the King (2) num. design. of onions, etc.

หัว *ond* หัว ร่อ (hooa' raw) to laugh เล่น — to play about

หัวรอ (hooa'raw) dam or defence against water

หอ (haw) [Chin.] *exclam. of approval*, 'tis well

หอ (haw) tower, residence of a superior noble — นั่ง reception hall เครื่อง — King's warehouse — ไตรย pagoda library — สมุก library

ห่อ (haw) to wrap up; a bundle (of books, linen, etc.)

หัว (hau) quickly

หอก (hauk) lance, javelin — ปลาย ปืน bayonet — ซัก short far-darting javelin

หอง *with* เย (chaung haung) proud, haughty

ห้อง (haung) apartment, room — เรือก

ante-chamber

หอน (haun) to howl

หอน (hon) [Laos.] never

หอบ (haup) [phon.] (1) to pant (2) to take up a bundle

หอม (haum) (1) sweet-smelling, scented (2) onion

ห้อม (haum) (1) to accompany (2) a figure by which a space is enclosed

หอย (hoi) shell-fish — กระพง bivalve — โข่ง snail — สังข์ a kind of shell trumpet; conch — อีรม oyster นา — to dive for shells

ห้อย (hoi) to hang down, suspended

หา (hah) to seek, look for ให้ — to get, fetch, procure ปืน — to complain of a person's absence; keep-sake ใช้ — to call, summon

หา มิ (hah mi') *and* หา ไม่ no, not หา มิ ได้ not at all

ห่า (hah) (1) abundant (of rain). copious (2) plague ผี — demon of the plague, plague fiend (3) num. design. of jars-full of water

ห้า (hah) [Chin.] five

หาก (hark) capable of

หาก *and* — ว่า (hark wah) supposing

that

หาง (harng) tail, extremity — ขี้ aloes — หาง corner of the eye — น้ำ second brew (of tea, etc.) — ไหล อังกรัย, a tree with medicinal bark ปิด — [cock-fighting term] to take up a cause, to back — เปีย Chinese pig-tail

หาญ (harn) brave, bold, audacious

หาด (hart) reef, shoal

หาร (harn) divisor [arithm.

ห่าน (harn) goose, swan

หาบ (harp) to carry on the shoulder; a load, 100 catties or pounds, hundredweight, quintal

ห่าม (harm) unripe

ห้าม (harm) and — ปราม to prohibit, forbid, prevent นาง — and — แหม royal concubines

หาย (hai) (1) to be cured (2) to rest — ใจ to draw breath, breathing (3) to be lost, to disappear — เหือด to diminish, to moderate

หาร (harn) arithmetical division

หารือ (hahrew) to hold council

หาว (hah'oo) (1) to yawn (2) proud, vain,

lewd กลาง — in the open air ล้ำ — and สาม — to speak impudently สาม — a plant with blue flowers

ห้าว (howe) (1) bold, impudent (2) over-ripe

หิง (hing) with มะหา assa foetida

หิง ห้อย (hing hoi) fire-fly

หิ้ง (hing) shelf — ติด ฝา shelf for fixing on wall, bracket

หิงษ (hing) [Pali] to hurt, damge, injure

หีน (hin) [Pali] inferior, bad, vile, wretched — ชาติ disreputable

หิด (hit) itching

หิน (hin) stone, rock — ลาย marble — แม่เหล็ก loadstone, magnet — เหล็ก ไฟ flint — ปากนก flint for gun

หิน (hin) [Chin.] gambling in lotteries

หิม (him) to prune, to cut off

หิมะ (himma') [Pali] snow, frost, dew — พานต์ and — วันต์ (1) Himalayas (2) snowy forests, fairy-land [Alab. C. 190]

หิริ (hi'ri') [Pali] to be ashamed, to fear

หิรัญ (hi'ra'n) [Pali] gold, bullion, treasure, riches

หิว (hi'oo') to be hungry, exhausted,

weak

หิ้ว (hi'oo') to carry in a hanging position

หี (hee) pudenda mulierum

หี (hee) and เหี่ยว withering, fading

หีบ (heep) (1) to press, crush ลูก — cylinder used for crushing (2) box — เพลง organ, piano, musical box — ชัก accordion — เหล็ก safe

เหีย (heeya') see ไร เหีย

เหีย (heea') land crocodile

เหียก (heea'k) semen humanum (opprobrious word, with อ้าย to men, with อี to women)

เหียง (heea'ng) a hard tree

เหียน (heea'n) to feel sick, nausea หัน — to turn, to whirl

เหียน (heea'n) to be worn out, spoilt, stripped

เหียม (heea'm) cruel, harsh

เหียว (heeoo') fading, withering

หึง (heu'ng') (1) to envy, jealous (2) [Laos.] (of time) long

หึง (heung) (1) a ball (2) [phon.] noise of bees, of a gong, etc., humming, buzzing, droning

หึง (heung) and หึง [phon.] resound-

ing, noise

หืด (heut) asthma

หืน (heun) rancid

หืน (heun) greedy ; lust

เหื่อ (heua') and หัว — sweat, perspiration

เหือด (heua't) (1) to be diminished (2) white spots on the skin

หุง (hoo'ng) to boil

หุง with ละ (la' heung) castor-oil plant

หุน (hoo'n) [Chin.] (1) (weight) the fifth part of a fuang (2) the eighth part of a niew or Siamese inch

หุน (hoo'n) hasty, violent

หุ่น (hoo'n) (1) form, type (2) puppets

หุ้น (hoo'n) [Chin.] and — ส่วน shares (in a business or company)

หุบ (hoo'p) to shut

หุ้ม (hoo'm) to cover, veil, clothe

หู (hoo?) ear ขี้ — ear-wax ตุ้ม — earring ใบ — outer part of the ear

หู (hoo) partly closed, partly open

หูก (hook) a weaver's instrument

หูด (hoot) wart

เห (hay?) to deviate, to be displaced, inclined

เห (hay) sound of a woman soothing a

child to sleep, to make a noise [espec. of men paddling the King's barge]

เห็ก (hett) mushroom

เหตุ (het) [Pali] circumstance, condition, event, cause, principle ลา — hatred, vindictive — ผล cause and effect — ว่า and — ด้วย because — ใก and — อันใก why ? — ไร what is the matter ?

เห็น (hen) to see — แก to suspect — ชอบ to approve of — ด้วย to agree — ๅ apparently, probably — รู้ to be sure, to be known — ว่า to think probable

เห็น (hen) with อี weasel

เห็บ (hep) small sand insect which attacks the skin

เห็บ (hep) and ลูก — hail, hail-stone

เหม (haym) canopy over a coffin

เหม (haym) [Pali] gold

เหม หง (haym hong) swan, large goose

เหมันต์ (hayma'n) [Pali] winter

เหรา (hayrah) dragon, crocodile

เหว (hao') valley, precipice ปลา — a fish

เหิร (hern) to fly over the land in a miraculous manner, to go, to travel

เหิบ (herp) to trickle

แห (haa?) cast-nest

แห่ (haa) to accompany, to walk in procession

แห (haa) noise of enraged animal

แหก (haak) to break open, to force open

แหง (haang?) bold, vigorous, courageous

แห่ง (hang) (1) place (2) of

แห้ง (haang) dry, faded

แหฅ (haat) [phon.] sound of lashes

แหน (haan) (1) to accompany, to guard ห้าม — royal concubine เฝ้า — to go to the King (2) to refuse

แหน (haan) [phon.] (1) action of gnawing (2) bark of a dog about to bite

แหบ (haap) (1) dried up, rough, hoarse (2) music

แหว (haao) Chinese truffle

ให้ (hie) (1) to give — ด with care — ให้ it is necessary ยก — to give up — สิ้น entirely — หา to call (2) to cause (with other verbs, as) — ดู to show (3) let (sign of the Imper.)

ไห (high) pitcher, small jar — ปั่รา collar-bone

ไห่ (hai) an aquatic plant

ไห้ (hie) and ร้อง — to cry, weep

ไหย (hai) [Pali] horse

ไหรญ (haironn) [Sansk.] gold, treasure, money

ไหหลำ (haila'm) [Chin.] Hainan

ไห (hoe) shouts

ไห (hoh) a fish

โหง (hohng) plague-demon

โหก (hoht) ill-tempered, peevish

โหม (home) to urge on, to rush in, violently

โหย (hoey) to cry, groan, lament

โหร (hone) and โหรา (hohrah) [San.] astrologers, soothsayers [Alab. 175]

โหรกา (hora'pah) a herb

โหร with มะ (ma'hohree) a musical instrument

โหระถึก with มะ (ma'hohra'teuk) [S.] a drum made (by the Kareans) of several metals

เหา (how?) louse คิ้ว — the eighth part of a grain of rice ไข่ — eighth part of the fore-going

เหา (how) to bark ง — venomous

snake

เหาะ (haw') to be carried in the air

หะ (ha') [excl. stopping a person.]

หะริ (ha'ri') [Pali] (1) green (2) enemy

หัก (ha'k) to break, to reduce, to deduct — ใจ to restrain oneself — ร้ to clear a field, jungle, or forest — เอา to set off (one debt against another) — หาญ and — โหม to oppose by force, to attack without fear

หัด (ha't) (1) to exercise, practise (2) a rash which comes out on children

หักถาถึก (ba'ttahneuk) [Pali] host of elephants

หัถิ or หถิ (ha'ttee) [Pali] male elephant — ลิงค์ vulture with beak like elephant's trunk

หถิ and หักถิ (hat) [Pali] hand, elbow สาย พระ ราช — the King's hand writing

หักถะยาส (ha'tta'bart) [Pali] string passing from elbow to elbow, the line of priests sitting in line, with this string connecting them

หถินี (ha'tteenee) [P] female elephant

หัน (ha?) to turn, reverse, deviate กัง — weather-cock กัง — and — เข

กาศ the last of the vowels, q. v. —
ใ๓ to draw one's breath

หั่น (ha'n) to cut in pieces

หับ (ha'p) to shut, to fold, to shut off

หัม (ha'm) to hold down firmly — หั๋ม
to hold with one hand and cut with
the other, to act imperiously

————◆◆◆————

ฬ

ฬ (*law bahlee* = Eng. *l.* and at the
end of a word *n.* Sansk. *l. and d.* A
low letter) — ฬาฬ็ namo of this
letter

ฬศ (lot) *for* โสฬศ half an att

————◆◆◆————

ฮ

ฮ (*haw checa'soon* = strong *h.* a low letter) — เฮ็ยะสุน name of this letter

ฮา (hah) [phon.] (sound of laughing)

ฮ่า (hah) [Chin.] (sound of pain, word
of disapproval)

ฮ่าโฮ่ (hah hoh?) [Chin.] expression of
triumph or defiance

ฮี่ (hee') [phon.] neighing of horses

ฮึก (heu'k) [Chin.] impetuous

ฮึ (heu) [Chin.] (1) groaning (2) noise
of moving, of a crowd, etc. — ๆ
vehemently

ฮึก (heut) [Chin.] panting, breathless

ฮึก (hoo't) [Chin.] (1) to blow (tinder)
(2) to lift up

ฮุย (hooi') [Chin.] (excl.) very nearly !
— เฮ shout of men pulling

ฮูก (hook) [phon.] (1) large horned
owl (2) to weave cloth

ฮูม (hoom) [phon.] roar of elephant,
report of cannon

เฮ (hey) shouts of joy — เฮ — ไฮ *and*
— ฮิ้ว shouts of workmen dragging
logs

เฮย (hoy) [Chin.] (excl.) come here !

เฮะ (ha') [excl. of surprise or prohibi-
tion]

แฮ (haa) (1) come here ! (2) escort of
many men

แฮ้ (haa) cry to attract attention

แฮน (haan) [phon.] neighing of horses

แฮะ (haa') (1) noise of laughing (2)
shout to attract the attention

โฮ (ho) weeping, wailing

โฮก (hoke) (1) sound of vomiting (2)
sound of an animal attacking

โฮเตล (hotenn) [Fr.] hotel

โหย (hoey) [in answering] here I am !

เฮา (how) [to elephants] stop and kneel

ฮะ (ha') (1) [exclam. of prohibition] stop (2) to shout out

ฮัก (ha'k) out of breath, panting

ฮัด (ha't) to sneeze

- - - - ◆ ◆ ● ◆ - - - -

อ

อ (aw = English short *a*. or more commonly short *au*. and short *o*. Sansk. short *a*. Reckoned by Siamese grammarians as a consonant, a Guttural and a middle letter)

อ (a') privative prefix, as in Greek and Sanskrit

อก (auk) breast, heart — ไก่ beam forming the peak of a roof — เอย alas !

อกนิฐ (a'ka'nitt) [Pali] greatest, highest, several, to abound

อกุศล (a'koo'sonn) [Sansk.] want of merit, sin, sinful

อกะตะ (a'ka'ta') [Pali] undone, unmade, wanting in merit, undeserving

อง (ong) subst. of personality — ไท่ and — บวน Cochin-Chinese priest พะ — ladder — อาจ bold, powerful, rash

อโขภินี (a'khopi'nee) *and* อโขเภนี [Pali] a very large number, army, host

องค์ (ong) [Sansk.] person, body, he [of Kings, priests, etc.] num. design. of Kings, princes, etc. พระ — title of a god, king. or prince พระ — เจ้า birth title of a King's son by a non-princess

องคชาติ (ongka'chart) [Pali] membrum virile

องคุลี (ongkoo'lee) [Pali] finger, finger's breadth, inch, half the thumb พระ — King's finger

องษา (ongsar) [Sansk.] sun

องุ่น (a'ngoo'n) juice of grape ลูก — grape ต้น — vine น้ำ — wine

อจินไตย (a'chintai) *and* อจินโต [Pali] inconceivable, incomprehensible

อชิตะ (a'chi'ta') [Sansk.] invincible

อณุกระเบียด (a'noo'kra'beea't) [San.] one eighth of a niew

อโณทาย (a'nohdart) source of rain, one of the seven great lakes of Himaphan [Alab. 296]

อด (ot) to bear, sustain, abstain from — ใจ patience — เข้า — อาหาร to fast — ออม patient, benign — ศีล fasting, Lent

อกทน (ottonn) to suffer, endure patiently

อกส่าห์ (otsah) [Sansk.] to endeavour, try

อกส (otsoo) shame, shameful

อดิต (a'dit) [Pali] past, the past

อดิศร (a'di'son) [San.] glorious, magnificent, great

อดิเรข (a'di'reck) [Pali] excessive, splendid, magnificent

อดุล (a'doo'n) [Pali] incomparable, admirable

อกุลย (a'doo'n) [Sansk.] dissimilar, unequal

อตโน (a'ta'no) [Pali] self, spontaneous

อติสาร (a'ti'sarn) nearly dead, at the point of death

อโทโส (a'tohsoh) [Pali] freedom from anger, absence of passion [Alab. 37]

อธรรม (a'ta'm) [Pali] lawless, irreligious

อธิกมาศ (a'ti'ka'mart) double month (8th) in the Siamese leap-year

อธิกรรม (a'ti'ka'm) [Pali] (1) great sin (2) a Pali book

อธิกราช (a'ti'ka'rart) [San.] supreme King

อธิการ (a'ti'karn) [P.] (1) office, authority, function, resolution (2) chief of a monastery or convent

อธิฏฐุรูยะ (a'titt-tayya') [Pali] to fix, set up, appoint

อธิฐาน (a'ti'tarn) to make vows, to make prayers, firm purpose, determination [Alab. 184]

อธิบดี (a'ti'bodee) [Pali] grandee, chief official, mandarin

อธิบาย (a'ti'bai) [Pali] (1) wish, intention, meaning (2) to publish, to explain

อดึก (a'teuk) [Sansk.] severe, harsh

อดิศีล (a'ti'seen) [Pali] eminent merit

อโต (a'toh) [Pali] under, beneath, below, low — ภาค lower side

อน (on) with ตัว an animal — อน oppressed in mind, perplexed, unable to make plans, at one's wit's end

อนง (a'nong) woman, fine woman

อนนต (a'nonta') and อนันต [Pali] indefinite, boundless, infinite

อนา (a'nah) within, within bounds

อนารักา and อนาเขต (a'nahcha'k, a'nahket) frontiers, boundaries

อนาคต (a'narkhot) [Pali] the future

อนาตมา (a'narta'mah) [Sansk.] not oneself, illusory, false [Alab. 227]

อนาท and อนาด (a'nart) to fear, to dread

อนาทร (a'nahton) [Pali] regardless, reckless, careless, desperate

อนารวม see อัณะราม

อนาวรณ (a'nahwon) [Sansk.] uncovered, unobstructed, manifest

อนิจา (a'nichah) [Pali] อนิจะ and อนิจัง not lasting, unstable, transitory, perishable [Alab. 160, 226]

อนิตยกรรม (a'nitta'ya'ka'm) [Sansk.] to die (of a Khun or Hluang)

อนิมิต (a'ni'mitt) [San.] without cause and without effect

อนิละ (a'ni'la') [Pali] wind, air — ปก sky

อนิยม (a'ni'yom) [Pali] uncertain, unusual, inproper

อนึ่ง (a'neung) therefore, accordingly, then

อนุ (a'noo') [Pali] according to, after, near, towards

อนุ (a'noo') [Pali] small, minute, a measure of 36 Paramanu

อนุกร (a'noo'kon) and อนุการ to act according to example or order, imitate

อนุกรม (a'noo'krom) [Sansk.] in order, in rank

อนุกูล (a'noo'koon) [Pali] to help, support, aid

อนุเคราะ (a'noo'krau') [Sansk.] patronage, help, assistance

อนุจร (a'noo'chonn) [P.] (1) to wander, to go about (2) attendant, follower

อนุชา (a'noo'char) [Pali] younger

อนุชาติ (a'noo'chart) [S.] according to one's kind, hereditary disposition

อนุญาต (a'noo'yart) [Pali] to consent, allow, permit, sanction

อนุปคมมะ (a'noo'pa'kha'mma') [Pali] going up to, getting close to

อนุพันธ (a'noo'pa'n) [Pali] consequence, succession, to follow, to tie together, to connect, to compose

อนุภาพ (a'noo'parp) [Pali] dignity, majesty, supernatural power, divine authority

อนุมาน (a'noo'marn) inference, conjecture, doubt

อนุโยค (a'noo'yohk) to question, to interrogate, to exert oneself

อนุโรท (a'noo'rote) and อนุโรไทย vuly. for อรุโณท etc.

อนุสร (a'noo'son) [Pali] to call to mind, think of, remember

อนุสนธิ (a'noo'sonn) [Pali] connection, application, to add

อนุสาสน์ (a'noo'sart) [Pali] to teach, instruction

อนุไสย (a'noo'sai) [Pali] inclination, disposition, tendency or bent of the mind

อนุสะ (a'noo'sa') *and* อนุสสติ [Pali] to think of, remember

อนุสัง (a'noo'sa't) [Sansk.] faithful, true, stedfast

อเนก (a'nayk) [Pali] more than one, several, many

อนไทย (a'nohtai) [Sansk.] sun

อโนะ (a'noha') [Pali] unerring, prudent

อนันต์ (a'na'n) *and* อนันตะ [Pali] endless, boundless, infinite

อนันตะระ (a'na'nta'ra') [Pali] uninterrupted, continuous; infinite series, eternity

อบ (op) to perfume, scent — รม (1) to incense (2) to take care of, to be kind to

อเชย (opchoey) cinnamon

อพยพ (oppa'yop) to migrate, emigrate, go into captivity

อบาย (a'baie) hell

อโป (a'poh) [Pali] water

อประภาค (a'pra'paht) portionless

อปรา (a'pa'rah) [Pali] unconquered — ไชย unvanquished

อไหกาศ *see* อักกาศ

อพะยพ (a'pa'yop) *see* อบพะยบ

อภารัง (a'pahra'ng) [San.] out of work, idle, at leisure

อภิ (a'pi') [Sansk. *abhi* Gr. *epi*] before, over, upon, over and above, more, most

อภิธาน (a'pi'tahn) [Sansk.] name, noun

อภิยาล (a'pi'barn) [Sansk.] to watch over, take care of

อภิรมย (a'pi'romm) [Sansk.] pleasure, satisfaction

อภิรุม (a'pi'roo'm) pomp, apparel

อภิลาป (a'pi'larp) [Pali] appellation, speaking to, conversation

อภิลาพ (a'pi'lahp) [Pali] reaping, harvest

อภิวาท (a'pi'wart) *and* อภิวันท์ [Pali] to salute, adore

อภิสเมยะ (a'pi'sa'maycha') [Pali] to comprehend, fully understand

อภิเสก (a'pi'sayk) [Pali] sprinkling, consecrating (of a King)

อโภกาศ (a'pohkart) [Sansk.] spacious, ample, a Heaven

อม (om) to keep in the mouth

อมร (a'monn *or* a'ma'ra') [Pali] Indra

อโมโห (a'moho) [Pali] freedom from folly, emancipation from ignorance, enlightenment [Alab. 37]

อมาจา (a'ma'tchah) [Pali] minister, courtier, magistrate

อยมุน (a'ya'moo'nee) [Pali] *see* กะรียมณิ

อย่า (yar) *and* หย่า (1) not, do not — เพธ

not yet (2) to separate, to depart, to
divorce

อย่าง (yarng) *and* หย่าง mode, way,
manner, kind, species, custom, fashion ตัวอย่าง pattern, specimen —
ะะไร how — ไง why — หนะ —ใก
in any way

อยุทง (a'yoo'tı) [Sansk.] invincible,
impregnable

อยุทธยา (a'yootta'yah) [Sansk.] Ayu-
thia, old capital of Siam

อยู่ (yoo) (*see under* ย) to remain, to be

อยู่พัก (yoopa'k) (*see under* ย) rest

อรรค (a'kk) [Sansk.] foremost, upper-
most, top, point, summit

อรรชุน (a'nchoo'n) (1) cloud (2) angel

อรรณพ (anopp) [Sansk.] ocean, sea,
lake

อรรถ *and* อรรถะ (a't, a'tta) [Sansk.]
lawsuit, cause, case, article, chapter, text

อร่อย (a'roy) savour, taste, savoury

อริ (a'ri') *and* อริณ [Pali] enemies

อริยะ (a'ri'ya') [Pali] venerable, holy,
pious ; saint

อรุณ (a'roo'n) [Pali] dawn, day-break

อรุโณท (a'roo'note) *and* อรุโณไทย [P.]
dawn, rising sun

อรูปะ (a'roopa') [Pali] formless, bodi-

less, inmaterial

อไร *see* อะไร

อลงกฎ (a'longkot) [Pali] adorned, em-
bellished

อลงกรณ (a'longkorn) [Pali] ornament,
decoration เฟ้าอลงกรณ ornamented hair-pin, Chulalonkorn (name of
H. M. the King of Siam)

อลมาน (ola'marn) tumult, disturbance,
riot

อลเวง (ola'wayng) outcry, uproar

อลอง (a'laung) clear, white, clean, fair

อลากพาก (a'lartpart) to scatter

อเลื่อยเนื่อย *better* เอลื่อยเนื่อย (a'leui'
neui') languid

อโลก (a'lohk) *and* อโลกา [Pali] seeing, sight, light, bright, shining,
clear, open

อโลโภ (a'lohpɔ) freedom from covetousness, absence of desire [Alab. 37]

อล่ำโภ (a'la'mpoh) snake-charmer,
King of serpents

อลังการ (a'la'ngkarn) [Pali] ornaments

อลัชชี (a'la'tchee) [Pali] impudent,
bold, brazen-faced, lawless

อวก (ooa'k) [phon.] sound of vomiting,
nausea, sickness

อวต (ooa't) (1) to show anything that
one is proud of, to divulge, to boast
— ตัว to make a show by dressing

up — อ้าง to call witness to one's character or in one's praise (2) vain, boastful

อวน (ooa'n) net ทำ — ลง — to throw the net

อ้วน (ooa'n) fat, full-blown อวบ — fat and white

อวม (ooa'm) to cover

อว่ม (ooa'm) white, full, fleshy อิอิ — full and pretty face

อวย (ooey) (1) to give (2) to wish

อวหาร (a'wa'harn) [Pali] to cheat, to steal

อวาหา (a'wah-har) [Pali] bringing a wife home, marriage

อวิชา (a'vee'chah) [Pali] ignorance, error

อวัยวะ and อวัยวะ (a'waiya'wa') [P.] limb, member, body

อวะ (a'wa') [Pali] from above, down from, from, of

อวะชาติ (a'wa'chart) [Pali] degenerate

อวะคาร (a'wa'tarn) [Sansk.] descending, swooping down, earthly manifestations of a divinity, Avatar; a name of Indra

อวะหาร (a'wa'harn) [Pali] to steal

อวิเอย (ooa' eea') languid, feeble

อสงไขย (a'songkhai) [Pali] unnumerable, infinite

อสรพิศม์ (a'sa'ra'pitt) [Pali] venomous animals

อสปถะ (a'sa'patta') oath, imprecation

อสุกรี (a'soo'kree) see วาสุกรี

อสุจิ (a'soo'chee') [P.] unclean, impure

อสุชล (a'soo'chon) [Pali] tears

อสุนี (a'soo'nee) and อสุนี etc. [Pali] thunderbolt

อสุภ (a'soo'pa') [Pali] ugly, nasty, disagreeable

อสุร and อสุรี (a'soora', a'sooree) [Pali] fallen angel, gaint (male and female), devil. [Alab, 192]

อโสกา (a'sohkar) [P.] free from sadness

อโสเภณี (a'sopaynee) see นครโสเภณี

อโสระพิศม์ (a'sohra'pitt) [Sansk.] venomous, venom, serpent

อสัญญ (a'sa'nya') and — กรรม [Pali] to die

อสัมพินพงษ (a'sampinpong) blood relations

อหิ (a'hee') [Pali] snake

อโหสิกรรม (a'hohsi'ka'm) [Pali] lost, utterly gone [Alab. 47,48]

อหังการ (a'ha'ngkarn) [Pali] selfishness, pride, arrogance, to boast, to threaten

อหัญชะ (a'ha'ncha') wo, us

ออ

ออ (au I) second of the vowels

เออ *and* ออ้ (au ?) oh I (word meaning "I understand")

ออ แอ (au aa) feeble, effeminate, indolent, idle

อ่อ (au) oh I

ออ้ (au I) oh I

ออ๋ (au I) (1) reed, rush, bullrush (2) to speak fluently — แออ feeble, effeminate, idle (3) only able to talk a little

อ้อ (au I) oh I (meaning "I recollect now ")

ออก (auk) out, away, exempt, to go out *or* away, to put forth, to utter — เงิน to spend money เขา — to go in and out, to go often backwards and forwards, to frequent — ชีร่า exempt from service — ลูก to give birth — ไฟ to rise from child-bed

เออก (auk) a large bird of prey

ออ๋ *and* อ๋อ๋ (aung) neat, bright

อ๋อ๋ แอ๋ง (aung eng) slouching about, manner of walking, speaking, etc.

เออก แออก (aut aat) (1) feebly, indistinctly (2) to complain

ออ่น (aun) soft, tender, feeble สี — light colour เมือ — *and* — หน่ออ่น *and* — ลง to get weak — น้ออ่น (1) to consent, yield (2) to be afraid นก — bird which builds edible bird's nest

ออ้น (aun) lachrymose, weak-minded, puerile

ออบ (aup) [phon.] croaking of frogs

ออฟฟิศ (aufiss) [Engl.] office

ออ้ม (aum) tortuous, winding, roundabout

ออย (oie) sugar-cane

ออรธาน (ora'tarn) all gone, to disappear

ออรานพ *see* อรรานพ lake, sea

อา

า *and at the beginning of a word* อา (lark kharng : third of the vowels : long a, as in English " grass," "path," etc.) ลาก ช้าง name of this letter

อา (ah) (1) (excl. of surprise and admiration) ah ! (2) younger brother or sister of the father

อ้า (ah) to deck oneself, to dress up — อาภ์ to put on full dress (of a Royal person)

อ้า (art) (1) to open (2) to hold up (3) [exclam.] ah !

อากร (ahkon) tax on gardens and monopolies นาย — tax farmer

อาการ (ahkarn) [Pali] appearance, symptom; character [Alab. 240]

อากาศ (ahkaht) [Pali] sky, air, atmosphere, space, open air, vacuum หน — name of the 18th vowel

อาเกียรณ (arhkeea'n) [Sansk] spread, diffused, scattered about

อากง (ah-keung) [Chin.] ship-builder, ship-writght

อากูล (ahkoon) [Pali] confused, troubled, dirty, odious, foul

อากังขา (arka'ngkhar) desires, bad desires

อากัป (arka'p) [Pali] manner, mode, fashion — อาการ character

อายโยก (a....u'yok) to join, joining

อาคเนย์ (arkha'nay) [S.] South-East

อาคม (arkhom) [[Pali] sacred forms; religion

อาคะ (arkha') [Pali] to come

อาฆะ (arkha') [Pali] sin, suffering, evil

อาคันตุกะ (arkha'ntoo'ka') [Pali] incidental, casual, mendicant

อาคัมน (ahka'mna') to call out for, to summon by calling

อาฆาฎ (arkhart) [Pali] malice, ill-will, revenge, anger, angry

อาง ขนาง (arng kha'narng) to hesitate, to be shy, bashful

อ่าง (arng) (1) large bowl, wide-mouthed jar (2) stammering, stuttering อึ้ง — [phon.] bull-frog

อ้าง (ahng) to rely upon, to use the services of สม — to agree in testimony รับ สม — to offer oneself as a witness in support

อ่าง ทอง (arngtaung) name of a Province (golden bowl)

อาจ (art) daring, bold, capable — สา มาท able, powerful บัง — rash, imprudent

อาจม (archom) [Pali] excrement

อาจาด (archart) soaked, preserved

อาจาร (archarn) [Pali] conduct, practice, manners

อาจาริย์ (archahria') อาจาริยะ and อาจาริ โย [Pali] teacher, tutor, preceptor

อาจิณ (archinn) [Pali] (1) to heap up, accumulate (2) continual (3) to become mad by thinking

อาจินไก etc. see อิจินไก

อาเจียร (archeea'n) to vomit, to be sick

อาเจลก (archeylok) [P.] naked ascetics

อาชา (archar) horse

อาชีวก (archeewok) [P.] naked ascetics

อาฎานา (artarnar) [Pali] shooting with cannon

อาญา (ahyar) [Pali] Royal order ลง — to inflict punishment ความ — important law-suit สาล — inferior tribunal

อาณาจักร (arnarcha'k) [San.] dignity, majesty, jurisdiction, sovereignty, dominion, dominions

อาก (art) [phon.] noise of a cart

อาดูร (ardoora') [P.] diseased, affected

อาตมา (ahtamah) [Sansk.] I, he, him, self — ภาพ I (of priests speaking to the King or to a person of importance)

อาถิน (arta'n) (1) relic buried in the earth (2) boundaries of a town or village, such as stones, pillars, etc.

อาโถง (ahtohng) see โอ่โถง ostentation, pomp, show, proud

อาทาศ (artart) [P.] mirror, telescope, microscope

อาทิ better อาธิ (arti') [P.] over, above, first, superior, excellent, more

อาทิตย (artitt) [Sansk.] and พระ — sun [Alab. 217] วัน — Sunday

อาน (arn) (1) to sharpen (2) to beat

severely (3) saddle

อ่าน (ahn) to read, to consider คิด — to calculate

อ้าน (ahn) clean, shining. bright

อานนท์ (arnonn) [Pali] (1) joy, happiness (2) a disciple of Buddha

อานาภาพ see อานุภาพ

อานาโรค (arnahrohk) [Pali] free from illness

อานิต (arnitt) [San.] pity, indulgence, compassionate

อานิสงส์ (arnisong) [Pali.] effect of good actions, reward, good result

อานุสัจ (arnoo'sa't) [P.] true, faithful, stedfast

อานุภาพ (arnoo'parp) dignity, authority, power, influence

อาบ (arp) [Sansk.] to wash, to bathe, to sprinkle — น้ำ to take a bath — เชิบ to be drenched, soaked — อบ to perfume — ทอง to gild

อาบิก (arbitt) a wine or liqueur

อาบุทฌา (arputchar) [P.] to ask leave to withdraw

อาบ่ำ(ahba'm) Malay cakes

อาบัติ (arba't) [Pali] sin, guilt - กัก absolution

อาป (arp) อาโป and อปั [Pali] water

อาพาธ (arpart) [Pali] illness, sickness, to be ill

อาพัก (arpa't) to bless (wine)

อาภรณ์ (arponn) *and* อาภรณัง [Pali] decorations, ornaments, vestments

อาภา (ahpah) splendour, ray; radiant, shining

อาภพ '(arpa'p [Pali] non-existence, deprivation, disaster, ruin, miserable

อามิศ (armitt) [Pali] object of enjoyment, bait, temptation, bribe

อามะ (ahma') [Pali] yes

อาย (aie) (1) vapour, emanation (2) leakage (3) shame, to be ashamed

อ้าย (aie)]Laos.] eldest brother

อ้าย (ai) [Laos.] first เกือน — the first Siamese month

อ้าย (ai!) *and* อ๊าย (ai!) [exclam. of pain] ah!

อายุสม์ (ahyoo') [Pali] age

อารติ (ahra'tee) [Pali] to refrain from sin

อารมณ์ (ahrom) [Pali] object of sense, thought, idea, affection, disposition, quality [Alab. 236]

อาราธนา (ahrahta'nah) [P.] invitation of priests

อาริย (ahria) *and* อารย [Pali] vener-

able, holy, sanctified, saint ศรี —

ไมตรี the Buddha who is next to come

อารุก กุกกิก (ahroo'k koo'kkik) rough

อารุ่ม (ahroo'm) (1) cloudy (2) Constantinople

อาโรก (ahrohk) a forest tree

อารัก (ahra'k) [P.] guard, guardian, protection; to guard, to watch

อารัญ (ahra'n) [Pali] wood, forest

อาหรับ (ahra'p) Arab

อาหลาด (ahlart) dispersed, scattered, disordered

อาลิงค์ (ahling) [Pali] to embrace

อาไลย (ahlie) [Pali] longing, desire, attachment, love

อาละมาร (ahla'marn) (1) half cooked, underdone, several persons acting together

อาละวก (ahla'wok) [Pali] a famous giant

อาลักษณ์ (ahla'k) [Pali] royal scribe, royal writer

อาลัด (ahla't) *and* อาหลาด scattered, dispersed

อาลัชชี (ahla'tchee) *better* อลัชชี [Pali] brazen-faced, impudent, lawless

อาว (ou) [L.] father's younger brother

อ่าว (ou) bay, gulf

อ้าว (ou) [intensifying the word which goes before it] very much, very (2) (excl.) hallo! ปลา — a small sea-fish

อาวาส (arwaht) *and* อาวาโส [Pali] dwelling for priests, monastery

อาวาห (arwah-ha') [Pali] wedding

อาวุธ (arwoo't *and* อาวุธา [Pali] weapons, arms

อาวไส (arwoo'soh) [Pali] brother [address of one priest to another]

อาสน์ *and* อาศนัง *see* อาษน์ etc.

อาศพ (ahsopp) [Sans] putrid corpse

อาศรม (ahsomm) [Sansk,] hermitage, cell, religious order

อาไศรย (ahsai) [Sansk.] to take refuge, to go to a house, to live, dwell, dwelling

อาษน์ (art) *and* อาษนัง *see* อาสน์ etc.

อาษา (arsah) assistance, auxiliary

อาสน (arsonn) note, bill

อาสน์ (art) *and* อาสนัง [Pali] seat (for the King or priest), mat

อาษาฬหา (arsarnhah) [Pali] constellation of the 8th month [Alab. 97]

อาสาฬ *sse* อาสาฬหา

อาสัตย (ahsa't) perjury, lying, lie

อาสัน (ahsa'n) [Pali] approach, propin-quity

อิ

อิ [so written at the begining of a word ; but in other cases the upper portion only is used, and is placed over the consonant which precedes the vowel sound]—short *i*, as in Engl. *in* ; fourth of the vowels พินทุ — *and* สระ — names of this vowel

อิง (ing) to lean upon หมอน — cushion กระดาน — back of a seat อ้าง — to call as a witness

อิง *with* สะ (sa'-ing) ornament worn as a scarf sideways

อิจฉา (itchar) [Pali] envy, jealous, covetous

อิฉุย *and* อิแฉก (itchooi, itchaak) to squander

อิฐ (itt) [Pali] brick

อิฐะ (itta') [Pali] to wish, desire

อินะ (inna') [Pali] debt

อิต (itt) *and* — โรย wearied, dispirited ระ — ระอา disgusted สะ — สะ เอียน (1) slighted, startled, horrified, averse (2) a measure of 12 niew

อิติ (itti) [Pali] (1) thus, in this way,

indeed (2) bad, unlucky, calamity

อิกะ (itta') [Pali] (1) patient (2) from this time

อิดี (ittee) [Pali] woman, female

อิทธิ (itthi') [Pali] miraculous power (as of going through the air, etc.) — บาท means of attaining this power [Alab. 196] — ฤทธิ์ supernatural power

อิทป (ittoop) a fish

อิทปะโก (ittᴄoppa'ko) [Pali] country

อิทะ (itta') [Pali] this, present, here,

อิน (in) a fruit tree

อินท อินท์ and อินทรา (inn, intra') [S.] (1) big, great (2) Indra

อินทรี (insee) (1) eagle (2) dorcy

อินทรีย (insee) [Pali] senses, faculties, moral power [Alab. 241]

อินทะนิล (inta'nin) black, very dark; sapphire กิน — a tree with hard wood

อินทะผาลำ (inta'pahla'm) [Malay] date (tree)

อิโปง (ippohng) [Chin.] spinning-top

อิม (im) satiated, surfeited

อิรม with หอย (hoi irromm) oyster

อิวา (irrah) (1) fishing eagle, osprey (2)

a kite (toy)

อิริ (irri') [Pali] officiating priest

อิริน (irrin) bird-trap

อิศวริยศ (issariyot) wealth, distinction, eminent, opulent

อิศวร (issooa'n) [Sansk.] excellent, lord, master; a name of Siva

อิศริยศ (isseeri'yot) [Pali] dominion, supremacy

อิศะวระ อิไร etc. (issa'ra', etc.) [Pali] principal, superior, chief, king

อิสาร (issarn) or อิสาน North-East

อิสูร (issoon) [P.] Asura, fallen angel, Titan

<hr>

อี [so written at the beginning of a word, but otherwise without the lower part] long i = English ee: fifth of the vowels พิณ — and สระ — name of this vowel

อี (ee) (excl. of one in pain) oh!

อี (ee) maid servant — กอก ทอง courtesan — เห้น weasel, stoat

อีก (eek) again, a second time มี — there is some left, there is more — ก again

อีกา (eekah) crow

อีกู (eekoo') a banana เรือ — a boat

อีเก้ง (eekayng) a small wild animal

อีโก้ง (eekohng) a large crane

อีดำ อีแดง (ee-da'm ee-daang) (1) measles (2) name given to male and female children, till their real names are given to them ; baby

อีทา (eetow) witch, poisoner

อีเหนา (eehnow) [Javan.] ruler, governor, king

อีเป็ก (eepett) a rowing boat

อีแปะ (eepaa.) [Chin.] small coin of copper, zinc, tin, glass etc.

อีเป้า (eepow) kite [toy]

อีแร้ว (eehyo) bird of prey, kite, hawk — กระไกร sparrow-hawk

อีวา (eeroh) a green bird with red neck and yellow beak

อีล้อม (eeloo'm) a handsome bird เว้า — a tailless kite

อีเลิ้ง (eeleung) fat and unwieldy ; a fat-shaped pitcher

อีสาน (eesarn) North-East

อีเห็น (eehayn) a large stoat or weasel which eats hens

อีแอ่น (ee-aan) swallow which makes edible bird's nests

เอียง (eea'ng) bent, leaning, inclined to ; bias

เอี้ยง (eea'ng) a talking bird

เอี้ยว (eeyo) to turn aside, to go on one side

อึ

อึ (so at the beginning of a word, but otherwise without the lower part) — short eu : no English equivalent but like Fr. eu in feu. Sixth of the vowels พีน — and สีระ — name of this vowel

อึ (eu) a word used by and to babies — อึะ exclaim. of one who refuses or pleads ignorance

อึก (eu'k) tumult

อึง (eu'ng) noise, aproar เสียง — noise, annoyance

อึ่ง อาง (eu'ng ahng) [phon.] bull-frog

อึ้ง (eu'ng) (1) deaf (2) silent

อึด (eut) oppressed in mind or body, harassed, impeded — ตัด blocked-up, embarrassed, hampered — โอย exclaim. of one who is afflicted

อึกทะปึ (eutta'peu) to abound

อึ (so at the begining of a word, but otherwise without the lower part : longer *eu*. No Euglish equivalen t but like Fr. *œu* in *c œur*. พึม — *and* สึ: — name of this vowel

อึก ๆ (eut-eut) noise of one groaning

อึน (eun) other เป็น — changed ผึ — other people, strangers

อึอ (eu) exclam. of assent, espec. when giving anything

อึอ ๆ (eu eu) (1) exclam. of one groaning (2) noise of lulling a child to sleep

อึอ (eu) deaf — อึง great uproar, tumult, confusion

เอิก เอิอ (eua' pheua') to attend to, to be kind to, help

เอิอง (eua'ng) a small tree

อึด: (eua'n) (1) a worm in fruit or in the intestines (2) nausea, vomiting

เอิอน (eua'n) to speak, to utter อึก — hesitating in one's speech, backward in replying

เอิอบ (eua'p) dried up

เอิอม (eua'm) to stretch out for, to long after what is unattainable, to wish hopelessly

---

อุ so at beginning of word, but otherwise without the upper part. short *oo* or short *u*, as in *foot*, *full*. Eighth of the vowels กุ — *and* สุ: — name of this vowel

อุก (oo'k) rash, bold

อุกฤษ ฐ (oo'kritt) [Sansk.] (1) inost, best. highest. supreme ॰) sovere punishment

อุกกาบาต (oo'kkarbart) etc. [Pali *and* Sansk] meteor, falling star

อุโฆษ *and* อุ ฆส (oo'kkoht) [San. *and* Pali] (1) to make a noise deep down in the throat (2) to reopen settled questions (3) to publish, relate, tell

อุง (oo'ng) convexity, concavity, — ฝึ concavity of the hand, handful

อุ ฯ (oot) (Pali) high

อุ จาระ: (oo'tchahra') [Pali] excrement, filth

อุ จาก (oo'chart) to act dirtily, disgusting, indecent

อุ ณหิต (oo'nhitt) [Pali] ornament for the forehead, turban, hat, crown

อุ ณาโลม (oo'nahlohm) [Pali] the forehead between the eyebrows

อุ ฯ ฯ (oo'nha') [Pali] hot

อุ ด (oo't) to stop up — หนุน to assist

with alms or with praise นำ —
front partition of a house-boat

อุกคลุก (oo'tta'loo't) confusion, disturbance

อุกกะพัก (oo'tta'pitt) a plant with
strong-smelling flowers

อุดม (oo'domm) [Pali] best, highest,
excellent, abundant, copious, plentiful, productive, fertile

อุดร (oo'donn) [Pali] higher, upper,
Northern ทิศ — North

อุกะกะ อุกกย etc. see อุกก

อุตริ (oo'ta'ri') to imagine evil, to act
improperly

อุตรี (oo'ta'ri') [Pali] higher

อุทก (oo'tok) [Pali] water

อุทกัง (oo'ta'ka'ng) [Pali] water

อุทธรณ์ (oo'tto'n) [Pali] pulling out
ลักขณ — rules of appeal

อุทยาน (oo'ta'yarn) [Sansk.] flower-
garden, pleasure-ground เนิน — a
Royal garden on the West side of
the river นันทวัน — R. g. near the
Palace

อุทร (oo'tonn) [Pali] (1) belly, stomach,
womb (2) accusation against the
Governor of a Province

อุทาน (oo tah-hon) [Pali] ejaculation,
interjection, utterance

อุทาม (oo'tahm) half-wild, fugitive

อุทาหรณ์ (oo'tah-hon) [P.] utterance,
interpretation, to foretell

อุทิศ (oo'titt) [P.] to select, to show a
preference for — แผ่ to shed one's
merits on others — ส่งไป to send
one's merits to the dead

อุทุมพร (oo'too'mponn) [Pali] fig-tree
(ficus glomerata)

อุเทน (oo'tayn) [Pali] name of a dignitary who plays on a banjo

อุไทย (oo'taie) [P.] Eastern mountain
behind which the sun rises, rising
sun, glittering, bright

อุธร see อุทธรณ์

อุ่น (oo'n) see อุดุน warm, tepid — ใจ
glad — ไฟ to warm up (food)

อุบ with ค่อย (toi oo'p) to strike with
the fist — เอา [of a fish, etc.] to
seize ปลา — a fish

อุบประไม (oo ppra'mai) see อุประมา

อุบล (oo'bonn) [Pali] waterlily, lily

อุบาท (oo'bart) [Pali] accident, misfortune, calamity

อุบาย (oo'baie) [P.] stratagem, device,
manœuvre

อุบาสิกา (oo'bahsi'kar) [Pali] nun

อุบาสะโก (oo'bahsa,ko) [Pali] monk

อุเบกขา (oo'baykkhar) [Pali] indifference to love and kate, single-mindedness [Alab. 168, 195]

อุโปสถ (oo'bohsot) [Pali] Buddhist Sabbath, usually called วัน พระ occuring at intervals of 6 to 8 days

กุบะ (oo'ba') bouquet

อุปัทติ (oo'batti') [Pali] misfortune, ruin

อุปการ (oo'pa'karn) [Pali] help, service

อุปฐาน (oo'pa'tarn) [P.] to look after, keep; attachment, adherence [Alab. 239]

อุปติ (oo'pa'ti') [Pali] condition of existence, source, origin [A. 212]

อุปนิไสย (oo'pa'ni'snie) [Pali] secret cause, tendency, faculty

อุปฐาก (oo'pa'tark) [Pali] attendant, servitor โยม — related to a priest

อุปถัมภ์ (oo'pa'ta'm) [Pali] stay, support, help

อุปทม (oo'pa'tom) siphilis

อุปทูต (oo'pa'too't) [Pali] second ambassador

อุปเทศ (oo'pa'tayt) [Pali] instruction, initiation, means of knowledge

อุปโภค (oo'pa'pohk [Pali] chattels, furniture

อุปริ (oo'pa'ri') [Pali] over, above, beyond [Gk. huper]

อุประ (oo'pra') near, to approach

อุประมา (oo'pra'mah) [Sansk.] as if, for example, similar, comparison

อุปสมบท (oo'pa'sombot) [Pali] priest's orders, ordination

อุปาชาย (oo'pa'chaiya') [P.] teacher, sponsor, ecclesiastical surety

อุปา (oo'pah) [Pali] refuge, help

อุปาณะ (oo'pahna') to compare วิทา — allegory

อุปายาศ (oo'pahyart) [Pali] vexed, annoyed, chagrin

อุปัชฌาไย (oo'pa'tchahyo) [Pali] head teacher, chief of a monastery, ordaining priest

อุปิเศก (oo'pi'sek) [Pali] sprinkling, conse ting, marriage

อุ้ม (oo'm) and — คิรรภ pregnancy, to be pregnant

อุหมย (oo'hmay) [exclam. of reproof to children]

อุโมงค์ and อุมงค์ (oo'mong) [Pali] subterranean passage or cave ปล่อง — shaft leading to a boring or passage or tunnel

อุย (ooi) a fish with yellow flesh

อุย หนา (ooi'nah) [exclam. of pain]

อุย *with* หนัก (ooi' na'k) weighted, weighed down

อุยยานุ่ง (ooi'yarna'ng) [Pali] garden

อุรา (oo'rah) *and* อุระ [Pali] breast, heart

อุรู (oo'roo') [Pali] thigh

อุไร (oo'rai') [Malay.] *with* ทอง pure gold

อุลโลก (oo'nloke) [P.] canopy, awning, ceiling

อุลามก (oo'larmok) immodesty, shameless action

อุลิต (oolitt) [high word) water-melon, pumpkin

อุโลก (oo'loke) a tree of which the wood is used for making common coffins

อุษณะ (oo'sa'na') [Sansk.] hot

อุษณาการ (oo'sa'narkarn) heat, feverishness, restlessness

อุสสาห (oossah) อุสาห *and* อุสาหะ [P.] patience, diligence, to endeavour

อุสุภ (oo'soo'p) (1) ox (of Indra) (2) length of 15 wah

อุอะ (oo' a') stammering, confused utterance

———————————

อู

อู (so at the beginning of a word, but

otherwise without the upper part, and placed under the consonant which in pronunciation it follows) — Engl. *oo* or long *u*, as in *fool*, *brute*. Ninth of the vowels) ทีฆ — *and* สระ — name of this vowel

อู (oo) (1) dock or large ditch opening on to a river แผ่ง — อ่าว — bays or bends in a river bank (2) cradle

อู (oo) rustling, roaring, sound of rushing [of heat, etc.], violent

อู (oo!) [Chin.] rich

อูฐ (oot) [Sansk.] camel

อูก (oot) noise of fluttering — ๆ noise of pigs grunting

อูม (oom) swollen

———————————

เอ

เอ so at the beginning of a word, but otherwise เ. Placed before the letter or letters which in pronunciation it follows [*mai nah* = English *a* or *ay* as in *shame*, *may*. Tenth of the vowels.] ไม้หน้า name of this vowel. Note that when the accent *lehk paat* is placed above the syllable in which this vowel occurs it is shortened to *e*, as in เห็น *hen*

เอ (ay) to bend, to bow, to stagger —

เๆ to stagger ไม้ — another name
for this letter

เอก (ayk) [Pali] one, first, superior,
excellent ไม้ — the first of the accents, as over น่า

เอกะทา (ayka'tar) or เอกัๆกา [Sansk.]
single-mindedness [Alab. 195]

เอกะเทศ (ayka'tayt) [P.] part, portion

เอกะลอย (ayka'loi) [San.] independent

เอกะสาร (ayka'sarn) [Sansk.] written
acknowledgement, note of hand,
sale-paper

เอง (ayng) and เอ็ง (eng) self, thyself,
thou, you (speaking to inferiors)
เป็น — spontaneously, of one's own
accord, voluntary

เอ็ด (ett) (1) loquacious, loud talk (2)
one กับ — eleven

เอน (ayn) bent, leaning, inclined

เอ็น (en) nerves, tendons เจ็บอก —

เอ็นดู (endoo) love, compassion, benevolence

เอม (aym) savoury, sweet ๆ: — a tree

เอย (eui') end of a verse, chapter, book,
etc.

เอ่ย (eui') and เอ่ย อิน to begin talking
or shouting

เอยยาสี (eui'yahsee') to summon by

calling, come here !

เอยยน (ayenn) [Engl.] agent

เอว (ayo) ส: — and เอว — loins, flank

เอวัง (aywa'ng) [P.] then, afterwards.
finally, in conclusion

เอื่อ (err) slack, motionless น่า —
slack water, turn of the tide

เอะ อะ (eh' ah') noise of a crowd, confused sounds

เอิกเกริก (erkka'rerk) to shout, to be
excited, to spread a general rumour

แอ

แอ so at the beginning of a word, but
otherwise แ: placed before the
letter or letters which in pronunciation it follows. (sara aa or mai
nah saung a'n = Engl. aa as
in Haafiz, Canaan, or like Engl.
a in hand, but much longer.
Eleventh of the vowels) ไม้ เเา สีอ

อึน name of this vowel. Note:
when the syllable in which this
vowel occurs has mai ayk over its
consonant the vowel is shortened
and becomes like Engl. e in yellow,
or rather a in tertiary or ir in
girl

แอ (aa) (1) closed up, serried, compact,
combined to obstruct or block the
way (2) shrieks of a child ก: —

child-language, inarticulate speech
— หญิ female devotee, nun

แอ (aa') (1) sound of a flute (2) expression of disbelief

แอ *with* ออ (aw' aa) (1) able to speak a little (2) feeble, effeminate, idle

แอก (aak) yoke of a plough — เกวียน pole (of a carriage)

แอง (aang) [Cambod.] thou, you

แอ่ง (æng) bay, strait, backwater — อู๋ dock

แอ้ง แม้ง (aang maang) tightly bound down, strictly confined

แอน (æn) out of the straight line, to bend — อีน swallow, swift, sand-martin อ̂ — bird which makes edible nests — หงาย leaning back so as to look upwards อก — pigeon-breasted เอ้ — loitering, delaying, loafing about, gadding about

แอ่น (aan) slender, graceful อ้อน — to totter

แอบ (aap) (1) to come near to, to steal up to, to put under the protection of กา — auxiliary words อ̂ง — to refuse to give evidence as desired (2) small box of wood or bamboo

แอว (aao) rather bent

แอ้ว (aao) shrill, out of tune, screeching

• ◆ •

ใอ

ใอ (sะ at the beginning of a word, but otherwise ใ : placed before the consonant which in pronunciation it follows) mai mɔɔa'n — Engl. *i* or *y*, as in *mine, why*: Twelfth of the vowels ไม้ ม้วน name of this vowel

---
• ◆ •

ไอ

ไอ (so at the beginning of a word, but otherwise ไ. Placed before the consonant or consonants which in pronunciation it follows) mai ma'lai. — Engl. *i* or *y*, as in *final, anodyne* Thirteenth of the vowels. ไม้ มะลาย name of this vowel

ไอ (i) to cough

ไอ (i) *with* ไม another name for mai ma'lai

ไอ้ (i) [Cambod.] child

ไอ้ (i) you fellow! that fellow [term of contempt used by common people to one another] — เร้า — ไง fool, stupid — ร้อย — ยาก rabble —

ไปรา [an imprecation] (2) [name of several birds and fishes] — จีๅ water-raven — ทก crocodile — ก a noisy kind of fireworks — ทก low fellow, vile person

ไอ้ (i!) [exclam. of fear or pain]

ไอยา (aiyah) [Chin.] exclam. of fear or pain

ไอยกา (aiya'kar) [Pali] grandfather, ancestor

ไอยการ (aiya'karn) [Sansk.] laws of the Kingdom

ไอยกี (aiya'kee) [Pali] grandmother, ancestress

ไอยวา (aiya'wah) ไอยรา and similar words [Sansk.] elephant of Indra, fine elephant

ไอยย (aiyay) madam (to a lady)

ไอยะ (aiya') [Pali] lord, master

ไอสวรรย์ (aisa'wa'n) ไอสวริย์ and ไอสุริย์ [Sansk.] property of the King, Government property, Royal domains, Royal treasure

— ◆ —

โอ

โอ [so at the beginning of a word, but otherwise โ: standing before the letter which it follows in pronun-ciation, = long o or oh. Fourteenth of the vowels.] ไม้ — and สระ — name of this vowel

โอ (oh) small basket-work basin or cup made of bamboo gummed or varnished over, and coloured black and red or yellow ส้ม — shaddock, pomelo ไม้ — a sweet-smelling yellow fruit

โอ โอ้ โอ๋ โอะ (oh!) etc.) [exlamations, signs of the Vocative.]

โอ (oh) [Pali] down

โอ้ (oe) proud, vain อ้า — and — โอ้ง pompous

โอ๋ (o) exclaim. of regret ไม้ — name of this vowel — โอ for a long time, protracted, lingering

โอการ (ohkarn) [P.] worthless, useless

โอกาศ (ohkart) [P.] occasion, opportunity, chance, opening

โอฆ (ohk) and โอโฆ [Pali] quantity of water, flood, inundation, overflow

โอ่ง (ohng) jar, large pitcher — อ้าง name of a canal

โองการ (ongkarn) [Pali] royal order or edict

โอช (oht) and โอชา (ohchah) [Pali] sap, juice, savour, sauce — รศ savoury, succulent

โอฐ (oht) [Pali] lip, lips

โอก (ote) to weep, to cry [speaking of actors]

โอโถง (ohtohng) pompous, dressed up

โอภาก (ohtart) [Pali] white, clear

โอน (ohn) [Pali] bent, stooping, inclined; to bend

โอบ (ohp) [Cam.] to embrace, encircle, surround

เโภาก (ohpart) [Pali] rays, radiance, lustre

โอย โอ่ย โอ้ย โอ๊ย and โอ๋ย (oh-i') exclam. of surprise or pain

โอรส (ohrot) legitimate son, King's son, son

โอวาท (ohwaht) [Pali] admonition, exhortation ราโชวาท King's rescript, Royal order

โอษฐช (ohtta'cha' [Sansk.] Labial

โอสถ (ohsot) [Pali] herb used in medicine, drug, medicine

โอหัง (oh-ha'ng) proud — มงกะโร haughty

โอฬาร (ohlar) [Pali] hanging down

โอฬาริก (ohlahrikar) and โอฬาร [Pali] thick, coarse, broad, large, unconfined

เอา

เอา [so at the beginning of a word, but otherwise with the omission of the middle mark, and having its first part ไ *before*, and its second part า after, the consonant or consonants which it follows in pronunciation = Engl. *ou* or *ow*, as in *foul*, *fowl*. Note however that when followed by the seventeenth vowel (sa'ra' a') is has the sound of aw' or au' with shortened breath—Fifteenth of the vowels.] สระ — name of this vowel

เอา (ou') [exclam. of encouragement] come on ! go on ! get on ! — ชิ *and* — วะ go on ! begin !

เอา (ou) to take — ใจ to flatter, to compliment — โทษ to punish — มา to bring — ไป to take away — ไว้ to keep — เยียง to imitate ไม่ — not to accept, to refuse ; no, thank you

เอา (ou) to cohabit

เอาภาร (owpahn) to make it one's business ; expert, capable

เอารส (owrote) โอรส and โอรสา [Pali] son — ธิราช Crown Prince

อำ

อำ (so at the beginning of a word, but otherwise without the อ and having the upper part partly over the consonant which it follows and partly over the า) s'ar'a a'm. Sixteenth of the vowels. No English equivalent, but like a in Fr. amour. สระ — name of this vowel

อำ (a'm) to keep silence, struck dumb with confusion — พราง not to speak the truth — ลา to ask leave to go ผี — night-mare

อำ (a'm) [Chin.] night

อำ (a'm) and -- อ้ำ to hesitate, to refrain, to repress, to abstain [from speaking]

อำแดง (a'mdaang) madam, mistress [usual title of a married woman]

อำนวย (a'mnooi') to bless, to bestow

อำนาจ (a'mnart) vulg. อำนาท [Pali] inspiring with fear, majesty, power, authority, power of attorney

อำนาม (a'mnarm) spoilt, weakened, decaying, going to ruin

อำนิฐ (a'mnitt) [San.] to wish, desire

อำนู (a'mnoo') [Camb.] to help, assist, lend a hand

อำนักษ (a'mna'kkh) [Pali] (stone) of inestimble value

อำพนน์ (a'mponn) adorned, endowed, gifted

อำพร (a'mpon) [Pali] (1) sky (2) cloth

อำพราง (a'mprarng) to tell lies

อำแพลม (a'mplaam) and อั้ง แพลม sulphur match

อำพา (a'mbah) [Pali] (1) mother (2) mango

อำพุ (a'mpoo') [Pali] (1) rain-water (2) misfortune

อำพุช (a'mpoo'cha') [Pali] (1) fish (2) lotus

อำพุช (a'mpoo'cha') [Cam.] embryo, birth of fish, flies, etc.

อำพุท (a'mpoo'ta') [Pali] rain-water, clouds

อำพะนำ (a'mpa'na'm) to keep back part of the truth, to tell only a little

อำพัน (a'mpa'n) amber [yellow and grey]

อำภา (a'mpah) อำไภ and อำภร [Pali] (1) fine, handsome (2) rays (3) water

อำเภอ (a'mpeu) magistrate's jurisdiction or district, magistrate, registrar — ใจ liberty, free will

อำมพฤก (a'mx'preuk) spleen ลม — disease of the spleen

อำมราช *and* อำมรินทร์ (a'mma'raht, a'mma'rinn) [Sansk.] names of Indra; archangel

อำมฤค (a'mma'reut) [San.] immortal น้ำ — nectar

อำม้าตย์ (a'mmart) [Sansk.] minister, councillor, courtier

อำมร (a'monn) [Pali] god, deva, angel ผี — phantoms, ghosts

อำมะพาก (a'mma'part) liver ลม — liver complaint

อำมะหิต (a'mma'hitt) cruel, savage, merciless, bloodthirsty

อำยวน (a'myooa'n) [Cambod.] to put off, defer, ask for delay

อำลา (a'm-lar) *see* อำ

อะ

อะ (so at the beginning of a word, but otherwise ะ Very short sound of *a*, with a check to the breath, as if *k* were to follow. No European equivalent, rather like *a* in Fr. *bats tabac*) Seventeenth of the vowels, สระ — name of this vowel

อะกะโต (a'ka'toh) [Pali] uncultivated, unformed, ignorant

อะกะตะ (a'ka'ta') *and other forms* [P.]

non-existence, absence of birth and dying

อะหงุ่น *better* องุ่น (a'ngoo'n) juice of grape ต้น vine ลูก - grape น้ำ — wine

อะกะเนสัน (a'kha'naysa'n) tumour on the back

อะชุตะ (a'choo'ta') [Pali] immovable, eternal, everlasting

อะญาณัง (a'yahna'ng) [Pali] ignorance

อะฐาบก *see* อิฐาบก

อะฐิ (a'ti) *see* อัฐิ bone

อะฐะ (a'tta') *and similar forms* [San.] eight

อะณู (a'noo) [Pali] the 8th part of a ธุลี or particle of dust = 36 paramanoo

อะเทสังสบา (a'deeangsab) [Cambod.] not yet learned, not yet understanding

อะดูล (a'doon) [San.] incomparable, excellent

อะติ (a'ti) *see* อะฐิ

อะตะยาก *see* อิตาระยาก

อะตะยา (a'ta'yah) [Pali] moderation, prudence, will, intention

อะติ (a'tti') [Pali] above, over, beyond, superior, more

อะนน *and* อนน (a'non) [Pali] *with*

ปลา gigantic fabulous fish which causes earthquakes

อะนาถา (a'nartah) [Pali] unprotected, helpless, miserable, unfortunate, poor ไฟ๊ : · mendicant priest

อะนามิกา and อะนามิกา (a'nahmi'kar) ring-finger

อะนิมิตตะ (a'ni'mitta') [Sansk.] (1) free from attributes, unconditioned (2) unseen, invisible

อะนิมะ (a'ni'ma') [Pali] angel

อะนี (a'nee) [Engl.] aniseed

อะนุเคราะ (a'noo'khrau') [Pali] to give assistance, kind

อะนัตตา (a'na'ttah) [P.] non-existence, incorporeal, unreal

อะบาย (a'baie) [P.] state of suffering, world of punishment

อะบะ (a'ba') [Pali] away from, without, [in compos. Privative]

อะภิโช (a'pi'choh) [Pali] race, family

อะไภย (a'paie) [Pali] fearless, safe, safety - - ไทษ pardon ขอ — to ask pardon

อะมนุษย์ (a'ma'noo't) [Pali] inhuman, superhuman

อะมะตะ (a'ma'ta') [Pali] deathless, immortal, heaven

อะเมริกัน (a'mayri'ca'n) [E.] American

อะมะหิก (a'ma'hitt) cruel, fierce, merciless

อะเย (a'yay) see อัยเย

อะยะนัง (a'ya'na'ng) [P.] road, motion, progress

อะยะมณี (a'ya'ma'nee) see อัญญะมะณี

อะวินนะ see ทวิ enemy

อะริยะมุน (a'ri'ya'noo'nee) [Pali] saint, highly educated

อะรัญ (a'ra'n) อะรัญยี etc. [Pali and Sansk.] forest, wood

อะหลอง etc. (a'laung) see อล๊อง

อะลิงโค (a'leungkho) [Sansk.] neuter, without gender

อะเหลอย เฉือ (a'leui' cheui') slow, tedious, dilatory

อะหลัก อะเหลอ (a'la'k a'leui') (1) to eat too much (2) hardly escaping from trouble

อลัง (a'la'ng) [P.] personal ornaments see อลงการณ

อะวะทาร (a'wa'tarn) [Sansk.] descent, appearance upon earth ; Vishnu

อะวะสาร (a'wa'sarn) [Sansk.] end, conclusion, perfect, most, best

อะไสเภน (a'sohpaynee) see นครโสภิน

อะโสกะ (a'sohka') [P.] free from sorrow

อะสะธรรม (a'sa'ta'm) [Sansk.] want of merit, sin

อะเหตุ (a'hett) [Pali] without a cause

อะโหสิ (a'hohsi') [San.] finished, done with, lost, effaced, pardoned, reconciled — กรรม neutralised, lost

อะหัง (a'ha'ng) ineffectual [Alab. 45]

อะหัง (a'ha'ng) [Pali] I, we — การ proud, boast

------ ◆━◆ ------

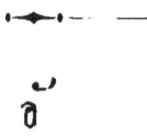

อ (see Preface. *mai pa't. ha'n ahkurt,* or *mai ka'ng-ha'n* = very short sound of *a*, as in *anon*. Eighteenth of the vowels) ไม้ผัด หันอากาศ *and* ไม้กัง หัน names of this vowel.

อัก (a'k) (1) instrument for spinning silk (2) noise of a blow — อวน feeling sick, ready to vomit, nausea

อักกะเริก (a'ka'rouk) *see* เอิกเกริก

อักขระ (a'kkha'ra') [Pali] letter

อักขา (a'kkhar) [Pali] die, dice, axle,

อักขี (a'kkhee) [Pali] eye

อักโข (a'kkhoh) *better than* อโข or อะโข [Sansk.] very many

อักคี (a'kkhee) [Pali] fire

อักคะเณ (a'kkha'nay) *better* อาคเณย์ [Pali] South-East

อักฎก• (a'ka'dok) [San.] poor, without any support

อักษร (a'ksonn) [San.] letter (of the alphabet)

อักนิฐ (a'kanitt) *see* อกนิฐ

อักเนสร (a'ka'nayson) *and* อักเนสร [Sansk.] a kind of boils on the back

อัคะเณ (a'kha'nay) [Pali] South-East

อัง (a'ng) to put near (so as to test the heat of a thing), to place before *or* near the fire, to toast

อังกนิศร etc. *see* อังกนิศร

อังกฤษ (a'ngritt) [Engl.] English

อังกา (a'ngkar) [Laos.] twelve letters or marks used in numbering the pages of a book

อังกาบ (a'ngkarp) a thorny shrub with flowers and medicinal leaves

อังกุ (a'ngkoo') [Pali] small drum, tambourine

อังกุ *or* อังกุษ (a'ngkoo't) *better* อังกุศ [Pali] hook for goading elephants

อังกูร (a'ngkoon) *better* อังกูร [Pali] shoot, sprout, family

อังกนิศร (a'ngkha'nitt) [San.] secretary who keeps the army list

อังคา (a'ngkhar) [Pali] members of the body

อังคาฐ (a'ngkhart) eclipse

อังคาร (a'ngkharu) [San.] (1) charcoal, live coal, embers (2) Mars (planet) วัน — Tuesday

อังคาส (a'ngkhart) [Sansk.] silent revenge, to brood over, rancune

อังคุฐ (a'ngkhoo't) [Pali] thumb

อังคุลี (a'ngkhoo'lee) [Pali] finger

อังคุละ (a'ngkhoo'la') [Pali] fingerbreadth, inch

อังคะจาก (a'ngkha'charta') *and other forms* [Pali] membrum virile

อังแพลม (a'ngplaam) sulphur

อังโล (a'ng-loh) *better* อังโล [Chin.] earthen-ware cooking apparatus

อังวะ (a'ngwa') Ava: old capital of Burmah

อังสา (a'ngsah) [Pali] shoulder

อังสะ (a'ngsa') priest's stole or scarf

อังสะกูฏ (a'ngsa'koot) [P.] upper part of the shoulder

อัจเลป (a'tcha'cla'p) grate, grating, stove-plate

อัจฉิ (a'tchi') [Pali] (1) flame, ray (2) fat, lard

อัจฉยะ (a'tcha'ya') [Pali] passing away, death, transgression

อัจฉรา (a'tcha'rah) [Pali] celestial nymph, houri

อัจฉริยัง (a'tcha'ri'ya'ng) [P.] marvellous, extraordinary, inexplicable

อัจฉา (a'tchar) [Pali] bear

อัชชะ (a'tcha') [Pali] to-day

อัจฉา (a'tchar) [Sansk.] transparent, clear, innocent

อัจฉาไศรย (a'tcharsaie) [Sansk.] (1) intention, inclination, temper, wish, will (2) polite จงบ — well acquainted with, good-tempered, agreeable

อัชะ (a'tcha') [Pali] goat

อัญ (a'n) [Cambod.] I, me - - ขอน (to royal persons) I, me - เชิญ to invite - - ขัน a plant จัด road, way

อัญชัน (a'ncha'n) a tree of the flowers of which collyrium is made

อัญญะมะนะ (a'nya'ma'nee) [Pali] one with another, mutually

อัฏโฏ (a'ttoh) [Pali] tower, fort

อัฏ (a'tta') [Sansk.] eight

อัฏ (a't) [Sansk.] the eighth part of a fuang, att: == nearly one cent

อัฏกาล (a'tta'karn) [Pali] the eight hours of the night; season

อัฐมะ (a'tta'ma') [Sansk] eighth

อัฐาบท (a'ttahbot) [Pali] chess-board

อัฐิ (a'tti') [Sansk.] bone

อัฐคราธ (a'tta'khrart) [Pali] partial eclipse

อัฐชั้น (a'tta'cha'n) crescent-shaped cupboard or side-board — ชั้นใด ladder

อัฐจันทร (a'ttcha'n) [San.] half-moon, crescent, semicircle; an odd number of steps

อัฐราตรี (a'tta'ra'tti') [San.] midnight

อันตะราย (a'nnta'rai) [San.] damage, injury, misfortune

อัณะราษ and อันาราษ (a'nahrart) [P.] people, citizens

อันทะ (a'nta') see อันทะ

อัด (a't) pressed, condensed, contracted

— อัด shut up, closed up, perplexed

— แอะ close crowd, throng

อัตถุ (a'ttoo') [Pali] substance, thing, property, wealth

อัตถุ (a'ttoo') [Pali] (1) letters (2) mousetrap (3) estates; to possess

อัตถัน (a'tta'n) boundaries of a town, village etc. (as a stone, a column, a relic buried in the earth, etc.)

อัตทร (a'tton) dull, desponding

อัตตา (a'ttah) self, oneself, individuality

อัตตะ (a'tta') (and other forms) [Pali] eight — ทัศ eighteen

อัตตะคัต (a'tta'kha't) indigent, needy, starving

อัตตะ (a'tta') and other forms [P.] eight — ทัศ eighteen

อัตรา (a'ttrah) continually, always

อัตลัต (a'tla't) a cloth

อัตตะกลับ (a'tta'kla'p) and อัตตะกลับ large Chinese hanging lamp

อัตตะกาน (a'tta'kahn) [Pali] for a long time

อัตตะคัต (a'tta'kha't) to be in want, in need of

อัตตะลัต (a'tta'la't) [Pali] red cloth embroidered or ornamented with gold flowers

อัตบาท (a'tta'bart) see หักกะบาส

อัตยา (a'tta'yah) and อัชฌา (a'tchar) [Sansk. and Pali] see อะทะยา

อัตติยาไสย (a'tti'yahsai) [Sansk.] see อัตตะ ไทรย

อัน (a'n) (1) who, which [relative pronoun] (2) something (3) num. design. of various small things —

ใก something, what? — กิ what
is good — ว่า that is to say —
หนึ่ง once, one piece — กับพนัน
afterwards, then เป็น — มาก a
great deal, very much เป็น — ขาก
absolutely, altogether, entirely

กัน (a'n) oppressed, anxious

อันฃาก (a'nkhart) altogether, entirely,
at all, absolutely

อันเชิญ (a'nchern) [Cambod.] to invite
to a house

อันคราย better อันตะราย (a'nta'raie)
danger, accident, calamity, misfortune

อันกิมะ (a'nti'ma') [Pali] last, final

อันใต (a'ntay) [Pali] within, in, among

อันโต (a'n'oh) [Pali] end, extremity,
last, biggest of a lot

อันกะ (a'nta') [Pali] below, lowest, the
lower bowels, end, death

อันตะร (a'nta'ra') [Pali] within, between, intermediate, under-cloth-
ing; heart

อันตะระถาน (a'nta'ra'tarn) [Paii] (1)
disappearane, covering up, vanish-
ing, (2) declensions of religion

อันทการ (a'nta'karn) see อันธะ

อันทะ (a'nta') [Pali] egg, testicle

อันทะชะ (a'nta'cha') [Pali] oviparous

อันทะพลึก (a'nta'pleu'k) a disease

อันธะ (a'nta') [Pali] dark, blind —
การ darkness

อันธะพาล (a'nta'parn) [Pali] stupid,
silly, doting

อันนะมะณี (a'nna'ma'nee) [Pali] property, effects

อันนัง (a'nnang) [Pali] boiled rice, food

อันโผฏนัง (a'npota'na'ng) to clap the
hands, applaud

อันร้าย (a'nraic) ill-tempered

อับปรี (a'pprec) see อัปรี

อับปาง (a'pparng) to be wrecked,
capsized

อับปัง (a'ppa'ng) [Pali] not much

อับศร (a'pson) [San.] celestial nymph,
houri

อับเพศ (a'ppayt) misfortune, calamity;
ominous, monstrous

อับปรา (a'ppa'rah) see อปรา

อัปรี (a'pree) [Sansk.] not beloved, un-
lovely, disagreeable; (a curse) accursed

อัประ (a'pra') [corruption of Sansk.
alpa] not much, a little, a few —
ยศ without honour, infamous —
ไชย vanquished

อัพภา (a'ppah) [Pali] fog, atmosphere, open air

อัพโภกาศ (a'ppohkart) [Pali] open air, open space

อภิญญา (a'pinyah) [Pali] superior knowledge, learned — ญาณ supernatural powers

อัมโพ (a'mpo) [Pali] mango

อัมพวัน (a'mpa'wa'n) [Pali] grove of mango trees

อัยเย (a'yay) madam

อัยยะ (a'ya') [P.] mother of a Governor

อัลละ (a'l-la') [Pali] damp, moist

อัศจรรย (a'ssa'cha'n) [Sansk.] wanderful, marvellous, inexplicable

อัศฎง (a'ssa'dong) [Sansk.] sunset

อัศฎางค์ (a'ssa'darng) [Sansk.] eightfold [Alab. 205]

อัศฎาทัศ (a'ssa'dahra't) [San.] eighteen

อัศกม (a'ssa'dom) [Pali] *with* ลม apoplexy

อัศดร (a'ssa'don) [Pali] fabulous horse, mule

อัศดิ *and* อัศดิลิงค์ *see* อัฐิ

อัศนีบาต (a'ssa'neebart) [Pali] thunderbolt

อัศวะ (a'ssa'wa') [Sansk.] *and* อัศ: [P.] horse — ราช superior horse — ณิก large collection of horses

อัศะวา *and* อัศวา (a'ssa'wa) *and other* *forms* [San.] horse — ณิก troop or crowd of horses

อัศโศ (a'ssoh) [Pali] horse

อัษฎางก (a'ssa'darng) [Sansk.] eightfold [Alab. 205]

อัษติ (a'sti') *see* อัฐิ [Sansk.] bone

อัษฌหา (a'ssa'nhah) (*and other forms*) a constellation [Alab. 97]

อัสัญหา (a'ssa'nhah) *and* สัญหา [P.] unamiable

www.ingramcontent.com/pod-product-compliance
Lightning Source LLC
Chambersburg PA
CBHW021115270326
41929CB00009B/895